AIR LINKS

AIR LINKS

G-ALDA

AKAROA

TEAL
AIR NEW ZEALAND

AIR NEW ZEALAND

GW00792228

And That's Another Story

GUY CLAPSHAW

RANDOM HOUSE
NEW ZEALAND LTD

ACKNOWLEDGEMENTS

The author gratefully acknowledges the many people he has encountered during his flying years and who have been reincarnated on these pages.

Random House New Zealand Ltd
(An imprint of the Random House Group)

18 Poland Road
Glenfield
Auckland 10
NEW ZEALAND

Sydney   New York   Toronto
London   Auckland   Johannesburg
and agencies throughout the world

First published 1997

Cover design: Kate Snushall
Cover illustration (clouds): L. Lefkowitz © International Press Photo Library
Cartoon illustrations: © John Weal

Printed by Wright and Carman (NZ) Limited, Wellington, New Zealand
ISBN 1 86941 324 5

CONTENTS

To my darling wife Colleen,
who held everything together and raised
Damon and Charles while I flew away

FOREWORD

If you were flying today and you saw Captain Guy Clapshaw coming down the aisle, you'd think, 'Mature fellow, safe hands,' and get on with the crossword.

The trouble is, Guy and I go back a long way — forty years, in fact — to a wind-swept airfield in Lincolnshire where scruffy erks were turned (or so ran the forlorn hope) into RAF officers, and later to Ternhill where we flew Percival Provosts in a manner Mr Percival had not envisaged in his worst nightmares.

We both 'passed out' (got our wings) flying the dearly beloved de Havilland Vampire. After National Service, I went into journalism and later authorship; Guy stuck with flying, joining the "If it's got a sharp end, two wings and a fan, I'll fly it" brigade: the charter jocks, shunting cargo and hapless tourists up and down Europe in aircraft that might even land on the same number of engines with which they took off.

All this and more has been described in the hilarious *A Likely Story*. With its sequel, which you now hold in your hands, Guy carries on the dodgy odyssey, introducing us to a one-Dakota airline called Air Links, heading back from a summer season in New Zealand to another summer in England.

At first all goes well: the tiny airline expands, acquires more modern (then) aircraft like the Argonaut, but finally plunges (the company, not the Argonaut) when the really big boys decide they want the growing tourist-package market all to themselves.

Faced with a career flying a desk at the National Provincial Bank, Guy makes one last job application — back to New Zealand where the national airline is expanding fast. This is a world where staff are actually trained and paid, and aircraft get the occasional check-over!

After that, it's respectability all the way. But *And That's Another Story* is chock-full of hilarious anecdotes, weird and wonderful characters, triumph and grief, some real hazards and merciful salvation, the way it used to be before things went terribly reliable.

There's even some pre-marital romance, which, when we were both teenagers, was completely impossible in a Vampire.

So, if you *are* flying and you *do* see this pillar of the community, nudging sixty, four glittering gold rings on each wrist, moving down the aisle; and if you are really holding this book in your lap and about to start, better ask the flight attendant for a stiff one with not too much soda!

Frederick Forsyth

Hertford, England, 1997

CHAPTER ONE
Some Sort of a Record

He was your typical level-headed Australian: rude and bad tempered with a chip on both shoulders. "Stayin' here long?" he challenged in fluent Strine, eyeing our British passports distastefully.

"No, just a day," Tony Butler, our captain, replied. "Then continuing on to Darwin and the UK tomorrow." He emphasised his words by pointing at our venerable Air Links DC-3 parked outside the Sydney Customs shed. I secretly hoped the customs man wouldn't typecast the four of us as a small band of travelling arsonists hell bent on destroying Australia in a day. The English test cricketers were beating New South Wales at the Sydney Cricket Ground and Australia, a nation of winners, was taking defeat badly.

"Got anything to declare?" he demanded belligerently.

"Nothing to declare," we assured him.

In the adjacent booth, his colleague was listening to the live cricket report on a pocket radio. A sudden burst of jeering and catcalling from the transistor drowned our reply.

"Harvey clean bowled by Trueman," the other officer called out indignantly to his colleague, who now eyed us even more distastefully.

His gaze lingered suspiciously on our crumpled appearances. Fourteen hours spent in the cramped cockpit of a Dakota does very little to improve anybody's image. My mouth tasted like the bottom of an elderly parrot's cage, our eyes were bloodshot from lack of sleep and the afternoon sun was making us perspire heavily.

The customs officer sat in contemplative silence while thinking up his next question.

"You all travellin' together?" he enquired suspiciously, directing his gaze at the four of us. We admitted we were. The revenuer brooded a while longer, glaring at our passports while trying to find a reason to detain us further. In the background, another roar from the transistor radio signalled the fall of another Australian wicket.

"No cigarettes, liquor or tobacco?" he persisted.

Tony was the first to respond. "Nothing. No cigarettes, liquor or tobacco," he enunciated slowly and distinctly. The customs officer's face scowled in distaste at the very pukka, English public school accent. We could sense Tony becoming irritated at this treatment. We still had an hour's work putting our aircraft away for the night before we could retire exhausted to the nearest cheap hotel for a few hours' rest before continuing on the next day. The officer eyed him challengingly, silently daring him to say something insolent. Tony fumed inwardly but managed to remain stoically silent.

The customs officer sighed resignedly and was about to stamp our passports when a last question occurred to him.

"Gotta crim'nal record?" he demanded abruptly.

Tony's patience suddenly snapped. Maybe the long tiring flight, the trauma of leaving good friends in New Zealand or perhaps just fatigue pushed him over the edge. He faced up to his tormentor.

"I didn't realise a criminal record was still a requirement to travel to Australia," he blazed back in his best British accent.

The effect on the Australian was instant and dramatic. His face erupted into a violent shade of indignant red as he beckoned four of his henchmen over to whisk us away to the examination rooms below.

It was eleven hours later by the time the Australian Customs and Immigration Department released us from their clutches. Most of that time was spent in subtle forms of torture — endless form-filling, countless interviews and repetitive questions, baggage searching, no food or drink, limited visits to the rest room, personal searches, and finally a half-hour harangue on what Australia thought of Pommies who came to their country causing trouble. We were finally released just before dawn.

The sour-faced customs officer who checked our documentation next morning could have been our earlier tormentor's twin brother.

"How long didjer spend in Sydney?" he demanded loudly.

A swift nudge in the ribs prevented me from answering, Too long.

"Just a night," Tony explained.

"Didjer enjoy it?"

"Well, er . . . yes, it was different."

The officer smirked with self-satisfaction as he stamped our passports. "Come back an' spend a lot longer next time," he suggested.

"Yeah, like ten years?" we muttered as we headed out to our aircraft.

We night-stopped in Darwin after thirteen hot uncomfortable flying hours, before continuing our flight back to the UK the following morning.

It was March, and the summer charter flying season was about to begin. We were anxious to get back to the UK in time for the lucrative summer months ahead.

We reached England in ten days, having routed via Bali, Djakarta, Singapore, Bangkok, Calcutta, Ahmedabad, Karachi, Bahrain, Damascus, Beirut, Athens and Rome. It felt good to be home after three months away.

The whole staff of our tiny airline, all three of them, were out at Gatwick to greet us on our arrival on a cold March morning. We completed customs formalities, then Denis Mills, our chief pilot and managing director, called us to his office for a business conference.

"We're going to make a small fortune," he assured us, pointing at the wall planner. The rest of us looked a bit sceptical; we all knew how most charter operators made their small fortunes — they started off with large ones!

Tony Butler scanned the wall board. "Seems like a lot of flying, but all for the same firm," he commented. "What do we know about them?"

It was a good question; the charter business in the 1960s was full of travel agents and others who would charter you and never pay.

"Horizon Holidays, travel agent with offices in the City of London, EC-4. They've signed the spring and summer contract and intimated there could be a winter programme to follow," Denis assured us.

Tony and I must've looked dubious. No charter company flew much in winter. The Spanish, Greek and French holiday resorts were too cold for the traditional British tourists, who always took their holidays between May and September.

"Who would want to go anywhere in winter?" Tony demanded.

Denis looked him squarely in the eye. "Skiers! In case you haven't heard, parts of Europe get rather cold in winter — cold enough for snow in fact. Horizon Holidays have a very progressive winter sports programme. They're leaders in the business and they've accepted our charter quote to fly passengers between London and Switzerland."

Tony and I exchanged glances. The prospect of flying in winter appealed enormously. Most charter companies in the fifties and sixties worked their crews like slaves during the summer, competing for the seasonal work available. Once the summer holidays ended and autumnal tints coloured the leaves, people tended to stay at home. Apart from the occasional sub-charter from the state-owned scheduled airlines and the occasional bit of freight work, pickings were pretty slim for independent operators like us during winter. Most companies hoped to have made enough money during the summer to bankroll them through the winter.

Some didn't make it through the winter and their crews would wait anxiously for new jobs to blossom in the spring. Air Links had been an exception, we had been lucky and found a winter flying job. The prospect of flying skiers to the major European cities had a definite attraction.

Denis began filling in the details of our windfall. "Orion Airlines folded last week," he volunteered. "Pegasus are reputed to be pretty shaky financially, their crews haven't been paid for a month, and there's a rumour going round that the fuel company is wondering whether to let them fly through the summer to reduce their debt or put them out of their misery now."

None of us were displeased at the news of the competition folding if it meant more work.

Denis gestured out the window to where Richard, our seventeen-year-old general factotum, was connecting a tractor bar to Kilo Echo's tail wheel.°

"Young Richard did all the spade work," he explained. "He convinced the travel agent we could carry their clients for a fraction of the cost they were paying the scheduled airlines. He got a few figures out based on a thousand hours' flying a year, and they couldn't wait to sign our agreement."

He waited while we digested this information thoughtfully. A thousand hours was a lot of flying for a one-aeroplane charter company. "We'll need a second aircraft if we're to do all the flying ourselves," he continued. "I've looked at what's available and there's a passenger/freight machine we can get from Field's that would suit us perfectly. We've checked the engineering records and modification state and it appears to be in good condition."

"What about a short-term lease with option to purchase at the end?" Tony suggested. Denis shook his head.

"I tried that but there's nothing much available at a reasonable price. Remember this is March; the summer inclusive tour season is about to start, and aircraft and pilots are in short supply."

I reflected on the irony of his statement. Life for pilots in the independent airlines was either a feast or a famine. In summer, every operator wanted to give you a job, promising the earth if you signed up with them. When autumn came, the situation reversed. Small private airlines were like Damocles, constantly threatened by overheads. As revenue from charter work diminished in winter, they struggled to reduce expenses. The three major expenses were aircrew salaries, fuel and maintenance. As flying hours diminished, fuel costs shrunk proportionally. Maintenance also reduced correspondingly, but the crew's salaries continued.

° Kilo Echo was the registration of our Dakota.

There were two options for the airline.

The first was to retain a full complement of aircrew for the minuscule amount of winter flying. Such a course of action would seriously deplete the coffers of any company and possibly drive it into insolvency. Airline pilots were perforce a disloyal breed; they had to be to survive. They would very likely abandon the company for more attractive job opportunities in the spring, leaving the airline short of cash and pilots.

The second option was to make most of the aircrew redundant in the autumn, throwing them onto the winter scrap heap of out-of-work aircrew. Most would somehow struggle through the winter in menial jobs as door-to-door encyclopedia salesmen, clerks, shop assistants or petrol station attendants. When spring jobs blossomed again in the back pages of *Flight* and *Aeroplane* magazines, they would fight among themselves to get back into the air.

Every year a small percentage didn't return to the independent airline scene. Some chose the security of a co-pilot's job in a state scheduled airline, others chose not to return to the rat race and pursued different careers, but most returned like grunion to the same spot every year.

Aircraft also experienced the feast or famine syndrome. Gatwick resembled an aeronautical museum in winter, with long lines of somnolent DC-3s, Vickers Vikings, Bristol Freighters, Handley Page Hermes, Argonauts, Avro Yorks, DC-4s, Airspeed Ambassadors and Constellations waiting for the spring. Now the industry was beginning to waken from the winter's hibernation. Ground engineers were busy on the tarmac, preparing aircraft for the coming summer season.

"We start the summer programme in three weeks," Denis told us. "So before then we'll have to complete every pilot's biannual competency check and bring the second aircraft into service."

Tony and I nodded satisfied. We had both invested money into Air Links and had a vital interest in its future.

The office door opened and our young operations clerk entered the office. His proper name was Richard but everybody called him Pickles. He'd been with us almost since the first day we'd started the company less than a year ago and had displayed a remarkable ability to organise the ground side of the airline.

Pickles directed his attention towards me. "Kilo Echo needs to be ferried to Biggin for servicing," he began. "Can you fly with Denis and he'll combine your biannual check with the ferry flight. Tomorrow afternoon okay?"

I assured him it was. Although I had pressing personal commitments waiting after four months overseas, the first lesson any employee in an independent airline learned was that your time wasn't your own. If there was money to be earned flying, everything else took a back seat. Many a relationship faltered under this selfish regime. Wives tended to get a bit crinkly lipped when their husbands were called out minutes before a dinner party or daughter's wedding, leaving them to cope alone. For a relationship to survive, and many didn't, both parties had to accept that the job came first.

Next day Denis and I ferried Kilo Echo to Biggin Hill, leaving Tony and his wife, Joy, to assist Pickles in the office. Joy doubled as an air hostess when required, although normally Denis's wife, Andrée or Christine, our receptionist/typist, flew as hostesses.

Within twenty-four hours of our arrival back in the UK we had resumed the busy work pattern of a small under-staffed private airline flying anything, anywhere, any time for anybody.

CHAPTER TWO
Days of Independents

By the time our summer flying schedule started, we had taken delivery of our second DC-3, Golf Alpha Papa Uniform Charlie (G-APUC), usually abbreviated to "Uniform Charlie", and had retained the services of Captain Laurie Chegwidden, a freelance pilot. We now had five pilots on our staff.

We also had two additional shareholders, who had financed the original aircraft purchase. Dr Ambrose Levitt, a prominent Harley Street physician, was a cultured gentleman who drove a beautiful late model Rolls-Royce. He was an extremely generous individual and always insisted on paying for lunch after company meetings. He contrasted markedly with our other shareholder, Stan Wilson, a West Hartliepool motor trader who had fought his way up from boy mechanic to proprietor of a large motor firm in the North of England. His first involvement with aviation had been as an RAF airframe fitter during the war.

They were as different as chalk and cheese in all but two ways. Both had a passion for aviation, although neither knew anything about the running of an airline, and both had seemingly endless amounts of money, which they were eager to invest in our little charter company.

Stan was happy to leave the day-to-day running of Air Links to us, in contrast to Dr Levitt, who constantly asked the reason for a particular course of action.

By mid-April we had flown 120 hours with our two aircraft. The second DC-3, an ex-British European Airways (BEA) "Leopard" convertible passenger-freighter model, was frequently called out on lucrative night freight charters when not transporting Horizon Holiday clients to their Swiss holiday destinations.

The tarmac at Gatwick early on a summer morning in the 1960s was always an exhilarating scene. A motley collection of ancient DC-3s, Vikings, Elizabethans and other aircraft would return shortly after dawn with their loads of sunburned holidaymakers. The scheduled airlines ignored Gatwick, choosing instead to fly into Heathrow. This left the new airport to the independents. Scheduled services then were almost exclusively run by the state airlines — BEA, Air France, Sabena (Belgium) and others. The Air Transport Licensing Board (ATLB) prevented independent airlines from flying schedules, lest they deprive the state airlines of passengers and revenue.

The independents retaliated by marketing "package" holidays, in which travel and accommodation were included in the one price. They called these inclusive tours (ITs). They then argued successfully that they weren't taking passengers away from the scheduled carriers because their IT passengers couldn't afford schedule airline fares and so could only fly on IT holidays. The ATLB reluctantly allowed the flights to take place, stipulating they could only operate outside scheduled airline hours. This meant IT passengers had to arrive at their holiday destination late at night and depart again two weeks later at some inconveniently early hour in the morning.

The only exception to the rule applied when a destination wasn't served by a scheduled airline. Then the independent operator could fly at any hour. The Horizon Holidays/Air Links organisation operated to such destinations, hence we could run a regular daily inclusive tour service.

Inevitably, once the holiday destination became popular the scheduled airlines applied to fly the same route, and the poor independent, having pioneered the new route, then had to plead before the ATLB to be allowed to continue.

The independents' argument that their passengers could never afford the scheduled airline fare was true. A two-week inclusive tour holiday in Palma-Mallorca, comprising hotel accommodation plus return air travel, could be purchased for less than the return scheduled airline fare. When Pickles sold the elder Mr Zucher (the travel agent) the idea of chartering Air Links to transport Horizon Holiday's customers to their summer destination, he effected a seventy-five percent saving in the firm's travel costs.

The IT charter trade was the handhold by which the private charter airlines were able to lever themselves more firmly into the post-war air travel business. Ex-military aircraft and crews were then in plentiful supply. Other opportunities followed — military trooping flights, pilgrims, government freight contracts — and eventually one or two private companies were allowed to turn their inclusive tour flights into scheduled services.

Now, thirty-five years later, the Gatwick scene has changed dramatically. The terminal has more than quadrupled in size, the ancient piston-engined aircraft flown by the struggling independents have given way to the latest glass cockpit jets of the state airlines, and few, if any, of the original charter companies remain. Trans-Air merged with Morton Air Services, Air Charter, Silver City and Britavia to become British United Airways. They eventually merged with Caledonian to form British Caledonian Airways, who in turn were absorbed into British Airways (which had previously been BOAC and BEA). Pegasus, Orion, Air Safaris and Overseas didn't last the distance and folded. Probably the longest-lasting charter company was Dan-Air, which, having started at the end of the war with ex-military Dakotas and Avro Yorks, continued into the jet age before finally collapsing under a gigantic debt load in 1992.

In the 1960s, a typical day's flying for Air Links would begin at seven thirty in the morning.

After calling into the office to check the telex for any charter enquiries, the crew would prepare the flight documentation before proceeding out to the overnight park, where both our DC-3s waited to be fed and prepared for the day's work. Oil and hydraulic levels, tyre pressures, and other items were checked and certified by the ground engineer, while the pilots turned the engines by hand through thirteen blades to check for hydraulicking then climbed up on the wings for refuelling. Meanwhile, the air hostess would check the condition of the cabin for cleanliness and supervise the loading of the catering.

Once the aircraft was ready for service, one pilot would taxi it to the boarding gate, while the other went to flight planning to check the weather and navigational warnings before preparing the flight plan.

Meanwhile, another member of the company, normally a pilot or hostess not operating on that particular flight, would begin checking in the passengers and their luggage. Air Links didn't have its own check-in counter, so we'd rent one by the hour from the more established airlines. Sometimes two flights departed close together, and we'd have to hire temporary staff from another organisation. If the particular flight was on behalf of another carrier, this could result in confusion for the passengers. The following public address announcement one busy August weekend typified the confusion: "Sun Seeker Holidays request Westpoint Airlines passengers flying by Air Links to Perpignan to please report to the Dan-Air counter, where an Airborne Aviation ground hostess will complete departure formalities."

The tarmac and buildings at Gatwick positively vibrated with the marvellous sound of powerful piston engines being run up. It was difficult to remember in the euphoria of the moment that summer would eventually give way to autumn and the number of flights would diminish, leaving the aircraft standing in the winter fog, resting from the season's activity. The less fortunate pilots and hostesses would lose their jobs for the umpteenth time and depart, resolving never to return to such a precarious living. Some would embark on courses to assist them into different careers, confident they had done the right thing, that there was no future in independent aviation.

Then winter frosts disappeared and Gatwick emerged from hibernation. Ground engineers began preparing the lines of waiting aircraft for flight once more, and pilots who had vowed never to return to the cockpit would pause and listen hypnotised to the distant sound of a Pratt and Whitney radial engine being run up to static boost. As they were drawn closer, the heady aroma of high octane aviation fuel would intoxicate them once again with the fascination of aviation and they would return like moths to a flame, their promises forgotten. We never questioned why we returned to a life with ancient aircraft, shaky management, impossible hours and irregular pay. To understand the reason, you had to be standing on the Gatwick apron on that busy summer morning and savour the smell of the Av-gas and listen to the engines of the Dakotas, Yorks and Wayfarers preparing for flight.

Though nobody could explain it in words, every one of us knew why we had returned.

CHAPTER THREE
The Big League

The winter sports season ended abruptly at the end of April, leaving us two weeks to prepare for the start of our regular services to the Costa Brava and the Greek Islands on charter to Horizon Holidays.

A spate of night freight charters boosted our revenue considerably at the beginning of May, but increased the office work load considerably. Meanwhile ground handling arrangements had to be made with the local agents in Corfu and Heraklion, our two Greek Island destinations. These agents would arrange Customs and Immigration facilities and ground transportation to the passengers' hotel and prepare documentation for the return flight, as well as arrange fuel, oil and any necessary maintenance.

Different agents had different charges. Sometimes the cost of ground handling could be the difference between a profit or a loss. Alternatively, to choose the wrong agents could often lead to pandemonium, with angry passengers stranded at their holiday destination without transportation, or waiting in Customs while some administrative blunder was sorted out.

At home base, our small staff had to sort such matters out during daytime office hours, then fly the regular freight run at night. Not that anybody minded. Work meant money, which kept us in business.

Mr Zucher's son, representing Horizon Holidays, came down to Gatwick one frosty morning to inspect our aircraft and facilities and to finalise contractual arrangements. Anybody who wasn't flying that morning made it their business to be near the office. Both aircraft were chocked in front of the office window on the North Park, looking rather smart in the Air Links red and white colour scheme. Pickles had the office operating at the peak of efficiency. Tony's wife Joy answered the phone, Christine was handling the morning mail, while Tony and I stood ready to meet Mr Zucher. Pickles would have been the best informed staff member to show him our organisation, but several of us had expressed doubts about his age. He had an instinctive genius for organising and running our charter business, but to the uninformed observer he was still a teenager.

Zucher arrived exactly on time. He was short — I estimated his height at only a few inches over five feet — very light skinned and, though young, was completely bald, even to his eye brows. Tony introduced him to each member of the team while Pickles hovered nearby, ready to fill in any required details.

Zucher seemed satisfied with the way we ran our office, for he said nothing during his inspection. Tony gave him the details of aircraft and passenger handling at Gatwick, Corfu and Heraklion then I took him out to the aircraft, where Denis and his wife Andrée waited. Denis and his wife had met when they both flew for Swissair, and the thoroughness of the Swiss cabin crew training became apparent as we neared the aircraft. A delicious aroma of fresh perked coffee hung in the air and a tempting array of hot snacks awaited us in the aircraft galley.

Denis suggested a cup of hot coffee to dispel the morning cold before the young Mr Zucher examined our machines. The gentleman agreed, and we stood crowded in the rear fuselage of Uniform Charlie, clutching steaming mugs.

Zucher was like a small kid around aircraft. Although he said very little, his eyes darted everywhere, and when Denis suggested showing him the cockpit, he hurried forward eagerly. We sat him in the captain's seat and gave him a simplified description of the aircraft's systems — throttles, flaps, under-carriage selector and flying controls. He sat there entranced, like a child opening its first gift on Christmas morning. Denis and I concluded he was a fellow aviation fan.

"I suppose you do plenty of flying in your job?" I ventured. Zucher shook his head vigorously.

"Only flown once in my life," he informed us. "That was with Mum and Dad to Glasgow . . . oh, and my sister came too. Mum's terrified of flying."

Denis and I exchanged surprised glances.

We then showed him the outside of the aircraft and he ended his inspection with a slightly briefer tour of Kilo Echo. He was very interested to learn that it had just returned from a charter to New Zealand.

"You mean New Zealand in Australia?" he enquired.

I replied that we had passed through Australia on the way and told him about the newly formed New Zealand airline we'd spent the winter flying for. He asked a series of questions about the trip, revealing an almost child-like interest.

We returned to the office to conclude the day's business. Zucher opened a conspicuously new briefcase and withdrew two typewritten pages of notes.

"Just a few points to clear up," he explained apologetically, and proceeded to read aloud a section defining which parts of the charter operation we were responsible for organising. None of it was particularly out of the ordinary; we were accustomed to organising and paying for the various ancillary services connected with charter flying. Denis explained this to him.

We concluded our business after less than forty-five minutes and waited to hear whether there was anything further to discuss. Young Mr Zucher sat awkwardly in his seat, fiddling with the handle of his shiny briefcase.

"Anything else you'd like to know or see?" Denis enquired. The young man shook his head. "No, that was super. I've never seen the cockpit of an aeroplane before."

"Anything concerning you about our operation that you'd like to discuss?"

Again the travel agent shook his head. "No, you seem very well organised. It's great the way you put the forthcoming flights up on the board."

Tony and Denis exchanged curious glances. Why the devil didn't he produce the contracts for signing?

The phone rang. Denis got to it first.

"Good morning, Air Links, can I help you?" He listened then gestured to Pickles urgently. "Fellow wants a quote for thirty-six passengers to Beauvais next Saturday." Denis handed him the phone and directed his attention back to our friendly travel agent.

"We'd like to finalise the contracts fairly soon, in the next couple of days," he explained. "Our ground handling agents must finalise various arrangements before we start flying."

Zucher seemed to come to with a bit of a start. He opened his briefcase and produced a folder.

"Yes, I'm sorry, I forgot in all the excitement. Dad's secretary gave these to me to get signed. She said it's important the signatures are witnessed." He produced two typewritten documents which Denis proceeded to read before passing to Tony. They were the charter contracts that we hoped were going to earn us untold riches during the forthcoming summer holiday season.

Denis had finished reading the documents. "Seems straightforward to me," he observed, passing the second document to Tony.

We got Christine to witness the signatures. We must have all looked rather smug after this, as we now had regular flying guaranteed through to the end of September, all at full revenue rates. There were also excellent prospects of similar work continuing through the winter.

Pickles interrupted our state of euphoria. "Alfie Cope of East West Airlines wants thirty-six passengers picked up early tomorrow morning from Leeds-Bradford for Glasgow. Football supporters. Says it's urgent and could become a regular thing."

Tony and I shook our heads. Alfie was one of the scoundrels in the charter business who rarely paid in full for work done. His former airline had gone into liquidation the previous autumn, owing thousands of pounds to local businesses and his own employees.

"Let's concentrate on the main chance," Tony suggested, pointing to the signed contracts on the table. I nodded my agreement, and Pickles told Alfie we didn't have anything available for him.

Mr Zucher collected his copies of the contract and replaced them in the briefcase. Denis escorted him down to the Gatwick rail terminal, leaving a band of jubilant Air Links employees in the office.

"This could really be the start of big things," Tony enthused. I agreed with him; both aircraft would be flying every day of the month throughout the summer season. Our continued existence seemed a stone cold certainty.

Apart from the first flight to Corfu, which suffered a one-hour delay due to late catering, the remainder of the Horizon Holidays IT flights went remarkably smoothly. Both aircraft performed faultlessly, thanks to the efforts of our maintenance contractor — Air Couriers at Biggin Hill. Crew flying hours nudged close to the 120 hours maximum allowed in one month, but never exceeded them, thanks mainly to skilful scheduling by Pickles in the office.

With so much regular flying, we became independent of the need to compete for the lucrative ad hoc charter market. These were last-minute charters for other operators who had broken down and ended up with a plane load of angry holiday makers anxious to get on their way. Other airlines continued to phone us whenever they needed rescuing in this way, but the frequency and number of calls diminished as we repeatedly turned them down.

One of the charters I felt bad about refusing was the Licensed Victuallers' Association. We had started the company on a shoestring in April 1960, and had questioned our wisdom when nobody wanted to fly for us. Eventually the drought broke and we became well known in the charter business. Our first charter had been the Licensed Victuallers. Now they were coming back for repeat business and we were turning them down.

By the end of August we had flown 450 revenue flying hours on the two aircraft. Horizon Holidays had paid us promptly at the end of every month and, after paying fuel bills, landing fees, maintenance, salaries and office expenses, we still retained £4700 in the bank account. But we all realised that the bonanza could end in the autumn and we needed to accumulate sufficient funds to see us through the winter.

I flew as Denis's co-pilot continuously throughout August. He used this time as a training period, acquainting me with the paperwork and other facets of flying a civil airliner. Then, on the first day of September, we combined a ferry flight with a base check to check me out as pilot in command. This gave us three full-time captains, plus Laurie Chegwidden — our freelance — and Les Smith, a co-pilot who had joined us at the end of the previous year.

My first flight in command of a DC-3 was a positioning flight from Gatwick to Stansted, to pick up a load of Horizon passengers travelling to Palma de Mallorca. Les Smith, now our only co-pilot, was flying with somebody else, so there was no other choice but to schedule Tony to come along as my co-pilot. It rather took away the importance of the occasion, but neither of us worried about it. We departed on time for Palma and I managed to cope with the reams of paperwork demanded by the Spanish immigration authorities at destination.

After depositing a return load of sunburned customers back at Stansted, I suggested Tony fly the empty sector back to Gatwick. It had been a long but satisfying day's flying, during which we'd found time to discuss our company's present and future plans.

The Horizon Holidays flights had gone conspicuously well, and two other travel agents had enquired whether we would fly for them next year. Although the prospect of more work was encouraging, it left us with a difficult decision to make. At present we were doing well, thanks to a combination of low overheads and hard-working staff. When we weren't flying, which was rare, we'd help out with the formidable amount of paperwork in the office. With a lot of hard work and dedication, we were able to handle both the flying and the office work, but to take on additional flights next year would require one or more extra aircraft and crews. The amount of office work would expand enormously, necessitating more staff, a larger office and more expense. The higher overheads would be met by revenue from the extra work, but if a recession occurred in the market, we'd be lumbered with heavy overheads from three or more aircraft and little or no income. Damocles was always waiting to drop his overheads on small businesses who expanded too fast too soon. Gatwick was littered with the relics of small private airline operators who had perished in this way.

I mulled this situation over in my mind during the turn-round at Stansted.

Customs was overloaded by the arrival of several other aircraft, so I waited patiently until the Waterguard officers could stamp our paperwork and allow us to ferry back to Gatwick. Outside the Customs shed, a Handley Page Hermes in Skyways colours was being connected to a ground tug. The Hermes was a British four-engined airliner, produced after the end of the war to compete in the civil market. BOAC operated them for a few years until better machines came along. They then sold them off to the independents at bargain basement prices. Skyways snapped them up and used three machines on Far East trooping contracts and IT flights similar to ours.

"Bleeding shame, ennit?" A ground engineer interrupted my thoughts, indicating the Hermes. I was about to question him, but was prevented by the Waterguard inspector arriving to process our documentation.

Ten minutes later we had completed customs formalities and were walking back to our aircraft. Tony settled himself in the left seat while I completed a hurried external inspection. After a longish taxi out to Stansted's South Westerly runway, ATC instructed us to wait at the holding point for a DC-6 on finals.

"Eagle doing a bit of crew training." Tony gestured towards the sleek four-engined monster approaching the runway. "Pity we couldn't afford something like that, we'd scoop the IT market."

The DC-6 landed in a cloud of blue smoke from its four mainwheel tyres, and we were cleared to line up and hold.

"Air Links Kilo Echo, Hermes under tow crossing the runway towards the fire dump, cleared for take off when it's clear."

We waited patiently while the stately four-engined aircraft crossed the duty runway towards the deserted far side of the airfield.

"Wonder why it's going over there?" Tony pondered aloud as he locked the tailwheel for take off. Our DC-3 gathered speed as he applied power and I didn't have time to consider his remark till much later.

We didn't know it then, but the answer to next year's flying problems had just passed before us. And neither of us had recognised it.

Back at Gatwick, Denis was waiting to congratulate me on my first command trip. We adjourned to the Aero Club for a celebratory drink.

"Another travel agent, Sunkissed Holidays, called today," he mentioned. "They offered us a six-month IT contract, flying to Nice and Barcelona once a week."

"That's four firms offering us work," Tony murmured thoughtfully. "What do we do, buy two or three more aircraft and expand rapidly or stay small?"

Denis reminded him of the attendant extra expenses that two more aircraft would incur. "We'd never find enough permanent pilots, we'd have to employ freelance crews," he commented. "And we couldn't pay ten pilots through the winter."

"Larger aircraft are the answer," Tony concluded.

Just when we didn't need it, the ad hoc charter business boomed. Our rival operators at Gatwick eagerly lapped up the business while we concentrated on our IT schedules. As summer flying continued into autumn, we tactfully reminded the young Mr Zucher of our willingness to fly his winter sports passengers to their destinations. We had now made more than a modest amount of money during the summer to guarantee our survival until spring, and winter work would be icing on the cake. Zucher senior phoned to assure us we'd get the winter contract and told us to start planning for weekly flights to Geneva and Zurich, starting the day after Christmas.

A week after my first command trip through Stansted, a strange incident occurred — almost providential. Les Smith, Christine and I ferried Kilo Echo back to Stansted on a Sunday afternoon. Next morning we were scheduled to Palma de Mallorca for Horizon. Pickles came along for the ride, to help with ground handling arrangements next morning.

We landed at 4pm and, after checking the four of us into a nearby hotel, I suggested wandering down the road to The Hop Poles, a local pub on the edge of the airfield.

It was a beautiful, still summer evening and we decided to take our drinks outside. Over the back fence of the beer garden, the crash fire dump lay less than a hundred yards away. I noticed a large four-engined aircraft parked among the blackened hulks used for fire crew practice.

"What on earth's a DC-6 doing on the fire dump?" Christine enquired curiously.

"That's not a Six, although it looks a bit like one," the co-pilot explained. "It's a Handley Page Hermes, Skyways are replacing them with new Avro 748s. They're 70 knots faster, turbine powered and pressurised."

"What's going to happen to their Hermes?" Pickles enquired.

Les shrugged. "Same as the other old aircraft there, I suppose. Somebody will put a match to it and the fire crew will put it out for practice, same as they do with the other old wrecks . . ."

A thought occurred to me. "How many passengers does a Hermes carry?" I demanded.

"About eighty or ninety," Christine said. "My sister-in-law flew in them when she was a hostess with Britavia."

Pickles and I exchanged glances. A Hermes could take two DC-3 passen-

ger loads. I finished my drink and called Denis from the phone box outside the pub. He listened without interrupting.

"It's probably time-expired and requires a complete overhaul," he suggested. "The cost would be out of all proportion, probably close to £30,000."

"But we could get it for practically nothing," I urged. "You can bet the Stansted fire department didn't pay for it. And it's probably still airworthy; it flew in here recently."

"How do you know that?" he demanded.

I told him Tony and I had been at Stansted when the aircraft arrived a week ago. He digested this piece of information thoughtfully. "Tell Pickles to have a sniff round tomorrow after he's despatched your flight. He'll have plenty of time and he's good at that sort of thing," he finally instructed. I passed the information on.

Our flight the next morning departed on time at 9am. I managed to have a quick discussion with Pickles about the Hermes before the hustle and bustle of preparing the aircraft for service drove everything else from my mind. Les and I did our own refuelling and documentation while Pickles checked in our thirty-six passengers. All this required two hours' hard work, but by doing our own ground handling we saved £30.

16

After take-off, when we were established in the cruise across France, I had time at last to think a bit more about the Hermes. A larger aircraft of this type only required two pilots to fly it but we'd need to employ flight engineers, since the aircraft required a three-person crew. The increased passenger capacity would also necessitate two hostesses in the passenger cabin, but since two DC-3s needed a hostess each, we wouldn't need to hire more cabin crew.

We deposited our passengers in Palma, having made a brief refuelling stop at Lyons on the way, and brought another load of British holidaymakers home to Stansted. Pickles marshalled us onto the parking area and wheeled the passenger steps up to the door as I cut the engines. Post-flight customs formalities took less than half an hour and, after topping up the main tanks, we were soon airborne on our way home to Gatwick. The tower had cleared us direct to Gatwick at 4000 feet and the ferry flight took exactly 30 minutes. After arriving, the co-pilot helped me secure the aircraft for the night and Pickles and Christine off-loaded the catering supplies into our company van. Only when all this was completed did I have a chance to talk to Pickles.

"I made a few enquiries about the Hermes," he told me as we walked away from our darkened aircraft. "Skyways have operated three of them during the summer season, but are replacing them with Avro 748s before next year."

"Why haven't they advertised them for sale?" I enquired.

"They traded them in for new 748s. Avro, the manufacturer, had three cancelled orders at the end of the production line and offered them to Skyways. They took the Hermes as trade-ins, so the manufacturers now own the Hermes and would prefer to see them taken off the civil register."

"Why's that?"

"To make room for the new aircraft," Pickles explained. "Neither Skyways nor Avro want somebody buying the old aircraft and competing for ad hoc charter business." He paused to let this information sink in before continuing. "I spoke to the senior officer at the airport fire station, and he told me that the East Anglian Air Museum at Southend was anxious to get the Hermes, but Avro wanted £750 to disassemble the machine and transport it by road to the museum site. If they can't raise the money, the aircraft will go to the fire dump for fire-fighter training."

We passed this information on to Denis and Tony in the office next morning.

"How long did they give the museum to come up with the money?"

"Three weeks. The time's up at the end of this month."

"That's only two weeks away; it doesn't give us much time."

"How many flying hours are left on the engines and airframe?" Denis wanted to know.

"The airframe is due for a major overhaul at 15,000 flying hours or the thirtieth of September next year, whichever comes first. Three of the engines have very little time remaining, but Skyways engineering have quite a cache of overhauled Hercules engines, which they're probably about to sell as scrap."

We knocked the subject around for another half hour before Denis and

Tony had to go flying. I stayed behind in the office to reduce the mountain of paperwork that continually tried to envelope us. Our flight records were a week behind and would take at least a full day to bring up to date. The Ministry of Civil Aviation had a nasty habit of dropping in on us occasionally to inspect our records and were not impressed if they found they weren't up to date. In best civil service style, they preferred the paperwork to be right even if it meant grounding the airline for days or weeks. The excuse that we were all too busy flying and earning a living cut no ice with them.

Denis arrived back from his flight after lunch and appeared in the office about three. Together we got the office back into some semblance of order.

"I've been on the phone to the East Anglian Air Museum," he explained as he arrived. "Their curator told me they've been unable to raise the money for the Hermes, so it looks like it'll be going to the fire school. He was most upset, said it was the last surviving example of the type."

"Why don't we buy it then?" I suggested. Denis winked conspiratorially.

"That's where we've got to be a bit crafty," he explained. "Neither Avro nor Skyways want the aircraft competing against their new 748s. I doubt if they'd sell it to us, and if they did, the price would be too high."

"So what do we do? Buy another Dakota for the extra work?"

Denis sniggered.

"Pickles came up with a good suggestion that I'll put to the shareholders. He suggested we buy the aircraft in the name of the museum and lease it back from them for a nominal sum."

I pondered the idea carefully. "Do you think the museum would agree?" I enquired doubtfully, but Denis assured me they'd do almost anything to eventually obtain the machine. "How long would they lease it to us for?" I said.

He shrugged. "Dunno and don't care. Have you ever heard of a museum that turned money away? They stand to win either way; as long as we hire the aircraft, they have a source of revenue. When we finally decide to stop flying it, they get another nice exhibit for their museum."

It sounded a great scheme. We could obtain a fully airworthy four-engined airliner for under a thousand pounds. It would need a lot more maintenance than a modern DC-6, Britannia or Viscount, but flying revenue would cover costs. The prospect of not having to beg for a bank loan also appealed. We discussed the matter further and decided to call a shareholders' meeting for the next weekend.

I flew through Stansted twice that week and visited the crash fire dump on both occasions. The stately Handley Page Hermes stood parked among the blackened hulks of several military and civil aircraft. It would be a shame to consign it to a similar fate.

After speaking to the duty fire officer in the station, I obtained his permission to go aboard the aircraft.

The interior was a trifle tatty after a busy season of flying holidaymakers to the Costa Brava and Mallorca. The aisle carpet had seen better days, and the ceilings and side panels bore the scars of innumerable scuffs and scratches. Making my way forward to the flight deck, I retrieved the technical log from the flight engineer's desk and scanned a few previous entries. The machine was getting high on flying hours but had been adequately maintained by its previous owners.

Surprisingly, the outside of the machine was in excellent condition, thanks mainly to a recent re-spray. The present owners had obviously appreciated the importance of keeping up appearances with their older aircraft.

By the end of my inspection I had concluded that with a new cabin interior — mainly carpets and head linings — plus our name on the side of the fuselage, we'd probably have a four-engined airliner on next year's flight line for less than £2000, which was a hell of a lot less than the £15,000 we'd paid for Kilo Echo, our first DC-3, a year ago.

The Air Links shareholders were divided in their opinion of the Hermes idea.

Stan Wilson, the pragmatic car dealer from West Hartliepool, was cautious. He wanted an assured clientele for the aircraft before putting any money down.

Dr Levitt was in direct contrast; he was ecstatic at the idea. "A four-engined aeroplane, able to carry eighty passengers," he chortled. "This is what I wanted right from the start. In another few years we'll be flying jets!"

Denis and Tony exchanged amused glances. There was going to be a lot of hard work before the aircraft carried revenue passengers. Legal agreements needed to be drawn up, our air operator's certificate would need to be amended to include the new type of aircraft, crew training courses on the ground and in the air would need to be conducted during the winter, and we'd need to hire more aircrew. Pilots experienced on that type of aircraft would be needed to help set up and run the training and checking organisation. Flight engineers would have to be hired and contracts with other travel organisations would need to be found. Our maintenance contractor at Biggin Hill, Air Couriers, would need more staff and equipment to service the aircraft.

We knocked all these points around at the shareholders' meeting and finally passed a resolution to buy the aircraft for the East Anglian Air Museum with a guarantee of being able to lease the machine back from them at an agreed rate.

Meanwhile we still needed to continue earning our living with two DC-3s.

With a few thousand stashed away in the bank, it was tempting to remain small, earning a living in the ad hoc charter market around Europe.

Horizon Holidays put the final seal on the Hermes deal for us. When the elder Mr Zucher heard we were re-equipping with four-engined aircraft, he sent his son down to Gatwick with a briefcase full of contracts.

Two of these were for weekly flights to Geneva, starting in late December and continuing through till the end of April. Our survival was guaranteed through another winter. Other contracts guaranteed a minimum forty-five hours a week.

The purchase of the stately Handley Page Hermes went relatively smoothly, but taking physical possession proved a little more difficult. We lent the Air Museum £750 to buy the aircraft on condition they leased it back to us for £1 an hour, the money to be deducted from the purchase price. Air Links retained the right to terminate or extend the contract as desired, provided the aircraft was eventually taken to the museum site and handed over to them when the time expired.

Griff, the chief of Air Couriers, managed to buy five overhauled Bristol Hercules engines at bargain basement price from Skyways Engineering, without having to divulge where they were going. He was also offered a large cache of spares at scrap metal price, which he quickly snapped up.

We handed over the cheque to the museum on the Friday and they promised to pay the purchase money the following Monday, October the first. We conscripted a ferry crew from the recently defunct Air Safaris to ferry the big aircraft to Air Couriers' maintenance facility at Biggin. Griff's men would check it over and paint our name on the side. Pickles and I drove them up to Stansted in the Air Links van. I was determined to fly on the first flight of our new toy, even if it was only a short hop across the Thames Estuary to Biggin. Pickles grumbled when I told him he'd have to drive the van back and muttered something about seeing about that.

Life was never meant to be easy in aviation. When we arrived at Stansted, the guard in a newly installed security hut at the main entrance asked for our proof of identity. Security was a lot more relaxed in the 1960s, hijacking was a relatively unknown activity in Europe and uniformed airline staff were free to come and go as they pleased without having to display identity cards.

Not so at Stansted on this particular morning. I explained to the guard we had come to collect our aircraft. He leaned against a fire alarm while peering at the Air Safaris crew behind me. He enquired where our uniforms were if we were airline staff. My explanation failed to persuade him to let us through.

A phone call to the duty officer at the crash fire station made a difficult situation worse. He informed me they'd heard nothing of the aircraft being purchased.

"Last thing we heard was the museum couldn't raise the money," he volunteered. "They had until the thirtieth, then the aircraft became the property of the crash fire service."

I realised with sickly dread that Sunday September 30 had come and gone. I assured him the purchase money had been paid today.

"Not in my book it hasn't," he replied jauntily. "Anyway, you've left it a bit late, we're just about to use it."

"Whaddya mean you're about to use it?" I demanded with alarm.

"New course of fire fighters have arrived from Heathrow this morning for practical training," he explained. "We're due to start in half an hour. Tarrah!"

A glance across the airfield confirmed my worst fears. Black uniformed figures were manhandling hoses from red and chrome fire tenders. Myriads of flashing red lights blinked their message round the Stansted Fire School's next victim — our Handley Page Hermes!

I tried appealing to the security guard's better instincts by again explaining that the aircraft about to be consigned to the flames had in fact been purchased by us. He remained unconvinced.

"Can I use your phone to call my company?" I appealed. He shook his head negatively.

"Sorry mate, no outside calls. There's a call box across the road." He gestured towards a phone box which three dishevelled kids were covering in graffiti.

I scared them out of the booth and dialled our Gatwick number. Christine answered.

"Tony and Denis are both flying," she apologised. "There's nobody here who can help. I'll leave a message for them when they land tonight."

"That'll be too late, they're about to set fire to our aircraft. We need to do something decisive now!"

Pickles was also crammed into the phone box, listening. Abruptly he left and sprinted back across the road as I began dialling the control tower. Maybe they could prevent the crash fire crew from igniting Air Link's next aircraft. The duty air traffic controller was unconvinced by my pleas.

"Our information is that Avro donated the aircraft to the fire school for training," he informed me. "We received a notam* that a fire-fighting demonstration was scheduled for 11am today. I don't have the authority to stop it, even if I believed your story, which frankly, I don't."

I thought desperately of something to do. Chaining myself to the aircraft was the most dramatic solution, but I couldn't get through the security gate. Phoning the Air Links' shareholders wouldn't achieve the desired result. Our aircraft was about to go up in flames and would be destroyed before they'd do anything. Not even the company solicitor could do anything in the short time available.

Reluctantly I concluded the situation was hopeless. Air Links was destined to soldier on as a small independent airline, living from hand to mouth until inevitably one long hard winter the money and work would run out and the bank would declare us insolvent.

And we had come so close to getting into the four-engined league!

* Notice to Air Men

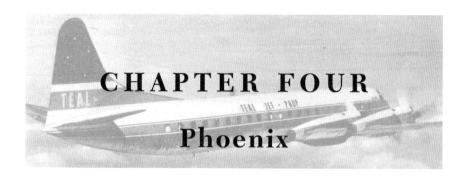

CHAPTER FOUR
Phoenix

Our winter sports programme commenced on December 26 and ran through till the end of April. Six pilots, including Tony, Denis and Les Smith, completed the Hermes technical course and got the type endorsed on their licences after a total of ten hours' flying training with an ex-Skyways training captain. We'd also hired four flight engineers for five months, with the assurance of permanent employment if we found sufficient work for our new aircraft.

Tony and Denis did the inaugural first flight, a Horizon Holidays IT schedule to Geneva with eighty excited skiers. Christine and Andrée were the hostesses, and a newly hired flight engineer, Joe Phillips, made up the crew complement.

Pickles and I checked the passengers in and completed pre-flight documentation. I took the load and trim sheet up to the cockpit for Denis to check and sign.

"Full load, eighty passengers, should make a nice bit of money for Mr Zucher," he observed with satisfaction, as he signed the form and handed it back to me.

I agreed with him, adding, "We were blooming lucky to get the aircraft. I thought it was going up in flames. If it hadn't been for that false fire alarm . . ."

Denis interrupted. "He's got a lot of initiative for an eighteen-year-old. Should go a long way in this business."

As I hurried down the passenger boarding steps, I pondered on Denis's remark and the last-minute miracle that had saved our aircraft from the ashes.

A light drizzle had begun to fall that day as I'd left the phone box and headed towards our van. The security guard leaned on the fire alarm post outside his security booth and eyed me with insolent amusement. As the first raindrops fell he extended one hand and looked skyward before scuttling into the shelter of his hut to watch television.

The Air Safari ferry crew waited beside the van as I returned. On the far side of the airfield, thirty or forty fire-fighters had finished laying hoses round our soon-to-be-cremated aeroplane. I explained to the crew what had happened and told them we'd take them back to Gatwick. They received the news regretfully; no professional aviator likes to see a perfectly serviceable aircraft destroyed, particularly when his job goes with it.

"Surely you can do something, phone your lawyer maybe?" Gibson, their captain, suggested.

I shook my head. "Not in the time available. They're about to set fire to it."

In the distance, we could see two figures in black oilskins pouring Av-gas over the wings and engine nacelles. The time was ten minutes to eleven and I didn't want to be around when they set the first match to it. I turned towards our three crew. "C'mon, let's get the hell outta here," I suggested. They seated themselves in the van as I looked round for Pickles.

The firemen had finished dowsing the aircraft with gasoline and were walking away to a safe distance, when the fire alarm sounded.

Absolute bedlam reigned as the Stansted Fire Section suddenly realised they'd been caught with their pants down. Two fire engines started moving away then remembered their hoses were laid out on the ground. Swarms of firemen began coiling them up again.

In the security hut the guard was talking excitedly on the telephone. He slid open his glass door and beckoned towards me. "Where's the fire?" he demanded. We were about to tell him we didn't know when Pickles appeared, nursing a cut hand.

"Where the hell have you been?" I enquired, but he ignored me and addressed the gate guardian.

"Fire in the Civil Aviation Flying Unit's hangar. Tell 'em to get over here quickly," he ordered the guard. The man ducked back into his security booth and spoke urgently into the phone. Across the airfield the first fire tender began lumbering away from the Hermes towards the flying unit's hangar.

We glanced in that direction but saw no signs of fire. An Air Ministry Dove aircraft stood parked outside on the tarmac, while an instrument-rating candidate pre-flighted it under the critical gaze of a flight-testing examiner. In the hangar, several ground engineers worked unconcernedly on the starboard engine of another aircraft.

"Looks like a false alarm," one of the ferry crew began to suggest, but Pickles cut him short.

"Tell 'em to bring every fire engine and make it quick! The whole hangar could go up at any minute if you don't," he ordered the guard. A second fire truck began its ponderous journey across the airfield as the security guard shouted into the phone.

While I was trying unsuccessfully to figure out what exactly was happening around me, a light-coloured Skyways van pulled up at the security point. A uniformed member of their ground staff climbed out and approached me.

"Air Links, I presume?" he observed pleasantly. "Ewbank, Station Manager, sorry I'm late but I had to drive up from Lympne and got caught in traffic."

"You were almost too bloody late," I told him. He shrugged apologetically and waved a security pass at the guard. As if by magic, the security barrier lifted and we followed his van round the airfield to our Hermes.

Behind us, five or six fire engines had surrounded the flying unit's hangar, while the airport fire chief discussed something heatedly with the testing unit's chief pilot.

Ewbank, the Skyways traffic manager, arranged a ground tug to tow our aircraft out of the fire dump onto the tarmac hard-standing. Our ferry crew boarded the aircraft to prepare it for the short ferry flight to Biggin. The flight engineer approached me as I chocked the nosewheel.

"We're going to wait an hour or more for the petrol fumes to dissipate," he explained. "Those fire wallahs did a great job of soaking the nacelles and wings in high-octane fuel. There's quite a fire risk from the exhausts on start up. It'll probably be after three o'clock before we get away."

I acknowledged the wisdom of his actions; it would be ironical to have the aircraft catch fire after escaping the firemen's match so narrowly. I looked around for Pickles to tell him I'd come back to Gatwick with him in the van. I found him aboard the aircraft sitting in the last row of seats, holding a blood-soaked handkerchief round his hand.

"What happened to you?" I enquired. He looked as if about to faint and mumbled something unintelligible about cutting his hand on a pane of glass. I told him to get in the van and I'd take him over to the medical section. He made no protest as I helped him down to the vehicle.

The doctor on duty gave him an anti-tetanus shot and inserted four stitches in the palm of his right hand. This took over an hour, and it was 2.30 before we got back to the aircraft.

Captain Gibson and his crew had pre-flighted the aircraft and were completing the last of the paperwork as we pulled up in the van. The smell of volatile high octane fuel had dissipated and the captain felt confident the risk of fire was minimal.

"But I'd like somebody standing by with an extinguisher until we've got all four engines running," he instructed. "And leave the aft steps in place just in case we need to get out in a hurry."

I motioned to Pickles to tell him to do that, then remembered his injured hand. He'd be unable to manoeuvre a heavy CO_2 extinguisher in his present state. I'd have to stand by with it during the start then manoeuvre the boarding steps away from the aircraft on my own. He'd be unable to drive the van home either, I'd have to do that. A thought struck me.

"You might as well travel in the aircraft and I'll pick you up at Biggin later this afternoon," I told him. His pale face dissolved into a smile; he'd got his wish to go on the first flight.

Ten minutes later all four engines were running as I struggled to manoeuvre the boarding steps away from the tail of the aircraft. The Skyways manager removed the wheel chocks and I gave the "thumbs up" signal. Gibbie acknowledged and the sound of the four Hercules rose as the Air Links Hermes moved away from its close encounter with destruction. In the jump seat, behind the captain, Pickles managed to extend two fingers of his bandaged hand at me.

I walked back to our van and drove round the perimeter track to the main gate. The same officious security guard was watching two technicians working on the fire alarm as I approached.

"Not going with 'em then?" he observed facetiously. I began to explain that one of us had to bring the van back and it had to be me because the other fellow was hurt. Then I stopped. A thought suddenly occurred to me.

"Did they find the fire and put it out?" I enquired. He shook his head.

"Naagh, false alarm, some blooming kids set the alarm off while I wasn't looking. One of 'em must've broken the glass with his bare hands 'cos there's blood everywhere." He gestured towards the technicians replacing a pane of glass in the fire alarm.

I commiserated with him and thanked him as he raised the barrier.

"Pleasure," he responded. "We're here to be of service."

Aviation historians have written many words of wisdom about the Handley Page Hermes. Even at a time when the British aircraft industry produced a multitude of unusual designs, the Hermes was unique among them. It was designed and built in the closing years of the Second World War and first flew on 12 December 1945, four months after the cessation of hostilities. It was intended as a peace-time long-range transport to compete with the American DC-4 Skymaster, which it closely resembled. It was a spectacular aircraft, with a wing span of 113 feet and an estimated maximum speed of 350 mph.

It supposedly incorporated all the lessons learned by Handley Page from designing wartime military aircraft, and used a revolutionary new high lift/low drag aerofoil section as well as patented Handley Page trailing edge flaps.

Test flying started at Radlett two weeks before Britain's first post-war Christmas. Like the Titanic, it started badly. The prototype crashed and burned on its first flight, causing considerable argument and consternation in the design office.

It took two years for Handley Page to pluck up sufficient courage to chance the second prototype in the air. Wind tunnel research had convinced the boffins that the probable cause of the accident had been control overbalance. Several modifications such as fuselage lengthening and repositioning of the tailplane had occurred.

Considerable argument and governmental indecision marked the gestation of this aircraft. Early examples had conventional tailwheel undercarriages, necessitating a main spar robust enough to absorb the landing shocks. Following a change in government, later versions were equipped with tricycle (nosewheel) undercarriages, requiring the rear spars to be strengthened to take the landing loads. This and other modifications increased the empty weight considerably, causing the first seven aircraft to be overweight and therefore unacceptable to BOAC.

Eventually (in February 1950) BOAC accepted its first example of the type. Despite its size and four engines the aircraft could carry only forty passengers. (Compare the Fokker F-27 Friendship which has two motors and carries the same number.)

It took BOAC another six months to complete crew training before introducing the type into regular line service on the London to Accra (West Africa) service.

Bristol Hercules engines were used on production Mark IV versions and the type began to earn a reputation for itself among passengers and crew. The early marks of Hercules engines encountered problems in the high temperature conditions and failed, causing more than one distraught flight engineer to call the Hermes "the corporation's best three-engined aircraft". (There were no three-engined aircraft in the fleet!) It certainly had great difficulty in getting airborne in hot conditions and required long runways so that it could use the curvature of the earth to become airborne. Hermes had more than their fair share of engine problems at that time, but these were eventually overcome by installing a different mark of Hercules engine. With these problems out of the way the Handley Page design team felt able to relax and concentrate on the design of the forthcoming "Victor" bomber.

The respite did not last long unfortunately, for a Hermes once again grabbed the headlines by crash-landing in the desert, several hundred miles off track.

However, the accident was attributed to pilot error, and Hermes were assigned to more and more of BOAC's routes. Ambitious plans were afoot to develop bigger and more powerful examples of Hermes, but fortunately for the travelling public these plans foundered in the quagmire of government indecision at the time.

By 1953 the type was operating on the West African, and East and South African services as well as London to Aden via Rome and Cairo. The type was never introduced on the North Atlantic run, because of a unanimous resolution by management and the manufacturer not to operate the aircraft far away from dry land.

The aircraft was unpopular with cabin crew, who complained the pronounced tail-down attitude required them to walk up-hill to provide service to the passengers. Pilots also complained that the aircraft "dragged its arse through the sky" unless higher than recommended power settings were used in cruise. The manufacturer's assertion that only the wing incidence was wrong was quickly rebuffed by BOAC executive captains, who maintained everything was wrong.

Late in 1953 the type was replaced in service by the revolutionary new British de Havilland Comet jetliner. Several accidents involving Comets caused the re-commissioning of the Hermes for a few months in 1954, but the type ended its BOAC service in December the same year, after an operational life of slightly over three years.

It was quickly snapped up by the independent airlines. Airwork used Hermes to carry troops to Kenya and the Suez Canal, Britavia acquired seven machines for both trooping and passenger work. Skyways, Kuwait Airways, Falcon and Air Safaris also operated the type with varying degrees of commercial success.

The independent airlines continued to operate the Hermes long after

BOAC relinquished theirs. Despite several more crashes, the problems associated with the government's first post-war British airliner were gradually overcome, enabling the private airlines to operate a cheap economical four-engined aircraft. An American's assertion at the 1953 SBAC Farnborough Air Show that the Hermes was a heap of rubbish (in Americanese, "a loada crap") was indignantly renounced by a very senior female member of the British royal family, who sternly advised the American gentleman that "It might be a load of rubbish, my good man, but it's British rubbish." He was then politely told to "naff off".

So the Handley Page Hermes, Britain's first post-war airliner — an overweight, underpowered ugly duckling — eventually turned into something rather beautiful. It was this aircraft that we spied over the back fence of an Essex pub and bought for less than a thousand pounds.

A lot of preparatory work needed to be done after obtaining the Hermes. Stan Wilson arranged for a coachbuilder friend of his to completely refurbish the carpets and ceilings. Air Couriers polished and cleaned up the outside and stopped most of the oil leaks. By the time they'd painted our name in red letters on the side of the fuselage and put the red Air Links chevron on the tail, the old girl looked pretty smart.

Denis, Tony and I worked together to complete the paperwork. The period between October and Christmas is a quiet time in the charter business so we completed it in less than five weeks. Griff, the head of Air Couriers, had used this time to check the Hermes over and install three overhauled Hercules in place of the high-time engines.

We hired several redundant Air Safaris crews, the first being Gibbie — the pilot in charge of the original ferry trip from Stansted. He was also a flight instructor and type-rating examiner, and proved invaluable in checking pilots out on the type of aircraft.

By the first day of December we had completed the last of the work involved in getting the aircraft into service. Crew training was over and we'd hired two more ground staff to help with the increased flying.

Tony suggested now would be a good time to have a get-together in the Gatwick Aero Club before we got busy. We announced it would be the following Thursday and Andrée arranged details of the food and drink with Vic the landlord.

It proved an excellent idea; we got to know our new staff and, more importantly, they got to recognise us. Towards the end of the evening I tore myself away from an unsuccessful attempt at charming a statuesque Caledonian hostess and fell into conversation with Gibbie, Denis and Tony. They'd been listening to Gibbie's account of the misunderstanding at Stansted six weeks ago.

"Anyway, that's all behind us now," I commented. "All the administration work's completed and we start flying in just over a month . . . sooner if we can pick up any charter work."

Everyone agreed except Gibbie.

"There's just one more important item," he began. "Probably the most important thing of all and nobody's thought of it."

"What's that?" I demanded with a feeling of alarm. I was beginning to get warning signals in my gut, the sort you get when it's your turn to buy a round of drinks and you discover you've left your wallet behind. My mind raced through all the possibilities: certificate of airworthiness, licensing board approvals, insurance, maintenance release, engine hours remaining . . . ? Nobody else seemed concerned, so I gave up. "What've we forgotten?" I demanded.

Gibbie smiled expansively. "A name for the aircraft. Same as BOAC and Pan American or Qantas. We're in the four-engined league now, so we've got to have a name for the Hermes."

I turned to Pickles for inspiration, but he was looking rather green around the gills. I suspected somebody had been spiking his ginger-beer shandies. Denis suggested "Dreadnought", which everybody pooh-poohed as too heavy. Somebody else came up with "Hermes", which we found too unoriginal, then somebody else suggested "Apollo", which we all rejected. "How about 'Flaming Arrow', like the 'Golden Arrow' but a bit faster?" a new flight engineer suggested. Various suggestions went round the group, until Tony suggested "Phoenix".

"Any particular reason? Who was Phoenix anyway?" I questioned.

"You've obviously forgotten all the Greek mythology we learned at school," he accused. "Phoenix was a beautiful bird that lived a hell of a long time then rose again from the ashes after being burned."

Everybody liked that; our bird looked as beautiful as any DC-6 or similar modern aircraft and it had certainly risen from the ashes, albeit the ashes of the other aircraft wrecks in the Stansted fire dump. Everyone but Pickles toasted the new name. He was fast asleep in a corner of the bar.

CHAPTER FIVE

Out of the Ashes

Although rather short of DC-3 crews, we continued to operate our two Dakotas on occasional freight and passenger charters. Because such work was almost non-existent in winter, we decided to advertise one DC-3 for sale, retaining Kilo Echo, the convertible passenger/freighter, for the small amount of flying available. The Hermes did the equivalent work of two Dakotas with almost the same number of crew and amount of fuel as two smaller aircraft. Other cost savings such as ground handling also resulted from the use of one aircraft instead of two.

The decision to retain the convertible freighter proved to be a good one, because Air France sub-chartered us to operate their nightly Heathrow to Lille freight service for six months. This kept Kilo Echo gainfully employed during December and for the first half of next year. The terms of the charter were pretty generous too: £40 per hour whether empty or full and fifty percent of the freight revenue.

It was a satisfying and exhilarating moment when our four-engined Handley Page Hermes, registration G-ALDA, departed for Geneva on Boxing Day, December 26. Dr Levitt, Stan Wilson, Pickles and I watched the sleek four-engined shape rise from Gatwick's westerly runway. I said I hoped this was the start of greater things for all of us.

The prestige of operating a large four-engined aircraft generated a lot of follow-on business. Enquiries for North Atlantic and Far East Charters came to our office, but we declined them. We didn't have aircraft time available, and to fly over such remote areas required the carriage of flight navigators, whom we didn't employ. We were also aware that our Hermes was a fairly ancient aircraft, liable to develop the occasional malfunction. When this occurred on the European routes, it was relatively simple to despatch an engineer and a spare part to the downed bird. Long-distance charters would be infinitely more expensive; the Hermes was a relatively rare type and American or Asian technicians would know little about it. A breakdown in those areas could bankrupt us.

We passed all long-range charters on to Caledonian Airways, a new company operating Douglas DC-7cs mainly on the North Atlantic. They were glad of the extra work and reciprocated by passing on to us the occasional European sub-charter.

A buyer for our second DC-3 came along early in the New Year: it was an airline that concentrated on carrying executives on specialist charters. They took delivery of the DC-3 in mid-January and ferried it to Air Couriers for a complete refurbishment and executive interior installation. The sale provided a further transfusion of funds into the company coffers.

Operation of an old aircraft like the Hermes was not without problems. By the end of the winter sports flights to Geneva, we had required two engine changes and had had several technical delays early on. As we gained experience with the new type, the problems diminished. In April, we had only one significant delay, caused by a tyre bursting on landing at Gatwick. Rubber debris damaged the flaps, and it took Air Couriers five hours to install replacements from stores. Griff had shown remarkable foresight when he'd bought the entire Hermes spares inventory from Skyways.

Summer IT work continued to keep us busy. Apart from Caledonian, we were the only other charter operator of pressurised four-engined equipment out of Gatwick, and travel agents were not slow to indicate their preference for our larger, faster and more comfortable machine. Our pilots also enjoyed flying the Hermes after the noise and discomfort of the Dakota.

Although plenty of work was coming in, we could not afford to forget that flying hours were running out on the machine. By autumn, the Hermes would be due for a major overhaul, an expensive item that would run into tens of thousands of pounds.

I drew the directors' attention to this fact several times, but they appeared unconcerned. Dr Levitt continued to bask in the prestige of owning a four-engined aeroplane, Stan Wilson couldn't think any further than our very healthy bank balance, and Denis winked conspiratorially whenever I mentioned it and assured me something would come up in the autumn.

I doubted his statement; it didn't make sense to spend our entire year's profit on renovating an old aircraft. Denis assured me, most emphatically, that he'd arranged something for the autumn.

"She won't cost us another penny," he assured me one evening, after we'd towed the aircraft to the overnight park.

CHAPTER SIX

Borrow a Pound

Borrow a pound and the bank owns you.
Borrow a million and you own the bank!
Anon

Our healthy bank balance didn't escape the notice of our hard-headed bank manager, who'd had years of experience dealing with impoverished airlines and crews. He cornered me one afternoon as I deposited two substantial cheques. He had lurked in the background until the transaction was done then had come forward.

"Cattermoull, branch manager, pleased to meet you," he began, ushering me towards an inner office. "Care for a cup of coffee? Tea maybe? You sure?"

We talked round generalities for a couple of minutes before he came to the point.

"Nice little operation you've got going. My daughter flew with you last week," he began. "I'm a great aviation enthusiast myself, know all the different types of aircraft. Always take an interest in what's going on at the airport. After all, aviation's the main source of employment in the local area. The National Provincial Bank always likes to participate in local business. There's lots of ways we can help our customers, advice on taxation, accounting, payroll, loans to buy aircraft and equipment . . ."

"Loans to fellows when they're out of work or between jobs?" I enquired curiously. He ignored the question.

"Yes, well we wondered how you paid for your new . . . er . . . DC-6, isn't it?"

I nodded absently. I was due to meet Griff at Air Couriers in an hour and I'd have to leave shortly.

"DC-6s don't come cheaply, I'd hazard a guess you must have paid a minimum of £80,000 for that aircraft." He gazed quizzically at me over his spectacles.

I told him we had paid a considerable sum for the aircraft. I didn't want him broadcasting the fact that we were operating a flying museum piece, which we'd rescued off the fire dump. The public were very sensitive about their own safety and would have shied away from flying with us if they'd known. In their estimation the only things that flew and went cheap were canaries!

"Thinking of buying any more aircraft?" he enquired sharply. I shook my head. "Not in the immediate future, in fact we've recently sold one of our DC-3s, which was surplus to requirement."

Cattermoull made a quick note of this then stood up and extended a limp handshake.

"Nice to have met you at last," he smiled. "Good to see the business is doing so well. Let me know if our bank can be of any assistance to you in the future."

I thanked him for his offer and went on my way, ruminating that life in the business community was either a feast or a famine. When you were short of cash or a job, nobody wanted to know you. When you had plenty of money, everybody wanted to lend you more.

The dramatic increase in flying hours quadrupled the administrative work for our small office staff. The payroll now listed twenty personnel, most of whom had to be paid weekly. Pickles, the only full-time member of the office staff, was fully employed with the day-to-day running of the flying side of the company, so Denis, Tony and I spent every non-flying hour in the office. After eight hours of tedious administrative work, two of us would then position our DC-3 to Heathrow to operate the Air France night freighter schedule to Lille and back to Heathrow. After the return freight had been unloaded at London Airport, we'd position the aircraft back to Gatwick, arriving early in the morning in time to go home for an early breakfast before taking the phone off the hook and collapsing exhausted into bed for a few hours.

It was after one of these night freighter runs that I first met Mr Koller, the head of security for the Bank of England. He was a smartly dressed individual in his early fifties. I found him talking with Pickles in the office when I arrived back at Gatwick after a night freighter run. Pickles introduced him and he came straight to the point.

"Her Majesty's Government are transferring two million pounds sterling worth of gold bullion from the Swiss Credit Bank in Zurich to the Bank of England. Bank policy dictates that the shipments will go by air for security reasons. The Swiss banking authorities customarily handle the transfer of the bullion from their vaults in Zurich onto the aircraft. The Swiss Federal Police, the Bundes Polizei, are then responsible for the safety of the shipment until the aircraft leaves Swiss airspace."

I listened semi-interestedly. We were obviously going to be involved in some professional way and I waited to learn how. It didn't take long.

"Scheduled airlines won't guarantee the security of the shipments," he continued. "And a trial consignment of boxes filled with sand aboard a chartered airliner was tampered with before it got to the bank's vaults in Cheapside."

I enquired how that could happen. The aircraft would be unloaded in a bonded Customs area, making it impossible for members of the public to gain access. Koller interrupted.

"Unfortunately the trade unions have run riot at London airport," he explained. "Demarcation of labour has resulted in all kinds of workers being allowed into the Customs area. Previously only aircrew, engineers, traffic staff and loaders were allowed access. Now there's just about every Tom, Dick and Harry wandering in and out at their pleasure. The Customs Service tries to avoid union disputes like the plague and rarely challenges anybody. The result is that anarchy reigns."

I enquired why Her Majesty's Customs couldn't deny them access. Koller laughed at the suggestion.

"London Heathrow is famous for two things. The first is the number of strikes and stoppages at peak holiday times; the second is the tremendous amount of theft of freight and baggage. It's got so bad that freight consignors now call it London Thief Row."

I had to admit I'd heard of problems in those areas, and these problems tended to compound. When a member of the ground staff was apprehended for questioning in connection with an alleged incident, the shop stewards would cry "victimisation" and call a stoppage. When this happened at a major European airport at peak holiday time, the effect on air travel was calamitous. Aircraft waited to be unloaded of their incoming payload, and when they weren't, the airport became log-jammed with outgoing freight, passengers and baggage. Meanwhile the arriving passengers became angry at not being reunited with their baggage and bombarded the airlines with complaints. It took less than an hour for complete chaos to envelope a major international airport in this way. Nobody needed that.

I told Koller I sympathised with him but wondered where Air Links fitted into the picture. The Bank of England had already used a charter airline, apparently with bad results.

The security man then told me Pickles had suggested Air Links could be of assistance. I looked across at Pickles, who had suddenly become rather self-conscious.

Pickles had met Koller and told him our Air France freight sub-charter was technically a scheduled service. He'd also suggested that we could extend our night freighter service on to Zurich, from where the gold could be flown direct to London Airport.

"What about the return freight out of Lille?" I demanded angrily of Pickles. "We're under charter to Air France and would have to call in at Lille again to collect the return freight for Heathrow." Pickles secretly signalled me to keep quiet, but I was damned if I was going to. "We can't leave the return freight behind," I advised Koller. "A lot of it is time-sensitive material like newspapers, bank records and documents that have to arrive that day."

Koller pursed his lips disapprovingly. "An en route stop would not be viewed favourably by the bank's officials," he informed me rather primly. "In fact I'd have to recommend that we do not ship the consignments if the aircraft has to stop en route."

I repeated that we couldn't leave return freight behind.

Koller then suggested blocking off the whole aircraft but I condemned the idea instantly. "The charterers would never agree to it; it would destroy the confidence and goodwill of the regular shippers if we treated them that way. They'd take their business elsewhere and probably never return. We can't leave freight behind just to accommodate your bank and, anyway, do you have any idea what it would cost? Thousands!"

The bank official looked regretful and muttered something about a lot of money being involved. Pickles had continued gesticulating at me while we spoke and now he drew me aside.

"It'd be a bad mistake to turn this job down too hurriedly," he began. "It'd be a very nice financial shot in the arm for us in the middle of winter."

I scoffed at the idea. "An extra two or three hours' flying for three or four nights at £40 an hour, plus a bit more for the freight, would be £500–600. Not exactly a fortune when you consider the bad effect it'd have on relations with our regular freight cons . . ."

Koller and Pickles interrupted me simultaneously.

"Because of the unusual nature of our shipments, the bank determines the revenue charges," Koller intoned. I was about to tell him our charter rate was £55 an hour but something in Pickles' expression deterred me.

"The rate for a transfer of this nature is a flat three-quarters of one percent of the gross value," Koller stated. I began to suddenly feel the accumulative effects of having been awake for almost twenty-four hours. I did a quick mental calculation but the result seemed absurd.

"You mean to say you'll pay just under one percent of £2 million pounds for this job?" I queried.

Koller nodded.

"Er . . . have I got an extra nought somewhere, 'cos I make that 15,000 pounds?"

Koller nodded his agreement, adding the consignment would be split into more than one load, each to go on a separate night. I enquired the weight of £2,000,000 worth of gold bullion and learned it was 3500 kilograms, including the crates and packaging. Half of that would be 1750 kilograms, which would easily fit into our Dakota's available payload and still leave a comfortable margin for our regular freight consignments. Fifteen thousand pounds for two night's work was a pretty favourable rate of return; our first aircraft, Kilo Echo, had cost exactly that much! I reminded myself that half of this revenue went to the charterers, Air France. Nevertheless, it was a lot of money when a DC-3 captain earned £2000 a year.

Unfortunately there was still one problem between us and half of £15,000 sterling.

"We'd still have to land at Lille," I insisted. "Unless we sub-charter another airline . . ."

Koller instantly dismissed the suggestion, explaining their underwriters stipulated the consignment must go by state airline. I briefly contemplated using another aircraft for the shipment, but our other Dakota had been sold and the Hermes was fully committed elsewhere. Air France would never agree to their regular customers being pushed aside, and I could see no way to carry the consignment on the bank's terms. I was about to relay this information to Koller when Pickles spoke up.

"That'll be fine then," he assured the bank official. "We'll extend our flights to Zurich when required and from there we'll route direct to Heathrow."

I was too tired to continue this argument, so I kept silent.

Koller looked pleased at the news. It was a pity I'd eventually have to disillusion him. As a director and shareholder of the company, I wasn't going to allow us to renege on the conditions of the Air France charter contract. Reputations are important in aviation and to ride roughshod over our regular customers would be commercial and financial suicide. Pickles had ushered Koller out of the door, otherwise I'd have told him so.

The phone rang and prevented me telling Pickles how I felt. The captain of the morning Geneva flight called to say his flight engineer hadn't reported for duty yet. A quick glance at my watch told me they were scheduled out in forty-five minutes. I assured the aircraft commander I'd alert the stand-by engineer and also endeavour to locate the tardy crew member. A short call to his home confirmed he'd left for the airport almost an hour previously by taxi. While I pondered my next move, an apologetic flight engineer raced into the office.

"Traffic jam on the A23 delayed us for almost half an hour in Horley," he explained. "There was no way to contact you en route. Sorry 'bout that."

I nodded sympathetically and he hurried out to his aircraft. I knew the ground engineers would have commenced refuelling and his pre-flight checks would normally take less than thirty minutes. There was every possibility of the flight leaving on time.

A charter airline's ops room can be a busy place, and several other matters distracted me from thinking any more about the lucrative gold shipments. I was exhausted from a full night flying and had no intention of getting trapped in the office. I headed for the door just as Tony and Denis arrived.

"Pickles has just told us about the bullion job," Denis greeted me jubilantly. "The bank balance is going to look very healthy if we can get a few more of those."

I felt too exhausted to discuss the pitfalls with him so headed home for a few hours' rest. I was scheduled to fly again that night.

Both aircraft were fully committed to winter flying programmes, and I was now the only pilot not checked out on the Hermes. I was keen to get a four-engined aircraft on my pilot's licence, so I mentioned this to Denis a day later. He pooh-poohed the idea.

"We've got enough pilots on the type and even if we could afford the limited flying hours to check you out, we need you for the Dakota operation," he explained. I suggested I could fly both types, but he shook his head.

"We're going to have to dedicate crews to a particular type," he explained. "The Horizon contract is ticking away nicely, and we can't take pilots away from it to fly the DC-3 as well. In addition, the Ministry of Civil Aviation has indicated some concern at our pilots being required to fly two different types of aeroplane."

I argued that Dan-Air pilots flew as many as three different types, but he seemed unimpressed. "Not four-engined types," he explained. "The Hermes is a relatively sophisticated type of aircraft, with four engines, tricycle under-carriage, three-man crew — sometimes four — and completely different technically from the Dakota. Frankly, I think the Dak is more demanding than the Hermes, particularly on a wet runway in a cross wind, but this tends to lend weight to their argument. I've gone along with their wishes; you'll stay on the DC-3."

I was bitterly disappointed at not getting my hands on our new toy but I could understand the reasons for keeping some pilots on the Dakota opera-tion exclusively. It meant a lot of night flying and I must have sighed resignedly at the thought of this because Denis then offered me a plum in compensation.

"I can't be chief pilot on both types," he went on. "And we're going to need to hire four new pilots for the freighter, one captain and two co-pilots. That'll bring the complement up to three complete crews with Chegwidden. I've offered the job of DC-3 chief pilot and training captain to Tony, but he prefers to stay on the Hermes."

He looked at me expectantly. I must have still showed signs of disappoint-ment at not getting on the Hermes, because he then nearly floored me with his next remark.

"What about taking over responsibility for the DC-3 operation?" he suggested. I looked at him in a startled fashion.

"There's nobody else in the company, and if you don't do it, we'll have to advertise for somebody from outside," he explained. "Think it over for a day or two then let me have your decision."

An incoming phone call terminated our conversation, and Denis left the office to prepare for a flight.

The caller was Koller from the Bank of England. He confirmed for me that Air Links had agreed to transport the gold shipments on his terms, with no intermediate stop at Lille. We discussed details for a few minutes, then I went in search of Pickles to question him about the matter. I spied him at the check-in counter, processing Denis's passengers. I left him alone until he had completed the task and returned to the office.

"Whose idea was it to take those bullion charters?" I enquired angrily. "Nobody told me and I've just had Koller on the line wanting a few details of the arrangements. We can't take the job. We're under charter to Air France and they'll be furious if we leave a load of return freight behind. They could easily call it a breach of contract and terminate the charters . . . possibly sue us too."

Pickles listened patiently, then motioned me into silence. He tried to assure me that no freight would be left behind.

"The Bank of England don't know that," I informed him. "Koller's just been on the phone and told me we've agreed to the freight charter on his terms, non-stop Zurich to Heathrow."

"That's correct," Pickles confirmed. "We collect the bullion in Zurich and fly it non-stop to London Heathrow."

"What about the damned freight out of Lille?" I demanded. He'd really fouled things up for us this time. Somebody was going to have to smooth things over with Air France's freight section.

Pickles seemed unaware of the strife he'd caused. "We pick up the freight from Lille and take it to Zurich," he explained quietly. "You can refuel there and fly non-stop to Heathrow. It'll take about two and a half hours. The Lille freight still gets to its destination okay, admittedly an hour or two late but that's never been a problem, and we earn a tidy sum from the gold shipment."

The figure of £7500 for a few nights' work kept going round in my head. I had to grudgingly admire the ingenuity of his scheme. I suppose I felt angry that I hadn't thought of it!

I didn't realise how short of DC-3 pilots we were until the co-pilot of the night freighter phoned in sick. I quickly scanned our rostering schedule to see who was available. Nobody!

Once again I placed the burden on Pickles' shoulder; he quickly phoned Dan-Air and arranged to borrow one of their pilots. The summer IT season had long since ceased and pilots were in plentiful supply. This was a windfall for us; with any sort of luck we'd be able to pick up four fully trained Dakota pilots.

I was flying the night freighter service, so decided to go home for a few hours' rest before starting the duty. I told Pickles to do something about hiring four more pilots as I left the office.

The night freighter service went uneventfully. While in Lille I enquired from the Air France freight agent whether it would matter if the freight was ever delayed a few hours en route. He assured me it wouldn't, but also suggested we could re-schedule our arrival and departure times.

"The freight consignors usually have everything here by 5pm," he explained. "The newspapers are here by 10, sometimes 10.30, so we could get you away an hour early if you wished. Any particular reason?"

I decided not to tell him about the bullion shipments. If security was a problem, the fewer who knew about it, the better.

We departed for Heathrow on schedule and I suggested to our borrowed co-pilot that he fly this sector. He readily agreed and proved to be a competent pilot. On the hour-and-a-quarter flight back I asked him about his background and experience.

Like a lot of new pilots, he'd paid to learn to fly at a civil flying club, working at a variety of jobs to finance his flying training. Finally he'd acquired the necessary commercial pilot's licence and instrument rating, qualifying him to start knocking on doors for a job. Like a lot of fellows before him, he ran up against the formidable 1000 hours' flying experience barrier. Nobody wanted a low-time pilot. They told him to come back when he had 1000 hours.

Two years of joyriding and instructing in the summer months and bar tending, waiting at tables and pumping petrol during the winter had kept body and soul together while he built up his flying hours. Once he'd achieved the four-figure total in his logbook, Dan-Air offered him employment as a DC-3 co-pilot on a temporary summer contract.

After observing him carrying out an accurate instrument-landing systems approach and smooth landing to Heathrow's runway 28 Left, I offered him the empty leg back to Gatwick. Once again he impressed me with his competence. I had calculated that his summer contract with Dan-Air must have expired, and if they weren't going to hire him, he was just the sort of fellow we needed.

On returning to Gatwick, I phoned Warren (Pluto) Wilson, Dan-Air's colourful chief pilot and told him that if Dan-Air didn't want this young pilot, we'd like to hire him.

Pluto was apologetic when he told me they were keeping him on.

"He's keen and a good operator," he averred. "We retained a skeleton staff to crew the aircraft during winter, and he was one of those I decided to keep on. He'll probably get a command when we get busy again in the spring." I said I was sorry he wasn't available and agreed with Pluto that he was an asset to the company.

I filed the paperwork from the night's flying and checked the incoming mail. Apart from a few bills from fuel companies and various charges from our handling agents overseas, there was nothing. The charter business had once again hibernated for the winter, with despondent groups of pilots huddled in the Greasy Spoon, listening for news of anything going on around Gatwick. I thought how lucky we were to have the freight schedule and the Horizon winter sports programme to bankroll us through winter. Pickles' entry into the office interrupted my reverie.

"We've placed adverts for one captain and three first officers in the Situations Vacant columns of *Flight* and *Aeroplane*," he informed me. "Denis says we'll be snowed under with applicants by Thursday. Somebody'll have to sort through the applications. Would you mind?"

I agreed to do it. Pickles was knowledgeable about commercial matters, but didn't possess the necessary technical knowledge to select aircrew. Tony and Denis couldn't do it either, they were fully committed to running the Hermes operation.

While we were hiring pilots as a necessity, Dr Levitt was using his leverage as a substantial shareholder in the company to place a nephew on the pay roll. Nobody else could fathom his reason for increasing our staff numbers when we needed to watch overheads closely. "Nathan will breathe fresh air into this company," he assured me. "He's a jolly good sportsman, played squash for Charterhouse, was commissioned in the Queen's Own regiment during his National Service, gets on well with anybody, but hasn't managed to find his niche in life yet." I recollected hearing that Nathan had worked for a stockbroker, insurance company and estate agent since entering the work force. I was doubtful he could contribute anything useful to our airline.

Thursday didn't bring Pickles his expected avalanche of job applicants. The back pages of *Flight* and *Aeroplane* gave the reasons: British European Airways (BEA) and Swiss Air were also looking for pilots. Both companies were excellent career prospects, infinitely better than some of the shaky independent operators. They were government-owned airlines with virtual monopolies on scheduled routes. They operated the latest aircraft and provided first-class training. Every pilot in the European independent airline scene would give his left testicle to fly for either of these prestigious airlines.

"I've phoned Dan-Air to see if they've got any Dakota qualified pilots they want to get rid of, but Pluto says they'll probably hold on to what they've got," Pickles said, breaking into my thoughts. "They expect to lose quite a few of their fellows to BEA."

It was strange there weren't any out-of-work pilots available in the depth of winter. In previous years they'd almost outnumbered the fallen leaves in autumn.

The situation changed slightly after lunch, when two pilot applicants arrived, in person.

I'd stepped back into the office and was greeted by a fellow I estimated to be in his early thirties. He spoke with a pronounced North American accent as he introduced himself.

"Cullenane," he said, extending his right hand. "I saw your advert in the magazine and decided to call rather than write."

This was a philosophy I had always endorsed; writing letters and filling in application forms merely put your name in the pile among a lot of others. Calling and talking to the people doing the hiring gave them a face and a voice to put with your application. Even if they sent you away to fill in the inevitable form, any intelligent being would do his best to ensure it ended on top of the heap.

Cullenane and I found two chairs and I began to take down his details.

Michael John Cullenane was born in Vancouver, British Columbia, twenty-nine years earlier. He told me he'd flown in the Royal Canadian Air Force, which he'd only recently left. I asked him his total flying hours and he admitted he hadn't totalled it recently. I sympathised with him; personal log-book keeping was a tiresome chore. My own log book was several months behind and the longer I left it, the harder it became to sit down and bring it up to date.

"Harvards and Thunderjets?" I enquired conversationally. He looked at me blankly. "Oh sorry, you probably called them T-6s and T-33 trainers. Is that what you learned on?"

He smiled quickly, nodding his head effusively.

I asked him what he'd flown after that and he told me he'd been a co-pilot on transports for three years before leaving to find a job in civil aviation. That had been three years ago. I could sympathise with him — Canada was reputed to be one of the most difficult countries to find employment.

I gave him a brief run-down on our operation, telling him how we'd acquired our two aircraft and describing the work they were doing. He seemed agreeably surprised at the salary for a DC-3 co-pilot, £1500 per annum, commenting it was over three times what he earned as a porter in a nearby hotel.

He seemed a reasonable enough sort of person, so I decided I'd recommend to Denis that we hire him. He readily accepted my offer to meet some of the organisation, and as both aircraft were on the ground, I decided to show him over Kilo Echo, our freighter DC-3.

He followed me down the terminal finger to where our aircraft were parked. Kilo Echo wasn't flying till evening, and as he'd be flying the Dakota rather than the Hermes, I decided to show him over it. I reflected he'd probably flown similar aircraft in the Canadian Air Force. My thoughts were interrupted by an announcement over the airport public address system; somebody wanted to contact me. I picked up a convenient courtesy phone.

"Hello, can I . . ." I began, but Denis interrupted.

"Guy, what've you done about getting more pilots for the Dakota?" he demanded agitatedly. "We need Les on the Hermes, and even if he stayed on the Dak, flight-time limitations would stop him flying after three weeks."

I knew what he was on about. The night freighter took about five hours flying a night and we were only permitted to fly 120 hours in twenty-eight days. The matter was urgent and I decided to discuss it with him there and then. I told Cullenane to go out to the DC-3 and I'd join him in a couple of minutes. I used the two minutes to explain to Denis that I was currently interviewing a pilot applicant and would meet him back in the office in half an hour. Ringing off, I hurried out to the Dakota.

There was no sign of our prospective pilot so I concluded that, like most aviators, he'd gone straight to the cockpit. I mounted the rickety aircraft steps and boarded the aircraft. He was nowhere to be seen. Glancing out of the cockpit slide window, I spied him standing by the nose wheel of our Hermes on the adjacent gate. I called out to him several times before he heard me and hurried over.

He came up to the cockpit and I pointed out various points about our control layout and radio set-up. We then went back into the cabin.

"We're fortunate that this aircraft is a convertible passenger/freighter," I explained. "We can whip out nine rows of seats and the galley equipment in less than thirty minutes." He looked at me in a puzzled fashion, so I explained that both freight and passenger work constituted our business.

I also took him round the outside of the aircraft, telling him about the new improved hydraulic brakes, larger passenger windows and the passenger-freight door. We then headed back to the terminal building. Denis met me at the office door.

"How was he?" He gestured towards Cullenane. I told him I thought he'd be all right, although he hadn't flown much in the last three years. Denis thrust a printed form in my hand.

"Then get him to fill in this application form and we'll take him," he instructed. "BEA are rumoured to be looking for 200 pilots, which could

40

really set the cat among the pigeons this summer."

I knew what he meant. The two state corporations, British European Airways and British Overseas Airways, were probably the best paying and most secure flying jobs in Europe. Virtually every licensed pilot applied to them in the hope of enjoying a well-paid career on the latest types of aircraft. Maintenance was good and the route structure was world-wide. Corporation pilots flew de Havilland Comets, Bristol Britannias, Vickers Viscounts and VC-10s, while we independents soldiered on in our venerable Dakotas, Yorks, Hermes, Vikings and other aeronautical antiques, few of which were under twenty years old.

Seasonal redundancy was unknown in the corporations, for no accountant would allow it after spending several months and thousands of pounds training their pilots to fly the modern types. Additionally, the state airlines flew world-wide schedules all year round. The business community didn't only travel during the summer months. Pilots in the independents fought to join the state airlines to enjoy these privileges, leaving a cornucopia of unfilled jobs in the private airlines for less fortunate pilots to fill.

The larger and more established private companies like British United, and Eagle Airways would have first choice of these applicants. Other operators like Dan-Air, Skyways, BKS Air Transport and Cambrian ranked slightly lower in the pecking order.

The smaller ad hoc operators like us in Air Links were bottom of the heap. Life in a company such as ours was a constant battle to trim costs against income so that sufficient funds accumulated to ensure survival through the winter.

The employment situation ran on a sinusoidal roller-coaster pattern, with a four-year gap between troughs and peaks. Whereas 1959 had been a disastrous year for low-time pilots seeking their first job, anybody who weathered the lean years quickly found secure employment when the pendulum swung the other way in 1963.

A knock on the office door interrupted me as I gave Cullenane the application form to complete. A tall rather slim fellow entered the office and introduced himself. "Michael Sommerpole, I'm looking for the personnel office," he explained in a quiet cultured voice. I tried unsuccessfully not to laugh. "You're in it," I assured him. "Personnel, flight operations, scheduling, rostering, it all goes on in this one office. Can I help you?"

He explained he was calling in connection with our advertisement for DC-3 pilots. I quickly found him a chair and asked him his particulars concerning licence and experience. He told me he'd recently gained his commercial pilot's licence with the Airways Aero Club at White Waltham. I enquired whether he also had an instrument rating.

"Not yet, although I've just passed the Ministry's Link Trainer Test and I've got a flight test booked for next Tuesday week."

"How much multi-engine time have you got?"

He admitted to only a few hours in a Miles Gemini. This placed me in a quandary. His qualifications were minimal in every respect; low on number of flying hours, probably very little actual instrument or night flying, negligible multi-engine experience and the instrument-rating flight test still to be passed. It was possible that he might fail one or more parts of the test and have to re-take it.

"I'm afraid we're looking for people with more experience than you," I told him regretfully. "The DC-3 is a bit different from a Chipmunk or Tiger Moth. It's heavy on the controls, marginal on one engine and you'd need two or three hours of instruction to become reasonably competent. In addition, you don't have an instrument rating yet, so we couldn't even consider you. Come back and see us when you've got 1000 hours."

A pained expression came to his face. "They all say that but how can I get the 1000 hours if nobody will give me a job?" he implored. I sympathised with him; less than three years earlier, I had found myself in the same situation when I left the Royal Air Force to take up civil flying.

"It's a problem," I admitted. "You'll just have to get whatever experience you can — joy riding, instructing, ferrying, crop dusting . . . I'm sorry I can't be more helpful. Look, what about applying to British European Airways or BOAC. They take low-time pilots and use them as second officers while they gain airline experience."

"I'm afraid that's out of the question. I've already worked for them," Mike Sommerpole interrupted, arousing my curiosity.

"Wouldn't that help? Surely they would look favourably at an in-house applicant?" I suggested. Mike shrugged his shoulders resignedly.

"'Fraid not. The corporations are very rank conscious, which cost me my chance of a job."

I pressed him for more details and heard an unfortunate story.

Mike's first flying job was as a BOAC steward on Britannias, Comets and Boeing 707s. The work was pleasant and the generous salary and time off enabled him to learn to fly on the Havilland Chipmunks at the company-subsidised flying club at White Waltham.

By the time he'd got his private pilot's licence, Mike realized he wanted to be a professional pilot. He began to spend every spare penny on increasing his flying experience to the total required for a commercial pilot's licence (CPL).

One sunny April morning he'd arrived at the aero club for a dual flying lesson. The instructor turned out to be Geoff Hickey, a BOAC captain.

"What're you doing here?" he asked Mike pleasantly.

"Learning to be an airline pilot — I hope," his student replied brightly.

Over the next few months, Mike flew regularly with the same instructor. His aircraft handling was confident and smooth enough to prompt his instructor to suggest he apply to the Corporation for a job.

At first he demurred; BOAC had the pick of the country's pilots to choose from.

Mike flew with the same captain several times on Far East trips. During the time away, they discussed Mike's career hopes and Geoff Hickey repeated his suggestion for Mike to re-muster to pilot.

"I'd be happy to endorse your application with a professional reference," the pilot assured him. "And I know a couple of other captains who'd be happy to recommend you."

With their encouragement, Mike applied. By now he'd accumulated the experience necessary for a CPL. Geoff Hickey assisted him to prepare for the examination and flight test.

By the time of his first interview, Mike had obtained his CPL and had begun working towards his instrument rating. The cost of flying training had now doubled as he had to learn to fly the club's twin-engined Miles Gemini. He also had to spend long tedious hours in the Link trainer, learning to navigate electronically along airways, in contrast to the map and compass visual navigation technique of the tiny Chipmunk elementary trainer.

Geoff Hickey monitored Mike's progress carefully.

"Got a date for the instrument-rating test?" he enquired.

"January the fifteenth."

Mike continued to fly as a steward; he had now progressed to the second round of pilot selection interviews.

Whereas the first interview had been a filter to screen out the obviously unsuitable, the second round was more demanding. Candidates were checked medically; it wasn't enough to have passed the CPL medical. The Corporation required it's pilots to meet their more stringent standards.

Mike had no problem meeting the medical standard and advanced to the second and third day. Aptitude tests, interview, debates and discussion groups on topical subjects filled these days. Once again he had no problems, thanks to patient tutoring from his flying instructor.

One point concerned him: fifty pilot positions were being contested by about 300 applicants. Mathematically his chances of success were six to one but he reasoned that the Corporation would also take flying experience into account. Applicants with several years' experience on multi-engined aircraft would have an infinitely better chance than a 250-hour flying-club applicant. The odds against him appeared formidable.

What he didn't know was the mass of moral support behind him. His annual confidential report portrayed him as conscientious, hard working and competent. Several appreciative letters from passengers who had benefited from his caring attitude to the job joined strong recommendations from three senior training captains including Geoff Hickey.

Just as he was feeling confident of passing the instrument-rating flight test, the British weather gods subjected southern England to a blizzard, halting air and surface traffic. Mike's flight test was postponed, along with thirty others, until the weather improved.

Fourteen days after the pilot selection interviews, an envelope bearing the Speedbird logo dropped into the mail box. Mike weighed it in his hand; he could tell it only contained one sheet, probably a standard letter advising his application had been unsuccessful.

I was becoming intrigued with this aspiring pilot's story so suggested going for a cup of coffee in the Greasy Spoon.

Mike had opened the envelope and extracted a single typewritten page. The Corporation was "happy to advise him" he had successfully completed their selection procedures and was now required to contact them to arrange a final interview.

The phone rang as he finished reading.

"Mike? Geoff Hickey here. Heard anything from the company yet?"

Mike read him the letter.

"Well thank Christ for that, we've been struggling to keep the secret until you heard officially."

"You mean you already knew?"

"Well, not officially," the captain blustered. "But walls have ears, y'know, and we had a pretty good idea. Anyway, what I really called for was to ask where the party is."

Mike looked around. The tenants of the other apartments, all airline staff, had appeared with various beverages to toast his success.

"Looks like it's just started," he told his friend. "Better get over here quickly."

The euphoria of being accepted as a pilot increased when Mike had to decide which fleet to apply for.

"You'll start off as a second officer," Geoff Hickey explained. "That's the third pilot who handles the navigation on long overwater sectors. You'll be sent on a six-month navigator's course, quite a good qualification to have."

On Geoff's advice, Mike applied for the VC-10, a British four-engined 125-passenger jetliner. It was the prestige fleet and only the most senior crews flew it. Simultaneously he resigned his position as a steward. The resignation evoked a letter from Cabin Services requesting him to return his uniform and equipment the following Thursday at 2pm.

Mike arrived at the stores a few minutes early and placed the items on the counter.

"Congratulations. I hear you're leaving us for greener pastures." A friendly female stores clerk approached him. "The Head of Cabin Services would like a word with you before you go. Why don't you pop in and see him while I check off these equipment items for you?"

Elliott Dempsey, the acerbic head of cabin services, grunted unintelligibly when Mike knocked and entered his office.

"Cabin Services not good enough for you?" he accused. "We've had your sort before. Join the company, have a bit of fun seeing the world then leave to enjoy yourself somewhere else."

Mike endeavoured to point out he wasn't leaving the company, he was transferring to another division. The explanation was wasted.

"Your type never stick at anything for long so it's good riddance. Hand your uniform and equipment in as you leave and don't ever bother coming back again." He finished writing something in Mike's personal file and dropped it into the "out" tray to indicate the interview was over. Feeling slightly deflated, Mike completed the remaining formalities and headed home, where he found a letter from the company instructing him to report to Heathrow flight operations the following Monday.

The day for the interview dawned sunny and clear. Mike joined three other applicants for the VC-10 fleet. Mike recognised one of them as a Britannia second officer seeking promotion onto the "Ten" as a first officer. They fell into discussion and Mike expressed the opinion that the interview was something of a formality; they'd been found suitable for employment and were now awaiting allocations to available positions. The Britannia second officer advised him otherwise.

"They can still turn you down if they don't like you," he cautioned. "Your first year is probationary, and if at any time they decide you're unsuitable, they can dismiss you without explanation. It doesn't happen often, but sometimes if one of the "barons" feels off colour he'll turn a bloke down. Happened twice last year . . ."

Further discussion was terminated by a secretary arriving to escort the first interviewee to the selection panel.

Mike was ushered into an office containing three captains. He recognised two of them: one was a check and training captain he recalled flying with as a steward; the other was Captain Rathbone, the VC-10 fleet manager and chief pilot of British Overseas Airways Corporation.

The third member of the interview panel, another VC-10 captain, made the introductions and gestured Mike to be seated. He then gave a brief but comprehensive description of the job vacancy.

"I see you've got your commercial pilot's licence and you're about to take the instrument rating test later this month . . .," the captain continued, but was interrupted by the chief pilot.

"Why haven't you taken your instrument rating yet?" he demanded, staring at his victim belligerently.

Mike explained how adverse weather had caused the cancellation of the first test and he'd had to go to the back of the queue again. His questioner grunted irritably and chose to ignore the explanation.

Questions from the other interviewers occupied a further ten minutes. Mike was asked to give the details of his flying training at the Airways Aero Club.

"So you've always wanted to be a pilot?" the second captain concluded pleasantly.

"Not much bloody use with 250 hours on light aircraft and no instrument rating," Rathbone suddenly growled. "When I was your age — What are you, twenty-five? — I had over 2000 hours on heavies."

Mike nodded quietly. Rathbone had probably been seconded to BOAC during wartime and gone straight into the captain's seat. Nowadays things were different; promotion to command went strictly on seniority and was measured in decades rather than months or years.

"How d'yer know you'd like the job, anyway?" Rathbone demanded. "Means a lot of time away from home, climatic changes, time zones, jet lag. Ever consider this when you applied?"

Mike patiently explained that his year's flying as a steward had fully acquainted him with the rigours of the job. The other captains nodded approvingly at the reply. Rathbone stared aghast at him and said nothing.

One of the others questioned Mike on a few generalities and emphasised that his employment would be conditional on getting an instrument rating. He then thanked Mike and turned to the third member of the panel.

"Got any questions for our new entrant, Charles?" he enquired.

"Don't think so, thanks Paul. All I can say is, work hard on the flight nav course, put all social engagements on the back burner until you've passed the exams, don't drink before flying and I hope to see you down the line in . . ."

He was cut off in mid-sentence by the irascible Captain Rathbone thumbing noisily through Mike's personal file. He snorted and grumbled to himself while turning the pages. The other pilot turned to his chief.

"Anything you want to add, Captain?" he enquired.

Rathbone finished reading the last page and sat forward on the edge of his seat. He eyed Mike belligerently for almost half a minute before speaking.

"If you think I'm having a blasted sandwich cutter in the cockpit seat beside me, you've got another think coming," he rasped unpleasantly.

A long pause ensued, during which time the other two pilots shuffled papers in embarrassment. Mike felt his whole world crumbling. Rathbone hadn't finished his fun yet.

"Two hundred and fifty hours, no instrument rating and a licence to make coffee doesn't qualify you for this sort of job. Cabin services don't want you and neither do we. Good day to you!" He flung the file at Mike and finished his sentence with a long hostile glance. Mike realised the interview and his career prospects were over. Summoning up what was left of his dignity, he rose and thanked the three captains for seeing him. The others shook his hand and smiled awkwardly while avoiding his gaze. One of them even wished him good luck. Rathbone ignored him completely.

Feeling utterly rejected, Mike drove home in a daze. It was early afternoon when he reached his tiny flat. He was glad to find the other tenants out; it would have been impossible to recount the details of the final interview to them.

A few items of mail had arrived. Two were for him: a monthly account of £25.10s from the Airways Aero Club and his weekly copy of *Flight* magazine. Dejected, he collapsed into an armchair and absently thumbed through the magazine. Like every true aviator, he began at the "Situations Vacant" column at the back. He felt a stab of pain when he saw that BOAC were still advertising for pilots. His gaze continued on down through the columns.

"And that's what brought you here?" I observed. Two cups of cold coffee remained un-drunk on the table before us.

He looked at me in embarrassment.

"Er . . . yes. Look . . . sorry for the sob story. I'm afraid it just suddenly all came out."

"That's okay, there are bastards like that in every walk of aviation — flying clubs, Air Force and airlines. The secret is learning to tiptoe round them. *Nil bastardi carborundum* — ever heard that phrase before?"

"You mean don't let the bastards grind you down? Yes, I have and thanks for the advice."

He got up to leave. I felt sorry that his gutsy determination had been thwarted in such a cruel way. BOAC had dangled a carrot before him and taken it away when he reached for it.

"What'll you do now?" I enquired quietly.

"First thing is to get my instrument rating before my money runs out. I'm out of work now and I can't get subsidised flying at the Airways Aero Club any longer. Once I've got the rating, it's find-a-job time."

I admired his tenacity. Even in the depths of his current despair he was thinking positively about the future rather than seething over the past. I wished we could have helped him, but Air Links needed people now and, as I'd pointed out to Dr Levitt when he had hired his nephew, we weren't a benevolent society. I wished him good luck and returned to the office.

My final piece of advice to him was to build up his flying hours and keep applying to the independent airlines, for I couldn't imagine him making it into the state airlines. Thanks to Captain Rathbone, that seemed a stone-cold certainty.°

Mike gained his command in British Caledonian, flying British-built BAC-11 jet passenger liners. He finally found himself in the command seat of a British Airways jet, thus proving for the umpteenth time that there is no such thing as a cold certainty in aviation. For this reason it is wise to heed the old adage: be nice to those you pass on the way up; you might meet them again on the way down.

Mike did get to meet Captain Rathbone one more time. Many years later, when Mike was Captain Sommerpole, he positioned up to Preswick for a duty. He found himself seated beside a very drunk male passenger. He recognised Captain Rathbone, who had by then retired.

The chief steward approached Mike quietly and apologised for the mistake in sitting him beside the objectionable drunk. "Traffic have decided to off-load him before he upsets other passengers, Captain," the chief confided to him.

Mike assured him this wasn't necessary. "I can keep an eye on him and make sure he won't be a nuisance," he volunteered. "I've had experience of this before."

The other crew member was relieved. "It'll be a pleasure to assist you Captain Rathbone," Mike assured the old ex-pilot. "Provided, of course, you don't mind having a blasted sandwich cutter in the seat beside you."

The drunken ex-captain belched and grunted unintelligibly — subtlety was wasted on him.

° Wrong, like most of my stone-cold certainties! Mike Sommerpole survived on a variety of flying jobs, progressing up the career ladder to British United. When BUA merged with Caledonian, he found himself in British Caledonian. Meanwhile, BOAC, his old company with antiquated views about ambition, merged with British European Airways (BEA) to become British Airways. Eventually, most of the independents (British Caledonian, BKS, Cambrian and others) were taken over by the new behemoth, British Airways.

CHAPTER SEVEN
A Golden Opportunity

Two other well-qualified applicants responded to our advertisement for Dakota pilots. Captain Frank Berg had returned to the UK after five hot years flying for Gulf Aviation in Bahrain; First Officer "Timber" Wood came to us from Westpoint Aviation down in the West Country. Both had considerable experience on Dakotas so I offered them immediate employment, subject to satisfactory check flights.

Pickles and I managed to corner Denis for two minutes to tell him he was required for an afternoon's crew training in a couple of days' time. He shook his head vehemently.

"Not me any more I'm afraid. I'm strictly a Hermes captain from now on. I've put your name up to the Ministry and they've approved you for check and training duties on the DC-3. So you'd better arrange your own training session!"

I thanked him for nothing! It would've been nice to have had some say in the decision but that was now history.

I arranged for Kilo Echo to have the main tanks filled after the night freight run. We'd get the training completed in about three hours.

Flying training and checking is an unproductive process that eats up fuel, money, engine hours, crew duty time and rubber tyres. Nowadays flight simulators do the job better than the real aircraft. You can take a simulator beyond the point of safe flight, even crashing it if necessary, then push the reset button and get the manoeuvre right next time. Furthermore, the use of full-time simulator instructors, usually recruited from retired pilots with a lifetime's experience in the air, ensures that line crews' flight time need not be expended in the instructing role.

Unfortunately, simulators were not available to independents in the early sixties, so all flying training had to be conducted in the aircraft. To minimise time spent pre-flighting the aircraft and taxiing out, several students were taught consecutively.

We arranged to take up five pilots. Chegwidden required a biannual check, which would take forty minutes, and I estimated our new captain, Frank Berg, would probably need about the same amount of time. Timber Wood's co-pilot's check was less comprehensive and therefore probably shorter, after which I'd check out Cullenane, the Canadian pilot, for his six take-offs and landings for a Group B co-pilot rating.

Pickles reminded me there'd also been a fellow enquiring about doing a Group B type rating conversion on our aircraft at his own expense. We contacted him and told him we could do it in a couple of days' time.

We were getting critically short of pilots for the DC-3 and had to borrow another first officer from Pluto Wilson's Dan-Air for the freight run.

"Looks like there could be a chronic shortage of aircrew this summer," Pluto had remarked conversationally. "Three of our full-timers have left to join BEA and I'll bet a lot of the seasonal pilots won't be coming back in the spring for the same reason."

I told him of the lack of replies we'd had to our advert.

"How many replies did you get?" he enquired curiously, and he nodded sympathetically when I told him there had been only four.

"None of your fellows," I assured him. "Just a captain from Gulf Aviation and a co-pilot who wanted to move away from Exeter and the West Country. We also had two other applicants, one of whom should be okay."

We discussed the terms for the loan of the Dan-Air pilots. The terms were fairly standard in the industry — £5 an hour for a captain and £3 for a co-pilot.

I must have mentioned that we were doing an afternoon's circuit training soon, because Pluto enquired whether we could squeeze in six take-offs and landings for one of his pilots.

"New fellow, came off Hastings in the Air Force so shouldn't be a problem. Just needs a co-pilot endorsement on the Dak. If you can do that for us, it'll save us having to get an aircraft up from Lasham."

I knew that Dan-Air scheduled their major maintenance in winter and most of their fleet would be at their Hampshire maintenance base, being prepared for next season's flying. I readily agreed to his request. Although competition was keen between rival independent airlines, time had proved that although we'd practically kill for winter revenue flying, it paid to co-operate on the operational and technical side.

Two days later, on a rather cold and windy afternoon, six of us assembled in the Air Links office for a pre-flight brief on what we were going to do. I decided to process Chegwidden first so that Berg could observe what he was required to do next. After that I'd do the three first officers' Group B co-pilot endorsement. The whole afternoon would probably involve twenty-four take-offs and landings. I also briefed on the speeds and power settings to be used. Everybody seemed to understand quite clearly.

The aircraft waited for us in the overnight park between a Pegasus Viking and a rather attractive privately owned Percival Proctor four-seater aircraft. Joe Phillips, now our chief flight engineer, had supervised the refuelling.

"Main tanks are full and there's about thirty-five aside in the auxiliaries," he greeted me.° "Should be more than enough."

° The DC-3 Dakota had four tanks, two in each wing, each holding approximately 168 gallons (716 litres). Full tanks (670 gallons) were sufficient for eight hours' flying.

I thanked him and checked the necessary paperwork; all was in order. I suggested to Chegwidden that he settle himself in the captain's seat while I did a walk-around inspection. I told the new co-pilots to accompany me.

The wind had now increased to twenty-five knots, so I told Cullenane to remove the elevator control locks and I'd leave the rudder lock in until we were ready to taxi.

We climbed aboard. Cullenane wavered indecisively round the tail, while the others boarded. For some reason he was fiddling with the rudder lock. I hurried over and took out the levator locks, reminding him I'd told him to leave the rudder lock in. He murmured something apologetic as he boarded the aircraft.

Chegwidden had completed the pre-starting checks before I clambered into the right seat. The door warning light went out and Joe gave the all-clear to start the starboard engine.

"Turning number two," Chegwidden announced as the three-bladed prop began to crank over. I moved the mixture to the run position as the reliable Pratt and Whitney radial engine grumbled into life.

When the second engine was running, Joe positioned himself to the left of the nose, holding up the rudder lock to signify all controls were now free. Gatwick Ground Control cleared us to the holding point of the westerly runway as he marshalled us out between the other aircraft.

Frank Berg, the ex-Gulf Aviation captain, observed all this from the jump seat.

Chegwidden's handling was smooth, his instrument flying accurate and, after his third approach, I gestured for him to let Frank into the left seat.

Frank had been flying round the Gulf for the previous five years and hadn't had the same exposure to bad weather as Chegwidden. Air Traffic Control cleared us to the Mayfield beacon for a practice hold, after which we requested an instrument approach. We made it a flapless approach to simulate hydraulic failure. Frank handled it perfectly adequately, and on the overshoot I throttled back the starboard engine to simulate engine failure. He handled this competently and after a single-engined approach I got into the left seat and Wood, the new co-pilot, took over the flying. He performed well, apart from a tendency not to allow enough drift for the strong winds aloft. We completed another approach and overshoot, during which I again simulated engine failure. Gatwick radar vectored us downwind for a single-engined approach and landing. Wood's handling was a trifle rusty so I got him to perform two more circuits before I was satisfied with the standard he'd achieved.

The wind had continued to increase in strength throughout the afternoon, but as it was down the runway I decided to continue the training. I glanced at my watch; it was three o'clock — we'd been airborne for an hour and a half. My cockpit seat was beginning to feel rather hard and uncomfortable.

The Dan-Air student flew next. I handled the controls while he settled into the right seat, and when he appeared comfortable I told him he had control.

"Continue climbing on runway heading, maintain 110 knots in the climb, and bring the power back to the climb setting," I instructed. We climbed ponderously up to circuit height, and I commenced the approach checks on the downwind leg.

The ensuing approach went well, taking into account his lack of experience on this particular type of aircraft. I talked him through the descent, telling him to hold 90 knots until over the airfield boundary. My hands and feet hovered close to the controls as we neared the runway. "Start the flare about now," I prompted the ex-Hastings pilot. "Wheel it on, power off slowly, raise the nose, raise it a little higher, power off, okay that's nice, keep her straight, I'm raising the flaps and we'll overshoot, power coming on slowly, keep her straight now . . ."

Once again we climbed back to circuit height.

So much flying had been hard work for everybody. We continued pounding the circuit until the student had completed six take-offs and landings to a satisfactory standard. Towards the end of the detail I lost count of the number of landings and take-offs we'd completed. A check of the fuel gauges told me we still had enough fuel for a further two hours' flying if required. The tower called us as we turned onto final approach.

"Kilo Echo is this a full stop or another touch-and-go?" they enquired. I turned to the figure in the jump seat.

"How many landings has he done?" I enquired. A voice from the back of the cockpit advised me this would be his sixth landing, after which we'd have completed all the training. I told the tower operator this one would be the final landing. He then cleared a Morton's Rapide to depart ahead of us.

The weather was now definitely a bit lumpy, with sudden downdraughts on short final approach. The Dan-Air student kept his airspeed higher than usual to compensate for the adverse conditions and did a good job of wheeling the aircraft onto the runway.

We slowed to taxi speed and were cleared back to the overnight park via the parallel taxi-way. The wind now began to buffet the aircraft quite severely as we taxied in. I told the student to relax and I'd take control. I was relieved we'd managed to complete all the training before the weather turned bad on us. Later I would regret not having kept a more careful account of the number of landings. An aircraft and lives would be endangered before I'd realise my mistake.

Pickles and Denis were waiting at the parking position as we taxied in. Once again I parked beside the Proctor. The door warning light came on before I had cut the engines and Denis hurried to the cockpit.

"Your friend Koller from the Bank of England is waiting in the office, so get up there as quickly as you can. He wants us to collect a shipment tomorrow night."

We turned everything off and I heard our engineer installing the chocks and control locks as we vacated the cockpit. Somebody had thoughtfully prepared the training paperwork for my signature, so I was able to head straight to the office with Pickles.

Koller rose as we entered. We shook hands gravely and he began to tell us the reason for his unexpected appearance.

"The bank would like you to collect a consignment of 1000 kilos of bullion from Zurich tomorrow night," he began. "Security is still proving a problem, mainly pilfering of the occasional box. When each box contains thousands of pounds worth of metal, you can understand our concern. For this reason we've decided to ship future consignments at short notice, before word can get round."

We discussed matters at some length and decided to adopt Pickles' scheme of flying the return Lille freight schedule via Zurich. The freight handlers at Heathrow and Lille had readily agreed to our request to depart an hour early so our arrival time back at London next morning would be set back the minimum time.

Koller now became very serious. He strode over to the door and ensured it was firmly closed before he spoke.

"Large bullion consignments are traditionally shipped in 1000-ounce ingots," he explained carefully. "Each ingot is packed in a wooden carrying case with rope handles. Because of its high density, gold is a very attractive target for thieves. As an example, a 1000-ounce bar, which is about the size of a builder's brick, is worth round about £17,000 sterling. It could easily be concealed in a briefcase or lunch box."*

I was impressed; one gold brick was worth more than the aircraft carrying it, and we were carrying a whole plane load. Koller continued, "We're still having problems with security at Heathrow. The Swiss authorities in Zurich have almost perfect security; we've never lost so much as a paper clip at their end. But London is a different matter. For that reason we've tended to restrict the number of people involved."

"Is that why you've only just told me about tomorrow night's shipment?" I enquired. Koller admitted it was.

"There are a few other arrangements you should know about," he continued. "Your young assistant here suggested carrying a dummy consignment in the cargo compartment and loading the real freight under the floor. Mr Phillips, your engineer, is checking the under-floor area for suitable locations now."

I immediately vetoed this idea, explaining that the under-floor areas were not stressed to carry heavy loads.

"The boxes could be thrown around in turbulence and damage the aircraft structure, maybe even restrict or jam the controls," I explained. "It would be better to load the genuine boxes in the forward radio compartments. There's ample space in the baggage lockers below the radio equipment and we could conceal it under other freight."

We discussed other technicalities until Koller was satisfied we had covered all eventualities. I voiced my concern about the freight-handling arrangements at Heathrow. Koller insisted we were responsible for the consignment

* Nowadays the same gold brick would be worth about £250,000.

until it was loaded into the bank's van at London Airport and an official receipt issued. After more discussion, we decided it was better to hand the genuine consignment over at Gatwick. The dummy consignment would still be unloaded at Heathrow.

I then returned to the aircraft and told our engineer where we'd be loading the genuine consignment. He thought it was a great idea to carry a false consignment.

"Can you imagine the thieves' faces when they find a load of lead in the boxes?" he chortled. I didn't tell him the boxes would actually contain bags of wet sand; lead was too expensive for our purpose.

As our three new pilots required a period of route training and checking, Pickles scheduled Cullenane to fly with Les and me on the next night's assignment. I arrived at the met office and found them completing the flight plan. The local oil company had already fuelled the aircraft sufficiently to allow us to fly Gatwick–Heathrow–Lille–Zurich without refuelling. I explained to Cullenane we'd refuel again in Zurich before loading.

We took off from Gatwick twenty minutes early, with Les doing the flying and Cullenane observing from the jump seat. The Heathrow loaders were waiting with the freight as we taxied in, so loading and documentation took very little time and we departed half an hour early.

At Lille the staff were delighted to get us away ahead of time. The total load was only 340 kilograms of newspapers and magazines, bound for London. Our flight was the last movement of the day, and by getting rid of us early, they'd have the rest of the evening free.

I had done the flying on the second leg, with Les in the co-pilot's seat. After landing at Lille, I suggested to Cullenane that he occupy the co-pilot's seat out of Lille. Les would ride shotgun° in the jump seat to assist if and when required.

"I'll fly the next two sectors, then after we've discharged the cargo at Heathrow, you can fly us home to Gatwick. How would you like that?" I suggested to Cullenane. He smiled in rather a sickly fashion at my suggestion.

Lille to Zurich took an hour and a half by the time we'd carried out an instrument approach to the southerly runway. It was a minute after 1am when Ground Control directed us to a discreet area away from the main terminal. Several vehicles waited in the shadow of a large hangar. A marshaller directed us into the freight-loading area, and a van moved up to the rear of the aircraft as the propellers stopped turning. A uniformed Swiss bank official, accompanied by a member of the Swiss Federal Police, greeted me as I emerged from the aircraft.

"Your papers are in order. It vill take twenty minutes to load your aircraft and we haf advised Air Traffic Control zat you vill depart at two o'clock," the official informed me. I politely told him the aircraft was going to be refuelled

° "Shotgun" is the name given to any crew member riding along to make up the correct crew complement when a pilot is being trained on a revenue flight.

before the cargo was loaded. He didn't seem to appreciate this bit of information.

"Zat is not how we haf planned it," he countered. "You can refuel while the cargo is being loaded. Now, you vill sign this receipt." He thrust a clipboard at me as he spoke. I gently informed him that I wasn't signing his receipt until the aircraft was refuelled and the freight checked aboard. He seemed to accept this, for he issued a stream of instructions in Schweizerdeutsch and a bowser petrol tanker rumbled towards us.

"We're going for a quick cup of coffee and will be back before the refuelling's finished," I told him. Les and Cullenane followed me towards a spotless Swiss coffee shop overlooking the tarmac.

A quarter of an hour later our Dakota had been refuelled and I gave the okay to load the precious freight in the front compartments. The other two pilots loaded some of the Lille freight on top of the boxes to make the bullion less conspicuous. Thirty-six boxes containing sand sat down in the rear of the fuselage where everybody could see them.

Once the bullion was aboard our aircraft, the Swiss official became agitated and urged me to sign the official receipt. Les had checked the number of boxes against their serial numbers and when he reported they were all there, I signed the document. The official snatched it from me and lost all further interest in the matter as he drove quickly away in his armoured van.

I checked the refuelling document and climbed up on the wing to ensure the fuel and oil caps were correctly seated. Les and Cullenane had finished loading newspapers on top of the bullion.

We taxied out ten minutes later. The airport was deserted save for a lone sweeper vehicle on the perimeter track. Air Traffic Control cleared us for immediate take-off as we neared the runway holding point. Cullenane was having a bit of trouble settling into his unaccustomed job, but with a bit of help from Les the pre-take-off checks were completed.

Our planned flight time back to Heathrow was three hours and forty-five minutes but Air Traffic Control cut corners for us and we shaved ten minutes off that time. Cullenane had no problem with the navigation and paperwork.

We landed on Heathrow's runway 28 Left and taxied to the freight terminal. I'd confided in the other two pilots that our problems were now beginning. There was no way thieves could have gained access to the bullion previously, but now hoards of loaders, traffic clerks, engineering staff and other hangers-on were about to swarm aboard the aircraft. I briefed Les and Cullenane to remain in the cockpit during unloading operations and not allow anybody past the flight-deck door.

"We'll let them unload the rear freight onto their trucks as if it was nothing special," I instructed. "You pass the bales of newspapers out to them in the cabin — there'll only be a few on top of the bullion boxes — and don't leave the aircraft until every person has left. That's most important because there's bound to be somebody wanting to steal anything hanging around."

I left them in charge of the aircraft and headed towards Customs with the cargo manifest and ship's papers.

By the time I returned thirty minutes later, our Dakota stood lonely and forlorn in the pre-dawn twilight. Les walked slowly round the aircraft, showing Cullenane what to look for in an external pre-flight inspection. In the rear of the aircraft, a refueller completed the fuel and oil uplift invoice.

"No problems?" I enquired.

Les assured me everything had gone smoothly. "Dunno how many of those boxes of sand will end up at their correct destination though," he added with a chuckle.

We climbed aboard our aircraft and I left the other two to close the bulky cargo door while I prepared everything in the cockpit. If Cullenane was going to fly us across to Gatwick, I wanted to make everything as easy as possible for him. I was about to turn on the battery master switch when I heard a scream down the back.

Looking aft, I saw Cullenane clutching his right hand to his chest. From the expression on his face, he'd injured it somehow. Les Smith hovered around anxiously as I hurried aft.

"Jeez, I'm sorry," Les began, then turned to me apologetically. "I shut his hand in the door, bloody stupid of me. How's it feeling?"

Cullenane continued to hold the injured hand close to his chest, his mouth contorted into a rictus of pain. He let me examine the hand and I was relieved to see there were no surface cuts or abrasions.

"Want us to get you to a doctor? Might be best to check for broken bones."

Cullenane shook his head. "Doesn't feel broken," he volunteered. "We've got to get the gold to Gatwick as soon as possible, so let's get going. I'll sit in the jump seat, and if it's still hurting when we get back to base, I'll go and see Doc Warnbeck."

I was impressed at Cullenane's selfless attitude. Les and I settled ourselves into the pilots' seats and started the checks.

"Sorry you didn't get to do any flying tonight, but there'll be other opportunities," I assured the injured co-pilot. I then gestured to Les to fly the leg back to Gatwick, which he readily accepted.

We landed on Gatwick's easterly runway after a flight time of less than fifteen minutes. The morning scramble hadn't even started by the time we'd landed.

Joe Phillips, Pickles and Koller waited as we taxied in. An armoured security vehicle stood parked a discreet distance away on the edge of the concrete. I opened my cockpit sliding window as the propellers wound down.

"Everything go okay?" Koller called up to me. I assured him it had been incredibly simple and he said he'd be up immediately to check the consignment. I got out of my seat to see what a third-of-a-million pounds' worth of gold looked like.

I wished I hadn't because when I removed the engine covers, pilots' briefcases and a few other extraneous pieces of equipment from the radio compartment, I realised it was empty!

Somebody, somehow, had managed to spirit away almost a ton of gold from beneath our very noses!

CHAPTER EIGHT
Plane Dealings

Koller chuckled to himself as he poured Worcestershire sauce over his eggs and bacon.

"Lots of people make your mistake," he explained. "They don't realise that 1000 kilograms of gold takes up a very small volume. It's a very high-density metal."

"Thirty-five bricks, not even enough to cover the floor of the radio locker," I admitted ruefully as Koller began to chuckle again. We were seated in the Greasy Spoon, enjoying a complimentary breakfast paid for by the Bank of England. I thought back to the traumatic discovery I'd made less than an hour ago.

After I'd removed various bits and pieces from the radio compartment and found that it appeared to be empty, I announced my discovery to the other two pilots. They peered into the darkened compartment.

"There's a few boxes in there but it looks like somebody's got away with most of the consignment," Les admitted sorrowfully. Cullenane reached into the compartment with his right hand and attempted to lift one of the wooden boxes out.

"It's fastened to the floor!" he exclaimed then used both hands to extract the box. "No, it's not . . . but crikey it's heavy! Must weigh fifty or sixty pounds."

Koller arrived in the cockpit and demanded to know what the problem was.

"Most of the consignment's gone," I told him. "Dunno how. Les checked the boxes aboard, and two of us remained with the aircraft all the time. Nobody's been in the cockpit except the refueller at Heathrow. We'll have him questioned. Unless there's somebody still aboard the aircraft, I can't imagine where the gold could've gone."

"Are you suggesting it could be hidden aboard the aircraft?" Les enquired hopefully. I scornfully asked him where anybody could hide half a ton of gold. Koller hushed us into silence.

"Listen to me a minute before you start looking for a big heap of gold bars," he implored. "Remember when I told you that gold was usually carried in 1000-ounce ingots?"

I vaguely remembered the conversation.

"Okay, 1000 ounces is about thirty kilos by the time you've added on the weight of the packaging. Now how many boxes would you need to make up 1000 kilos?"

"About thirty-three, thirty-four maybe?" I suggested.

"Thirty-five actually. Now tell me how much space thirty-five building bricks would occupy?"

"About nine bricks by four, that's . . . er . . . about three feet square, maybe a little bit less."

Koller nodded in agreement. "Correct. Now might I suggest you count the number of boxes left on the floor of the radio compartment before you call in Scotland Yard?"

I'd already begun counting.

"Thirty-five!" I announced jubilantly. Koller nodded in agreement.

"Precisely, thirty-five bricks worth over £300,000. Make it up to a nice round hundred bricks, Captain, and it'd be nearer a million. Let's check them against my inventory, then we can get going. My ulcer's telling me it's breakfast time, and when it speaks, I listen!"

Two uniformed bank staff had entered the freight compartment and now began lifting the boxes out. Each staggered down the fuselage under the weight of one box, which he deposited carefully onto a conveyor belt running into the security vehicle. The transfer took less than fifteen minutes. Koller signed a receipt, gave me a copy, then obtained a similar document from the senior of the two security men.

"Right, where can we find a good breakfast?" he demanded. I headed us towards the Greasy Spoon, while Les and Cullenane retrieved our flight satchels. Les passed them back to Cullenane and I heard him ask how the hand was feeling.

"What hand?" Cullenane enquired blankly.

"The one you hurt on the ground at Heathrow. Is it giving you any trouble? Tell us if it is and we'll get you over to the doc."

Comprehension suddenly lit the other's face. He laughed self-consciously. "Oh that, no . . . I think it'll be fine. Just a bit of bruising." He picked up the three satchels and followed us to breakfast.

Denis, Pickles and Nathan Warnup, our new commercial manager, joined us in the crew restaurant.

I still needed to be convinced that Nathan was contributing anything productive to our operation. His uncle's assurances that his nephew's connections in "The City" would bring us increased business remained to be proved. The nephew's contribution so far had been to entertain a motley crowd of travel agents and other hangers-on to expensive business lunches in the airport restaurant overlooking the aircraft manoeuvring area. When not running up large expense accounts in the bar or restaurant, he spent long hours on the phone to his chums overseas.

Characteristically, he came along when he heard about the free breakfast.

Denis asked me how Cullenane's route training had gone and I told him I'd found no problems.

"What's his flying like?" he enquired. I told him about his accident at Heathrow, which had prevented him doing any flying. Denis frowned disapprovingly at this bit of information, until I assured him there'd be plenty of other opportunities for him to demonstrate his flying ability. Further discussion was interrupted by the restaurant manager of the Greasy Spoon advising us there was a phone call for Koller. We waited curiously while the bank official took the call. He could barely conceal a smirk when he returned.

"Good news or bad?" I enquired.

"Both, I suppose," he replied. "That was the manager of the bank's vaults in Cheapside. The first consignment has just arrived and two of the boxes are missing. He doesn't know of our little deception so he's a little agitated. Security are busy checking back to where a box could've been scooped off. My guess is that once again the problem is at Heathrow. It's a good thing your young colleague had his bright idea." He directed his approving gaze at Pickles as he spoke.

Nathan Warnup listened to all this with an incredulous expression on his face. "That's preposterous!" he blustered. "You mean to say we've lost a gold brick? It can't just have disappeared into thin air, have they double checked the numbers?"

Koller and I exchanged confidential glances. In accordance with Koller's wish to involve as few people as possible in the operation, we had not included our new commercial manager in the information loop. Both of us felt reluctant to divulge highly confidential information to a newcomer who spent most of his time in the bar exchanging airline scuttlebutt with members of the travel industry.

Koller pressed his finger to the side of his nose as he spoke in a quiet monotone loud enough for only those closest to hear.

"There'll be another shipment in two weeks' time," he confided. "You can't use the same ruse again, it won't work a second time. Our underwriters are watching the operation very closely and will refuse insurance cover if they feel uneasy. Give the matter a bit of thought over the next week." He directed his gaze predominantly at Pickles as he spoke.

Nathan Warnup had tried unsuccessfully to catch this conversation. "What was that about?" he demanded. "Have you got a lead on the crime? Sounds like an inside job to me. I'll have a word with a friend of mine in Hatton Garden. His father's one of the biggest diamond merchants in the Garden and he's forever transporting stones between Amsterdam and London. I'll take him to lunch and see what he has to suggest about our problem."

Pickles spoke before I could tell Nathan to keep our problems to himself.

"There's no problem as far as we're concerned," he chortled. "The thieves got away with a couple of boxes of wet sand. The real consignment was hidden in the radio compartment up front and is now on its way to the Bank of England from Gatwick. We'll get a couple of new boxes made to replace the ones stolen and we'll pull the same trick again . . ."

Only a hefty kick under the table from me shut him up. But it was too late, the news was out.

"You mean we put a false consignment in the fuselage, where everybody would see it, and hid the real gold somewhere else?" Nathan exclaimed. Koller and I looked daggers at Pickles but he seemed oblivious of us.

"Yeah, we put identical boxes down the back, loaded with wet sand to make them heavy. The thieves saw what they expected to see, grabbed a couple and scooted off. It could be days before they open the boxes and find their mistake."

Nathan broke into convulsions of laughter which attracted the attention of diners at other tables. "I think that's hilarious. Wonder what the thieves will say when they find they've stolen boxes of wet sand?" He chortled away to himself for several minutes.

I was furious with Pickles. Quite uncharacteristically he'd divulged confidential information. Soon the news of our little deception would be all round the airport.

Koller excused himself to depart for the city, and conversation changed to operational matters. The Hermes operation was going well, with no major delays in the last two months. Horizon Holidays, our main customer, seemed delighted with our on-time performances and were anxious for us to fly for them again through the summer IT season. I reminded Denis there wouldn't be sufficient flying hours left for the whole summer season. Once again he looked at me mysteriously and assured me he had the matter in hand.

"This time next year, you could find yourself flying four-engined aircraft," he added.

"You mean you're going to check me out on the Hermes?" I enquired excitedly. He looked at me and said nothing.

It had been a long night and I was scheduled out again that night with Timber Wood, on route familiarisation to Lille. It was time to get some rest. I bade everybody goodnight, thanked the Bank of England for a very good breakfast and headed home.

The others also had things to attend to; Pickles returned to our operations office with Denis. Joe Phillips had two aircraft to prepare for the day's flying.

Nathan Warnup looked round indecisively, glanced at his expensive Rolex watch and hurried off in the opposite direction to the main passenger terminal, where a few of his professional contacts waited for him in the bar.

When I got home, two letters waited in the mail box. The first was from a friend we'd flown for in New Zealand a year ago. I had tentatively suggested repeating the charter during their busy southern summer season.

I quickly opened it and devoured the news of a country I'd enjoyed so much. Regrettably his airline, South Pacific Airlines of New Zealand, was also finding it hard to compete against the government airline. The other envelope bore the logo of British European Airways, the British government's designated European scheduled carrier. Three years previously, I had applied to them for a job after leaving the Royal Air Force. There had been no vacancies then, but now circumstances had changed and they needed aircrew. They instructed me to contact their personnel officer to arrange a suitable interview date.

This posed a problem for me. There were two career paths down which an aspiring airline pilot could progress. He could either join the independent airline movement and progress rapidly from co-pilot to captain or he could join the state airlines and progress slowly through the ranks of second officer, first officer (co-pilot) and eventually make captain. This might take ten or fifteen years.

There were trade-offs in either choice. Fast promotion in the independents was gained at the expense of job security, lower salaries, minimal training and older aircraft. Most pilots flying for the independents regularly lost their jobs when the company they were working for folded, and they were forced to compete against their colleagues for another position.

In contrast, the state airlines offered secure employment, excellent training on the very latest aircraft and good working conditions. A co-pilot's salary in the corporations would be equal to or higher than a captain in an independent airline. The only negative thing about working for the government was the long years as a co-pilot.

Now I was required to make that decision. Did I want to give up my present nomadic existence to work for the government airline? Air Links depended on each of us and was doing extremely well at the moment. Maybe we could break out of the independent mould and become an established reputable airline. Others were doing that. Over on the south side of Gatwick, Freddie Laker's British United Airways (BUA) was reputed to be re-equipping with modern jet equipment, as was Harold Bamberg's Eagle Airways at Heathrow. Both companies had graduated from ad hoc charter work to military trooping flights and now were about to get a slice of the scheduled flying work.

Or would Damocles raise his sharp sword one autumn day and cut the thin thread between profit and loss, thus putting us out of business? I made a mental note to phone BEA that afternoon.

Heavy rain had begun to fall when the alarm clock woke me late in the afternoon. I needed to attend to a few matters in the office before starting the night's flying, so got out to the airport two hours before the scheduled departure time.

The Heathrow loaders were on another "go slow and work to rule" so we could expect delays. Pickles had rostered Les to ride along as shotgun once again while I checked out Timber Wood on the route. They arrived in the office shortly after me. I told them tonight would be the normal return freight run to Lille. Wood had plenty of DC-3 experience so I didn't anticipate any problems with his route check. They listened attentively then headed off to the met office to start flight planning.

Our positioning flight across to Heathrow was a domestic one and therefore did not require customs clearance, so I took the short route out to the aircraft through the baggage section. A vaguely familiar figure in white overalls waved as I passed.

I recognised Mike Sommerpole, the ex-BOAC steward who'd applied to us for a pilot's job.

"Gotta new job, eh?" I observed conversationally. "How did the instrument-rating test go?"

He told me he'd passed it and was now the holder of a commercial pilot's licence with multi-engine and instrument ratings. He'd had to take a job as a baggage loader to support himself financially while he hunted down that elusive first job.

"It was quite fortunate really," he explained. "I managed to get a job at Heathrow, which enabled me to stay in my flat. Occasionally we have to help out at Gatwick, which is why I'm here now. The airline provides a coach to bring us over and take us back to Heathrow. As a matter of fact, I'd better get moving because it leaves in fifteen minutes."

I jokingly told him we could give him a lift to Heathrow if he missed the bus. He looked at me intently but said nothing as he hurried away into the rain.

It took me forty minutes to get our Dakota ready for the short hop across to Heathrow. Joe Phillips was busy with the Hermes so I had to do everything myself. I reflected how nice it must be to work for the government, where everything was done for you. A job with BEA seemed a lot more attractive when you were pre-flighting your aircraft at night in pouring rain and wondering whether the air-conditioning system was going to freeze your bollocks off or cook you medium rare in flight.

I had just begun to pull the starboard propeller through by hand to check for hydraulicking, when a white-overalled figure approached me.

"Want a hand? That looks rather hard work," Mike Sommerpole enquired, pulling down on the next blade.

"What happened to you, did you miss your coach back to Heathrow?" I puffed as I fought against the motor's compression.

"I deliberately missed it. Well, actually . . . I told the driver I wouldn't be travelling back with him. Anyway, I hope you meant it when you offered me that lift?"

I assured him he was welcome to come along for the ride if he wanted. Some people would have said he was crazy to fly aboard a noisy draughty freight aircraft when he could travel home by luxurious air-conditioned coach. I didn't; sometimes you had to be mad to work in aviation.

With Mike helping me on the pre-flight, we were soon ready to depart. Les and Wood arrived from flight planning and I told Wood to occupy the right seat for the short ferry flight. I told Les I wanted him to monitor every-thing from the jump seat and Mike Sommerpole could look over his shoulder to see what went on. It was a bit chummy with four of us crowded into the tiny cockpit.

It took an unusually short time to load our aircraft at Heathrow, which enabled us to depart ten minutes ahead of schedule.

Wood had no problem in demonstrating his route competence. He flew the night sector from Lille back to Heathrow and after observing how he handled the approach in heavy rain and crosswinds, I had no hesitation in certifying him as competent. When unloading and other formalities had been concluded at Heathrow, I invited Les to fly us home to Gatwick.

The sun had risen as we got airborne. The Heathrow Departure Controller handed us over to Gatwick Director, who vectored us onto the instrument approach path for runway 08. The morning airborne commuter rush between the major European cities hadn't begun as we proceeded across the City of London's business district. I thought of Koller's precious gold lying in the Bank of England's vaults 2000 feet below us as Big Ben on Parliament Tower indicated 7am.

In the jump seat, Wood was filling in the night's paperwork while Les savoured the handling of the DC-3. His right hand moved the control yoke right as Gatwick manoeuvred us towards the runway centre line.

"Is that fellow a friend of yours?" he suddenly enquired.

"What fellow?"

"The chap who came along and helped load the freight at Heathrow," he explained. I hadn't realised Mike had stayed behind to help at Heathrow; after an eight-hour shift at Gatwick, he couldn't really have wanted to load another aircraft. I began to tell Les how I'd met him.

"He nearly got accepted into BOAC," I continued. "But bad luck intervened I'm afraid. He's going to have to fight his way into the independents. I would've liked to offer him a job but he didn't have an instrument rating when he applied. It's too late now, we've got the three extra pilots we need. Maybe he'll get something in the spring. Dan-Air might take him."

Gatwick Director broke into our conversation at that moment to turn us onto final approach.

"Kilo Echo turn right onto one two zero to intercept the final approach course and change now to tower on one one eight one. Have a good day!"

Gatwick Tower cleared us to land and another night's work was over.

A busy day was brewing up in the office. A rival operator up at Leeds Bradford had sub-chartered us for a passenger trip to Beauvais, which made it necessary for us to convert Kilo Echo back to a passenger aircraft. Joe was installing the seats and Pickles was hurriedly rounding up a DC-3 crew by telephone.

Nathan Warnup was enthusiastically arranging the paperwork for the charter. He chortled as he told me how much we were going to earn from his piece of commercial acumen.

"Two and a half hours' flying at £55 pounds an hour," he gloated. "That's damn nearly 150 quid." We were all pleased with his success; winter charters were very competitive. An extra £100 or so in the kitty would help our cash-flow problem.

Pickles located Frank Berg to command the Beauvais charter. It was now 10am and I decided to creep out of the office before I became embroiled in some important matter. After flying all night I needed to catch up on my sleep, especially if I was going to be called out again that night.

I heard Pickles talking to Cullenane on the phone as I left the office. Nathan Warnup headed off for important discussions with his travel agent cronies in the bar.

I drove home with the uncomfortable feeling that something was not quite right about the Beauvais charter.

The letter from BEA still lay on the kitchen table when I got home. I hadn't had time to decide on the best course of action. I knew most of my colleagues around Gatwick wouldn't hesitate to take a secure job in the government airline rather than oscillate from job to job in the independent sector. My case was slightly different; I'd invested capital and faith into a company that now depended on me. With several independent airlines making it into the big league, there was no tangible reason to think we in Air Links couldn't achieve the same success.

Nevertheless, I was reluctant to reject the offer of a secure job with BEA. I dialled the West Drayton number and arranged a preliminary interview with their personnel officer in ten days' time. It was better to have the offer of a job and refuse it than never to have the opportunity.

Christine phoned at 4pm to advise me Chegwidden and Timber Wood were doing the night's freight schedule and I would operate a second charter to Beauvais the next morning.

"Take-off time is eleven but Mr Zucher junior would like to talk to the directors about something," she added. "Tony and Denis are scheduled back from Geneva about then but could take half an hour to clear customs. Could you be in the office at nine when Mr Zucher arrives?"

I assured her I could. The Beauvais flight wouldn't take more than an hour to prepare, so I could spend an hour with the travel agent before having to start work.

Zucher had arrived on an earlier train and was waiting in the ops office when I arrived next morning. We shook hands and I gestured for him to be seated at our table. Christine was assembling the paperwork for the Beauvais charter later that morning. Zucher gazed with fascination at the aircraft parked on the tarmac. Our DC-3 had just arrived from Heathrow, and I watched Berg and Cullenane as they walked across to Crew Customs.

"I believe you wanted to see the directors?" I enquired curiously. Zucher directed his attention from the tarmac back into the office. "Er . . . yes, Dad thought this might interest you." He proffered a thin wad of typewritten foolscap sheets. I began to read them carefully.

"Lourdes, that's in the southern part of France, or is it Spain?" I mused aloud, looking up at our wall map.

"Southern France, at the foot of the Pyrenees," Zucher explained readily. "It's a popular place for pilgrims to visit."

I listened as he told me the story of Lourdes.

"It's been one of the greatest pilgrimage destinations in the world," he explained, "ever since the middle of the last century when the figure of the Virgin Mary appeared to Bernadette, a young French peasant girl, in a grotto in Lourdes. Since then, the sick and handicapped have gone there in search of a miraculous cure."

The young Zucher filled me in on the details of the miracle of Lourdes. Whether or not anybody ever received a magic cure in the grotto, the fact remained that thousands of pilgrims a year travelled to the little town in south-western France. Most of them were physically handicapped in some way, some very severely, making travel by surface means an inconvenience. Demand for air travel was building up fast. And air travel was our business.

I re-read the documents. They were for a series of weekly return flights to Tarbes, the nearest airport to Lourdes. The contract stipulated twenty-five passengers. The travel agent had correctly calculated the round trip as seven hours' flying, for which the contractual price would be £385 — about £11 per head. I pointed out that our aircraft could carry thirty-six passengers. Zucher shook his head regretfully.

"Dad allows extra seats for the nurses and assistants, plus all the equipment."

"What equipment?"

"Wheelchairs, stretchers, crutches, oxygen tanks, things like that. Remember, these people are handicapped and require assistance to move."

We discussed a few other items on the contract until Denis and Tony arrived.

"Weekly charter flights to Lourdes. We'll land at Tarbes, and the travel agent will arrange surface transport the rest of the way. Seven hours a week is 350 hours a year, quite a nice little earner," I explained. They nodded approvingly as they read through the contracts.

"We're going to have to review our aircraft utilisation," Tony observed. "This and the Air France freighting will amount to thirty-five hours' flying a week with no down time allowed for maintenance."

The matter had also occurred to me. We were also going to be critically short of aircrew at a time when everybody else was hiring in anticipation of a shortage in the summer.

It was now time for me to leave the other two directors to settle the contractual business with young Mr Zucher and start preparing for the Beauvais flight. I hurried down to the weather office. A familiar figure greeted me as I passed our check-in counter.

"Mornin' Cap'n. Nice loada passengers for you today as well as yesterday."

I must have looked startled at recognising Alfie Cope, one of charter aviation's rascals. We'd done a lot of sub-charter work for him when he'd run North-South Airlines two years ago. Alfie's business technique was to pay nobody and liquidate his company in the autumn, when creditors began pounding on his door. The bailiffs then moved in and confiscated a few items of office equipment for the creditors to fight over. The same creditors then began to suffer cashflow problems and found themselves unable to pay salaries, fuel bills and other essentials. This drove them into bankruptcy, leaving Alfie Cope a fresh market in which to start another airline in the spring. We'd endured the same treatment from him, ending up with him owing us £1500 at the end of the IT season. Word of his reputation got around and he finally ran out of airlines who'd fly for him. That was when Pickles came up with the ingenious scheme for us to fly for him — provided he paid cash in advance. We never recovered our original £1500 but we made a lot of money from subsequent charters, while everybody else either refused to fly for him or went broke doing so.

A nagging doubt about the Beauvais charters had troubled me since yesterday. I approached Alfie suspiciously.

"Are we flying for you, Alfie?" I enquired. His self-satisfied smirk was my reply. I hurried back to the office to check with Pickles. If Nathan Warnup had arranged this charter, I wanted to know whether we'd been paid in advance.

Pickles looked sullen when I confronted him.

"If we don't get cash in advance, he'll never pay us," I warned. "He makes a handsome living out of small airlines like ours, pocketing the charter money and not passing it on to the operator. He did the same thing last year when he ran North-South and he'll do the same thing now."

Pickles had remained unusually silent during my harangue. Now he spoke.

"I've already told Mr Warnup that but he overruled me. I told him his uncle said we weren't to fly for Alfie Cope or North East Airlines but he said Alfie was a personal friend of his and had given him an assurance the money would be paid. Something about a gentleman's word being his bond . . ."

"Where's Nathan Warnup now?" I demanded. "Get him on the phone and we'll sort this out right away."

"He's probably in the bar with his old school pals," Pickles countered.

I hurried back to the passenger terminal and found our commercial manager in his usual position at the bar, surrounded by a small crowd of hangers-on. It sounded like he was telling them something about a new restaurant when I interrupted his dialogue. I ignored his injured look.

"Who's paying for the Beauvais charters?" I demanded.

"North East, up at Leeds Bradford," he assured me. "Run by Alfie Cope, a friend of mine. Lots of experience in aviation, good businessman, drives a Bentley Continental and got a son at . . ."

"Has he paid in advance?" I demanded.

Nathan looked hurt. "Of course he hasn't. We'll invoice him at the end of the month and he'll . . ."

"He'll never pay!" I exploded. "He owes money all over the country and has no intention of paying his creditors. That's his style. That's why he drives a Bentley."

"Might I remind you he's a very good client of Air Links?" Nathan replied pompously. "You did quite a bit of flying for him last winter when work was scarce."

I admitted we had earned a lot of money from Alfie but assured him it had always been on a cash-in-advance basis. I then insisted we get money in advance before I took off for Beauvais. Nathan shook his head sadly.

"It's a bit late for that, Guy. The passengers have begun checking in. We can't turn them away, and in any case I don't know where Alfie is. He's most likely up at Leeds."

"He's downstairs and we're going to see him now," I replied. I exited the bar rapidly, dragging our unwilling commercial manager with me.

We found Alfie out at the aircraft, basking in the undisguised admiration of the Beauvais passengers as we approached him.

"And after the tour you'll be taken to a typical French luncheon at the Brasserie . . ." He faltered in mid-sentence as I grabbed his arm and steered him to a quiet corner under the wing.

"That's a bit rude, Captain," he pleaded. "I was doing a nice line in public relations work until you butted in."

"I've just heard you haven't paid us yet." I got straight to the point. "You know our rules. We'll fly anything anywhere at any time, but our terms are cash in advance."

Alfie looked at Nathan indignantly. "What's all this about then, Nat?" he pleaded. "Won't you honour our gentlemen's agreement?"

Nathan shuffled his feet awkwardly. "Course I will. We've just had a small disagreement in the office, that's all."

"There's no disagreement," I assured Alfie. "The directors of Air Links are delighted to fly for you on our terms. Cash in advance."

The passengers were waiting to board the aircraft while we spoke. Several gazed enquiringly at the travel agent.

"Look, let's get the flight away then we can discuss terms. There's no reason to inconvenience the customers," Alfie beseeched.

"Yes, okay. Let's get them aboard then we'll settle this matter between us amicably," Nathan readily agreed.

"Negative to that. Once these passengers are on their way, we've lost all the leverage in our argument. I prefer payment now before we take off. I can't discuss it afterwards, I'll be half way to Beauvais."

Alfie looked daggers at me. He was going to have to find a lot of money in a hurry. Two white-overalled figures approached. The younger cleared his throat nervously. "Er, sorry to interrupt you, Captain, but I just wanted to let you know we've loaded all the bags in the rear luggage compartment. There wasn't very much, just a dozen small bags, so I don't think it'll affect the longitudinal trim," Mike Sommerpole informed me. He nodded his head at Alfie and began to walk away.

"Doing a bit more work at Gatwick, then?" I remarked.

He then explained he'd also come over for another reason.

"Mr Cope's aeroplane needed to be taken over to Biggin for servicing." He gestured towards the attractive four-seater Proctor that had languished in the overnight park for several days. The Proctor was a pre-war design from the drawing board of the versatile Edgar Percival. Many record-breaking designs had emanated from this man's genius.

"And you're flying it over there for him?" I ventured. Mike confirmed that he'd readily agreed to ferry the machine over to Biggin to keep in current flying practice.

I directed my attention back to Alfie Cope. "Cash in advance are our terms," I repeated. "You already owe us for yesterday's charter, so that's £300.

We're not leaving until we've been paid, so I suggest you pop over to the bank and draw some money. "

The passengers had begun to board the aircraft.

"I'll give you a cheque. Much more convenient than handling large quantities of cash," Alfie responded.

I advised him we'd have to cash the cheque before departing. He looked crestfallen.

"Be a bit reasonable, can't you?" he pleaded. "The passengers are aboard and waiting to depart. We can't tell them the trip's off, they've paid their money and everything . . ." Alfie suddenly put his hand to his mouth; he'd inadvertently let the cat out of the bag.

"Okay then, if you've been paid, we can take your cheque over to the bank and cash it," I agreed. Alfie grimaced as if in acute pain.

"Er . . . the money's not actually in the account yet," he spluttered. "Takes five working days for the cheque to clear, by which time you'll receive your payment."

"Cash in advance, I'm afraid. We prefer to remain on the ground rather than incur fuel costs and landing fees then not get paid. We don't pay to fly; you pay us."

I almost felt sorry for Alfie as he struggled with his self-made dilemma. The charter money had obviously been spirited away to a secret account and he didn't have £300 in ready cash. I began to weaken.

"Look, we'll wait here while you work it out," I suggested. "Phone the bank in Leeds and arrange something. There's still twenty minutes to go, I'm sure you can find an answer."

Nathan Warnup had rapidly departed the scene when the going got tough. Alfie hurried away to the terminal building, leaving Mike Sommerpole and me on the tarmac. I wandered idly over to the Proctor and ran my hand over its beautifully streamlined form.

"I've always admired Percival's designs," I confided. "I learned to fly on Percival Provosts. He produced some great designs."

"Vega Gull, Mew Gull, Percival Q-6, Jet Provost . . . He certainly designed a lot of good aeroplanes. This one's a little beauty to fly."

Mike climbed onto the left wing and opened the cockpit door. Inside, beautiful leather-covered seats and a walnut veneer dashboard imparted the impression of a vintage automobile.

"She's a fast little beast. One hundred and thirty knots cruise at ten gallons an hour." He settled into the pilot's seat and grasped the spade grip control column. "Long legs too; this particular Proctor's got extra wing tanks, so it could go almost a thousand miles without refuelling."

We continued to admire the lines of the sleek craft while waiting Alfie's return. The Proctor epitomised everything I admired in private aeroplanes. It was sleek and good looking, fast, powerful and demanded a moderate amount of skill to fly. If you couldn't afford your own personal Spitfire or P-51, a Proctor would make a good second choice. War-surplus Proctors were still around in large numbers, and Alfie had probably snapped up this example for the price of a second-hand car. Proctors were raced by their owners in the annual King's Cup Air Race. If I'd wanted to own an aeroplane, this Percival design would have been high on my wish list.

The sight of a distraught Alfie Cope hurrying back to the Dakota broke my reverie. I beckoned to him and he altered course towards us.

"The bank manager's on holiday and his deputy's at lunch," Alfie began. "I can't raise 300 quid in a few minutes. Your bloke shouldn't have accepted the job without first telling me it was cash on the knocker."

I glanced towards the Dakota. A plane load of excited passengers waited for us to fly them away from their humdrum nine-to-five existence for a few glorious hours. They'd already paid for the flight and if we refused to fly, they'd be the losers. Alfie had already squirrelled their money away. I'd hate to be responsible for their loss. I wavered indecisively.

"How much have you got on you in ready cash?" I asked. He extracted a wallet and counted out six £5 notes.

"What about the other pocket?" I snapped. He guiltily produced a slim billfold containing another £20.

"That's everything, fifty quid, unless you want to take my return train ticket as well," he whined.

Fifty pounds. Not even enough to cover our bare operating costs for today's flying. I hesitated further. Over at the aircraft, two or three passengers had emerged to find out what was going on. The taller of them, a typical north country pub bouncer, resembled a 200-pound gorilla — broad-shouldered, florid-faced and probably a bit short-tempered. His companion was ten or fifteen years older, short, bespectacled and obviously the spokesman.

"Everything okay? Not going to be late departing, are we?" he enquired pleasantly. I stepped aside — they were Alfie's problem.

"Just finalising a few last-minute formalities," Alfie assured him. "The bank draft hasn't arrived yet. Mere formality, won't take very long."

I saw the short gentleman nudge the gorilla. "Yer mean yer 'aven't paid 'em our mooney?"

The gorilla advanced menacingly on Alfie.

"No, of course not. Nothing of the sort. Your pilot here's all ready to depart. Now if you'd like to return to your seats, you'll be on your way soon." Alfie's eyes begged me to extricate him from his predicament. Mike and I gazed at the ground.

"Look, here's the fifty quid and my gold watch, real gold, Swiss-made, cost 200 quid when I bought it. Take it and get going before Tarzan feeds me to the ape."

I hesitated momentarily. Alfie's watch wouldn't be worth much more than £50 at a pawnbroker's shop, but that plus the other fifty would just about cover today's operating costs. The long-suffering passengers would get their trip but we could wave goodbye to the rest of the money he owed us. Behind him, the short passenger was endeavouring to coerce the gorilla back aboard the plane.

"It's all I've got on me," Alfie blubbered. The gorilla hesitated on the steps and listened intently. "There's nothing else!" he pleaded. The gorilla took one step down.

I'd have to make the most of a bad situation. After all, Air Links was ultimately responsible for Nathan's mistake in giving Alfie credit. I was about to agree when an interruption occurred.

"The Proctor," Mike Sommerpole whispered. I looked at him questioningly. "That's worth something. It's in nice condition. Must be worth three or four hundred pounds on the second-hand plane market . . ."

"Awlright, take it, it's yours!" Alfie begged. He hurried across to the light aircraft and returned with a wallet containing logbooks and documents.

"Here's the important one, the certificate of registration." He pulled out a document and scrawled his signature on the back. "Fill in the rest of it, the aeroplane's yours. Now please get going." He thrust the paperwork into my hand and stepped back.

In the Dakota, Les Smith, Christine and the gorilla awaited my decision. I accepted the Proctor documents and boarded the aircraft.

"Okay, we're on our way. Mike, can you remove the steps please?"

The Gatwick loader supervisor had come over to Mike and ordered him back to the baggage centre. "This ain't yer bloody flying club, sonny," he informed Mike. "There's two aircraft arriving in fifteen minutes and only three men to unload them. Get yerself over there smartish. You're paid to heave baggage, not look after passengers. Now move yer arse over to the terminal. Quick!"

I gestured to Mike from the cockpit window to remain and move the boarding steps away from the aircraft. Alfie had hastily departed the scene and there was nobody else to do it. He placed one hand on the side rail and was reprimanded by his supervisor and told to get back to the loading bay.

"He'll be with you in less than a minute," I assured the supervisor. He ignored me completely.

"I said now!" he bellowed at Mike.

"He'll first remove the steps before he does anything else," I instructed. The supervisor shook his head and glared up at me insolently.

"Not while I'm in charge he won't," he bellowed back. Mike looked pathetically embarrassed. He knew the supervisor could make life hell for him, even get him fired if he wanted to. In a moment of anger I made a hasty decision. "You're not in charge of him any longer," I replied.

"You're not fit to be in charge of a herd of cows. Mr Sommerpole now works for Air Links!" I gestured to Mike to move the steps away.

He wheeled them away and stood in front of the aircraft, squinting up at the cockpit. His world had suddenly fallen apart; he'd quite likely lost his job as a loader and was probably wondering whether he was really employed by Air Links.

"Clear on number two," he called, looking miserable as he held up two fingers.

"Welcome to Air Links," I called down to him. "You've just started with us."

"What as?" he implored. I thought furiously. What could we use him for?

"A pilot. Isn't that what you wanted?"

His face lightened into a broad smile. "Yes! When can I start flying?" he called.

I removed the Proctor document wallet from my briefcase and dropped it down to him.

"Now. Take our new aircraft over to Biggin for me. I'll see you in the office tomorrow."

His reply was drowned by the sound of the starboard engine bursting into life as I energised the starter.

On the way to Beauvais I had time to wonder how I was going to justify another name on the payroll to Dr Levitt and my fellow shareholders.

Despite our delayed departure we arrived at Beauvais on schedule, and our passengers continued into Paris by autobus. Les borrowed the airport manager's car and drove us into the village for a leisurely lunch, after which we basked in the sun and watched the world go by. This gave me additional time to wonder how I was going to explain my reasons for hiring Mike Sommerpole. I could already envisage Dr Levitt's response.

CHAPTER NINE
Fixed by the Fickle Finger of Fate

Fate sometimes flexes her fickle finger to alter events dramatically at the strangest times. I delayed getting into the office next morning because I hadn't resolved yesterday's dilemma. Another co-pilot on the payroll would increase our outgoings considerably, and it was all my fault. After my tirade against Dr Levitt for hiring Nathan, I wasn't looking forward to being confronted by the angry physician.

Fortunately for me, more urgent matters were under consideration. I heard the sounds of raised voices even before I'd reached our office. Chegwidden was berating somebody. I entered and walked straight into a heated argument.

"He bloody nearly wrote the aircraft off twice," the captain was explaining angrily to Denis. "I let him do the take-off out of Heathrow and he nearly went off the edge of the runway. He's too slow in his responses. He didn't use power and rudder to keep straight, so we began to drift off the runway until I took over, then he froze on the controls. That's only a small part of the story. His instrument flying is bloody awful — I had to take over during the approach to Lille because he was so hot and high."

While the captain listed other faults of his co-pilot, I checked yesterday's crew roster to see who he was talking about. It was Cullenane.

Chegwidden finally ran out of things to say, and Denis turned to me.

"Did you have any problems with this fellow during conversion training?" he enquired. I thought back to the afternoon several days ago when we'd endlessly pounded the circuit. I couldn't recall anybody being particularly bad; everybody had previous heavy aircraft experience, and I seemed to recall they'd all coped adequately with the DC-3. Chegwidden had also been aboard the aircraft and he'd have remembered anybody substandard.

"Not that I can recall," I replied. "We had five or six pilots under instruction that afternoon and I can't recall any of them standing out in any way. If he'd been below standard, I'd have given him a bit of extra training, but nobody needed it."

Chegwidden now directed his anger at me. "There's something just not right," he declared. "I don't mind helping new co-pilots but this one's downright dangerous and shouldn't have been let loose on the line. Find out who did his route check and ask him how he did then."

I told Chegwidden I'd checked him less than a week ago and couldn't remember any problems. I went to the filing cabinet and drew out his personal training file.

"I checked him out a couple of nights ago. He struck me as very keen and conscientious, eager to learn about our operation."

"What was his flying like?" Chegwidden demanded. I cast my mind back to that night. Les had ridden along as shotgun with us. Part of the route check required the pilot under check to demonstrate his flying competence. I suddenly remembered Cullenane's unfortunate accident when he'd jammed his hand in the cabin door mechanism, preventing him flying the last sector. I ruefully admitted he hadn't done any physical handling that night.

"Yet you signed him out as competent?" Chegwidden accused. "Why the hell did you do that?"

I reminded him we were critically short of co-pilots so I'd had to bend the rules slightly. There would be plenty of other opportunities later on for him to fly the aircraft. This didn't please the irate captain. "So you falsely signed him out, without confirming yourself that his handling was up to standard," he exclaimed. "Then I get him as my co-pilot and he nearly writes the aircraft off on his first take-off. That could've cost me my licence and livelihood."

I thought furiously during this tirade. If this co-pilot was as bad as Chegwidden said, why hadn't I noticed it during his circuit training? I thought back to the afternoon when we'd checked him and several other pilots and couldn't remember any of them not being up to standard. Oddly enough, I couldn't remember anything about Cullenane's flying, but this was hardly surprising when five pilots had done over thirty landings.

Chegwidden concluded the meeting by announcing he was putting in a report on the night's incidents with a recommendation that the co-pilot should not operate as a line pilot until he'd received additional training to bring him up to standard. My assurance that this would be acted upon seemed to satisfy him and he left.

I was left alone in the office with Denis, who demanded to know how this could have happened. I was at a loss for a reply but did point out rather feebly that Cullenane hadn't flown for three years. Denis remained unimpressed.

"You'd better do another route check on him and report back. If he's as bad as we've just heard, there's something afoot. I'll check with his previous employer — he may have a whole lot of P-51 time in his logbook.° If that's the case, we'll replace him."

Further conversation was interrupted by the simultaneous arrival of Dr Levitt and Mike Sommerpole. The doctor was in a cheerful mood as he greeted us.

I remembered with sickening dread that I was going to have to justify my reasons for hiring another pilot.

"Good morning, gentlemen. Nathan tells me yesterday's charter went very well and we've already been paid for it. That's excellent news, now what else is new?"

° P-51 time. False entries in a log book to increase a pilot's apparent experience.

Denis briefly recounted the bare bones of our recent conversation about Cullenane. The doctor's nose twitched disapprovingly at the news.

"He must be replaced then," he insisted. Denis mumbled something about giving him further training. I sidled over to Mike Sommerpole and questioned him on yesterday's flight in the Proctor.

"Everything went fine," he assured me. "Air Couriers have the aircraft in their hangar . . . oh, and they want to know whether to transfer the ownership to you or the company."

I thought quickly; Air Links didn't need the expense of another aircraft on their books, but they did need prompt payment of yesterday's charter flight. I decided to buy the Proctor and pay Air Links the money owing for the Beauvais charters. I'd keep the aircraft until I could sell it. I was secretly rather looking forward to owning and flying such a sleek machine, so I phoned Griff and told him to re-register it in my name.

Levitt had now become involved in the subject of Cullenane's training. I tried to explain that the lack of familiarity with the Dakota had probably been the problem. Levitt didn't appreciate that experienced pilots were getting scarce and soon we'd have to accept what we could get. I mollified him by telling him I'd take the co-pilot on another route check and report on how he fared. This seemed to satisfy the doctor and he headed off to congratulate our new commercial manager on his business acumen. This delayed my having to announce Mike Sommerpole's recent recruitment.

Somewhere down in my subconscious a hidden instinct was telling me something was not quite right with Cullenane. Further contemplation on the matter was interrupted by Pickles telling me he needed me to ferry Kilo Echo to Biggin for urgent maintenance. He'd already rounded up Timber Wood by phone. An idea suddenly struck me.

"Mr Sommerpole can bring us back in the Proctor," I announced. "Tell Mr Wood to go straight to the aircraft when he arrives. I'll get it ready."

I took a set of Pop Speller's DC-3 notes from the filing cabinet and handed them to Mike.

"Have a read of these when you get a chance. I've got a funny feeling we're going to need your services soon." He began to say something, but stopped when I hurried out to pre-flight the aircraft.

Pickles had long ago adopted the policy of using non-revenue (empty) flights for training purposes whenever possible. On this occasion there was no training commitment outstanding except for Cullenane, who was off duty. I decided to let Wood fly the aircraft over to Biggin and I'd fly it back later.

Mike checked the fuel and oil quantities for me while I completed the necessary paperwork. It would take Wood three-quarters of an hour to reach the airport, so once we had completed everything I just sat and relaxed. Mike, in contrast, seemed rather fidgety. I had just begun to tell him we'd give him the necessary flying training as soon as he'd passed the Dakota technical exam when he interrupted.

"I thought an opportunity like this might crop up one day so I took the exam just in case. I borrowed a flight manual and a set of notes and managed to pass."

This put a very different complexion on things. With a current commercial pilot's licence, and multi-engined and instrument rating, he could legally be checked out and employed on the aircraft. I thought for a moment.

"I'd like to put you in the seat and get you to fly it to Biggin, but we should really run over the controls and things first," I explained. He reminded me he'd witnessed our operations when he'd flown as unpaid baggage handler a few nights ago.

"I've memorised most of the speeds and power settings," he assured me. "I just need to handle the controls. You can only learn so much from the books."

That made sense to me. My watch told me we'd be waiting another half hour for Wood so I suggested we sit in the cockpit and run through a few drills and procedures. He became quite elated at the suggestion.

I put him in the right seat and ran through everything he needed to know — even how to adjust the seat, turn the instrument lighting on and off, de-ice the props, turn on the pneumatic wing de-icers and set the cabin heat. Finally we ran through the normal and abnormal procedures.

"The most critical phase of flight is engine failure on take-off, so make sure you identify the correct engine before shutting it down," I emphasised. "The Dakota doesn't climb very well with one dead engine but it flies even worse with two! Take a few moments to decide which engine has failed and get the other pilot to confirm it before doing anything drastic." Mike nodded his understanding as I pointed out the various emergency controls. I then ran through the sequence of events for today's flight. He would start the engines and taxi us out to the runway while I performed the co-pilot's checks. I repeated the technique for keeping straight on take-off and reminded him I would take over if necessary.

Further discussion was interrupted by the arrival of Wood. I introduced Mike and explained what we'd planned. Wood would sit in the jump seat and ensure everything went smoothly. Within five minutes we were taxiing for the take-off point.

Given Mike's minimal experience on multi-engined aircraft and my limited time as an instructor, we did all right. My hands and feet hovered nervously over the controls during take-off but he got airborne without any interference from me. He forgot to call for the undercarriage to be raised but that was normal for someone who hadn't flown a retractable landing-gear aircraft very much. Gatwick Director gave us a course to steer and told us to change frequency to Biggin when over Redhill.

The rest of the flight went as I'd expected. Mike established himself on final approach in the correct configuration after a little bit of prompting from me. The rivulets of perspiration running down his face told me he was feeling nervous, but his first landing in a heavy aircraft rated a six out of ten, which was pretty good in my estimation. I waited until he'd slowed the aircraft to a walking pace and turned off the runway before taking over and taxiing the rest of the way to Air Couriers' maintenance base. It had been a stressful but satisfying twenty minutes for Mike, and I told him to relax.

Griff came up into the cockpit after shut-down and discussed the forth-coming maintenance.

"The Air Registration Board issued an airworthiness directive on the fire warning systems," he explained. "I got the fellows in the electrical shop to make up two looms, which we should be able to install in two or three hours, provided we don't run into any other problems. You can have her back after lunch."

I decided to wait and ferry the aircraft back to Gatwick when ready. We discussed the details of the work involved, and I drew Griff's attention to a few other snags on the squawk sheet.

He then very diplomatically suggested we get out of the way and leave him to get on with the job.

"Go and play with your new toy," he suggested.

"What toy?" I looked blank as Griff nodded towards the hangar.

"Your Proctor. The office girls checked the documentation and we've transferred the registration to you. Everything else is okay, we've had it in here for a check so it's in good shape. Go and enjoy yourself for an hour."

I raised a questioning eyebrow at Mike. "Think you could check me out on this machine?"

He assured me he could. Timber Wood said he preferred to stay on the ground but helped us push the trim monoplane out of the hangar. Once again I had an opportunity to admire the sleek lines of my new purchase.

Like most of Edgar Percival's machines, the Proctor had classic lines. Alex Henshaw had flown a Mew Gull in the pre-war King's Cup air race, then broken the London to the Cape record in the same machine. New Zealander Jean Batten had used her Percival Gull Six for a London to New Zealand record and other record-breaking flights. Another female pilot, Beryl Markham, had used a Percival Vega Gull to conquer the South Atlantic. When war broke out in 1939, the Air Ministry recognised the Vega Gull as an ideal light communications aircraft. It was fast (150 mph cruise), carried a pilot and three passengers, had good range and was built of non-strategic materials (wood, fabric and ply), as metals were at that time required for bomber and fighter production. The Royal Air Force modified the aircraft to their speci-fications and re-named it the Proctor. Alfie Cope's aeroplane had been converted to civilian status after the war and had been owned briefly by an ex-bomber pilot, who had eventually tired of flying and sold the aircraft to Alfie.

Mike and I walked round the aircraft, while he pointed out the items to check in a pre-flight inspection.

The long sleek nose cowl concealed a six-cylinder, 200-horsepower de Havilland Gypsy Queen engine turning a metal two-bladed propeller. The undercarriage was enclosed by streamlined spats to reduce air resistance. Pilot and passengers entered via doors on either side of the cabin.

The aircraft smelled of a delicious essence of wood, cellulose dope, high octane fuel and genuine leather. In its day the Proctor had been a very competitive design; even today it would do better than many light aircraft with respect to cruise speed, range, payload and cabin area. I felt a heady

sense of excitement as we prepared to fly this machine. The leather-covered seats imparted a touch of luxurious comfort to the aeroplane. A spade-type control column, Second World War-type instruments and a set of earphones reminded me this was no American Spam can; this had been a military aeroplane.

Mike pointed out the various controls before suggesting I start the engine. I flipped on the electrical master switch and the radios suddenly came to life.

"I normally give the engine about five primes," he volunteered, pointing to a Ki-gas priming plunger. "Quarter of an inch of throttle and release the starter once she's running."

The starter motor whined in protest before the Gypsy Queen suddenly snarled into life like a grumpy feline. We taxied the short distance to the westerly runway and held a short while, allowing the engine temperatures and pressures to stabilise in their operating range. Mike used the time to brief me on the take-off technique.

"Bit like the Dakota in a way. Lots of coarse rudder to keep straight initially, then once the tail's up you'll find she tracks down the runway quite easily. Lift her off at fifty-five to sixty knots and allow the speed to build up to eighty in the climb. She should climb out at 800 feet per minute if you do that."

The Proctor proved delightful to fly. We climbed to 4000 feet and slowed almost to a stall. On Mike's recommendation, I didn't allow the stall to fully develop.

"Lotta Proctors have a tendency to drop a wing and spin, especially when they're tail heavy," he explained. "Once they're in a spin, you could have problems. Lots of people have been killed that way. It pays to watch your speed when turning onto final approach. Get too slow in a turn and this aircraft will bite you!"

I heeded his advice conscientiously. The Proctor was a bit like a pedigree racehorse — fast, headstrong, ready to bite you at any opportunity and needing a firm hand. Despite these characteristics, it was an exhilarating aeroplane to fly.

Mike's nerves must have become a bit frayed after my sixth landing, for he suggested we stop for lunch. I was having so much fun I hadn't noticed the time. We taxied back to Air Couriers then joined Wood in the Greasy Spoon. Griff had assured us the Dakota would be ready in an hour.

"You can leave the Proctor in our hangar," he graciously offered. "That'll be better than leaving it out in the weather at Gatwick. I might even get some executive charter work for it if you're interested."

I thanked him, and after a quick lunch we were airborne and heading back to Gatwick in our Dakota. Mike's next landing was a greaser, probably as a result of gaining a bit more confidence. As he taxied back to the north park, I could see he was more relaxed.

"Thanks, I enjoyed that," he muttered after we'd stopped the engines. I told him we'd try to get him the rest of the landings as soon as possible. Denis arrived in the cockpit at this moment.

"There's another bullion charter scheduled for tomorrow night," he confided quietly. "I'm not too happy about the security arrangements. We can't hope to pull the same trick we used last time. Pickles shot his mouth off afterwards and the story spread like wildfire; it undoubtedly got to Heathrow. We'll have to carry an additional person to keep watch. I'm contacting one of the security firms to provide somebody."

"Why not use one of our own fellows?" I gestured to Mike. "We've got a fully qualified loader, familiar with Heathrow and Gatwick, working for us. He'd be delighted to ride along and he'd know the ropes a lot better than anybody we could hire. Besides which, I don't think Mr Koller would want another organisation involved in this confidential matter."

Denis agreed to this when I explained Mike's status in the company.

Pickles, Denis and I discussed the matter in the office before phoning Koller at the bank and agreeing to collect another 1000 kilos of bullion from Switzerland. Pickles had checked the loadings out of Lille and confirmed we had sufficient payload available. In the interests of security, I selected Les Smith as co-pilot for this assignment and Mike Sommerpole would accompany us as security guard and loadmaster.

Until this moment, I had forgotten the problem with Cullenane. Sooner or later I was going to have to fly with him to decide whether his flying skills could be brought up to the required standard. I made a note to fly with him the following night; the empty sectors could be used for training. I instructed Pickles to advise tomorrow's rostered crew they wouldn't be required that night.

By the middle of April, both aircraft had earned us a substantial bank balance. The Dakota was fully committed to the night freight schedule and Lourdes pilgrims, while the Hermes concentrated on a series of long-haul flights to Corfu and Heraklion in Greece.

The administrative pressures of the DC-3 operation prevented me taking any interest in the Hermes, although I did privately wonder what Denis had planned when it ran out of flying hours.

The bullion charter took place as scheduled, but resulted in quite a few surprises for everybody.

Koller had insisted the cargo be consigned to Heathrow this time. I'd had a few sharp words with Pickles again and told him not to discuss company business in public areas where conversations could be overheard. I was disappointed at the way he'd shot his mouth off over the details of the previous bullion job.

"News travels fast around here and undermines the confidentiality of the operation," I cautioned him. There seemed no point in hiding the bullion to thwart thieves if everybody knew about it. He listened with sulky disinterest.

We positioned Kilo Echo over to Heathrow in the late afternoon and once again I put Mike in the right seat to get him another take-off and landing towards his type rating.

Pickles had loaded the bogus bullion boxes in the forward baggage hold before we departed from Gatwick. He spent a considerable time briefing Mike where to put them when we departed Zurich. Mike handled the short flight to Heathrow without problem; his flying was getting more confident with every flight. After shutdown, he climbed out of the co-pilot's seat and donned a pair of loader's white overalls to supervise the freight loading.

I let Les Smith fly the next sector to Lille with Mike observing from the jump seat. The reduced payload out of Lille would allow us to carry the bullion out of Zurich. We refuelled there to minimise time on the ground in Switzerland.

On arrival at Zurich the same solemn guards waited for us. Mike was the first out of the aircraft, before we'd even shut down the engines. He was issuing instructions to the Swiss as Les and I left the aircraft. We checked the return weather in the briefing office and activated our return flight plan. The senior of the Swiss security guards handed me two copies of the cargo manifest and a receipt for my signature. I was agreeably surprised on checking inside the aircraft to find Mike had already positioned the bulky boxes of gold and was now checking the fuel and oil levels.

He handed me the fuel docket and muttered something unintelligible about the loading. I suggested we climb aboard our aircraft and head home to London.

The Swiss guards seemed to watch our departure with amused interest. Air Traffic Control cleared us to depart via the northerly runway, which reduced our taxiing time to less than five minutes. I had decided to fly this sector, and Mike could do the final empty leg back to Gatwick. It would be daylight by then and the weather was forecast fine for our arrival.

We lined up on the 12,000-foot runway and had time to admire the thousands of coloured lights marking the extent of the paved area. Les engaged the tailwheel lock as ATC cleared us for take-off. I applied power and we began to accelerate ponderously down the runway.

The tail seemed to take an unusually long time to come up, which I attributed to Zurich's 1400-foot elevation, yet the aircraft almost leaped into the air when I lifted it off at eighty knots. Two complete turns of forward trim were required to stabilise the speed on climb-out. At 2000 feet I engaged the autopilot and turned to Mike in the jump seat.

"She seems a bit tail heavy," I commented. "Are you sure the boxes are secured correctly?"

He assured me the loading had been done precisely to Pickles' instructions. As the aircraft was now performing satisfactorily, I dismissed the matter.

The return flight took a little less than two hours and we were parked back in front of Heathrow's freight terminal before dawn. I told Mike we'd delay our departure till after daylight to make things a bit easier for him when he flew us home.

The arrival of five enormous baggage loaders interrupted me before I'd finished. To my alarm, one of them stood and jammed the aisle behind Mike and supervised his colleagues as they unfastened the webbing straps across the forward baggage compartment. I struggled to get out of my seat but was blocked by his bulky form.

I waited anxiously as the thirty-six boxes in the forward compartment, each containing a large fortune, were swiftly transferred to a waiting trolley and hauled away.

A black armoured car sidled up to the rear door of the aircraft, and three guards began placing the other bullion boxes inside. To my consternation, all the remaining freight, including the boxes from the forward hold, had been whisked away while we had sat trapped in the cockpit. I searched around desperately for a member of the airport police or security staff but none were to be seen. I briefly considered calling for help on the aircraft radio but decided it was better not to broadcast our £300,000 problem to the world.

I could only watch helplessly from the aircraft as the trolley containing thirty-six boxes of gold bullion vanished into the freight terminal. I wondered how many of those boxes would emerge from one of Great Britain's most notorious crime areas. By the time the consignment had been picked over by various thieves and criminals masquerading as clerks, drivers and baggage loaders, we'd be lucky if even the trolley was left. I finally managed to fight my way out of the cockpit and proceed to the rear of the aircraft, where Mike waited unconcernedly. He handed me a foolscap form.

"Receipt for the bullion," he volunteered. "Didn't take long, did it?" I took the paper and beckoned him to get up to the cockpit. There was no point in telling him the guards had taken the wrong boxes; he was going to fly us back to Gatwick and it would be counter-productive to cloud his mind with other issues.

As I settled into the left seat, I idly wondered how long it would take a third of a million pounds of gold bullion to reach the underworld.

I thought I sensed trouble as soon as I saw Koller, Pickles and Denis waiting on our hard standing. Mike taxied Kilo Echo into the parking area and cut the engines. Joe Phillips had arranged for the aircraft to be refuelled and reconfigured for passenger use. Today was our first pilgrim charter to Lourdes.

Zucher's son also appeared as the engines slowed to a stop.

I delayed getting out of my seat, confident that Koller would be up in the cockpit to castigate me for losing a fortune in gold. The insurance underwriters were probably only a short distance behind. Somebody outside called up to me in the cockpit.

"Chocks are in, release the brakes and throw us down the pins," Joe called. Behind him, Denis and Koller were laughing at something Pickles had just said. Feeling very weary and disheartened, I clambered out of my seat and prepared to face a storm of criticism. Mike and Les followed behind.

Strangely, Koller and the others didn't take an awful lot of interest in us as we exited the aircraft. I walked up to him and shrugged apologetically. To my surprise he extended a congratulatory handshake.

"Well done, captain. Fooled 'em again, eh?" he chortled. I looked quizzically towards Denis but his expression told me nothing. Koller directed his attention to Mike.

"And I believe you were partly responsible for the success of the operation." The banker pumped Mike's hand enthusiastically. I looked around for somebody to enlighten me and ended up confronting the banker.

"Are you telling me the gold consignment arrived at its destination safely?" I enquired suspiciously. Koller adamantly assured me it had. I muttered something non-committal. There was something here I didn't understand. If £300,000 worth of gold had gone through London's Thief Row airport undisturbed, there was something afoot I didn't know about.

Koller excused himself almost immediately, leaving the rest of us to proceed to the office. Once inside, I shut the door firmly and addressed everybody.

"For your information, the wrong consignment's gone to the bank," I announced grimly. "As soon as we'd landed and parked, half a dozen heavyweights came to the cockpit, jammed us in our seats and emptied the forward freight compartment. The gold was whisked away before I could do a thing. We couldn't even get out of our seats. This must've been an inside job."

I turned to Mike. He hadn't been much help at all. I was about to register my disappointment in his attitude when Denis interrupted. "The bank phoned half an hour ago and confirmed the gold had arrived safely," he assured me. "I dunno what happened to the fake consignment, it's probably on its way to Algeria by now . . ." Behind him, Pickles appeared to be silently convulsing at some private joke.

My look of utter disbelief caused Zucher to interject. "The thieves took the wrong consignment again," he tried to explain, but I interrupted before he could finish.

"The boxes in the rear fuselage went into the armoured security vehicle and the hidden consignment up front got whisked away from under our very noses. This was definitely an inside job, five big fellows crowded into the cockpit and kept us in our seats while their accomplices filched the gold," I announced angrily. I turned to address Pickles. "And part of the blame is attributable to you for talking too much. Walls have ears and somebody heard what we did previously."

Pickles listened while I raved on. He appeared to have problems keeping a straight face. Several times he glanced across at the younger Zucher, who also had difficulty not laughing.

"The bank's deputy head of security phoned and confirmed the consignment arrived at 9.16am," Pickles announced. "I enquired whether they'd checked the contents of every box and he just about came down the phone at me. The gold is now locked safely away in the bank's vaults."

"What about the fake consignment?" I demanded. "Where did that end up?"

Pickles shrugged. "Dunno, but from what you've told us, it had plenty of attention. They'll probably dump it somewhere when they find their mistake."

I remained puzzled and tried to question him further. The office was now becoming quite crowded as several crews arrived to collect the paperwork for their day's flying. Outside the office window on the apron, ground staff were replenishing the Hermes with fuel and catering. Soon it would head off to the Mediterranean holiday resorts. Further away, our DC-3 waited on the north park for the next crew to taxi it over to the passenger terminal, where Lourdes pilgrims would be assisted to embark. It was impossible to continue the conversation amidst so much noise and confusion, so I decided to go home and get some rest. The others left with me.

Once out of the office I turned on Pickles angrily. "I dunno how the gold arrived safely at its destination but . . ."

Pickles gestured me to silence. "I had to use a little guile," he admitted. "After you gave me that rocket for talking about it in public, I did a bit of thinking. I realised the details of how we hid the gold under tarpaulins in the forward freight compartment would have fallen on wrong ears. It was too late to undo the harm done so I, well we, decided to fight poison with poison. Know what I mean?"

My blank countenance prompted young Zucher to speak. "He got them to swap the consignments around. This time the bogus boxes were up front in the forward baggage hold . . ."

"And 300,000 quid's worth of gold bullion was left down the back in full view of everybody!" I exclaimed incredulously. Several passers-by paused to glance at us curiously. I quickly lowered my voice.

"Do you realise what could've happened if somebody had stolen those boxes down the back?" I whispered at Pickles. He turned on me indignantly.

"But they didn't, did they? They were more concerned with finding the load hidden up front. You fellows behaved perfectly, taking no interest in what was down the back but becoming quite agitated when the stuff up front disappeared."

I had to admit the audacious scheme had worked admirably. "But it'll never work again," I cautioned. "Don't accept any more bullion charters, they'll outsmart us next time."

Pickles agreed with my sentiment but pointed out correctly that we were richer by £15,000. The annoying thing was he was right.

We had reached the main concourse in the passenger terminal building. I headed left towards the staff car park while Pickles and his friend Zucher continued to the passenger check-in area. A thought suddenly struck me.

"Whose idea was it to change the consignments over?" I demanded petulantly. The two youngsters stopped and stared back at me awkwardly.

"It was his idea." Zucher pointed at Pickles, who shuffled awkwardly and muttered unintelligibly.

"Well, it worked," I admitted. "Okay, well done, it was a brilliant idea."

"I er . . . actually I got it from a book he lent me . . ." Pickles pointed at his friend.

"What book?" I enquired curiously. Pickles turned away in embarrassment, leaving Zucher to reply.

"Ever heard of Captain W. E. Johns?" He held a slim volume aloft.

"The author of the Biggles books? Of course I have. I probably read every one of them when I was a teenager. You're not going to tell me you . . ."

"Ever read *Biggles and Co*? They had the same problem."

My mouth must have nearly crushed my foot in amazement because I became incapable of coherent speech for thirty seconds.

"You mean to stand here and tell me you copied the antics of some blooming fictional air hero to formulate the policy of our airline?" I accused him loudly. "You gambled with £300,000 of somebody else's gold?"

"Well, it worked, dinnit?" Pickles had overcome his embarrassment and turned on the defensive. "And keep your voice down when you're discussing company business in public areas. Walls have ears, y'know . . ."

Ginger Hebblethwaite and his friend Biggles turned and headed towards the check-in area, so I couldn't see if they were laughing at me.

CHAPTER TEN
"I Do Declare"

The customs boys at Gatwick had obviously received some sort of tip-off. In addition to the usual number of uniformed staff, we noticed several plain-clothes branch (PCB) members patrolling the passenger arrivals hall.

The crew of our DC-3, consisting of the co-pilot, hostess and myself, waited patiently by the crew counter. We'd been up all night and another half hour wasn't going to matter.

Eventually a middle-aged two-ringer hurried over. "Sorry to hold you up, Captain," he apologised distractedly, shuffling through our documentation.

"Something up?" I enquired conspiratorially.

The customs officer looked up in confusion before admitting there was a bit of a panic on.

"Just had a last-minute tip-off that somebody rather interesting is coming in on a false passport," he confided. "Unfortunately Interpol didn't give any details of flight, airline or anything else. So head office have decided to call out all available staff to ensure he doesn't slip through our net. Blooming inconvenient on a Sunday."

He resumed checking our documentation, leaving us to ponder what sort of person would need to enter the country clandestinely.

"Got a stamped copy of the General Declaration?" he enquired. I rummaged among the ship's documents for the required piece of paper.

"Definitely had it somewhere," I apologised. "Remember signing it just after we left Rome. Must be in among the aircraft papers. Hang on a minute while I check." I opened up my flight satchel and removed a manilla envelope containing the used navigational documents from our flight — met briefing, flight plan, notams and engineering record. Aviation has made sweeping changes since these events of thirty-five years ago, but even Concorde can't arrive or depart until the paperwork is right.

While we waited, we eyed the constant stream of passengers filing past.

"Got a name or description of the person?" I enquired. The customs officer frowned slightly; he shouldn't have revealed what he had.

"Drug baron. Fled the country 'bout three years ago. Broke bail," he eventually confided. "Normally such people hole up in the south of Spain or the coast of North Africa with their ill-gotten gains, but this fellow's decided to return. We've got plenty of photos taken when he was in custody, but he's most likely changed his appearance by plastic surgery or grown a beard since then."

"What about fingerprints?" I suggested. "They won't have changed."

The revenuer nodded his head in regretful agreement. "But who's going to fingerprint every passenger who goes through here in a day?" he asked. "At peak times there are over a thousand travellers arriving in an hour. Imagine how long it'd take us to print every male suspect. Meanwhile more and more passengers would arrive and be subjected to long delays. Pretty soon the Sunday papers would hear about it, the airlines would complain to the minister of Civil Aviation and somebody's head would roll."

"So he'll probably slip through undetected?" the co-pilot suggested. The customs chappie shook his head.

"Naagh, we'll get him somehow. There's more than one way to skin a cat."

I thought he looked rather self-confident when he said that. I continued watching the seemingly endless string of passengers arrive by air at Gatwick's terminal. Insignificant PCB members merged among them. A bearded fellow in his late thirties hobbled in on crutches, looking distinctly suspicious. A PCB joined the queue behind him and signalled to a uniformed colleague at the barrier. A button was pressed to alert the rest of the staff as the suspect leaned one of his crutches against the inspecting officer's rostrum. He retrieved a new-looking British passport and handed it to the inspector. A senior uniformed branch member approached and took the document from his colleague. A short exchange of words resulted in the suspect hobbling away to a distant interview room with two other officers.

"Think that was him?" I wondered out loud. My other two crew members agreed he looked pretty suspicious. Our customs officer remained silent. PCB continued to mingle among the passengers. Only now did I notice police officers strategically positioned at every exit.

I continued rummaging in the flight satchel until I found the missing document in the previous flight's documents.

The two customs officers returned from their business with the man on crutches. I saw one of them shake his head quickly at the others on barrier duty. The suspect appeared, indignantly clutching his passport between clenched teeth. A robust-looking elderly lady eyed the policemen at every exit while her passport was checked.

The crew customs officer was about to stamp our documents when a red warning light glowed at his console. Dropping his official stamp, he hurried to where the elderly lady was showing signs of agitation. As he and another officer approached, she broke away and sprinted with remarkable agility towards one of the exits. An alert police constable caught her in full flight and restrained her until the customs men arrived. After a few short exchanges, she was escorted away.

Customs clearance was going to take a little longer today. A British United Airways Viscount crew arrived behind us and enquired impatiently the reason for the hold-up.

"Somebody coming in on a false passport," we explained. "They've stopped two people while we've been waiting."

84

Five minutes later our inspector returned, looking rather smug.

"Got 'im dead to rights," he smirked. "The CID boys are on their way to take him into custody. He won't be allowed out on bail again."

"They never learn, do they?" his colleague chortled. "They can grow beards, change their names, obtain false passports, undergo reconstructive surgery, have fingerprints removed, but one thing they never think to change."

"Yeah, he won't be the last we catch that way," the other remarked. "He even changed his sex. Now that is unusual."

"How did you detect him then?" we asked.

"We had a good description of him — height, weight, age — and this isn't the first time somebody's come in disguised as the opposite sex," the senior customs officer explained.

"So what tipped you off?" I persisted. The customs man shuffled awkwardly, while we waited enthralled.

"Well, voice for a start. But there's one thing they never think to alter, which gives them away more times than anything else."

"And that is . . .?"

The customs officer held up our sheaf of passports gleefully.

"Date of birth in their false passports. Our computers keep an eye open for anybody of either sex answering to the approximate description, and when somebody with the same birth date comes along, we check closer. Worked like a charm this time and it'll work again."

The crew of our DC-3 exchanged wondering glances at this revelation, as the inspector returned his attention to our crew search list.

"Now then, anything to declare, gentlemen?" he enquired.

CHAPTER ELEVEN
Phoney Experience

Two problems awaited me when I got home.

Christine phoned to enquire whether I could fly with Cullenane that night to assess his competence. I told her that would be fine. Three more sectors under supervision should bring him up to standard.

The second problem was harder to resolve. British European Airways had written confirming the date of my interview in a week's time. I mentally noted to keep the day free, a difficult thing to accomplish in the air-charter business.

I slept till late afternoon, then prepared a light meal before setting off back to the airport. Fine drizzle had begun to fall as I drove the short distance to the terminal. Cullenane and I arrived in the office simultaneously, and I greeted him cheerily. I had decided it was best to adopt a casual attitude to his problem, for I felt confident we could overcome it together.

"A frontal system's coming in from the west," he volunteered. He'd already been down to the met office to check the weather. "Could make our return into Heathrow a bit difficult." I made a mental note to load a bit more fuel for the flight. Bad weather becomes even more of a problem when fuel reserves get low and you have to resort to desperate measures to get back on the ground.

We walked to the briefing office together, and I told him of the concern expressed about his flying ability. I suggested he do all the flying tonight with the intention of improving his handling skills.

"We'll treat it as a training flight, except I won't be failing any engines or doing anything nasty. I'll act as co-pilot and I'll also help with anything else that occurs. Happy with that?"

He nodded silently and we sat down to prepare the night's flight plan.

Darkness had fallen early in the inclement weather conditions and we got a lift out to the aircraft in the company van. The machine had flown that afternoon and the refuellers were finishing their task as we arrived. Cullenane made straight for the cockpit, leaving me to do the external inspection.

I first checked the paperwork before inspecting the outside of the aircraft. From the technical logbook I learned that Chegwidden had flown the aircraft that afternoon and snagged the VHF radio. Joe Phillips had changed it for an overhauled unit and signed the defect off. Apart from that, and a severe case of old age, the aircraft was serviceable. I checked the outside then settled into the left seat; Cullenane had prepared the navigation log and the required charts for the short hop across to Heathrow. I picked up the navigation clipboard from the space between us and told him not to worry about the paperwork.

"Enjoy yourself. You're doing all the flying tonight and I'm going to have to sit here and do all the hard work for you. Okay then, ready for some pre-starting checks?"

We read through the pre-starting checklist and he performed the drills faultlessly. A ground engineer gave us the all clear to start engines.

When both motors were idling smoothly and the checks had been accomplished, Gatwick Ground Control cleared us to the runway holding point. I gestured to Cullenane to start taxiing. He inched the throttles forward as he released the brakes. The aircraft rolled forward, but failed to respond as he applied full right rudder and brake to turn out of the confined parking space. He applied power to the port engine but the aircraft still refused to turn. A ground servicing vehicle loomed dangerously close to the left propeller as I applied full braking to prevent a collision. My right hand felt for the tailwheel lock and released it.

"Tail wheel was still locked. Common mistake. Don't forget to release it before turning," I cautioned. "We all make that mistake now and again. Okay, we're cleared out to the runway."

A strong northerly wind buffeted the controls, causing us to weave our way down the taxiway. I locked the tailwheel for him again once we straddled the centre line and this helped a lot. He remembered to take it out again as we turned into the run-up bay for our power check.

The tower operator cleared us for take-off as soon as I called him, and I gestured to Cullenane to taxi onto the runway. He lined up well to the left of the centre line, until I suggested rolling forward until the mainwheels straddled the white runway centre-line marks.

"Okay, we're cleared for take-off. Advance the power gradually at first and use plenty of coarse rudder to keep straight initially."

His left arm advanced the power levers and the sound of our two radial engines increased to a deafening roar. The tail came up and the runway lights streamed past the cockpit side windows in an indistinct blur. The engine instruments had reached the full power setting. Cullenane continued to push the throttles forward. I placed my right hand over his arm to prevent the maximum permitted settings being exceeded.

"Okay, pull 'em back to forty-eight inches," I cautioned, applying a touch of right rudder to help us keep straight. The needle of the airspeed indicator passed eighty knots as I gave the signal that we'd achieved flying speed. He pulled back on the control column and the Dak left the ground.

"Wheels up?" I suggested, noting the signs of stress on his sweat-beaded face as we left Gatwick's bright lights behind and climbed up into the night. I retracted the landing gear and reminded him of the correct climb-out speed. We had entered cloud, and light turbulence was affecting the aircraft.

"Concentrate on the flying and I'll handle the power," I suggested. He had made no effort to reduce power to the climb setting. I fiddled with throttles and pitch levers until they stabilised at the correct figures.

"Maintain 3000 feet on reaching," I told him. "Lower the nose slightly to maintain 110 knots." I pointed at the airspeed indicator which was showing ninety. He looked across at my flying panel and mouthed something.

"Can't hear you . . . use the intercom," I instructed, pointing to the three-position switch on his control yoke.

Suddenly his voice sounded clearly in my earphones.

"Can't see the blind flying instruments very well from this side," he said.

I nodded sympathetically; there was only one set of flight instruments on the Dak and they were set in front of the captain. The co-pilot had to squint across at the other pilot's panel when he flew.

I cranked in a quarter of a turn of nose-down trim, and on my suggestion he engaged the auto-pilot. The airspeed settled at the correct figure and shortly afterwards we levelled at 3000 feet. On contacting the Heathrow approach controller, he gave us radar direction onto the final approach path, and at twelve miles from touchdown I tuned the radio aids for the approach. The latest aerodrome weather broadcast gave light rain with a cloud base of 1000 feet. The instruments indicated we were aligned on the extended centre line and approaching the glide path from below; a normal situation.

"Ready for some approach checks?" I enquired helpfully. Cullenane looked at me blankly.

"Better get the approach checks completed," I instructed, reading from the list. "Fuel? Okay, I've checked the contents and we're feeding from the main tanks. Pressures normal. Mixture?"

Cullenane failed to respond to the checklist calls. I completed them silently and drew his attention to the flight instruments.

"Coming onto the glide slope, better start slowing down and think about getting some gear and flap out. Pull the power back." He moved the levers back a small amount. "We'll need a lot less than that, glide path is active, pull the power back to twenty inches." He retarded the throttles further.

"Quarter flap," he commanded and I moved the hydraulic selector. We were now nine miles from touchdown and the glide slope indicator had centred.

"On the glide path," I reminded. "Start descending, don't get too high. Okay, I'll extend the landing gear for you." I leaned across and selected the landing-gear lever down. The hydraulic system grumbled and wheezed while the gear extended, but finally the pressure stabilised. I centred the lever and locked the safety latch; two green lights confirmed the undercarriage was down and locked. I redirected my attention back to the flight instruments.

"Start descending, we're getting too high," I cautioned.

He tweaked the autopilot pitch control and the Dakota began descending. "Half flap, make that three-quarters," he commanded, but the speed was too high. We had now flown through the glide path and were high on our approach profile. I gestured for him to reduce power as we got even higher on the glide slope. He rotated the autopilot controls to increase the rate of descent but in doing so allowed the speed to increase.

At 1200 feet the runway approach lights began to appear through the broken cloud base. We were much too high and fast. I announced I was taking over control. Closing the throttles completely, I disconnected the autopilot and raised the nose. The speed quickly dissipated back to the approach figure and I was able to extend full flap. Pushing the propeller pitch levers into full fine increased our rate of descent at the cost of increased engine wear.

I had hoped to hand control back to Cullenane once we became established on the correct approach path, but we never achieved that situation. Crossing the runway threshold at 300 feet, indicating 95 knots, we touched down three-quarters of the way down the wet runway and required moderately heavy braking to avoid running off the end.

I turned off at the last taxiway and glanced across at my co-pilot. He showed signs of tremendous stress; rivulets of sweat coursed down his face, although conditions in the cockpit were cool. He had left his intercom switch on and I could hear his laboured breathing.

It had been an abysmal display of airmanship on both our parts, mainly mine for not recognising his limitations and taking over sooner. I decided to take a more dominant part in the flying on the next sector. His handling was of a poor standard and, equally important, his anticipation was inadequate.

While we taxied the long distance from the far end of the runway to the freight terminal, I tried to alleviate any gloom by remarking on the difficult conditions on approach.

It took the loaders an hour and a quarter to load the outbound freight. The wind had increased in strength and now blew across the runway. The next departure would be a difficult manoeuvre, requiring dexterous manipulation of rudder, ailerons and asymmetric power to keep straight. No line pilot would delegate such duty to his co-pilot; I told Cullenane I would perform the next take-off.

"I'll hand over control to you at 1000 feet once we're established in the climb," I explained. "Conditions are worse than forecast, and I don't expect you to be able to cope with them."

The relief on his face convinced me this was the right decision.

We took off towards the west and Cullenane handled the co-pilot's duties. At about 1100 feet, with climb power set and the aircraft climbing satisfactorily at 500 feet per minute, I told Cullenane to take over when he was ready. He glanced across at me anxiously and placed hands and feet reluctantly on the controls.

The height was passing through 2000 feet when Departure Control cleared us direct to Dover. I tuned the automatic direction finder to the Dover beacon and told Cullenane to home onto it. He was slow to react.

"Turn left onto about 100 degrees and keep the needle on the nose," I prompted. He commenced a cautious left turn, applying less than ten degrees of bank. Very slowly the Dakota began to turn onto the required heading. I prompted him to increase the bank angle as we were still almost on the reciprocal of the correct heading. He turned the control yoke and the angle increased to twenty-five degrees. On the front panel, the compass card began turning faster.

"Watch the speed," I prompted gently. The needle of the airspeed indicator had increased to 130 knots as I eased back on the yoke.

The hour and a quarter flight to Lille was more like an initial flying lesson for a beginner. Every manoeuvre required prompting from me and I found it almost inconceivable that a pilot could get so psyched up on a check flight.

On my suggestion, we started our descent slightly early into our destination. I initiated the checks, extended the flaps and landing gear and constantly prompted him on speed and power management. Under our combined efforts the aircraft crossed the airfield boundary at the correct height and speed. A brisk wind down the runway would slow our touchdown speed to less than sixty knots and further assist our stopping. At fifty feet, everything looked good. I began talking to Cullenane slowly.

"Keep her straight . . . down the middle, power slowly off, take the power off . . . now begin raising the nose." Both pairs of hands were on the controls now as we settled onto the runway. Touchdown was satisfactory, and once we were on the ground I kept straight with rudder and occasional stabs of brake. As we slowed to a walking pace, I relinquished my hands on the controls.

"Not too bad. We weren't so rushed that time, were we?" I pointed out. He remembered to release the tail lock and taxied off the runway towards the terminal buildings.

The return flight to Heathrow was no better or worse than the previous one. He performed adequately when told what to do but didn't seem to possess initiative or any sense of airmanship. Instrument flying required constant reminders from me to monitor height, attitude or heading.

The weather had improved sufficiently to allow a visual approach and landing at Heathrow. Again I had to prompt him to do everything, and once again the landing was a two-person affair. I delayed the next departure until after daybreak. I anticipated it would be a short hop across to Gatwick in generally clear conditions with little or no traffic at that time of the morning.

We had time for a cup of coffee in the works canteen and I took the opportunity to discuss the night's work.

"You're feeling pretty tense about this check flight," I began, "which is hampering your performance. Try to relax and enjoy the flying, I know you can do it, I saw you perform satisfactorily a couple of weeks ago in the circuit." He gave me a strange haunted look and was about to say something, then thought better of it.

After coffee, we proceeded back to the Dakota. The sun had risen and bathed the wet taxiways and runways in a blinding glow. A frontal weather system had passed through during the night, leaving clear blue skies and virtually no wind. Perfect flying conditions and a lightly laden aircraft; I wished I was flying this sector.

I noticed Cullenane perspiring heavily and his hands shook as we strapped in. He picked up the checklist and began calling out the items. After engine start, he released the brakes and attempted to move the throttles unsuccessfully.

"Slacken off the friction control if they're too hard to move," I suggested, pointing to the friction nut. His left hand fiddled with the control.

I performed the pre-take-off checks silently, leaving him to concentrate on taxiing. Air Traffic Control cleared us to line up after a departing BEA Viscount. Cullenane aligned us on the runway and locked the tailwheel. In my peripheral vision I noticed he was still sweating profusely and his shaking hands clasped the controls as if he were hanging from them.

"Okay, let's make this flight the best one of the night," I suggested. "Bring the power up gradually to forty-eight inches, keep straight with rudder, and lift off at eighty knots. Maintain ninety knots until the gear's up, then increase speed to 110 and leave the throttles for me to look after. Got that okay?"

The Heathrow controller then cleared us for take-off and Cullenane's reply was drowned by the increase of engine noise. The Dakota accelerated down the runway and I felt him pedalling the rudder lightly to keep straight. The tail came up, and at eighty knots I indicated that we had achieved flying speed. He eased back on the yoke and the aircraft left the ground.

"Gear up?" I suggested. I had waited until 200 feet for the order, but he appeared not to hear me. We hit a patch of wake turbulence from the preceding Viscount, and he used both hands to clasp the controls tightly. With full power still on both engines and the airspeed indicating ninety knots, we climbed out at 1000 feet a minute. I reached down between the seats to manipulate the landing gear controls.

To raise the undercarriage of the DC-3, the non-flying pilot must accomplish two actions. He must first release a locking lever on the floor before selecting the retract lever to "Up". The action is rather like opening a locked door; first unlock the mechanism before moving the handle. As I reached down to start the retract sequence, my head and eyes fell below the level of the instrument panel.

I fiddled with the locking mechanism and suddenly sensed a decrease in engine noise. I looked up in alarm and saw the airspeed had decayed to eighty knots and the rate of climb had dropped to zero.

"I can't get it to climb," Cullenane called.

I pushed the yoke forward to maintain airspeed and we began descending. Both engines had suddenly and inexplicably stopped producing power, an almost impossible thing to happen . . . unless pilot error had caused it. I instinctively performed the emergency drill: trim for ninety knots, check fuel supply. Both cocks were selected to the fuel main tanks. Mixture controls? They were correctly in auto rich. Fuel pressure? Indicating okay. Ignition? Both magnetos were on. A quick glance at the engine instruments revealed nothing amiss. Temperatures and pressures were normal and rpms were still at 3000. Only the boost pressure gauges and the rate of descent revealed the engines weren't producing power. I shouted that I had control and looked forward for a place to land amidst the power lines and buildings of suburbia. Our precious height had now dwindled to well below 200 feet. I spotted the only available place to go.

About a mile ahead and off to the left the smooth waters of the Wraysbury reservoirs offered the only hope of a survivable landing.

I tried to bank left and discovered Cullenane had frozen on the controls. Shouting to him to let go achieved nothing. He stared glassily ahead through the windshield as the ground rose up to meet us. A sudden recollection of once overhearing two instructors discussing the best course of action when a student freezes on the controls came to me. Bunching my hand into a tight fist, I called out to him to let go as I struck him hard on the left temple. Involuntarily, his hand sprang to the source of pain and he released his vice-like grip on the controls. In the background I heard the tower controller enquiring if we had a problem.

With the landing gear still extended and the propellers in full fine pitch, we seemed unlikely to clear the lip of the reservoir. I reached across to the hydraulic control panel and selected full flaps. The aircraft ballooned up and cleared the grassy bank by a few feet.

We skimmed across the surface of the water indicating less than sixty-five knots and I raised the nose to minimise our touchdown speed. The dangling undercarriage would almost certainly turn us onto our back, making escape rather problematical.

Trimming the machine tail down, I reached for the throttle levers to cut any residual power. Even with only a trickle of power on, the aircraft would skim across the water in ground effect and impact into the vertical face of the far bank. Of the two options I preferred a water landing.

To my surprise the throttles were already in the closed position. I tentatively pushed them forward and was rewarded with the glorious sound of the two Pratt and Whitney radials spooling up to full power again. With flaps full down and the main wheels inches above the water, we skimmed across the reservoir. On the far bank a fisherman watched anxiously as we bore down on him. I raised the nose a few degrees and we cleared the far bank by about twenty feet. The fisherman had thrown himself down the grassy bank just before we passed over him.

We climbed through 200 feet and I gestured to Cullenane to raise the landing gear. He removed his hand from the side of his head and manipulated the gear levers in the correct sequence. Once again the hydraulic system wheezed and protested as it pulled the landing gear up into the nacelles. The airspeed began to increase with the reducing drag . . . seventy knots . . . seventy-five . . . If an engine decided to fail now, we were dead men.

"Kilo Echo, are you declaring an emergency?" an anxious tower operator enquired. A curt assurance that everything was under control satisfied him. I struggled to maintain a positive rate of climb.

"Milk the flaps up, slowly," I called to Cullenane. He looked at me questioningly, but did nothing. Taking my right hand off the throttles, I raised the flaps to the half position. The engine noise suddenly subsided and the aircraft settled into a descent. I put my hand back on the throttles and found they had moved back to the closed position. I pushed them fully forward again to the maximum power position.

"Tighten the throttle friction," I implored. The aircraft had begun climbing again and airspeed was now a respectable eighty knots and increasing. Cullenane fiddled under the throttle pedestal. Now the levers remained in the forward position, enabling me to raise the rest of the flaps.

Neither of us said a word as we climbed through 1000 feet. Cullenane was preoccupied with his bruised temple, and I flew the aircraft as if I were alone. The tower operator handed us over to Heathrow Director who gave us a course to steer to our destination.

A few minutes later, when levelled out at 3000 feet, I mentally reviewed the events of the previous five minutes. Cullenane had coped with the first part of the take-off, but had suddenly closed the power levers as I bent down to reach the undercarriage retract levers. He must have been oblivious of his actions for I recalled him saying the aircraft wouldn't climb.

"What happened to the throttles?" I enquired.

"I really don't know. They must have closed by themselves."

"Did you tighten the friction nut before take-off?" I demanded. He admitted he hadn't. The throttles would have moved back towards the closed position as soon as he removed his hand.

We returned to Gatwick in silence, me flying the aircraft single-handed, leaving Cullenane to recover from the recent horrifying experience.

After landing, we parked in our usual position and I told him we'd discuss the flight in the office. Joe Phillips waited at the aircraft steps to tell me Denis and Levitt wanted to see me in the office.

Both directors were pacing back and forth like caged tigers when we reached the office. Levitt began a carefully prepared speech, but was cut short by Denis.

"What the hell was the idea of doing training out of Heathrow?" he demanded. "ATC have probably filed an incident report and the commandant will want an explanation. There's a hefty fine for this kind of thing plus a few other . . ."

"We didn't do any training." I waved him to silence. "It was a genuine emergency."

"But you told ATC there was nothing wrong when they called you," Levitt insisted.

I briefly explained the details of the take-off. I wanted to discuss the flight with Cullenane first, because there were several things I couldn't fathom. Levitt, however, had tasted blood and insisted on discussing the matter more fully. Denis seemed in agreement and nodded his head repeatedly. Cullenane had disappeared from the room. So reluctantly, I sat down and recounted the details of the whole ghastly night's flying. They listened intently until I had finished.

"And what do you recommend?" Levitt demanded.

"I really don't know. Captain Chegwidden was right when he said he was bloody dangerous. To let him out on the line with line captains while he's in his present state would be disastrous . . ."

Conversation was interrupted by Timber Wood arriving to collect pre-flight documentation for his duty. I bade him a perfunctory good morning and returned to the subject under discussion.

"He was unfortunately under an awful lot of stress. I could detect it. He's been out of aviation for three years and is obviously terribly anxious to excel at this job. He's very keen, conscientious, but when it comes to physically flying the aircraft, he has to be told to do everything. He can't even plan a descent and approach, yet the strange thing is, he didn't seem to have any problems when we did the circuit training. I can't believe a person's flying ability can deteriorate so rapidly."

Wood was obviously highly embarrassed at overhearing confidential personal matters discussed in his presence. He hurriedly gathered together a file of documents and prepared to leave as Denis spoke.

"So he didn't have any problems with you in the circuit?" he enquired. "Are you sure you didn't have to take over or give him additional training?"

"Definitely not. I'd have remembered if I had, but everybody achieved a satisfactory standard."

Levitt wrinkled his nose disdainfully. "It would appear we've hired some-body unsuitable," he observed. "In which case we must replace him as soon as possible."

"That's not quite as easy as it sounds," Denis told him. "Qualified pilots are being snapped up by the bigger airlines and, frankly, I don't think we could find an experienced DC-3 co-pilot at the moment. There's also the question of what to do with him; do we give him another check flight with a different captain, or do we just fire him?"

The question had occurred to me. Different people interrelate together in various ways, and maybe he couldn't learn from me. I suggested Denis could take him for an hour's circuit training before a decision was made.

Unbeknown to us, while this discussion was taking placed, Cullenane was resolving part of the problem for us.

Denis displayed deep reluctance to become involved in the matter. His duties as chief pilot of the Hermes operation already occupied him seven days a week. Additional duties would further increase his work-load. He suggested we discuss the matter with the pilot involved. I looked around for Cullenane but he was gone. A check of the passenger hall and coffee shop failed to locate him. I phoned his digs and left a message to phone in when convenient.

I decided now would be a good time to advise my fellow directors of my decision to hire Mike Sommerpole, but Dr Levitt had very conveniently beaten me to it. I returned to the office to find him deep in conversation with Denis.

"Just the sort of young fellow we need," he assured him. "Well educated, extremely keen and has all the licences and ratings. I was talking with him yesterday and he struck me as just the sort of chap our company needs."

Denis turned to me enquiringly. "Do you know this fellow Sommerpole? Who's he working for at the moment?"

Levitt interrupted to tell us he'd recently resigned from BOAC. "No doubt because he wanted to break away from their antiquated promotion system. Young fellows out of the Air Force start as navigators until they become senior enough to become co-pilots. It then takes another fifteen or twenty years to become a captain. Now this young fellow's got initiative and decided he wants to be a pilot now."

I could see things turning my way. I made a few complimentary remarks about Mike, and Levitt urged us to consider hiring him. Denis looked at me enquiringly.

"I must admit he has the necessary qualifications," I began. "And he's not frightened of hard work." I briefly recounted how he'd helped us on the second bullion charter. Levitt looked at us beseechingly.

"Ex-BOAC, so he won't leave us to go and join them when the opportunity arises. Fully qualified and, by your own admission, very keen . . ."

"Does he have any DC-3 experience?" Denis enquired. I admitted he did have some time on the aircraft.

"Seems like just the fellow we need," he observed. "Call him and offer him a job immediately. Give him a competency check next time we have the aircraft available, and I'll leave you to complete the other formalities in your own time."

Levitt looked at me smugly, with an expression that asked why I hadn't thought of this obvious solution. I managed to look suitably humiliated, while inwardly rejoicing that my dilemma over Mike had resolved itself. I consulted the wall chart and worked out when we could complete his remaining training and checking. I then derived great pleasure from phoning him and telling him he'd start flying in two days' time.

It was now mid-morning, and I felt exhausted from the night's events. Double engine failures and almost having to ditch after take-off are not everyday events in an airline pilot's life, and I felt a strong desire to go home and collapse for a few hours. Cullenane and the problem at Heathrow could wait until tomorrow.

It was 10am when I bade everybody goodnight and fled the office.

Timber Wood waited in the corridor as I emerged from the office. He approached rather timidly and asked if I could spare five minutes. I asked kindly whether the matter could wait until tomorrow.

"It's been a rather stressful night," I explained, aware that Wood had overheard some of the earlier conversation. "I'd prefer to wait until tomorrow unless it's really urgent."

He assured me the matter could wait a day and we headed off in our different directions.

Next morning I returned to the office feeling refreshed after a twenty-four-hour break from the rigours of working for a charter airline. I phoned the Air Traffic Control Centre at Heathrow and managed to talk to the controller who'd been on duty the day before. I assured him we hadn't been doing any training that morning and our sudden disappearance from his radar screen had been a real emergency.

"Wasn't wake turbulence?" he enquired anxiously. "I cleared you for take-off immediately behind the BEAline Viscount. We're supposed to wait three minutes . . ."

I assured him he wasn't the sole cause of our narrow escape. "Loss of power on both engines plus a bit of wake turbulence after take-off, mainly pilot error I'm afraid. The co-pilot was flying and I took over and retrieved the situation."

"Sounds like a mistake at both ends," he remarked helpfully. "We haven't submitted anything official at this end yet. No noise monitors were set off so the matter is closed. Oh, except that a rather angry fisherman phoned in and complained you dive-bombed him and knocked him off his stool. Wanted to make an official complaint until we reminded him that fishing is prohibited by the Thames Conservancy Board. Seemed to lose interest after that so he's probably decided not to take the matter further. Okay, thanks for calling back, we can now consider the matter closed."

This was a relief. The inhabitants around Heathrow were becoming increasingly vocal in their protests about noise pollution. New aircraft like the Boeing 707 and de Havilland Comet were proving a greater source of annoyance than their piston-engined predecessors. Jet aircraft were subsequently required to follow predetermined departure routes and reduce power immediately after take-off. Noise monitors were positioned either side of these routes, and any aircraft exceeding the maximum allowable decibel reading incurred a substantial fine for its company. I reflected that we probably hadn't generated much noise as we glided down with both throttles closed. After the exchange of a few pleasantries, I thanked the controller and rang off.

The next matter requiring my attention was Cullenane. I pulled his training documents out of the filing cabinet and read through them carefully. There wasn't much to read. Christine had copied down the details of his licence number, type, period of validity, aircraft type ratings and date of birth. Next I read through the job application form he'd filled in when I first interviewed him. Large gaps had been left in the flying experience column but he'd listed T-6 and T-33 training aircraft plus the DC-3 in the "types flown" section. I now recalled him saying he'd flown transport aircraft in the Canadian Air Force, which he'd left three years ago. Even allowing for the fact that he was out of current flying practice, nothing could explain his almost complete ineptitude for flying the Dakota. I dialled his phone number and spoke to his landlady.

"He's left," she told me. "Arrived back yesterday morning looking very tired after his night flight. Then he told me he'd been transferred at short notice. He threw his things into a suitcase and flew out the door without even saying goodbye or thank you."

"Do you have any idea where he might have gone?" I enquired. She thought for several moments.

"He might have said something about 'nearer home'," she admitted. "One thing's certain, he was in the dickens of a hurry. Must've had a bus or a train to catch. Fortunately he'd paid his rent up to the end of the month. Doesn't say much, does he? Spent an awful lot of time studying. Must be a good pilot. Must go now."

My gaze had flicked across the pages of his documentation and discovered something significant. The details copied down by Christine differed from those provided by Cullenane.

"There's a discrepancy in his birth date," I exclaimed aloud. Sure enough, the date copied from his commercial pilot's licence differed from what he'd written on his job application form. I suddenly remembered what the customs boys at Gatwick had told me. One thing they never think to change.

A discreet cough reminded me there were others in the room. One of them was Timber Wood.

"I know you're very busy, but this could be important," he began hesitantly. I dropped Cullenane's paperwork and invited him to pull up a chair.

"Is this the same thing you wanted to talk to me about yesterday?" I enquired.

He nodded. "Yep, I'm sorry but I couldn't help overhearing you discussing Mike Cullenane yesterday," he began. "Look, I know he's had a spot of trouble with his flying and, er . . . well, this is none of my business, but I heard you say he performed satisfactorily when we did our circuit training."

"That's right. Are you saying he didn't?"

Wood waved the suggestion aside emphatically. "No, no, I'm not saying that, but I thought you ought to know he didn't do any flying that day. When his turn in the queue came up, he let the next fellow take his place. What I'm saying is, he never sat in the seat so he never flew the aircraft. We all thought he came along for the ride to observe. I couldn't understand why you said he performed okay in the circuit. He held back to the end, and when the time came for you to sign the paperwork, you must have signed him off too."

I remembered that something urgent had cropped up and I'd had to hurry straight to the office. It would have been simple for anybody to put an extra form in the pile for my signature. You tend to lose count of how many people have done how many landings after three or more hours and thirty plus landings. "Are you saying he didn't fly the aircraft at all?" I looked at Wood directly.

"Yes, I am," he returned my gaze unflinchingly. "And there's another thing that struck me as odd at the time, which may have some relevance. Do you remember telling him to remove the elevator locks?"

"Yes, that was because I wanted the rudder lock left in till after we'd started engines. There was a strong wind blowing if you remember and I didn't want the rudder buffeted around. Anything wrong with that?"

"Okay, okay, fair enough. I understand all that. But the curious thing was that Mike Cullenane didn't know which were the elevators."

"That's preposterous!" I exclaimed. "Every pilot knows what an elevator is. Are you suggesting something?"

Wood hesitated before continuing. Professional loyalty made him reluctant to inform on a fellow pilot but lives could be at stake in this instance. "I'm just telling you a few facts," he emphasised. "He didn't fly the aircraft on the day in question. We all thought he didn't require a check, so nobody commented on it until I heard you say he'd performed okay that day. We were also a bit surprised at some of the gaps in his technical knowledge, but I suppose we thought they used different terminology in Canada and America . . ."

"Like undercarriage and landing gear, you mean?" I suggested. He nodded his assent.

"Precisely. Lifts are elevators in the USA, and cars are vehicles. Anyway, I decided it might be important you knew about the circuit training. Now if you'll excuse me, I'd like to go home for the rest of my day off. I promised my wife I'd spend it in the garden with her."

I thanked him for coming in. His revelations had convinced me of something I'd suspected since a couple of nights ago. The co-pilot we'd hired had little or no flying experience. How he'd gained a commercial pilot's licence was a mystery. More important was the fact he must not be allowed near one of our aircraft again. I phoned Denis at home.

"I've had time to think about this co-pilot who's having problems with his flying," I began. "I don't know who he is, or even where he is right now, but I'm adamant he's not going to fly one of our aircraft again. Chegwidden was correct when he said he was bloody dangerous. I'll take the new fellow out tomorrow afternoon for a few circuits and I'll do his route training next week. He can fly with some of the other captains too, and I'll give him a final route check as soon as he feels confident enough."

Denis had listened, but chose not to question my decision about Cullenane. I felt positive we'd never hear from him again. What did concern me was he might pop up somewhere else and pass himself off as a pilot. I felt tempted to call the Ministry of Civil Aviation, maybe even the police, and discuss my doubts. Wisdom prevailed, and I filed the whole episode under experience. I couldn't afford to be asked why I had signed him out as competent. Small charter companies didn't need ministerial flight inspectors looking too closely at their operations.

We never unravelled the mystery of Cullenane and although aviation is a small community, I never saw our mystery pilot again. He may have returned to his native country to escape any investigation. We'll never know because we never knew his correct name, only his birth date.

CHAPTER 12
Gifts from the Gods

The following day Mike Sommerpole completed an hour's circuit flying to get the DC-3 endorsed on his commercial pilot's licence. I also completed his biannual competency check, during which we practised several emergency procedures. Taking into account his very limited experience, he achieved quite a satisfactory standard. By eleven o'clock we'd fulfilled all the requirements and he was on his way to the Ministry of Civil Aviation to get his licence stamped.

Before I could congratulate him, Denis and Tony cornered me in the office for an urgent shareholders' meeting. We found a quiet corner in the Greasy Spoon, where Levitt joined us and informed the meeting that Stan Wilson, our other director, would join us up at Burnaston.

"Burnaston? What's he going there for?" I demanded. Tony and Denis exchanged meaningful glances.

"We thought you might enjoy a lesson in Greek mythology," Denis explained. "You know, Hermes, Jason and the Argonauts."

"Why the hell would I be interested in the blooming Argonauts?" I had a lot of important things to complete that day and wasn't in the mood for light conversation. I told them both to get to the point.

"Okay, well, we all know the Hermes is running out of hours soon. In fact, it won't make it through the winter."

I nodded but remained silent. Several well-meaning friends and colleagues in other companies had warned us the cost of overhauling the Hermes would swallow all our profits. I'd reminded Denis repeatedly that we needed to find a replacement urgently. Until now he seemed to have ignored the impending problem.

"Tony met Ron Paine, the managing director of Derby Airways . . ."

"You mean the racing pilot?"

"Correct. They were at the Royal Aero Club's cocktail party and Ron mentioned his company were looking at re-equipping with jets."

I scoffed at the idea. Comets or Boeing 707s would cost hundreds of thousands of pounds. Derby couldn't hope to make enough money in the summer IT season to keep up the finance payments through the winter.

"Sounds like the drink talking," I suggested. "We all like to impress the opposition, and Ron's probably no exception. They could never afford 707s . . ."

Denis gestured me to silence. "They're not getting 707s. Ever heard of the BAC One-Eleven?"

"You mean the new bus-stop jet? Freddie Laker's supposed to be getting some of them but nobody knows exactly when. Early 1964 maybe . . ."

"According to Ron Paine, the British Aircraft Corporation, which is the new name for Vickers, Bristol, English Electric and a whole load of other aviation manufacturers, are anxious to get more initial orders for their new bus-stop jet. Unlike other jet aircraft, this one can operate efficiently on shorter routes at twice the speed of Viscounts or Heralds."

This was an interesting piece of news, but I didn't see where a bus-stop jet fitted into Derby's route network. "They're IT operators, like us," I protested. "Why would they want an aircraft that can do lots of short sectors?"

Denis explained that the Conservative government had offered Derby a number of main-trunk scheduled services if they re-equipped with the British-built aircraft.

"Can you imagine the effect a 500-mph jetliner would have on the IT market?" he enthused. "A single crew could operate to Majorca twice in a day . . . and when they aren't cashing in on the lucrative IT market they still have their scheduled services to support them in the off season."

"And where do we fit into all this?" I demanded. There was no way we could consider One-Elevens. We couldn't afford it. Denis lowered his voice to an excited whisper.

"Ron Paine said they were looking for a buyer for their Argonauts. That's a DC-4 with Rolls-Royce Merlin engines. About the same size and performance as the Hermes. Tony immediately thought of our need for a Hermes replacement, and thinks the directors of Air Links should go up to Derby and take a look."

The prospect sounded attractive to me. The Argonaut was a Canadian built version of the American Douglas DC-4 Skymaster. The American engines had been replaced with Rolls-Royce Merlins, similar to those used in war-time Spitfires, and the cabin was pressurised, enabling the machine to fly higher.

"Griff has already been up to examine the engineering records," Denis continued. "He says there are still plenty of Merlins available and Derby have a comprehensive supply of other spare parts. There are three aircraft available, so we could use one as a Christmas tree."*

I must have looked interested because Tony then suggested the four of us go up to Derby and talk to their commercial manager.

"But it'd take us three hours to drive there," I protested. "It's a good 200 miles by road. We'd do well to get there by tea-time."

"Not if we fly," Tony suggested. "What about flying us up there in that velocipede of yours, the Percival Proctor? It shouldn't take more than an hour at the maximum."

"It's over at Biggin," I countered.

"Then get somebody to bring it over here. Phone Air Couriers and ask one

* Aircraft used as a source of spare parts

of their pilots to bring it over as soon as possible. We'll grab some lunch while you wait."

Somebody had already done a bit of fixing because when I phoned Air Couriers, the chief pilot told me my aircraft had been refuelled and would be at Gatwick within a half hour. This barely gave me time to collect the necessary maps and charts, check the en route weather and make out a flight plan.

En route flying conditions were good enough to allow us to fly visually below airways until we got to Lichfield. Tony sat up front beside me and navigated, while Denis and Dr Levitt dozed in the back seats. We averaged 140 knots on the way up and landed soon after 2pm, after a flight time of fifty-two minutes. Three Argonauts were parked outside the Derby Airways hangar in various stages of disassembly. Derby obviously did their major maintenance in winter, like most other charter operators.

Nobody came out to marshal us in so I parked in front of the tower beside a smart-looking Miles Hawk Speed Six. After less than an hour in a fairly comfortable cockpit, we felt considerably less tired than if we'd driven up by road. Levitt was ecstatic at flying somewhere by private aeroplane.

"Executive air travel, that's the thing of the future," he enthused. "You can be up and back in half a day. Just think of the savings in executives' time and expenses. No overnight hotel accommodation and you could visit two or more cities in a day. There's no reason why we couldn't fly to the Continent. Paris or Brussels are not much farther than Derby. Just think what a fleet of machines like this could achieve."

I pointed out that air travel didn't come free. "Something like this jaunt would cost £5 for fuel and oil, plus maintenance costs and pilot's salary, landing fees . . . You'd have to charge £10 for today's flight. Imagine what it'd cost to carry on to Edinburgh or over to Brussels, it'd be the best part of £25."

Levitt tried to convince me that some people's time was worth considerably more than £25 a day.

"Lawyers, politicians, managing directors, architects and doctors earn that much in an hour," he assured me. "Why, if executive travel really caught on, you'd have the heads of industry travelling round the world in private jets!"

I smiled indulgently. Everybody is entitled to their private dreams but some of his were absurd.

Stan Wilson, the other Air Links director, had already arrived and talked with Derby Airway's commercial manager. They both came out to greet us, and he eyed the Proctor with interest.

"Is that what the modern airline executive comes to work in?" he enquired. Levitt repeated his lecture on executive air travel, while we followed the manager into the hangar.

Stackpole, Derby Airway's commercial manager, repeated what Denis had already told me.

"BAC have offered us three of their new One-Elevens on very favourable lease terms," he began. "We need to phase out the Argonauts as soon as possible to give us time to train up aircrew and engineering staff on the One-Eleven.

Initially we'll borrow ground engineers and pilots from BAC. Our staff will undergo factory training then work alongside them, learning from experts."

I reflected how different this was from most training in the independent sector. Normally a set of questions and answers plus a borrowed aircraft flight manual was all the ground training we got on a new type.

"We're pretty cramped for space here so we're looking for a purchaser for the Argonauts. It's still a good aircraft. We earned a lot of money with three aircraft last year and whoever buys them can do likewise. They're economical to operate and a lot cheaper than a DC-6 or a Constellation. Mr Griffiths came up yesterday and went through the engineering reports. He can give you an unbiased opinion," Stackpole volunteered.

The five directors of Air Links exchanged thoughtful glances. All of a sudden we were being offered a "ready to go" airline fleet. We already had sufficient work for one machine once the Hermes ran out of hours.

"Horizon Holidays have been urging us to get additional aircraft," Tony pointed out. "This could be just what we need."

We discussed tentative terms and conditions of purchase for the three machines. Stackpole, Derby's commercial manager, was perfectly frank and told us the aircraft had been amortised over a period of seven years. "Their book value is a pound apiece but their scrap value is considerably more than that," he assured us. "Aluminium, brass, copper, high-grade steel and various high-grade alloys have substantial scrap value . . ."

We listened while he convinced us the Argonauts would be an ideal replacement for our almost time-expired Hermes. After our discussion, we sat in Stan Wilson's Jaguar and talked over details of how to finance the Argonaut deal. It was agreed that tomorrow Denis and I would approach our bank manager and discuss financing. He had asked to be considered when and if we ever needed capital for expansion.

Ninety minutes after landing at Burnaston, we were on our way back to Gatwick. I was looking forward to the flight back in a classic aeroplane like the Proctor. As we settled into our seats prior to departing, I happened to glance towards the hangar.

In some ways I wished I hadn't, because at that moment Ikey Silverstein, an infamous antique dealer, bookmaker and aircraft spare parts dealer, hurried into the hangar in search of Mr Stackpole.

Denis had also noted his arrival and displayed similar dismay. If Ikey also bid for the Argonauts, we were going to have to pay top price to outbid him.

We departed at quarter to four and again proceeded under visual flight rules until entering the London Control zone. On contacting London Approach Control for a clearance, we were directed overhead Heathrow at 3000 feet, thence direct to Gatwick. As we flew across the passenger terminal, which sat in the centre of the complex of intersecting runways shaped like the star of David, I gazed down at the host of modern aircraft below.

In the BOAC maintenance area, Britannias, Comets, Boeing 707s and VC-10s were being prepared for flight. Other modern types around the terminal building resembled bees round a honeycomb. Tridents, Caravelles, Viscounts,

Vanguards and DC-8s seemed to outclass the more prosaic Friendships, Heralds, Electras and Convair liners.

My envious gaze moved across to the BEAline hangar where Viscounts and Comet IVs were receiving attention. In another hangar the nose and engines of a solitary DC-3 peered out anxiously at so many turbine-powered competitors. The sight of the BEA logo on the hangar roof reminded me of something rather important.

Today was the date for my initial employment interview with British European Airways. In the excitement and haste of the Argonaut deal, I had completely forgotten.

After landing back at our Gatwick base, it was another three hours before we finished discussing the Argonaut purchase and headed to our respective homes. Although we were unanimous in agreeing the Argonauts presented the ideal solution to replacing the Hermes, we needed to establish whether Mr Zucher's Horizon Holidays travel agency would guarantee us sufficient work for additional aircraft.

Tony pointed out we also needed to determine the number of pilots available. A few other smaller problem areas became apparent as we discussed the overall deal. It was finally agreed Denis and I would try to raise the necessary finance, leaving Tony to recruit air crew and additional engineering staff. Levitt promised to instruct his nephew and commercial manager to solicit work for two additional aircraft.

As we talked so animatedly of the future, I became convinced that I could make a successful career with Air Links. Private charter companies had an abysmal survival record, but there were exceptions to every rule.

Next morning I was woken by the sound of letters dropping into my letter box. The time was 8.30. I phoned the National Provincial Bank and told them I'd like to see the manager as soon as convenient. Cattermoull himself came on the line and asked whether 9.30 would be too early. I checked our bank balance and was agreeably surprised to see we had over £11,000 deposited with them.

I collected Denis on the way. The bank manager greeted us effusively when we arrived. He ushered us into his office and beckoned for a staff member to bring tea and biscuits. He gestured for us to help ourselves.

"Business seems to be ticking along very nicely indeed," he commented, consulting the file before him. "Got plenty of IT work for the summer?"

Denis briefly told him of our contractual arrangements with Horizon Holidays. The manager listened quietly, occasionally jotting down a few notes and figures.

"Sounds like a very business-like arrangement," he commented and waited for us to reveal the reason for our visit. My fellow director seemed to have run out of words, or maybe he wasn't used to having to borrow money; until today he'd been an investor rather than a borrower. I decided to do a bit of the talking.

"You're correct when you say we've got quite a profitable operation going,"

I admitted. "The future looks quite bright for us. We've established an excellent working relationship with our major customer, Horizon Holidays. We've worked for them for almost the whole year and we're one of the very few charter companies to have a winter sports programme to keep us occupied through the winter."

"And?" The bank manager's eyes gleamed hungrily.

"And they have urged us to take over a bigger portion of their work."

The banker's eyes were wide with greedy anticipation as he impatiently gestured for me to continue.

"That would mean expansion, which means more aircraft," I explained. "Unfortunately, both these factors result in increased costs. We've got to spend money to make money."

His face positively beamed at this news.

"And that means your money," Denis interjected.

The beaming smile vanished from the manager's face.

I briefly explained that our unique arrangement whereby we all doubled as office staff, check-in clerks, ground staff and any other task that needed performing would not work in a larger operation.

"We'd need clerical staff to maintain records of flying hours and pay expenses and salaries. Then a proper commercial department would need to be set up to handle the charter enquiries. Plus a flight operations department to handle training and checking. All this would require more staff and office accommodation. This would take a considerable amount of money."

"How much?" Cattermoull interjected abruptly.

"I don't know, but our present bank balance wouldn't be enough to cover both the initial setting-up costs and finance the aircraft purchase.

"Aah, so you are thinking of buying new aircraft?" Cattermoull positively beamed at this news. His usurer's brain had balked at the idea of lending money for office leases and salaries, but aircraft represented tangible assets. Like motor cars and homes, they could be repossessed if loan repayments fell behind.

"Aircraft and a whole lot of attendant necessities," I confirmed. "Like engine and airframe spares, specialised servicing equipment . . . things like that."

Cattermoull spoke into a phone briefly before interrupting me in mid-sentence. "Aircraft finance is a substantial part of this bank's business," he began. "But naturally it isn't handled from this branch office. A transaction of this magnitude would have to go through our head office in the City."

I must have looked impatient at this news, for he held up a hand begging my patience.

"Coincidentally, today we have a member of the aviation finance division visiting this office in connection with another deal on the airfield. I've asked my assistant manager to try and locate him."

A tap on the door brought the bank's aviation finance expert into the conversation.

"Blob-bottom!" The words escaped from my mouth while the brain was temporarily disconnected. The recipient of the greeting eyed me curiously for a micro-second before recognition lit his face.

Cattermoull hastily intervened and made the appropriate introductions.

"This is our Mr Evans from head office," he began anxiously. "And these gentlemen are Mr Mills and Mr . . ."

The rest of the introduction was lost in loud guffaws of laughter. Melvin, better known as "Blob-bottom" or just "Blob" to his friends because of his curious shape, had previously been a member of my National Service pilot's course four years ago. At the conclusion of the two-year course, the RAF disgorged us back into civilian life to pursue whatever career we chose. Many had returned to their previous jobs as solicitors, accountants, school teachers, office workers or clerks. A few, whose brains had become addled from two years spent breathing pressure oxygen and aviation fuel, went into civil aviation. Blob-bottom had returned to his secure former job as a clerk with the National Provincial Bank, where he'd enjoyed the security of a safe job in an established and reputable banking organisation. Although we had scoffed at his ultra-conservatism at the time, I subsequently had to admit he hadn't had to endure the heartache of examinations, flight tests, endless job interviews and the nagging anxiety of wondering how long the current flying job would last.

Blob sat opposite the manager and eyed us reflectively.

"Last time I saw you, you were out of money and a job," he began. "So you did manage to find something eventually?" I nodded and briefly explained I'd been embroiled in the charter business for almost three years. I thought I detected a sniff of disdain as I spoke. Blob put great emphasis on financial security.

"And what about you? Did you eventually manage to break the chain on your pencil and get through the anodised bars?" I enquired half jokingly. Blob grinned good-naturedly. During our early days back in civilian life, several of us had begun to scrape the bottom of the financial barrel while getting our commercial flying licences. We'd approached the bank for a small loan to help finance the necessary tuition, exams and flight tests for our licences. Blob just happened to be working at the branch office where we'd applied. He'd delivered us a serious but well-intentioned homily on the necessity of a secure job. He'd then helpfully suggested we consider a career in banking, where a life filled with luncheon vouchers, subsidised sports clubs, guaranteed low-interest mortgages and two weeks' annual holidays in August would continue tediously and uneventfully until the bank pensioned us out to pasture when we got too old. We'd decided writing in the ledger in pencil was only slightly less boring than watching paint dry, and had told him where to stick his pencil.

Now, four years down the track, I was back again, asking for money.

Cattermoull, fearing the meeting was about to dissolve into an exchange of acrimonious abuse, intervened.

"Mr Evans is our assistant deputy chairman of the aviation finance desk," he explained. "The bank's Millburn office in the City's financial district handles a significant part of the funding for all the leading aircraft manufacturers, both here and overseas. Currently the bank is supporting the British Aircraft Corporation, Hawker-Siddeley, British United, Boeing and Rolls-Royce . . ."

"Must be a lot of money involved," I admitted, having already calculated that Blob's well-cut three-piece suit and pencil-slim attaché case would have made an oversized dent in my monthly pay cheque. He modestly shrugged the compliment off.

"Okay, let's get down to business, shall we? Money running a bit short in the winter, is it?"

Cattermoull gave him a mild kick under the table and turned a ledger sheet towards him. Blob's gaze shot straight to the bottom line and his eyes opened wide in surprise.

"Looks like you could lend us some money," he observed, a new tinge of respect in his voice.

I gave him a brief run-down on Air Link's history. I thought Cattermoull's eyes were going to pop out of his head when I told them we'd bought our Hermes for less than a thousand pounds. He pointed out that was less than he'd paid for his Rover. Even Blob-bottom was craning forward to catch every word.

"This is slightly different," I explained. "The Hermes was like a dinosaur — outdated and uncompetitive against other designs. We were lucky to get all the spare engines and parts we were likely to need, so maintenance wasn't a major item. Neither was finance. We paid cash for it. So our only major expenses were fuel and salaries. This enabled us to undercut the competition by a significant margin."

Cattermoull resembled a lizard about to eat a fly as he licked his lips hungrily. Blob-bottom took notes while I talked. Finally I came to the reason for my visit.

"We have guarantees of even more work if we get additional aircraft," I told the audience. Blob remained silent; only Cattermoull spoke.

"Why not buy a few more aircraft off the dumps?" he suggested rather crudely. I convinced him this was not feasible.

"Our Hermes was a chance in a lifetime," I explained. "It was £1000 from us or nothing from the Stansted Fire School. Quite an easy decision really. But now, if we get more aircraft, we need to expand our ground organisation."

Blob now came back into the conversation.

"If you can produce letters of understanding from established travel agents, stating they will charter these aircraft for a guaranteed number of flying hours per year, plus a cashflow forecast, I may be able to recommend to the bank that we finance you. Subject of course to an inspection of the aircraft, and a sensitivity analysis and personal guarantees from the directors. Where did you say the aircraft were?"

"Burnaston, just outside of Derby. The aircraft are there for winter overhauls, so their engineering records can be inspected at the same time. Our maintenance chap's been up there and reported back already. There are plenty of engines and spares but we need to move fairly quickly if we want to secure them. I believe there may be another party interested."

Blob-bottom consulted his diary. "Burnaston, hmm, probably take the best part of a day getting up there. Might be better to go up overnight. Then I'd need to spend a morning with the accountant, plus the afternoon looking over the aircraft and equipment . . ." He flipped through pages of his diary as he spoke. "I'll have to allocate three days for the project and the earliest I could get up there would be . . . the middle of next month, probably the thirteenth."

I told him that was absolutely useless; we needed to move quickly to secure the aircraft and vital spares. Derby Airways were heavily committed to their jet re-equipment and needed the hangar and workshop space immediately. If we came up with a reasonable deal, they would most likely agree to it. Blob-bottom looked doubtful.

"We're talking about tens of thousands of pounds here," he protested. "Things have got to be done properly if I'm going to recommend this loan to my directors."

"But it can still be done quickly and correctly," Denis suggested. Blob shook his head doubtfully. I could sense that a few short years in the bank had withered the initiative and resourcefulness he'd displayed as a young jet fighter pilot. We knocked the subject around for another ten minutes and achieved nothing.

I even turned to Cattermoull in exasperation and demanded to know why he'd ever suggested his National Provincial Bank as a source of finance. He quickly darted for cover.

"Holiday Air Travel is a vibrant new business," I finally protested to the bankers. "Sometimes decisions have to be made rapidly. Surely you fellows have to move quickly and decisively at times?"

"Like when?" Blob-bottom enquired unhelpfully.

I was temporarily stuck for an answer, but Denis came to our rescue.

"When a currency fluctuates up or down, or political instability enmeshes a country. The international banking community isn't slow to act decisively then," he suggested. "What about the BAC One-Eleven deal that everybody's whispering about? You couldn't have afforded three weeks to decide that one."

We'd touched Blob's source of vanity. He nodded his head in agreement. "That was an important deal," he admitted proudly. "Both the British Government and the aircraft manufacturer were desperate to find a first customer for their bus-stop jet. Unfortunately, in business and trade, companies are reluctant to take a chance. BEA positively refused to buy the aircraft, they were already committed to the Trident. BOAC rightly said it was too small and didn't have sufficient range for their routes. Meanwhile, the government, with an election due next year, was desperate to save 120,000 jobs at BAC Weybridge and Rolls-Royce. All the European airlines — Alitalia, Air France, Aer Lingus and Swissair — are waiting in the wings, trying to decide whether to buy American or British. I went to the factory, spoke to their financial analysts, inspected the production line and even went up on a couple of test flights in the co-pilot's seat."

"How did it handle?" Denis and I demanded simultaneously.

"Very nice, bit like the Vampires we flew in the Air Force but a lot bigger. Good control harmonisation, plenty of power, we climbed at 4000 feet per minute initially, although I think the test pilot was trying to impress me — which he did. It's a nice aircraft."

I could sense Blob warming to his subject.

He finished his description of flying the One-Eleven and returned to the subject of our discussion. "I can confirm a definite appointment for the thirteenth," he suggested helpfully. "I know it's important to you fellows." I felt like saying "like life or death". Unless we replaced the Hermes, we were going to end up with a lot of angry holidaymakers, no suitable aeroplanes and an expensive lawsuit to fight.

"That's no bloody use to us," Denis interrupted angrily. "Guy's right, we've got to move quickly and decisively on this, and frankly I don't think you're capable of . . ." I held up my hand to stop him turning the meeting into a slanging match. It would be better to conclude the discussion amicably and go elsewhere. I was about to say this when Blob spoke.

"You're being a bit harsh, y'know. There's a lot of other airlines needing financial support and they're content to wait. We'd like to help you in this deal. In fact, I can tell you I've been told to give you almost anything you want, even the top brick off the chimney if you want it, but I can't just take three days off my schedule to look at a bunch of aeroplanes up north. If I had a private rocket-ship I could do it almost immediately, but you seem to forget there's a couple of days' travelling involved."

I scrawled a quick note and handed it to Cattermoull. The bank manager read it and disappeared from his office.

An idea had suddenly struck me. "What are you doing after this?" I asked.

Blob revealed he had to return to London to complete his report on the BAC One-Eleven deal due the following Monday. "And I've got a dental appointment at five. Why do you ask?" he enquired.

"Because we have our own private rocket-ship which can get us up to Derby before lunchtime and have you back in the dentist's chair by 5pm," I almost roared.

Denis looked at me as if I were insane. "What are you talking about? You're not suggesting we use Kilo Echo to get up there? It's on its way to Tarbes at the moment."

I could sense Blob was becoming quite interested.

"Not Kilo Echo, we'll take Alfie Cope's aircraft we bought."

"You mean the Percival Pro . . ."

"Yeah, we could be there in less than an hour. Pickles will tell 'em we're coming, and they'll have everything ready for Blob to look at. Mike's getting the aircraft ready now. Cattermoull just phoned him for me."

Blob's eyes began to shine. "Did you say a Percival Provost?" he enquired excitedly. "I could always finish the BAC report over the weekend," he volunteered.

"What about the dentist? They don't like to be kept waiting, you know,"

Cattermoull had returned to the office. Blob shrugged and said he'd cancel if necessary.

I turned to Denis. "Okay, let's get to the airport. You can drive us straight to the aircraft and I'll depart for Burnaston immediately. Will you confirm that somebody has advised Derby of our ETA?"

We bundled Blob into the back of the Air Links van and Denis deposited us beside the aircraft in record time. Mike had pre-flighted the machine, and he handed me a flight plan and set of maps as I stepped onto the wing.

"Both wing tanks are full so you won't need to refuel at the other end. I've run her up and everything's fine. Weather's okay and you should get there in under an hour . . ."

I had slammed the door before he'd finished. A quick check round the cockpit and I cranked the starter. The six cylinders of the de Havilland Gypsy engine burst into song and I released the brakes. There had been no need to attend to Blob; he'd strapped into the other pilot's seat almost before I'd finished listening to Mike.

Stackpole marshalled us up onto the hard standing behind two Argonauts when Blob taxied us in at Burnaston. Blob had subjected me to increasingly imploring glances in flight, until I'd reluctantly agreed to him taking over control. His handling was smooth as he flew northward leaving me to navigate. I let him join the circuit and fly the approach. Then, because he was doing so well, I forgot to take over for the landing. Two years' expensive Air Force flying training had ensured he hadn't lost his flying skills overnight.

Stackpole had gathered all the information required for the proposed Argonaut purchase, and Blob was soon able to establish the size and worth of the deal. Since the National Provincial was also bankrolling Derby Airways' BAC One-Eleven deal, it was very likely that no money would physically change hands.

By late lunch-time, Blob had seen enough evidence to support his decision to recommend financing our purchase. He spent a further fifteen minutes with Stackpole, while I examined the three aircraft. They were in reasonable condition, much better than the Hermes had looked on the fire dump, and would only require a fresh coat of paint in our colours before we could start crew training. Blob came over and joined me while I examined the third aircraft. We somehow ended up in the cockpit, where he told me we could now regard the aircraft as belonging to Air Links.

"They'll actually belong to our leasing company," he explained. "You'll pay for them over a period of five years. The total package deal will be worth £150,000 financed at eight percent."

A quick calculation told me our initial payments would be around £2300 per month or £28,000 a year. If we could achieve 4000 flying hours a year with three aircraft, the payments would represent a relatively insignificant percentage of our overall costs.

It was 3pm when we taxied into our parking area back at Gatwick. Blob had flown us back, grabbing the left seat before I could protest. He'd

managed to squeeze three days' work into four hours, thanks to the use of our Proctor. He said something about getting a private pilot's licence and using a light aircraft to get around the various airlines he visited in the course of his work.

"How much would something like your Proctor cost?" he enquired.

I told him a good one with low hours and good radio aids could probably be picked up for less than £500. Blob seemed quite preoccupied by this bit of information as we walked towards the terminal.

"Think you could make some enquiries for me? And I'd need some idea of operating costs. Today's been a bit of an eye-opener; using a light aircraft has saved me two half-days' travelling plus overnight accommodation. I'll be interested to see how that compares with the cost of today's flying."

He finished discussing the matter as we entered the terminal building. I decided to leave a quick message for Denis, then head over to the Gatwick Aero Club for a well-earned beer. I was about to suggest Blob join me, but another thought occurred to me. I took his arm and steered him towards the railway station.

"You'd better hurry if you want to get there by five," I reminded him.

"Get where? I thought we could have a couple of beers somewhere and talk about . . ."

"Some other time, Blob. I'd hate to make you late for the dentist."

It had been a satisfying day for Air Links and I knew Blob had enjoyed going back to flying again, even if only for a day.

Next morning I swapped my scheduled Tarbes flight for the night freight run to Lille. I rounded up Pickles, Tony and Nathan Warnup and told them we'd hold a company meeting at 10am. Denis had just returned from a flight to Greece, and Levitt would probably be around by then.

I briefly related yesterday's events before we discussed the various tasks that needed to be delegated. Tony landed the job of interviewing prospective flight crew. We calculated we'd need eight full crews, captains and first officers. The Argonaut didn't require a flight engineer in its crew complement, so there would be a small saving over the Hermes in that area. Denis suggested we hire additional captains if sufficient co-pilots weren't available. We told Nathan Warnup to get letters of intent from Horizon Holidays guaranteeing 2000 hours a year for the two aircraft. Denis also suggested soliciting other travel agents like Thomas Cook, Arrowsmith, Lords and Clarksons.

Other members of the firm ended up with other jobs. Pickles would locate additional office space and equipment, Denis would help Tony arrange the necessary ground and flight training for our crews, and I would arrange for Air Couriers to move the vital Argonaut spares to Biggin.

Zucher learned about our aircraft procurement from Pickles and immediately gave us a letter guaranteeing enough work to keep the Argonauts flying through summer and winter. We didn't hear from any other travel agents, and I secretly wondered whether Nathan Warnup had contacted them.

By early December our first Argonaut was ready to enter airline service. Five senior and rather elderly Derby Airways' captains had chosen to spend their final years flying Argonauts with us, rather than go through the hassle of converting onto jets. Seven co-pilots joined us from Aden Airways, but the remainder of the new employees were not type-rated and would require ground and flight training.

Denis insisted on flying the last hours off the venerable Hermes before introducing the new type into service. We'd managed to get a three-month extension on flying hours. So Delta Alpha, the world's last airworthy example of the type, flew its last revenue flight on December 13 after a refuelling stop in Brindisi. Nine days later Denis and Tony flew it to Southend, where it was enthusiastically welcomed by the members of the East Anglian Air Museum.

It was fortunate for us that the Argonauts carried the same number of passengers as the Hermes — eighty-two. This was particularly convenient considering the coaches conveying our passengers to and from the airports held forty adults apiece.

The five Derby captains handled all the initial flying, assisted by the seven type-rated co-pilots. Denis had arranged a four-week ground-school course to be held in our newly established flight operations department in the "beehive" building on the south side of the airfield, and the necessary flying training was completed at Stansted during a spell of fine weather in January.

Denis, Tony, Frank Berg and I were scheduled to start on the first course on 1 January. Les Smith and Timber Wood were offered the choice of DC-3 commands or co-pilot positions on the Argonauts. It was a difficult decision; four-engined experience was a valuable commodity in the pilot job-market but so was multi-engined command time. Timber Wood chose the captain's seat of the Dakota; Les converted onto the Argonaut as a co-pilot; Mike Sommerpole stayed on the DC-3, accumulating a lot of valuable flying experience, and Chegwidden, our freelance captain, continued to fly the Dak on an hourly basis.

The January Argonaut course started one student short after I broke an ankle while skiing in Scotland. By the time I was fit to fly again, the course had been completed and I was stuck on the Dakota once more.

The first Argonaut revenue flight took a load of Zucher's Horizon Holidays customers to Switzerland for a fortnight's holiday. Dr Levitt made quite a big deal of it by inviting the aviation correspondents of the leading national newspapers to a luncheon in the airport grill restaurant. Nathan Warnup and a bevy of newly hired air hostesses did an excellent job of sewing them up with champagne cocktails, so although they never even looked out the window where our first aircraft, G-ALHT, was preparing to depart, all of them wrote glowing articles about our company. Derek Dempster of the Daily Express described us as "the little people's airline" and reported that our passengers could never afford to fly on the scheduled airlines. Although highly embarrassing, there was some truth in what he wrote: the scheduled IATA fare to Zurich was more than double the cost of the entire holiday with Horizon Holidays.

The other two Argonauts, LHH and LHI, were ferried to Biggin. LHI, which we referred to as "Hotel India", was painted in our colour scheme. LHH never flew for us commercially and became our Christmas-tree aircraft.

Only one thing blighted the excitement of introducing two four engined aircraft into service. Although Blob-bottom had arranged for his bank to finance the aircraft purchase, this had not included the comprehensive spare-parts inventory offered with the planes. It was only during casual discussion with Air Couriers that we learned the spares had already been snapped up by Ikey Silverstein, the aircraft spare parts dealer with rather questionable business ethics. Nobody doubted he'd demand top dollar for any components we were forced to buy from him.

Derby had worked their aircraft hard but maintained them well, and Denis was quick to emphasise to Griff at Air Couriers that this practice was to continue. By the time LHI, the second aircraft, came into service in January, the aircraft were each averaging twenty flying hours a week. The bulk of this flying was at weekends, enabling necessary maintenance work to be completed during the week. The hardy Merlin engines, almost identical to the legendary Spitfire's power plant, performed faultlessly, and our major consumables were fuel, oil and tyres.

The total lack of interest from other travel agents rather surprised me, so while I recovered from my ankle injury, I made a few enquiries. Five of the major travel agents confirmed my suspicions; none of them had been advised of our extra available charter capacity.

"Clarksons, Lunns and Lords Travel didn't even know we still existed," I told Pickles indignantly. He shrugged dejectedly and said he'd mentioned the matter to our commercial manager.

"He couldn't have been less interested," he revealed. "Fortunately I don't think we'll need them. Zucher's determined to fly the pants off us during the summer, and the winter too if we perform satisfactorily. The old man worries about reliability, but his son's our most ardent supporter and always convinces his father we're just as good as the scheduled airlines . . . if not better. I told him we've now got three four-engined aircraft, with one on permanent stand-by if another goes unserviceable."

I managed to conceal a smile when I heard this; the third aircraft was technically airworthy at present, but wouldn't be once we began pulling bits off to keep the other machines flying.

Pickles mentioned that the younger Zucher was keen to inspect our new aircraft. "He wants to come down during the Christmas holidays, so I'm meeting him off the train tomorrow. I thought of offering him a trip in the jump seat, say to Geneva and back on a Saturday. We don't carry an engineer and he'd really love it."

I agreed to allow the son to fly as supernumerary crew on one of our flights. I'd noticed he and Pickles seemed to be developing quite a rapport together.

"Getting to be quite a friend of his, aren't you?" I observed casually. Pickles looked at me quizzically. "Well, yes. I suppose so. We do share a few common interests."

"What time's he arriving tomorrow?" I asked. Saturday was our busiest day and somebody had to man the office.

"On the 10.30 train so I'll be out of the office till lunch time."

I told him I'd stay in until he returned.

"Offer him a flight in the Proctor. Mike can take him up. But don't borrow any more Biggles books from him," I implored jokingly.

CHAPTER THIRTEEN
A Cuckoo in the Nest

The shortage of pilots became more acute towards the end of the year. BEA were still recruiting and so were Caledonian, Eagle and British United. Even Dan-Air now offered permanent year-round employment; they couldn't afford to let pilots go in the winter. The aircrew employment market was rising up to a crest.

Blob-bottom visited us on several occasions to check progress. On two of these occasions an Argonaut was scheduled for an air test, and he leaped at the opportunity to go up in it. Denis must've put him in the right seat, because he came back raving on about the Argonaut's heavy controls.

"Not enough elevator authority for me and too much adverse aileron drag," he informed us knowledgeably. Tony commented he knew an awful lot about aerodynamics for a City banker. We had gravitated to the Gatwick Aero Club for a few beers after work, and I explained to Tony that Blob and I had gone through airforce pilot training together.

"And I now hold a private pilot's licence," Blob informed us proudly, holding aloft a buff-coloured booklet. "Four hours in Guy's Proctor and another two hours dual with old Pashley at the Southern Aero Club was all it took."

"Better keep it handy, we might need to borrow you for more test flights at the weekend," Denis joked. Blob dismissed the idea instantly; nothing would replace security in his set of values, and working for a major bank was demonstrably a lot safer than operating a fleet of flying museum pieces!

The second Argonaut entered service with the minimum of trouble. Derby Airways had maintained them to an excellent standard and this policy paid handsome dividends for us.

Its first commercial service departed on Christmas Eve, 1963, with seventy-eight members of the Combined Services Winter Sports Association bound for Geneva and Zermatt. The Argonaut was similar to the Hermes in general appearance, and when painted up in our Air Links colour scheme, the casual observer probably didn't even realise we had introduced a different type of aircraft into service. Two ex-Derby Airways captains operated the service, with Christine and a new girl serving in the passenger cabin.

Pickles and his friend the younger Zucher watched the departure from the airport viewing gallery. Nathan was busy cementing future commercial relationships in the bar with a motley collection of hangers-on who called themselves travel agents, so he didn't actually get to see the aircraft depart. I sat at a table in the Gatwick Brasserie restaurant with the elder Zucher, Tony, Dr Levitt and Stan Wilson. Everybody was ecstatic about the new aircraft except Zucher senior.

"Can we rely on these old aircraft to keep going throughout the whole year?" he worried aloud.

I reminded him the aircraft had Rolls-Royce engines and had operated reliably for the last fifteen years. "But won't they wear out eventually?" he enquired nervously.

Pickles and the son had come in from the viewing gallery, and between the six of us we managed to allay the father's fears. He departed shortly after that, muttering something about scheduled airlines having the aircraft and resources to back up any breakdowns. Pickles accompanied them to the exit, issuing reassurances on the reliability of our recently acquired aircraft.

During the two months my ski injury kept me out of the air, I was able to devote my total energies to administrative work. The DC-3 operation still ticked along nicely through the winter. Our involvement in the Air France scheduled freight service had brought our name to the attention of quite a number of freight consignors and shipping agents, which resulted in two or three freight charters a week. The Tarbes pilgrim flights had finished until spring, so we kept the aircraft in freighter configuration to ensure it was ready at short notice if required.

Other travel agents began making tentative enquiries about chartering us for the coming summer IT season, but we refrained from committing ourselves financially to them. Summer charter work was relatively easy to pick up, and I preferred Horizon's regular all-year-round business. It would have been foolhardy not to afford them first priority, especially as they had virtually guaranteed to keep us busy through summer and winter. I mentioned to Blob-bottom we were turning other people's business away. He had arrived at Gatwick looking rather smug in a sleek twin-engined Miles Aries, which he occasionally used for getting round the country on bank business.

"We could expand further, but I don't know how your bank would view another application for a large loan," I ventured, aware that our current monthly outgoings to his bank were equal to my annual salary. He asked a few questions and became rather thoughtful at my answers. I noticed he jotted something down in a diary.

Both Argonauts gave sterling service throughout winter and early spring so we didn't need to cannibalise parts from our Christmas-tree ship over at Biggin.

Monthly use was almost a hundred hours per aircraft during the first three months of 1964. I attended the next Argonaut technical conversion course, which was held in a spare office in the "beehive" building. Doc Warnbeck examined my ankle at the beginning of April and declared me fit to fly again. Flying hours tapered off in April, and Gibbie used the vacant time to take three of us up for the conversion flying training, to get the Argonaut type endorsed on our licences.

The Argonaut was easier to fly than the Dakota. The tricycle undercarriage and nosewheel steering helped the pilot cope with crosswinds and wet runways. Failure of an engine on take-off caused only a twenty-five percent loss of power against the Dak's fifty percent. It was a more exhilarating and faster aircraft to fly, and the sound of the four Merlins at take-off power made the hairs on the back of my neck stand up.

After two training sessions with Gibbie on consecutive days, we had completed the conversion syllabus and he signed us out. His only advice to us had been a caution to remember we didn't have a flight engineer to rely on any longer so we had to be careful to do everything "by the book". I tactfully reminded him I'd never had one on the DC-3 either and he explained that his comment really applied to the other students, who had converted from the Hermes.

Apart from the occasional sightseeing flight to the Dutch bulb fields, April in the air charter business is a transition time between winter doldrums and the frenetic pace of IT summer flying. We had managed to circumnavigate the doldrums, thanks to Horizon's winter sports flights, but by April, when alpine flowers replaced skiers on the mountain meadows, our flying hours wound down to only a few a week.

Griff used this slack time for both aircraft to be ferried to Biggin for minor maintenance. When an aircraft is in continuous service for months at a time, small defects like hydraulic leaks or inoperative gauges tend to be deferred until maintenance staff can work on the aircraft without interruption.

"Leave 'em with me for a couple of days and you'll get 'em back as good as new," he promised. It was an excellent idea in principle, but it would prove to be the catalyst for something rather unfortunate.

Zucher hadn't provided precise details of flights planned for the summer months. We knew Horizon were promoting holidays in Genoa, Venice, Milan, Barcelona, Palma de Mallorca, Athens, Basle and Perpignan, and a cautious calculation confirmed our two aircraft could handle the amount of flying.

I managed to corner our commercial manager mid-morning, before he became embroiled in his busy day's schedule in the airport bar, and urged him to get Zucher's signature on the contracts. When we hadn't heard anything back from the travel agent by the middle of the month, I left a message for Pickles to follow the matter up.

He must've done a good job, because next morning Zucher senior arrived at the airport unannounced, clutching a briefcase full of documents. Nobody except the office girls were in attendance when he arrived with a companion.

"We'd like to wander over and examine the aircraft, if that's all right," he told them. "Mr MacLachlan would very much like to look over one of the machines."

The receptionist explained both aircraft were over at Biggin Hill getting fixed.

"Not both aircraft, surely? Whatever's wrong?" the travel agent enquired with concern. Nathan chose this moment to pay the office a fleeting visit. He pushed rudely past the visitors and rummaged in a desk drawer.

"Keys of the company van," he interrupted the girl as she was about to speak. "Who's got them?"

The receptionist paused in mid-sentence to point to a set of keys hanging from a wall hook labelled "company van".

"Mr Warnup is our commercial manager and can tell you more about the aircraft," she explained to Zucher and his companion. Nathan stopped in mid-flight to glare at the visitors.

"Bit busy at the moment." He breathed alcohol fumes over the visitors. "Both aircraft are down for maintenance. There's a public viewing gallery where you can watch planes all day. Why don't you?"

"Mr Zucher hoped to see our aircraft," the secretary explained. Nathan looked at her blankly.

"Well he can't, can he? Both planes are over at Biggin getting fixed," he pointed out to her irritably. Zucher's face registered concern and surprise.

"But supposing a charter flight came up at short notice, what would you do then?" he enquired curiously. Nathan laughed aloud.

"The passengers would have to wait until the aircraft were fixed," he guffawed in Zucher's face. "Maintenance is only one of the problems of running a fleet of old aircraft. Finding spare parts can be a nightmare for some of the older machines around here."

Zucher exchanged glances with his companion.

"Look, you'll have to excuse us, we're a bit busy at the moment." Nathan held the office door open as a rather unsubtle invitation for them to leave. Zucher and his companion took the hint, and departed with two briefcases containing our summer contracts.

"Who the hell were they?" Nathan enquired as the door closed behind them.

News of Zucher's visit reached my ears next morning. Denis was furiously berating Nathan for not getting the contracts signed. The commercial manager tried to excuse himself by pointing out he hadn't known who they were.

"If somebody had told me a client was coming down to see us, I could have arranged to meet him," he remarked petulantly.

"You mean fill him in at the bar then take him to lunch at the Airport Brasserie?" Denis suggested bitingly.

"Well yes, either there or the Gatwick Manor, they've got a new chef there, supposed to be Turkish, and the food is super," he admitted. Denis interrupted him by suggesting if he spent more time in the office and less at the bar, he might recognise our major clients better. Nathan slunk out of the office, leaving us to devise a scheme to retain Zucher's business.

As usual, the solution lay with Pickles, who spoke to the travel agent's son next morning.

"He's really keen to go for another flight in one of our new planes, so I've suggested he come on one of the ferry flights from Biggin," he explained. "Show him round the aircraft first, point out the Rolls-Royce engines, show him how much time is spent on preventive maintenance, then put him in the jump seat for the flight over. I'll meet him here when he arrives and between us we can convince him how reliable our aircraft are."

118

Denis and I collected the first aircraft during mid-morning. We picked young Zucher up from Redhill railway station en route to Biggin.

On arrival at Air Couriers, Griff detailed the work carried out on the aircraft.

"LHI had a cracked rudder torque tube so we replaced it with the rudder on the spare aircraft," he informed us. "Apart from that they only needed minor maintenance. Number four oil temperature gauge was over-reading so we replaced it with a new item from stores, we've changed the port landing light and we've fitted a new nosewheel tyre while we had the machine here. The aircraft's had a servicing check and is as good as new again."

He handed Denis the technical log book, open at the last sheet. His chief engineer had written "nil defects" across the last page and signed the entry with his name and licence number.

Griff walked out to the aircraft with us while Denis extolled the virtues of the Argonaut's Merlin engines.

"Developed during the war years in all sorts of aeroplanes," he explained to our passenger. "Very light and reliable, powerful too, and more streamlined than the big radial engines on the American DC-4s and 6s."

"And a lot quieter than some of the jets coming into service," I added. "The Speys in the BAC One-Elevens are real screamers. Still very much in the development stage of course."

By the time we'd landed back at Gatwick, our passenger was sold on the Argonaut.

"Same engine as the Spitfire," I heard him tell his friend Pickles as they walked away from the aircraft. "Very reliable and much more streamlined than those big round engines on all the other aircraft."

Pickles steered him to the office where Tony and Nathan waited. Tony asked him how he liked our new machine, emphasising the "new". Our visitor was about to enthuse on the new aircraft when the phone interrupted. Tony picked it up.

"Somebody for you," he said, and handed the receiver to Zucher.

"Hello . . . Oh hello, Dad . . . Yes I did . . . Oh, very impressed. Vastly superior to other aircraft, even the new jets," he told his father. "I overheard the engineer say they're as good as new. Yes, much faster than the DC-4."

"Pressurised to fly above the weather," Pickles mumbled in his free ear.

At the conclusion of the phone conversation the travel agent opened his briefcase.

"Dad says to discuss the European flights with you," he began. "Caledonian are doing the trans-Atlantic flights . . ."

"We can do those as well," Nathan interrupted, anxious to make his presence felt. "North Atlantic, Far East, Australia, did you know we've even flown to New Zealand . . ."

A kick in the shins silenced him. Denis then explained to the meeting that we preferred to concentrate our efforts on the European market. He didn't need to mention we weren't licensed to operate over the areas mentioned by Nathan, and anyway the Argonaut lacked the range to cross the Atlantic non-stop. To have entered into open competition with our colleagues in Caledonian would have created more problems than it was worth.

"We're a European airline. We have the ground-based organisations in all the European destinations and we prefer to concentrate our efforts within our area of expertise," Denis convinced the travel agent.

Zucher had begun producing papers from his briefcase while Denis spoke. He arranged them on the desk before him.

"Palma de Mallorca has increased to twice a week this year," he informed us. "Perpignan, Athens and Corfu are weekly flights. So is Basle, and Tarbes will continue with small loads in the DC-3."

By afternoon tea-time we had signed contracts for forty flying hours a week from May through till October. Denis and Zucher signed each document, and one of the office girls witnessed their signatures.

Pickles escorted his friend to the railway station and Nathan hurried to conclude something vital in the bar, leaving behind an ecstatic roomful of Air Links employees congratulating each other. The pile of signed agreements on the desk served as a certainty of our survival until the winter. All flights were at full revenue rates of £140 per flying hour. If Horizon also used us for their winter sports flights, we would be in remarkably good financial shape by the Spring.

Denis and Tony were positively radiant at the good news. I pointed out that a lot of the credit should go to Pickles.

"Zucher senior had doubts about our aircraft," I reminded everybody. "Especially when he arrived unexpectedly one day and found nobody to talk to in the office and both aircraft apparently grounded. It's fortunate his son doesn't share his misgivings and, thanks to Pickles, is able to convince his father we're a reliable airline. Pickles deserves most of the credit for today's work."

Everybody was unanimous on that point.

We then discussed Nathan's unfortunate first encounter with Zucher senior.

"Don't let that ever happen again," Tony implored. "Nathan nearly lost us our best customer."

"Yeah, keep him away from the customers at all costs," somebody suggested facetiously, but the remark was wasted. Nathan was already back in the bar.

Our summer flying schedules started with a hiss and a roar. One moment we were quietly waiting for the IT season to start, then suddenly we were doing four flights a day to European destinations. Most of our long flights departed and arrived over the weekends. Friday night saw both aircraft depart simultaneously for Greece, one to Athens and the other to Corfu. On their arrival back the following morning, one was quickly replenished and sent off to Basle, while the other went to Perpignan that evening. Three-quarters of our revenue flying was done between Friday and Monday, leaving three days free for crew rest, minor maintenance and the occasional ad hoc charter for various other organisations, one of whom was the Ministry of Defence.

A Lieutenant-Colonel Fitzwilliam phoned on the second Monday in April to enquire whether we could convey sixty grenadier guards to Gutersloh in Germany.

"Military trooping flight," he explained. "The government prefers to use you private operators as a sort of back up to RAF Transport Command in the event of something blowing up somewhere."

"You mean World War III starting?" I enquired jokingly. A muffled guffaw from the other end indicated the caller had a sense of humour.

"Not quite as drastic as that, or at least I hope not," he explained. "Troop movements mainly, plus wives and families. Freddie Laker's BUA and British Eagle do most of it in their Britannias, but we've been instructed to share the work around a bit among you smaller fellows. Besides which, sixty is rather a light load for a Brit."

He described the nature of the work, which was basically the leftovers that BUA and Eagle couldn't handle. On hearing that most of it was over the weekend, I reluctantly had to tell him we didn't have spare capacity.

"But I thought you charter chaps flew anything, anywhere, at any time," he protested.

"For anybody." I finished the statement for him. "Well yes, you're right, but we've only got so many aircraft and crews and at the moment they're fully employed."

"This could be a regular source of revenue for you once you're on our books," he promised.

I understood and appreciated his point, and promised to discuss it with the other Air Links directors. An outfit like ours needed as many strings to its bow as possible. Trooping was a year-round business which had helped many a private airline survive a bad winter. If Horizon Holidays decided not to use us in the winter, then Ministry of Defence trooping would be a welcome source of revenue.

Next morning we convened an impromptu directors meeting in the small office overlooking the tarmac.

"There's no way we can afford to let Horizon down," Denis insisted. "Zucher's seen our aeroplanes and he knows we can carry his customers for a quarter of the cost of the scheduled airlines."

The consensus of opinion of the meeting was that we turn down the troop-ing flights. I remained thoughtful at this decision; anybody who's been in the charter business for more than a season hates to turn bona fide customers away. Even if you can't do the job, sub-chartering it to a competitor will result in a small commission. The Ministry of Defence was a reliable if rather slow payer. But on the other hand, Horizon had promised us work all year round. I silently wondered whether we should consider bringing our third aircraft, the Christmas-tree machine, back into service.

While this and other thoughts went through my mind, a de Havilland Comet IV jetliner taxied past our window. It seemed to be in BEA colours except for one small difference: the name on the side of the fuselage said British Airtours.

CHAPTER FOURTEEN

One-Elevens

I flew just under the 120-hour maximum allowable figure in May, and by the end of the month I felt a bit punch drunk with so much flying. The final flight had been a Palma de Mallorca return flight, landing back at Gatwick at 8am after nine hours' flying, most of it at night. The fellows in Gatwick Ground Control must have guessed we'd had a busy night, because they parked us on Gate 17, right outside Crew Customs. We only had to carry our bags a few yards to where the Waterguard officers waited to clear us through arrival formalities.

As we exited the customs shed, two men approached me. The taller, a slim bald-headed man in his early fifties, addressed me.

"Edwards, British Aircraft Corporation." I heard only the end of his sentence above the noise of an arriving aircraft.

"Good trip?" his companion enquired pleasantly, extending a welcoming hand. "Jock Bryce, also with BAC. We wondered if you had five minutes to spare?"

I looked at them rather dazedly. After so much night flying, I wasn't thinking as clearly as I would've liked. These two fellows probably had a spot of charter work for us, most likely heavy freight, which we weren't particularly well equipped to handle. I wondered why they didn't give it to their best customer, Freddie Laker, who'd subsidised their BAC One-Eleven bus-stop jet.

"Come up to the office," I invited, leading the way.

I was quite surprised to find Denis and the other directors of Air Links waiting there for us. Pickles arrived as we entered. Dr Levitt approached the taller man and positively fawned at his feet.

"Sir George and Mr Bryce, delighted to meet you, I'm Ambrose Levitt, delighted to make your acquaintance." He turned and introduced the rest of us: "Mr Wilson and my other fellow directors, Captain Mills, Captain Butler . . . and you've already met Captain Clapshaw. Oh, and young Richard here's in charge of the office."

Surprise now registered on my face. I had recognised our two visitors.

"You're Sir George Edwards, chairman of BAC," I told him unnecessarily.

The taller gentleman admitted he was and introduced his companion.

"Captain Jock Bryce, our chief test pilot."

Tony and Denis were smiling. They'd recognised the two famous British aviation personalties immediately. George Edwards had joined Vickers Super-marine, manufacturer of the immortal Spitfire and Wellington, as a lad in the design office before the war. After the war, Vickers Supermarine had produced the Attacker naval jet fighter, the Swift, which captured the world airspeed record, the Scimitar fighter and the Valiant V-bomber. They also produced a line of post-war civil airliners; their Viking, designed as a DC-3 replacement, was purchased by BEA and several other carriers. When turbine engines came into production, Vickers produced the Viscount, powered by four Rolls-Royce Dart turbo-prop engines. The Viscount had proved a world-beating design and was soon in service all over the world. Now the BAC One-Eleven bus-stop jet was coming into production to replace the Viscount. There were even rumours floating around of a proposed supersonic airliner on the drawing board. Jock Bryce, Sir George's companion, had succeeded the legendary Mutt Summers as Vickers' chief test pilot. Vickers had become part of the British Aircraft Corporation a few years ago.

"We've been admiring your operation here." Sir George started the proceedings going. "Your aircraft seem to be permanently on the go. Argonauts, aren't they?"

We admitted they were, while wondering what interest these two leaders in post-war aviation could possibly have in our small fleet of antiquated piston-engined airliners.

"Excellent design." Jock Bryce entered the conversation. "Has all the design experience of Douglas plus the expertise of Canadair and Rolls-Royce. Been in service for twenty years now. Had any problems with your machines?"

Denis assured him we'd had excellent service in the short time we'd oper-ated them. "The Rolls-Royce Merlins run like well-oiled Swiss watches," he observed. "Apart from routine servicing, we can fly them ten hours a day and they come back asking for more."

"Operating mainly round Europe, we gather?" Sir George queried.

"That's correct, we prefer to stay within our own patch, so to speak. Greece is about as far as we normally go."

The conversation went back and forth for ten minutes while we tried to guess what our distinguished visitors had come for. Finally Tony broached the subject.

"If you're thinking of chartering us for something, we're fairly heavily committed at the moment," he explained. "However, we never turn work away, even if we have to sub-charter it to our rivals. What did you have in mind?"

Sir George smiled as he listened.

"Nothing at all, actually. We haven't come here to buy, we've come to sell you something. We're taking a tentative look at your operation to see if our One-Eleven would fit into your route structure. From what we've seen so far, it'd be admirably suited to your short- to medium-range sectors. With your permission, we'd like to take a closer look at your operation to see what would best suit you."

You could have heard a pin drop when Sir George said that. I exchanged astonished glances with the other two pilots. Dr Levitt and Stan Wilson were staring at Sir George, willing him to say more. He remained silent while we absorbed this momentous piece of news.

"Jet airliners!" Levitt was the first to speak. "We'd be a jet airline." His words hung in the air like silken threads. Tony brought us back to reality.

"We're a small charter company operating three aircraft in the cut-throat air charter business. We have no scheduled services, no long-term contracts, no trooping contracts, and we survive by trimming our costs to the bone. That means using old aircraft that we buy very cheaply, operate until their hours are run out, then throw away. We cannibalise other aircraft for spare parts, we employ as few staff as we can get by on, we delay paying our bills as long as possible. In winter we fly for less than it costs us in fuel, oil and wages, just to keep the cashflow going, and we somehow manage to survive on a hand-to-mouth basis."

"But you've been busy summer and winter since you began operating," Sir George pointed out. Denis muttered something about the luck of the draw.

"A week ago, we didn't have a single flight booked for the coming season," he explained. "We couldn't possibly afford your One-Elevens. The loan payments would bankrupt us in less than . . ."

"Listen to us for a moment." George Edwards beckoned him to silence. "You know the British Aircraft Corporation are manufacturing the One-Eleven to compete against and eventually replace the hundreds of Viscounts, Convairs, Caravelles, Friendships and other earlier designs. You've probably heard that Boeing and Douglas are also competing for a share of the market. Boeing is producing their 737, a sort of mini-707 with two engines, and Douglas are coming out with the DC-9. The three of us, Boeing, Douglas and BAC are competing to get the first order from a major airline. Every airline is looking sideways at the others to see which design they're going to buy. None of them wants to be the first to take the plunge, but when they do, the others will follow."

He paused to gain breath. Nobody spoke.

"We need to be the first in the market," the manufacturer continued. "Normally the British Government would support us with a substantial first order, but unfortunately they've subsidised de Havilland's Trident. The One-Eleven is a better aircraft, but it's a private venture with all the attendant risks. We've got to win this race to survive."

"Bit like us and the state airlines," I remarked a little sardonically. "We're playing Monopoly with our own money against civil servants with nothing of their own to lose."

"Precisely, which is why we popped over from Weybridge today," Sir George affirmed. "We've only taken a quick look at your operation, but we quite like what we've seen so far."

"You're making money out of a shoestring operation, if you don't mind me being perfectly blunt," Jock Bryce interrupted. "We believe that if you were seen to increase your profits considerably after introducing One-Elevens, all the other airlines waiting in the wings might jump on the band-wagon and copy you."

"And we'd be prepared to lease you one or more aircraft on favourable terms, just for the attendant good publicity."

"But how much would all this cost?" the ever practical Stan Wilson wanted to know. Owning a large motor business up north had taught him how machinery costs could cripple a business.

"Not a damned thing!" Jock Bryce assured him. "Our statistics department would analyse your route structures and the anticipated load factors. They'd then come up with a passenger/mile cost below that of the piston-engined equipment you're currently operating. How many passengers can you get into an Argonaut? Sixty, maybe sixty-five?"

"Eighty. They're in one-class high-density configuration," Tony interjected. Jock Bryce hesitated in his sales pitch.

"Eighty? Crikey, that's a hell of a lot of people in an Argonaut. The hostesses must use shoehorns to get them all in."

"How many passengers can your One-Eleven carry?" I asked.

"Seventy in dual configuration at present in the One Hundred series, but that'll go up when we get the new Rolls-Royce Speys. We're already working on a fuselage stretch, which could be in service in time for next summer's IT season. In the meantime, we'd like to look at the feasibility of leasing you an aircraft on a passenger-seat per mile basis."

"What does that mean?" Stan Wilson interrupted.

"You'd only pay for the number of passengers and the distance you carry them."

"Supposing we have an empty flight?" Denis asked. Usually a few initial flights had to return empty at the start of a season. Then again, we usually had to fly an empty aircraft out to pick up the last load of passengers at the end of the season.

"No passengers, no pay," the test pilot assured us.

"You mean to tell me flying an empty aeroplane back from, say, Athens in six hours wouldn't cost us a thing? That's over a thousand miles."

"A thousand miles multiplied by no passengers was zero when I went to school," Bryce assured him. "Oh, and by the way, it wouldn't take six hours to get back from Athens. You're entering the jet age, remember, and we cruise at 500 mph."

"How much would it cost to lease a One-Eleven then?" Tony challenged.

"Ten percent less than your Argonauts. We'd make certain our figures came out significantly below your present operating costs. Remember this is an advertising exercise for us, we can't afford to let you fail," Sir George emphasised.

We ruminated on his words.

"Crew training, additional ground handling equipment, all those sort of costs would be absorbed by our commercial development department. Think of it as a business lunch," he murmured.

"Whaddya mean?" Wilson's ears had pricked up at the mention of a free lunch.

"Well, when we take clients out to lunch at an expensive London restaurant, we don't do it to make friends, we do it to generate business. If we launch Air Links into the jet age with the One-Eleven, that'll generate a lot of other business. Think of it as advertising."

"Same as you're doing for Derby Airways?" I suggested. Both visitors nodded in agreement.

"What about the free lunch?" Stan Wilson enquired. The idea of eating in a swank London restaurant at another firm's expense had considerable appeal for him.

"That too," Bryce promised laughingly.

The meeting broke up shortly afterwards. Edwards and Bryce flew back to Wisley in their company Dove, Tony and Denis headed towards the weather office, and I went home for eight hours' rest. Pickles was left to manage the office.

Although I was dog-tired after being awake for more than eighteen hours, I found it impossible to sleep. The prospect of getting jet aircraft for next summer or maybe even as early as this winter, kept racing through my mind.

CHAPTER FIFTEEN
Daylight Robbery

Next morning was a Saturday, and although I was out of flying hours until the end of the month, I could still work on the ground.

Both aircraft had just returned from Athens and Corfu when I arrived. Our staff were over-extended trying to handle two arriving flights and check in eighty other passengers for the mid-morning departure to Basle. I entered the load-control office behind the check-in counter to begin preparing the load sheet. The only other occupant of the office was a petite brunette in Air Links uniform. She eyed me expectantly as I entered.

"Did you bring the list of crew names for the General Declaration?" she enquired. I admitted I hadn't brought the information with me, but as I usually assisted Pickles with the week's rostering, I was able to give her the names from memory. The typewriter clacked away rapidly as she typed the information onto the printed form.

I began filling in the flight details on the load sheet form. Date, aircraft registration, captain's name, destination, flight number were all recorded. Outside the office I could see the checking-in process wasn't going particularly fast with only two staff on duty. At that moment a distraught female check-in clerk burst into the office.

"Either of you speak Swiss German?" she appealed. "Family of four are checking in and have only brought three passports. I can't get the message through to them that they each need a passport. Why does this sort of thing have to happen at weekends?"

The other girl stopped her typing and left the load sheet office. I heard her talking in Swiss German. After a two-minute rapid-fire exchange, the passport problem appeared to be resolved. She returned to her desk.

"No problem with the passports?" I enquired conversationally.

"None," she replied, shaking her head. "The youngest child was an infant travelling on her mother's passport."

The phone rang at that moment, and the captain of the outgoing flight gave me the fuel load and estimated consumption. I entered the figures onto the form as a member of the check-in staff arrived with the passenger numbers and baggage weights. I continued my calculations until the load sheet was completed.

The typist slipped the completed documentation into the ship's papers envelope and took them out to the aircraft. Ten minutes later she returned to the office and relaxed into a chair.

"Busy place on a Saturday morning," she observed. "Pity the Basle flight can't be scheduled out an hour later."

"Why's that?" I enquired, although I thought I knew the answer.

"Not enough staff to handle the incoming and departing passengers. If the Basle flight went later, we could concentrate on processing the incoming passengers from Mallorca and do the job properly. If you hadn't come in and helped out, we'd have had a delay on our hands. By the way, I'm Olivia Noble, and I don't think we've met." She extended an elegant hand and I introduced myself.

"Been working long for Air Links?" she enquired conversationally. "Haven't seen you around here before."

I explained I was usually flying rather than helping out in the office. "Unfortunately, this month I allowed my flying hours to mount up too rapidly, so I can't fly for another four days."

"Wish they'd place a limit on our flying hours," she observed wistfully. "This is the first day I've had on the ground in fifteen days."

"And you choose to spend it in the office?" I observed with surprise. She shrugged.

"Well, you know how it is. In a small company like ours, it's a team effort, we all pitch in and help each other. The girls and boys couldn't have coped with three aircraft movements in an hour, so I decided to come in and help. What about you? You didn't have to come in, did you?"

I explained I was a shareholder in the company, so if the company didn't succeed, I would be out of a job. She digested this piece of information quietly.

As the next scheduled arrival wasn't until 4pm, when our aircraft arrived back from Basle, I suggested we break for lunch. She declined the invitation.

"Sorry, but my sister's picking me up at two. We're going to Epsom."

"What's on there?" I enquired and Olivia told me her father's horse was running.

"Daddy's a horse-racing fanatic and his latest two-year-old looks like a real winner," she advised me. "It's running in the three-thirty. Are you a gambling man?"

"Yes, but only on aeroplanes. I don't know enough about horses to gamble hard-earned money on them," I informed her. She frowned lightly.

"Pity, 'cos Daddy might have a winner today. The trainer says our horse is in top form. The trainer is very confident of its chances — says it's a certainty."

"What's the name of this certainty?"

"Stone Cold. Remember the name."

We had walked across the terminal to the main entrance, where a silver-grey Jaguar waited in the prohibited parking area. An expensively dressed girl of about thirty climbed out.

"Get in and change when we get there," she ordered her sister impatiently. Olivia turned to me.

"My elder sister, Georgina. This is Guy."

I said something appropriate.

The elder sister acknowledged me briefly, then hurried her passenger into the car. I was left watching the sleek sports car accelerating out of the airport.

After a late lunch in the Greasy Spoon, I called into the office to check the teleprinter for messages. Our DC-3 was managing to survive on a diet of ad hoc freight charters, most of which reached us via the teleprinter.

Pickles was doing arithmetical calculations while talking to somebody on the phone. He concluded his conversation and turned to me. "Did you know Air France asked us to quote for the freight service again?" he enquired a trifle indignantly. I shook my head.

"Haven't heard a thing, but that's hardly surprising. My feet have barely touched the ground in the last month. How did you hear about it?"

"Their freight manager just called to ask why he hadn't heard back from us. I didn't know what he was talking about, but I told him we were finalising our figures and would get back to him shortly."

"Good thinking," I remarked. "It could be quite lucrative, it certainly kept Kilo Echo busy last winter. Wonder who their manager spoke to."

Even as I said that, I suspected Nathan had taken the initial enquiry.

"Give them a written quote by teleprinter," I urged, gesturing at the telex machine. Pickles shook his head regretfully.

"Too late, I'm afraid. The Frenchman says the tenders had to be in by yesterday. That's why he wondered why we hadn't responded. He says it looks like Westpoint will be awarded the job. They have a daily service between Exeter and Heathrow, which should connect rather nicely with the freighter service."

I mentally cursed we hadn't got the contract. One of the problems with our expansion had been our inability to maintain contact with everything that happened in the airline. In the early days, when we had one aeroplane and only half a dozen employees, everybody helped where required. Now that we had a staff of forty, the intimate nature of the company had disappeared.

"A hundred and forty pounds for a round trip." Pickles finished his calculations. "Five nights a week would have been £700 a week. Pity about that."

Unfortunately that was now water under the bridge, and we needed to look ahead for more work.

We discussed the prospect of operating BAC One-Elevens next year. Pickles pointed out that the bus-stop jets carried less passengers than our Argonauts.

"The travel agents base their costs on multiples of coachloads," he explained. "Their coaches usually carry forty passengers plus their bags. So our Argonauts carry two coachloads. The One-Eleven only carries seventy."

"In dual class configuration," I interrupted. "And I'll bet BAC can increase that number to eighty if they install high-density, all economy-class seating. Anyway, they hope to have a stretched version out soon."

"Why mess around with expensive new aircraft?" he implored.

The door opened and Dr Levitt and his nephew joined the conversation.

"We know exactly what we're doing with the Argonauts," Pickles continued. "New aircraft have teething problems that cause breakdowns and we can't afford delays."

"We're entering the jet age!" Levitt interrupted rather abruptly. "The new generation of passenger jet aircraft fly in pressurised comfort at twice the speed of our present aeroplanes. Flight times will be halved."

Nathan nodded in obedient agreement as his uncle spoke. I suspected Levitt had absorbed a bit of BAC sales propaganda from some of their brochures.

"BAC are only offering us their research and development aircraft as a publicity exercise," Pickles pointed out to the doctor. "Once they start to get airline orders, they'll lose interest in us and concentrate on keeping their bigger customers happy. That could leave us with no aircraft."

"Then we'll order One-Elevens ourselves!" Nathan breathed alcohol fumes over the group of us. "We'll make enough money in the first year to buy a whole fleet of aircraft."

"One-Elevens are a bit more expensive than Hermes or Argonauts," I cautioned. "I'd say at a rough guess two aircraft would represent an investment of nearly a million pounds."

Levitt dismissed the idea as preposterous. "What do you think, Nathan?" He turned to his nephew for confirmation.

"Oh . . . er, no, nothing like as much as that, and don't forget they fly faster so they get there sooner. That must make a difference, doesn't it?" He petered out and suddenly sat down very heavily in a convenient chair.

Pickles pointed out the importance of establishing the operating costs if we decided to get One-Elevens. Levitt listened to him without interest.

It was obvious he held Pickles' opinion in very low esteem. He wanted the prestige of owning a jet airline and he was accustomed to getting what he wanted. He produced a large silk handkerchief and wiped it across his brow. It seemed he'd joined his nephew for a liquid lunch in the bar.

"Damned lies and statistics," he muttered angrily. "We need positive action here, somebody with the courage to make the decision to buy One-Elevens. It'll prove itself once it's in service, same as their Viscount did. Gentlemen, I believe the One-Eleven will be the aircraft of the future." He emphasised his remarks with a loud burp. In the background, Nathan nodded his head, either in agreement or more likely from the soporific effects of his recent lunch.

"Okay, let's discuss methods of raising capital for expansion," Pickles began, but the doctor interrupted him.

"That's hardly your department," he suggested sternly. "Leave that to Nathan and the directors." He paused and directed his attention towards Denis, while Pickles looked to me for support.

"Do we have a coffee machine in here, I'm feeling badly in need of a cup of coffee," the doctor demanded suddenly.

Denis shook his head regretfully. "We've always been a bit short of space," he explained. Levitt turned to Pickles and told him to bring them five cups of coffee.

"Make that six, one for yourself," I suggested. Pickles left the office, and Levitt turned to me angrily.

"That boy's a pest around here," he complained. "Too big for his boots. Thinks he knows it all. Totally negative, never prepared to listen to new ideas and suggestions."

I pointed out that, on the contrary, Pickles had been the kingpin of our organisation, the one who had first sold Horizon Holidays the idea of cheap charter-flight holidays.

"He also runs the office while everybody else is away," Tony pointed out.

"Whaddya mean by that?" Nathan suddenly aroused himself from a light doze to rejoin the conversation. "I'm the commercial manager around here. Who do you think gets all the business, eh?"

Denis conceded that Nathan seemed to have covered most of the airport bar trade. Fortunately the remark was not heard by the rest of the room.

Levitt staggered clumsily to his feet and addressed his fellow directors.

"Gentlemen, Nathan and I have decided Air Links are going to be the first all-charter airline to order the One-Eleven. Isn't that right, Nathan?" He turned to his nephew for verification.

Air Links commercial manager gazed up at the speaker.

"Isn't what right, uncle?" he slurred. Levitt grimaced, but otherwise ignored his nephew's total lack of interest.

Pickles arrived back with the coffee just as a Comet IV jetliner taxied past the window. Levitt paused in his delivery as we all admired the aircraft. Its red, black and white colour scheme emphasised its menacing sleek lines as it taxied by.

Five of us watched the marshaller guide it onto its parking position. In its day the Comet had been the leader in jet-age travel, enabling airlines like BOAC to leap in a single bound from piston-engined aircraft cruising at 250 mph to commercial passenger jet aircraft able to cruise at twice that speed.

"What's BEA doing in here, must've diverted from somewhere?" Denis muttered curiously. Our eyes followed the machine as the marshaller finished guiding it onto the white lines. He crossed his batons, giving the order to stop, and the noise of the four Avon engines suddenly decreased.

"Who the devil are British Air Tours?" Tony wondered aloud. Levitt gestured out the window.

"Gentlemen, that is where our future lies," he announced dramatically. "Jet aircraft. We are about to enter the jet age."

We drank our coffee and Pickles and I left to assist with our next flight arrival.

Next day was Sunday and I'd planned to help with the early arrival from Perpignan, then take the rest of the day off. My flying hours would soon be below the maximum twenty-day total allowed by the regulations, and I'd be able to operate the Genoa return flight the following day.

Mike Sommerpole had accosted me in the Aero Club a few nights previously and offered me a complimentary VIP pass to the Biggin Hill airshow.

"Busman's holiday, just what you need," he'd convinced me. "Watching somebody else doing the flying, while you sit and relax in a comfortable seat with a cold drink. Pickles suggested the oil company might like to invite one of their best customers to the show."

"Typical of him. What did the fuel company say? 'Get lost!' I would imagine."

"On the contrary, they came up with five passes to their VIP tent! Captain Mills and Butler are away flying, Nathan says he isn't interested, so we've got three spare tickets."

He extended one to me.

"Should be a good show. The Black Arrows are performing, plus the Tiger Club and a whole load of other aircraft. Why don't I see you there?"

I thanked him and accepted one of the passes. The remainder would be offered to other off-duty staff members. It would be good to get away from Gatwick for a day.

Unfortunately, fate flexed her fickle finger yet again and decreed that things would go very differently.

Our Argonaut arrived back from Perpignan half an hour behind schedule. Stronger-than-forecast head winds over France had added an extra half hour to the scheduled flight time, so the aircraft finally arrived on chocks at a quarter to eight.

Ground Control were having a hard day coping with more than the usual amount of weekend charter flights. They assigned our aircraft to a distant stand, where the tail protruded out into a position aligned with the main parallel taxiway. The incoming crew must have omitted to apply the control locks correctly after landing, because jet blast from a taxiing jet turning onto the taxiway buffeted the Argonaut's tail and damaged the rudder.

I was about to depart for the air show when the phone rang.

"Joe says we'll have to install a new rudder," a voice announced.

"What are you talking about? Would you mind telling me what's going on?"

"Oh sorry, didn't you hear that LHI's rudder's been struck by jet blast? The chief engineer's borrowed a gantry and thinks it might be damaged. He's going to remove it and send it away for crack testing."

"That'll take a couple of days."

"More like two weeks. We'd be better off to instal a replacement from stores. Shouldn't be a problem, Derby Airways had plenty of airframe spares."

"Better to use the one off the Christmas tree. I'll contact Air Couriers and tell 'em to remove it and get it over here pronto," I assured him. "Tell Joe we should have it here by lunch-time. Meanwhile, we'll reschedule the other aircraft for the next flight."

Griff wasn't at home when I phoned, but his daughter gave me the after-hours number of his engineering manager.

"Shouldn't be a problem," he assured me. "We'll have it over there by two o'clock at the latest. Leave it to us."

He rang off and I prepared to depart for the Biggin Hill airshow with Pickles. The phone rang again, while I was waiting for the rudder to arrive. Something told me it was bad news.

"Air Couriers here again, Guy. I'm afraid you don't have a spare rudder. We installed it on one of the aircraft a week or so ago when we found stress cracks in the original item."

"Damn! Yes, I forgot. Okay, I'll get onto Derby Airways and see whether they've got one in stock. I'll phone you back."

I was surprised when Derby's Burnaston number was answered on the first ring. I asked to be put through to stores.

"Air Links, Gatwick, here," I began. "Bit of a problem with one of our Argonauts. Need a replacement rudder in a bit of a hurry."

"Sorry but we sold all our Argonaut and Merlin spares. We're re-equipping for the new jets and disposed of everything — aircraft, engines, propellers, airframe spares. Needed the storage space. Sorry."

A dreadful feeling of doom enveloped me as I rang off. I remembered who had bought the entire Derby spares inventory.

Ikey Silverstein!

I gazed out the window like a prisoner seeking a glimpse of sky. Biggin Hill was going to be one spectator short today.

"All ready to go then?" Pickles and Mike Sommerpole breezed into the office. Les Smith and one other person trailed behind in the corridor. Pickles noticed my facial expression.

"Let me guess . . . a last-minute charter?"

"Wish it was. LHI needs a new rudder."

"That's impossible. Griff fitted one on its last check."

"True, but that one's just been damaged by jet blast, and I can't locate a replacement."

"Derby Airways must have a bundle of spares left over, might be worth trying them." Pickles had already picked up the phone. I placed a restraining hand on his arm.

"I've spoken to them. They sold everything to Ikey Silverstein."

"Damn. He'll want an arm and a leg for anything. Aviation Traders at Southend may have a DC-4 rudder left over from one of their Carvair conversions. Maybe we could fit one of those?"

A quick call to Southend revealed Aviation Traders did have two DC-4 rudders, but they weren't compatible with the Argonaut.

"Same basic design but manufactured by different companies in different countries," their chief engineer explained. "Why not try SAC at Blackbushe? They have parts for almost everything, at a price."

A ray of hope glimmered for a moment.

"SAC? Never heard of them, are they new?"

"Silverstein Aircraft Components. You must have heard of Ikey Silverstein, surely?"

I admitted I had heard of the person. I didn't mention that all our previous dealings with him had been bad. Joe Phillips came into the office while I spoke.

"Any chance of getting the other rudder repaired?" I enquired hopefully.

His pessimistic look was my answer.

"Not in a few hours. We need the aircraft back in service tonight. I've swapped aircraft so the other one can do the next flight, but that's only postponing the problem."

"Doesn't matter, this is an hour-by-hour existence. We'll probably have to sub-charter a few flights to other operators." I turned to Pickles.

"See if Dan-Air can do it. If they can't, try Caledonian."

"There's also that new outfit just started up, Lloyd International. They use a DC-4 to position ships' crews all over the world," Mike suggested. Pickles had already picked up the nearest phone and soon began speaking to Dan-Air's flight ops department. After thirty seconds, he replaced the receiver.

"Not a thing, they're too busy with their own work. I'll try Caledonian."

Further phone calls to various charter companies revealed that nobody had a spare aircraft that weekend.

"I'll phone Ikey and see if he's got a rudder." It was Pickles who volunteered for the unpleasant job. He dialled the parts dealer's twenty-four hour number, and after some initial confusion was put through to him. I could imagine Ikey lurking like a greedy tarantula waiting for us to approach his web.

"Good morning," he gloated over the phone. "Is this a social call or business on a Sunday?"

"Social," Pickles lied. A devious thought had crossed his mind. "We wondered if you'd like a complimentary pass to the Biggin Hill airshow?"

"Thanks, but no. I've already been offered half a dozen in case I wanted to watch aeroplanes on a Sunday afternoon, which frankly I don't."

"Fair enough, just thought we'd ask."

"Got a spot of trouble and needing a spare part in a hurry?" Ikey suggested greedily.

"No, nothing like that. We were just about to leave for the airshow when Joe Phillips mentioned your name."

"Joe working on his day off? You have got trouble. Okay, tell me what it is and I'll see if I can help."

"Er . . . well, while you're on the line you might like to let us know if you've got an Argonaut rudder."

"I've got six," he interrupted. "Complete with all documentation. When do you need one?"

"We used our spare one a couple of weeks ago and prefer to keep a spare handy. How much do you want for one delivered to Gatwick?"

"Why Gatwick? Your maintenance base is Biggin. Hmm . . . yes, I think I smell trouble. Something wrong with the new rudder, is there? Why not fit one of mine?"

"How much for it to be delivered to us here at Gatwick?" Pickles demanded.

"When did you say you wanted it?"

"Today would be fine."

"Ooh, so it's very urgent, is it? Sounds like an aircraft-on-ground job to me. Funny how they always come up on weekends, isn't it?"

"It is rather inconvenient," Pickles admitted in an unguarded moment, then wished he hadn't.

"And expensive. Triple time for my lads on a Sunday, plus travelling time, but we could get it over to you by . . . er, let's see. What time is it now? We could get it over to you by four o'clock."

Things began to look good for a few moments until we asked the price.

"Twelve hundred quid!" Pickles repeated the figure to me. The tarantula had baited its trap.

"That's ridiculous." I grabbed the phone. "We could've bought the whole spares inventory for a few thousand."

"But you didn't, did you?" the arachnid replied.

"No but . . ."

"And I did. The price is twelve hundred, take it or leave it." In the background I thought I heard the sound of a motor horn. "Come on, make up your mind. The family are waiting in the car, we're supposed to be going rabbiting this afternoon? Do you want it, yes or no?"

"Twelve hundred is daylight robbery and you know it," I protested.

"Then why not go elsewhere if you think you can do better? You and I know there's nowhere else to go, is there? Now do you want me to get it over to you or can I go out for the afternoon?"

"We've got to take it," Pickles urged.

"Okay, we'll take it," I agreed miserably. "Get it here as quickly as possible."

"And the cash? Don't forget this is a Sunday."

"No problem, the airport bank's open seven days a week. We'll have the money waiting for you."

We finalised the details and I turned to Joe.

"He's holding us to ransom, but we'll just have to pay. Ikey will have the replacement here by four. How long will it take to install?"

"Four hours if I can borrow the right ground equipment from BUA. I'll contact a few friends over there and we should be ready for it when it arrives. Provided nothing goes wrong, we should have the aircraft back in service by 9pm at the very latest."

"Spot of trouble?" a different voice enquired. I turned and saw the younger Zucher's bald head in the doorway.

"Minor technical problem," I assured him glibly. "Engineering are working on it now. Should have it fixed in time for the flight at nine."

"We were going to the airshow." Zucher turned to Pickles with disappointment. "What about the gold passes?"

"We've got yours here," I reassured him, handing him my pass. "Richard . . . er . . . Pickles will have to stay behind, but Mr Smith can still take you there in his car. Better get going if you want to see the start of the show."

Pickles muttered a few words of apology to his friend before returning to the office.

"Silverstein is still our cheapest option," he assured me. "There are no scheduled flights to Palma so we'd have to arrange something from Barcelona. That'd come to considerably more than the cost of the new rudder. The one-way fare on Iberia is £21 a head, then there's the cost of the onward travel. And we'd still have to get the aircraft fixed."

I agreed we'd chosen the cheapest option, especially if insurance paid for it.

The rudder arrived late afternoon in a truck driven by Ikey. The aircraft had already been towed over to BUA's hangar, where a small team of engineers waited to begin work. Ikey gave me a wide leer as he approached with his right hand extended. He gave the signal to start unloading the component as I handed him an envelope full of bank notes.

"Anything else we can help with? Just let me know if there is. You've got my twenty-four-hour number?" He counted the notes as he spoke.

"Thanks, but I think we're okay now." I turned away rather sharply to watch the replacement part being manoeuvred towards our aircraft.

The rudder was installed without problem, allowing our evening flight to leave on time, and I finally got home at 10.30.

Next morning brought three lots of trouble.

I was scheduled to operate the Monday morning return flight to Genoa, using the substituted aircraft returning from Mallorca. While I was in the office, Nathan was conversing animatedly on the phone. Levitt and Denis listened agitatedly.

"Yes, I agree it looks like a reject from a tin-can factory, but we had to do something quickly. We were jolly lucky to locate a replacement bit from a chappie at Blackbushe who runs a sort of scrap yard full of bits and pieces off old aeroplanes. Without him we'd have been grounded for a week or more." He put the phone down.

"That was Zucher," he informed us gravely. "He's not very happy."

Levitt and Tony turned to me accusingly.

"I bet he's not. Have you seen LHI recently?" our chief pilot demanded angrily of me. I looked across the apron area to where our aircraft had recently arrived and was now disgorging sunburned passengers. The red and white Air Links colour scheme clashed glaringly with the emerald green and white Derby Airways colours on the rudder. The effect made our aircraft resemble something assembled from left-over spare parts. Several plane spotters in the viewing gallery were pointing at it with amusement.

"Why the devil didn't they spray paint the rudder before they installed it?" Denis thundered. "It looks bloody awful."

"There wasn't time. We had to race against the clock to find a replacement part and get it fitted in time. Everybody did a tremendous job, and the aircraft was back in service that evening."

"What was the hurry? I understand from Nathan that the other aircraft was available as a back-up."

"The hurry was to get the aircraft repaired in time for the evening flight.

Joe and his team achieved miracles in the short time available," I assured him. Levitt looked very unhappy.

"The sooner we get modern aircraft the happier I'll feel," he muttered. "Every time one of our machines hiccups, we wonder whether we'll be able to fix it. They're a bit like old motorcars, held together with chewing gum and bits of string."

Pickles pointed out that our aircraft were a lot better than that, but Levitt waved the explanation aside.

"One-Elevens are the aircraft for us," his nephew recited like an obedient parrot. "Five hundred miles per hour, cruising above the weather."

"But not as economical as our present aircraft," Pickles pointed out. "We're the little people's airline — remember what the press boys wrote about us? We carry the people who can't afford to go on holiday at scheduled airline prices. Factory workers, clerks, storemen, packers, shop assistants — there are millions of them out there who can only afford to go on overseas holidays with the IT operators. If we bought jets, we'd have to increase our costs and we'd lose most of our customers."

Nathan said something unintelligible about old piston-engined aeroplanes.

"Pickles is right," Denis interrupted. "We need to concentrate on our niche market, leaving the bigger boys to carry the wealthier passengers in their Britannias and Viscounts."

"The important thing is to keep Zucher happy with our present set-up," Tony observed pragmatically. "Somehow he found out about yesterday's fiasco and isn't very happy. Maybe somebody should pay him a visit and reassure him we can do the job satisfactorily."

"That shouldn't be a problem, he's coming down to Gatwick tomorrow," Nathan announced unexpectedly.

"Blimey, good thing you told us. We'd better prepare a bit of a reception committee for him. Show him over the aircraft, he hasn't seen them yet."

"I can take him to lunch afterwards and tell him about our future plans," Nathan volunteered. Nobody reacted very favourably to his suggestion.

"We'd better get LHI across to Biggin to get the rudder sprayed," Pickles interjected pragmatically. "There are no flights scheduled for tomorrow, so maybe two of you can fly her across this afternoon. I'll confirm with Air Couriers they can do it first though."

"Would you mind doing it?" Denis looked at me. "While you're there, ask Griff if it's worth getting one of the damaged rudders repaired to keep as a spare. He'll probably say it's cheaper to buy replacement parts as and when we need them," he added, recalling the Hermes days of a year ago when Griff had been able to buy hangars full of engines and airframe spares for virtually nothing. I hated to disillusion him this time.

"Silverstein's unfortunately bought up Derby's entire spares inventory," I revealed reluctantly. "He waits like a greedy spider for us to get desperate for a component, then he produces it and demands an exorbitant price."

"How much did a rudder cost us yesterday?" Denis enquired and nearly fell over when I told him.

138

"That's more than we paid for our Hermes!" he protested indignantly.

"Who authorised the purchase?" Levitt suddenly demanded.

"Well, Pickles I suppose, but I went along with the decision," I replied. "The matter was urgent."

"That was a decision for the commercial manager, not the office boy," Levitt reproved me.

"Nathan wasn't here. It was a Sunday."

"I was playing golf at Woodcote Park," Nathan protested sanctimoniously.

"Well, it's all water under the bridge now," I told them. "I've got to go flying now, but I'll be back by half past five to ferry LHI over to Biggin." I exited the office and found Levitt already waiting in the corridor.

"I'm very concerned at the way you leave the young office boy to make major decisions." He fell into step beside me. "Nathan is the commercial manager and is better equipped to make commercial decisions."

"He's never around the office when we need him," I pointed out. "And when he does make a decision, it takes two of us to repair the damage."

"Nathan has enormous potential that hasn't been realised yet," his uncle replied patronisingly. "I don't think you're giving him a fair chance."

I almost told Levitt you only got one chance to make a right decision in aviation and if you got it wrong, the result could be financial death. Fortunately common sense or sheer cowardice prevailed and I kept silent. We directors of the company couldn't afford to fall out with each other. I bade the doctor goodbye and turned right towards the weather office. Levitt caught the next train back to Harley Street.

I arrived in the despatch office to find the co-pilot had already completed the pre-flight documentation and proceeded to the aircraft ahead of me. On arrival in the cockpit I was greeted by a familiar female face.

"Good morning, Captain, I didn't realise who you were the other morning," an attractive female voice greeted me politely. I recognised Olivia Noble from the previous morning in the load-control office. "I've just made a fresh pot of coffee if you'd like a cup."

"A cup of hot coffee would be rather nice. I forgot you flew too," I replied, then turned to the co-pilot. "Les, what's the flight time today?"

"Two hours fifty. Weather's okay at the other end, but I loaded return fuel. The price of Av-gas in Italy is astronomical."

Olivia Noble returned with the cups of coffee.

"Cream and sugar on the tray behind you," she said.

"How did your father's horse do on Saturday?" I enquired.

She smiled ruefully. "It didn't. The trainer withdrew it on race morning, so it was a non-runner. Most disappointing, but it'll do well next time."

"Should we keep an eye open for it then?" I suggested, and she nodded.

"My sister and I didn't see you at the Biggin Hill airshow," she ventured timidly.

"Last-minute problem just as I was about to leave," I explained. "Bit like your dad's horse in a way. I bet it was a good air show?"

She nodded. "Treble One squadron did a twenty-two aircraft formation loop for the first time, Vickers had their Spitfire there, and Bill Bedford did a brilliant display in the Hunter. Pity you missed it all, it was a great show."

I said something about there being other opportunities, then Les and I became involved in the pre-flight checks.

The ensuing flight was uneventful. The Argonaut's pressurisation system enabled us to fly the direct route. Clear weather gave the passengers a spectacular view of the Alps.

The flight operated ahead of schedule and we landed back at Gatwick by afternoon tea-time. After clearing customs, I thanked the two hostesses for a pleasant trip and headed back to the aircraft.

"Not another flight?" Olivia enquired in surprise. I explained it was just a short ferry flight over to our maintenance base.

"No passengers, just Les and me. Short flights like this are rather fun, I'll put Les in the left seat and he can get a bit of command practice."

"It does sound rather fun, doesn't it?" Olivia agreed. "Where are you going?"

I gestured north-eastward towards Biggin Hill, explaining that our maintenance was done there.

"Biggin, near Westerham?" the hostess enquired. "Any chance of coming along for the ride?"

"Er . . . yeah, I suppose so. What about your car at the airport though?"

"I'll leave it here until I fly again. How will you get back from Biggin?"

"British Rail probably. Air Couriers will drop us off at the station. Okay, let's get going." Les and I picked up our flight bags and headed back to the aircraft, leaving Olivia Noble speaking to somebody on the telephone.

Les handled the short flight well. If the company continued to expand we would soon need more Argonaut captains, and Denis was keen to promote from within the company. If he had Les in mind, I would certainly endorse his suggestion.

Olivia had arrived at the aircraft shortly after us and she strapped herself into the middle jump seat while Les prepared to start the first engine. Soon the distinctive grumble was emanating from our Rolls-Royce Merlins as we performed the post-start checks. Gatwick Ground Control cleared us to the holding point of the westerly runway, and the grumble increased to a snarl. I turned to Olivia.

"Same engines as the Spitfire," I shouted above the noise. "Merlins, marvellous sound, isn't it?"

"Sort of like listening to classical music," she nodded. "Gives me goosebumps up and down my back."

The tower cleared us for an immediate take-off after a landing Bristol Freighter, so I didn't have time to respond. The snarl of the four-engines increased to a deafening roar as Les advanced the throttles. The empty aircraft accelerated then climbed away easily as Gatwick Director vectored us northeastward. We were cleared to join downwind for Biggin's runway 29 and were back on the ground again within fifteen minutes. It was early evening and the airfield was deserted save for three figures waiting at Air Couriers.

140

"Short and sweet, I'm afraid," I announced as the propellers slowed to a stop outside the hangar. The excitement on her face betrayed her as an aviation fanatic.

"Short but wonderful," she agreed. "I really enjoyed every minute. I'm getting my private pilot's licence, so it's really interesting to see how large aircraft are flown."

We discussed the difficulties of learning to fly, while a ground engineer connected a towbar to the nose wheel-fork. Slowly we were towed into the hangar by tractor.

Griff met us at the top of the steps after we'd parked, and promised us we'd have the aircraft back on the line by the following evening. I looked at Les questioningly.

"Want to ferry it back tomorrow?"

Les nodded.

"Does that invitation include me?" the third member of our crew enquired hopefully. I assured her it did.

Griff had sent the original rudder to Aviation Traders at Southend for repair.

"We can keep it in stores until you need it," he suggested. "Now, do you need a lift to the station?"

"My sister's picking me up, we live nearby," Olivia said.

A rather languid-looking female with shoulder-length ash-blonde hair had stood smoking while we'd talked. Now she ground out her cigarette and approached our group.

"Dinner's at eight and the old man wants us both there," she informed her sister.

"My elder sister, Georgina," Olivia said. Her elder sister eyed me speculatively, as if measuring me up for a suit — or a coffin. From the disdainful expression on her face, I guessed that my rumpled appearance must have placed me somewhere between a train driver and a plumber in her social estimation. Les and Griff did slightly better than me. She acknowledged me with a short and somewhat impatient hello.

"Guy and Les need a lift into Westerham, so I thought we could take them," Olivia said, interrupting Georgina's appraisal. "I've just ridden in the flight engineer's seat on the flight over. It was . . ."

However, Georgina had already turned towards her car. Les said he'd go with Griff into the village, leaving me to travel alone with the two sisters.

Georgina drove recklessly, talking animatedly, while I remained silent in the back. After nine or ten minutes, we turned into a gravelled driveway leading to a large country house. The Jaguar pulled up in a scrunch of gravel, and Georgina hurried out.

"She's forgotten you want a lift," her younger sister apologised. "I'll take you to the station."

A distinguished-looking gentleman in his early fifties approached and opened both passenger doors. He beamed as his daughter kissed him affectionately.

"Max Noble, pleased to meet you," he said, turning towards me. "Come and have a drink while I supervise the barbecue."

Before I could decline, he'd returned to the house. Max Noble was not accustomed to having his suggestions refused. I turned to Olivia awkwardly.

"Don't worry about it. I'll phone a taxi," I assured her, not wishing to intrude on a family occasion.

"Come and have a drink first," Olivia suggested.

The offer was too good to refuse; I hadn't relaxed over a cold drink for more than a month and had nothing planned for the evening. I followed her through the house to a patio area overlooking a small lake.

Max Noble was obviously very successful at whatever he did. A white-coated barman waited attentively for our drink orders. Behind him, other members of the household staff manned a large barbecue. The owner of all this introduced us to his wife, referring to her as "Mrs Noble".

"We're all drinking Pimms," she began. "Here's yours."

"Look, I don't like to intrude on your family evening," I said. The others were dressed in casual evening clothes, and I felt downright uncomfortable in black uniform trousers and a rather grubby white shirt.

"You're not intruding," Mrs Noble assured me. "We're spending an evening with our two children. We don't get the opportunity to enjoy that very often now. Max is away more than he's home. Georgina . . . well, she's always away somewhere, and Olivia, our youngest, seems to spend all her time flying."

Max Noble came over and we discussed generalities for ten minutes until both daughters arrived back. Olivia had changed her Air Links uniform for a simple dress, in contrast to her sister's slinky black evening outfit.

"Olivia told me about your horse," I began. The father's face wrinkled philosophically.

"Yes, bit of a letdown, I'm afraid. We bought it as a foal and were expecting great things from its ancestry, but we've only had bad luck so far. You a racing man?"

I informed him I wasn't. He assimilated this piece of information thoughtfully.

"We've entered him in the Ascot Gold Cup," he explained. "That's next week. Scobie Breasley's down to ride him, and we should stand quite a reasonable chance if the trainer can get him to the post."

"I don't think Guy's remotely interested in horses, are you?" Georgina interrupted. Her father smiled indulgently.

"Very wise, cost a lot of money, but then there's always the chance of a win. Quite a thrill when it happens; no wonder they call it the sport of kings. You should go to the races one day, you might enjoy it."

Olivia's parents were excellent hosts, able to make any guest feel at ease. We spent a pleasant hour listening to Olivia's account of learning to fly with the Surrey and Kent Flying Club. Georgina listened to our exchanges, chainsmoking and saying very little. My most determined attempts at engaging her in conversation were met with total lack of interest. As the evening

142

drew to a close, I thanked the family for their generous hospitality and told Olivia I'd call a taxi. She was adamant she'd take me to the station.

"I'm afraid you must have been bored stiff listening to Daddy's horse-racing talk," she sighed regretfully. I assured her I'd thoroughly enjoyed the evening.

"One of my business acquaintances is very involved in the racing scene," I assured her, thinking of Silverstein. "Unfortunately most race meetings are held at weekends when I'm busy flying. I've been to one or two and thoroughly enjoyed them."

We drew up outside British Rail and I thanked her for her kindness.

"See you at work." I waved as I entered the station.

Next morning I told Denis about the spare rudder and said I'd be happy to collect Hotel India later in the day.

"Griff says we can have it in the evening. Les and I are happy to collect it then."

"Thinking of dropping in for tea at the Nobles en route?" he suggested slyly. "Tea with Max on the back lawn maybe? There's rumours he'll get a knighthood in the New Year's Honours List."

"Whaddya mean? One of his daughters flies for us. She gave me a lift to the station."

"Yes, that's Olivia, sweet girl. I've flown with her a few times. Good worker, keen on flying and only too happy to help on the ground when she's not flying. Lovely person — unlike her sister, who's a real man-eater, been married three times and is about to divorce her latest husband. The two sisters are as different as chalk and cheese. Olivia's a little sweetie, but her sister Georgina's a dangerous vixen, out for everything she can get."

Reluctantly I had to admit his statement contained some truth. The trouble was, for some totally inexplicable reason, I'd become completely infatuated with Georgina!

CHAPTER SIXTEEN
A Cheap Lesson

Things didn't go quite as we'd planned them next day. Griff phoned to say the aircraft wouldn't be ready until the following morning. Then Levitt came down to try and force us all to agree to the One-Eleven deal. Stan Wilson paid one of his rare visits to the airport, and Levitt used the occasion to call a directors' meeting.

No flying was scheduled, so we five directors assembled together in the office with Pickles. Levitt arrived last, with a reluctant Nathan in tow. He opened an attaché case and spread a number of sales brochures across the table.

"British Aircraft Corp have just sent me the details of their larger 200 version of the One-Eleven. The prototype has flown, and they're prepared to guarantee firm deliveries by next April. It has 200 miles extra range, eighty seats in mixed first- and economy-class configuration, ninety in all-economy, and has a passenger-seat per mile cost lower than our present aircraft."

"It can do Athens to Gatwick non-stop," Nathan added. From the way they recited facts and figures, I suspected they'd carefully rehearsed this speech before calling the meeting.

Pickles scanned the performance graphs in the sales catalogues. "What about on a plus-twenty day? Athens can get to thirty-five or forty degrees in summer," he pointed out.

Aircraft take-off and climb performance deteriorates badly in high temperatures. BAC's graphs were drawn for standard sea-level conditions. Levitt turned to his nephew for help.

"The One-Eleven will cruise above the weather," Nathan volunteered inanely.

"But it's got to get up there first," Denis pointed out. "We've had this problem with high temperatures at Palma, Athens and Corfu ever since we started. We would either have to limit the payload, which means leaving passengers behind, or load less fuel and make an en route stop. Either course of action is economic disaster, and Zucher wouldn't go along with that sort of thing. The One-Eleven burns a lot more fuel than the Argonaut."

"The alternative is to reschedule flights to ensure night-time departures, which would also be unpopular . . .," Pickles began, but Levitt rudely interrupted him in mid-sentence by reminding us that this was a directors' meeting.

"These are important decisions for the directors to make if we are to re-equip with jet aircraft," he said, directing his remarks at Denis, Tony and me. "Hundreds of thousands of pounds of shareholders' money is involved. This is not a matter for just any member of the staff to decide on."

Denis, Tony and I shuffled our feet awkwardly. Levitt's autocratic attitude was becoming difficult to accept. His enthusiasm was beginning to outweigh commercial common sense. Nobody would have denied that a lot of preliminary groundwork had to be done before we could consider the introduction of expensive jet aircraft, but Levitt wanted to buy first and work out the details later. "Derby Airways are also getting One-Elevens," he informed the meeting.

"And government approval to operate several scheduled routes," Denis reminded him. "They hope to make money both ways, subsidised scheduled services all the year round and tour traffic in the summer."

Levitt had no reply. The meeting gradually disintegrated into a disorganised rabble. Attempts by any of us to introduce an ounce of common sense were overruled by Levitt. The final straw came when he told Pickles to keep his opinions to himself.

The meeting broke up. I was preparing to leave the room when the phone rang. It was for me.

"Is that you, Guy? Olivia Noble here. Any chance of a lift to Gatwick this afternoon. My car's still there."

"You mean on the ferry flight? 'Fraid not, the aircraft won't be ready till tomorrow. What about then?"

"Well . . . er, I was going to ask you something else. Remember we discussed horse racing yesterday?"

"Vaguely, yes."

"Well, you mentioned that all the meetings were at the weekend when you were busy flying."

"Yes, I remember that. The Derby, Oaks, St Leger are all held at weekends to draw the biggest crowds. Why, what's all this about?"

"Well I hope you won't think this a bit cheeky but Royal Ascot is coming up next weekend and I, er . . ."

"And you want to take time off in the weekend to see Daddy's horse win?" I suggested rather unkindly.

"No, of course not. I'll probably be busy flying then and wouldn't ask for time off, but Ascot week runs from Monday till Saturday. I wondered . . . er, that is, my sister and I wondered if you might like to come tomorrow for Ascot Heath?"

"Your sister said that?"

"Er . . . well, I . . . yes, we both wondered if you'd enjoy a day at the races. Daddy takes a box for the whole Ascot week but only uses it for Royal Ascot, that's Gold Cup Day when the Royal Family attend. The rest of the time he lets us use it with our friends."

The thought of meeting the delectable Georgina again was too good to miss. I accepted.

"Where do I meet you?"

"Eleven-thirty in the grandstand. I'll leave your ticket with the attendant."

"Sounds fine, I'll pick the aircraft up at 8.30 and go straight from the airport."

"Er, there's just one other thing you should know." I could detect the hesitation in her voice.

"What's that? Don't say I can't land on the race track?" I joked. A giggle at the other end preceded her reply.

"No, not exactly, silly. I thought I'd better mention that it's formal."

"So I would imagine. Don't worry, I do possess other clothes apart from a uniform. I promise I'll wear a tie and a clean shirt."

"I'm afraid formal means full morning suit," she informed me solemnly.

"You don't mean grey top hat and wedding outfit, do you? Where am I going to get that?" I protested.

"Hire them. Any of the military tailors, Moss Bros, Alkits, Gieves, they have hundreds of suits available. Just tell them what it's for and give them your size. They'll do everything else. Now, will we see you there? You'll thoroughly enjoy it, I promise."

Indecision raced through my mind for a micro-second. Pickles could find somebody else to do the ferry flight tomorrow morning, and I could get fitted for a poncy-looking grey morning suit and topper this afternoon. The thought of a whole afternoon in the company of the luscious Georgina clouded my judgement, and I accepted.

"See you there then, 11.30."

Olivia rang off and I cornered Pickles to tell him I was taking a day off tomorrow.

Next day dawned bright and clear. I'd checked the synoptic meteorological chart before leaving the airport the previous day and was pretty confident of good weather. After breakfast I tried on the rented morning suit and admired myself in the mirror. I didn't want the other residents of the flats to see me in such a fancy-looking outfit so I carried the top hat and long-tailed jacket down to the car.

I'd anticipated heavy traffic west of Reading, but it was worse than I thought, causing me to arrive quarter of an hour late.

The ticket awaited me, and I ascended in the elevator to the fifth level. A young character in footman's outfit, complete with powdered wig and white stockings, relieved me of my ticket and ushered me through a numbered door.

"Mr Clapshaw," he pronounced with some difficulty in a phoney upper-class accent. Beyond the door, about a dozen people were drinking and talking animatedly. Six of them were women in their mid to late twenties, all trying to drown out each other's voices.

The male members of the species were ten or more years their senior.

Olivia spied me as I took a tentative step into the box.

"Oh good, you made it at last. I thought you might have changed your mind. Let me introduce you to everybody."

Another footman approached, with a tray of filled glasses.

"Champagne, sir?"

"Yeah, thanks. Cheers." I removed a glass and held it aloft. A rather bibulous looking fellow stumbled towards me.

"Gordon-Clarke, Rupert. Oops . . . sorry if I spilled some of my drink." He appeared to be having difficulty focusing his eyes as he extended a limp hand. "Jolly pleased to meet you. I race cars. Jolly pleased to meet you."

"I'm Guy Clapshaw. Pleased to meet you too."

"And this is Waterford, Tony. He doesn't do much but back horses, do you, old chap?"

An older fellow of about forty approached me and eyed me speculatively. "Tony Waterford, friend of the family. Haven't met anywhere before, have we?" He spoke in an indeterminable accent.

"I don't know. Might have. Where do you work?"

Waterford had already melted silently away before I had completed the question.

"I race cars," Rupert again volunteered, struggling to remain vertical. If he was a professional racing driver, I was a ballerina. I nodded politely and looked around for Georgina.

"I race cars. What do you do?" Rupert-bore persisted.

I said that must be great fun. I had just located Georgina in the centre of the crowd. Olivia joined us at that moment.

"What do you do then?" Rupert ended his sentence with a burp. He wavered a little as he waited for my answer.

I struggled to think of a hobby or interest.

"Well, I . . . er, don't do much."

"Gosh, how terribly boring. What do you do all day then?"

"Work mainly, then in the evenings I read or go out."

"Did you say work?" he enquired curiously.

"Yes, I did."

Rupert spun on his heels and nudged the back of the man behind. "Bert, you must meet Guy," he insisted.

"Guy, this is Bert Cherry-Downs. He plays cricket, don't you Bert? Quite good actually, played for I-Zingari."

Bert and I shook hands.

"Guy works!" Rupert announced. The other fellow's interest immediately perked up. He looked like a startled hen.

"Really? Gosh, that's jolly interesting." He turned to the girl beside him. "Guy works."

Several others turned round with polite interest to view the strange sight of somebody who worked for a living.

"Olivia works. Doesn't need to, but she does. Have you met her?" another girl enquired conversationally.

I told her we had met a few times. Then I moved away. I was more interested in establishing communications with the delectable Georgina.

"Hi, got any good tips for the first race?" I had managed to make my way through the other guests to a position beside her.

She looked at me like something the cat had brought in.

"Oh hello, it's you." She drew on a French cigarette as she spoke. "Didn't think you went in for this sort of thing. Bit plutocratic and all that, isn't it?"

"Not at all. I enjoy a day out as much as anybody. Makes a nice change to get away from work for a day, doesn't it?"

"Does it? I wouldn't know. I find the whole thing rather boring. Lot of smelly horses chasing each other round a race course for lots of money. Look, would you mind doing me a favour?"

"Certainly, what is it?"

"Grab me another drink, then come back here." She handed me her empty champagne glass. "I don't want to talk to that wimp Castairs, he's been trying to get into my pants the whole week."

I passed her a full glass and renewed my attempt at conversation.

"Not keen on horse racing, then?" I began, but she'd turned her attention to someone else. I found myself beside two other guests.

"Ever been to Ascot before?" a voice on my left enquired. It was Waterford.

"No, this is my first time. Always been too busy. What about you?"

"Oh I've been here more times than I can remember," he replied, directing his attention at a female on his left. "Used to ride a bit myself until the old war wound began playing up." He pointed at his right knee.

"Tony was in the army. Pay Corps, wasn't it?" the girl explained. Waterford glared at her irritably.

"Navy actually," he corrected. The girl retreated in confusion.

"Sounds interesting," I prompted. "Where did you serve?"

"Oh, Mediterranean mainly."

"How interesting, one of my school teachers served there. I think he was on destroyers. Rather dangerous, I believe?"

"Oh, incredibly so. German subs everywhere, shelling us with their six-inch guns."

The young girl's eyes widened as Tony Waterford wove a tale of what sounded suspiciously like humbug to me.

"What ship did you serve on?" I asked him.

"Oh, I can't remember all their names, *Ark Royal*, *Glorious*, we changed around so much."

"That's unusual."

"Yes, well, I was on the flying side mainly, had to go from aircraft carrier to aircraft carrier. Operational necessity I think we called it. Fighters mainly . . . oh, and torpedo bombers. Exciting though. Sunk a tanker off Malta once."

I resisted the urge to enquire whether it was one of ours. The afternoon was becoming interesting.

"Seafires?"

"What was that?"

"Seafires?" I pronounced slowly.

"Oh yes, saw plenty. Once the oil exploded there were plenty of fires. Chaps swimming in the water to get away. Flames everywhere."

A small crowd of admiring females began to congregate round the speaker,

148

eager to listen to anything vaguely interesting. I detected the unmistakable odour of bullshit and turned away.

"Enjoying yourself?" Olivia approached me with an anxious smile. I assured her I hadn't felt so relaxed for a long time.

"Been working too hard recently, forgot what fun's all about."

"The fun's just about to begin," she assured me. "Lunch is served, then the first race is at half past." She manoeuvred me to a seat beside her. I noticed Georgina had placed herself between two harmless-looking chinless wonders.

"Bit different from the box lunches on an Argonaut?" Olivia whispered to me as the smoked salmon arrived. At the other end of the table the erstwhile Seafire pilot was entertaining his companions with an account of torpedoing the *Tirpitz* single-handed.

At the conclusion of an excellent meal, everybody abruptly left through the door at the back of the room. I turned to Georgina, the only other remaining guest.

"Where's everybody gone?" I enquired.

"To place their bets." She eyed me with disdainful amusement. "Aren't you going to follow them?"

"I'd rather stay and talk to you than throw money away," I assured her. The compliment was met with a look of complete indifference as the first guests dribbled back to their seats to watch the first race.

The afternoon passed pleasantly enough until after the last race. Guests collected their handbags, binoculars or hats and prepared to leave. Olivia approached me.

"Going near Gatwick by any chance?" she enquired timidly.

"Going past it, yes, but I'm not calling in wearing this outfit. It'd be just my bad luck to get called out for a flight. Can you imagine the reaction?"

We chuckled at the vision of somebody flying an Argonaut in full morning suit.

"Mind if I come with you?" A few spots of rain had begun to fall as she spoke. "My mini's still in the staff carpark."

"That'll be fine," I assured her. "I'll get the car and meet you outside the grandstand. Save you getting wet. Give me ten minutes."

The pleasant prospect of Olivia's company for the tedious journey home was better than driving alone. I soon located my car and drove slowly past the grandstand. I recognised the taller form of Tony Waterford before I saw Olivia.

"Not going near town by any chance, I suppose?" He'd opened the door before I'd stopped. "The Aston-Martin broke down in Windsor and I'm due at a regimental dinner at my club this evening."

"No, but I could drop you off at East Croydon if that's any help?"

His face brightened as he assisted Olivia into the front seat. "Frightfully decent of you," he assured me, getting into the back.

By the time we'd completed a quarter of the journey, I'd developed a newfound respect for our uninvited passenger. He regaled us with accounts of his successful money-making ventures, most of the talking being directed at Olivia.

"Must be a gift of mine," he concluded. "Everything I touch seems to turn up trumps. I even backed that long shot in the third race. People come to me to make money for them."

"Olivia's father may be interested in a new chromium-plating process one of my companies has perfected," he continued. "Cheaper and more durable than the present process. Has enormous potential in the manufacturing industry, which of course Max is involved in."

Olivia displayed complete indifference to the conversation, while I listened spellbound.

The journey as far as East Croydon took slightly less than seventy-five minutes in light traffic. Waterford was recounting the details of a successful dive for gold in the Caribbean as I drew up outside the ticket office. I waited as he finished his account of the venture.

". . . so five of us shared half a million pounds, well actually I got slightly more than the others because my experience as a naval frogman was largely responsible for our success."

"You should make it in good time," I said, pointing at the station clock.

"In time for what?" he enquired blankly.

"Your regimental dinner. Trains depart for Victoria every fifteen minutes, you'll be there by 6.30."

"Oh yes, that's right, plenty of time." Waterford began ferreting in his pockets.

"Damn and blast, know what I've done?" His voice had dropped to a confidential whisper. Olivia gazed out the window as he spoke.

"What've you done?" I enquired, watching him pat his pockets.

"I've left my wallet in the Aston-Martin. Jolly embarrassing." He laughed. "I suppose you couldn't lend me a fiver to get me home?"

Olivia rolled her eyes skyward while Waterford floundered away in the back. I began to remove five £1 notes from my wallet.

"Couldn't possibly make that a tenner, could you?" he whispered urgently. "Got to play golf at Royal Berkshire tomorrow and might not be able to get near a bank. Pay you back, of course. I've got your address, haven't I? Oh, I say, that's awfully kind of you. Better hurry, there's a train due in a couple of minutes."

Waterford and my £10 disappeared into the station as I drove away.

"You got a bargain," Olivia announced five minutes later as we sped down the A-23.

"Whaddya mean? He'll pay me back. He was a naval officer."

"Rogues come in all shapes, sizes, sexes and denominations. Tony Waterford is a professional leach who borrows from Peter and never pays Paul. If you were fooled by his sales patter, you've learned a good lesson and it only cost you a tenner. Yes, you got a bargain; some people have paid thousands of pounds for the lesson you've just learned."

She was right. Rogues don't always have working-class accents and wear flashy suits. They come in all shapes and sizes.

CHAPTER SEVENTEEN
Problems

Next morning I returned to a disaster at work. The office door was still locked when I arrived at 9.30. The phone rang in the office while I was feeling for my key. It had stopped before I could get there and pick it up.

"Where the hell's Pickles?" I demanded as our two typists appeared outside the door. "He's supposed to open the office at 8.30."

The girls exchanged nervous glances. "I don't think young Richard's coming in today," the taller girl ventured nervously. I muttered angrily that somebody else should have opened the office.

"We arrived at 8.30, but the door was locked," she explained.

"Mr Warnup has the other key, but he doesn't come in till much later," her companion chipped in. "We don't have a key so we waited outside."

I decided to have a word with Pickles when he arrived. Punctuality was his strong point and it was totally out of character for him to be so late.

"He must be ill or something," I concluded. "Did he look all right yesterday?"

The women exchanged embarrassed glances as the phone rang. It was Denis.

"What the dickens happened to Pickles yesterday?" he demanded.

"Dunno, I'm trying to find out. I think he might be sick . . . hold on a minute."

Levitt and his nephew Nathan had strode into the room during this exchange. Nathan looked rather pleased with himself as Levitt confronted me.

"There have been one or two administrative changes around here in the last twenty-four hours," he announced solemnly. "Nathan reluctantly had to exercise his managerial authority yesterday."

"What does that mean in plain English?" I demanded impatiently as warning bells began to ring in my brain.

"Your young office boy, Richard whatever-his-name-is, was downright impertinent to Nathan yesterday."

"What happened?"

"Nathan accepted a very lucrative charter from a friend of his up north. We've done a lot of work for him in the past."

I cursed inwardly. Levitt was describing Alfie Cope of North East. "Your office boy told Nathan we couldn't do it."

"And could we?" I enquired with concern. Pickles did most of the aircraft scheduling and would have known whether we could spare an aircraft.

"We accept work first then decide whether we can do it or not," Nathan piped up.

"Not if it conflicts with our bread-and-butter business at weekends," I reminded him scathingly. "Horizon Holidays can guarantee us continuous year-round work. We can't afford to let them down. When was the flight scheduled?"

"Friday evening. North East have sixty passengers for Dublin, returning late Sunday evening."

"Pickles was probably right then, we can't possibly spare an aircraft for a whole weekend, that's our busiest time. Dublin is less than three hours' flying for us. Who did you say the charter was for?"

"North East Airlines, out of Newcastle. We've done work for them before."

"Yes, I feared it was probably them. We always work on a cash in advance basis with them," I reminded him. "Tell them we can't do it before Monday."

"Too late, I've telexed our acceptance."

"Is that what the row with Pickles was about?" I turned on Levitt angrily.

"He's a bit too clever for his young boots," the doctor tried to convince me. "He lacks the maturity to deal with matters of this nature."

"And Nathan of course possesses all the maturity and experience we need?" I suggested sarcastically.

"Well . . . er, yes. He has the social contacts and is in daily communication with other colleagues in the travel industry."

"Let me get this right," I pleaded. "Nathan has committed one of our aircraft to a three-hour charter, tying it up for the whole weekend?"

"More than that," Nathan protested. "The passengers are up at Leeds."

"Did you quote full revenue rates?" I demanded.

"Er . . . no, not yet. We haven't discussed the price yet."

"But you've committed us to the charter. No wonder Pickles got excited. Alfie Cope is a notoriously bad payer and we're going to have to sub-charter another airline to fly for us. That'll cost plenty and we probably won't get paid by Alfie. Let's get hold of Pickles quickly and get him to sort it out for us."

"I'm afraid that won't be possible," the doctor informed me gravely.

"Why not? Not ill, is he?"

"No, but Nathan had to dismiss him yesterday. He doesn't work for the company any more."

Angry sounds from the telephone in my hand reminded me Denis was still waiting on the line.

"You'd better get in here quickly. We've got a bit of a problem on our hands," I told him and rang off. I faced Levitt and his nephew angrily.

"You're telling me Nathan came into the office yesterday for a fleeting visit, put our weekend flying programme into complete confusion, then fired young Richard — the only person who could put it right?"

"Nathan can put matters right," Levitt announced stiffly. "He's happy to accept additional responsibilities . . . with a commensurate increase in salary, of course."

"Nathan couldn't organise a piss-up in a brewery," I informed him. "If he tries to run the office, things will dissolve into total confusion. He's already proved it several times. I'll get hold of Pickles . . . er, Richard, and persuade him to come back."

"There's no way I'd agree to him coming back," Levitt insisted, turning to his nephew for reassurance. Nathan nodded obediently.

"Without him, we'll have to work twice as hard," I cautioned. "And we'll need additional office staff to replace him. We'll never find anybody else with his blend of skills."

"Be that as it may, we are not having Master Bransom back. The company is better off without him. We'll make this a first-rate airline."

I looked across the tarmac area at the various Vikings, Dakotas, Wayfarers and our two Argonauts parked to the north.

"I reckon Richard Bransom could have made this a blooming good airline," I muttered angrily to myself.

Denis, Tony and I discussed the latest bombshell to hit the office. We were unanimous in our opinion that Pickles must be reinstated. Two of us went round to his mother's house.

"He's moved up to London," she explained. "Said he wants to get away from Gatwick and aviation for a while."

We returned to the office and began sorting out the matter of the Dublin charter. Denis suggested positioning the aircraft on Friday night to do the evening Athens flight. Meanwhile I tried to contact Alfie Cope to remind him of our preference for cash in advance. He was unavailable whenever I called.

We repeated our instructions to Nathan never to poke his nose into the office again. Somebody diplomatically pointed out to him that his real forte was in the field of public relations. He readily agreed to our suggestion to concentrate his energies on the social aspect of the air charter business.

The Dublin charter went off all right but involved another three hours of non-revenue flying. I landed back at Gatwick just in time to hand the aircraft over to the Athens crew. Denis met me at the bottom of the steps.

"Zucher senior's sniffing around, worried his precious passengers will be delayed."

"Shouldn't be a problem tonight. Both aircraft are going well," I assured him.

"Hmm . . . well, let's hope it continues. We really need one of us permanently in the office to monitor things. The trouble is we can't afford to take a pilot off the roster at weekends, which is when problems occur."

Both flights departed on time and Zucher left the airport a slightly happier man.

Saturday's flying programme went off without a hitch but Sunday was a bit tense. Denis positioned an empty Argonaut to Dublin on Sunday afternoon and collected the Leeds passengers. The aeroplane arrived back at Gatwick an hour before the scheduled Mallorca flight at 9pm. We had somehow managed to complete every flight without disruptions, but any delay would have had an accumulative effect on the whole weekend's flying.

After further discussion with the other two flying directors, it was agreed that one of us would man the office at all times to handle everyday administrative matters. Since most of the revenue flying was done at weekends, this meant we would have to do two jobs simultaneously.

The first week went fine. Two freight charters came up for the DC-3 and a last-minute sub-charter for seventy stranded British United passengers cropped up on Wednesday. We tried advertising for an office manager to replace Pickles, but nobody suitable applied.

I had agreed to man the office on Friday and Saturday while Tony and Denis did the Greek flights.

Jock Bryce, BAC's chief test pilot, phoned on Friday afternoon to tell me they were publicly unveiling the 200 series stretched One-Eleven.

"Eighty-nine seats in the all-economy configuration," he informed me. "Just what Air Links needs. Want to come and have a look? It's only forty minutes away by car."

"I'd like that very much. When do you suggest?" I replied.

"We're having a final design conference over the weekend, tidying up all the small details. You'd really get a good idea of what the new machine's capable of if you came to that. I'll phone you back and let you know when it is. Okay?" He rang off.

I was down at the newsagents in the main terminal when I noticed a familiar silver-grey Jaguar pull up outside.

"Looking for somebody?" I asked the elegantly dressed Georgina Noble. She gave me a surprised look, obviously not recognising me.

"Just picking somebody up." She dismissed me with a contemptuous wave. "Won't be more than . . . oh, here she comes now."

Olivia had suddenly appeared on the kerb beside me. She greeted me with a big smile.

"Off for the rest of the day?" I asked enviously.

"Birthday party tonight then off to Basle tomorrow," she explained. "Want to come to my party tonight?"

Out of the corner of my eye, I noticed her elder sister glancing at an expensive watch. My mind raced; a party would be another opportunity of getting to know Georgina better.

"Love to. What time does it start?"

"Seven thirty, and it's informal — that means casual."

"Okay, fine, I'll be there," I promised, eyeing Georgina as she slid back into the sports car.

"Oh good. I'll enjoy that, and so will you, I promise. See you there then."

Her words were lost as the Jaguar's engine snarled into life. Georgina pulled her sister into the passenger seat and roared off.

I left the office at 5.30, after giving the switchboard operator an after-hours number where she could contact me.

Olivia's birthday party was peopled by the same sort of folk I'd met at Ascot. I thought I saw Tony Waterford when I first arrived, but if I did, he remained elusive for the remainder of the evening.

I'd arrived a few minutes after eight o'clock. Olivia's parents welcomed me.

"Good to meet you again, Olivia tells me you all had a great time at Ascot," Max Noble greeted me. I confirmed it had been a most enlightening experience.

"Only lost ten pounds on the whole day and your daughter tells me it was worth every penny," I assured him obliquely.

"You remember Rupert Gordon-Clark?" Olivia's mother interrupted to introduce me to the man I recognised from a previous afternoon. I smiled at Rupert.

"Yes, of course I remember him. Famous racing driver, isn't he?" Rupert's brow furrowed into a puzzled frown as he struggled to place me.

"What did you say your name was? Guy? I'm sure I met somebody with a name like that recently, now where was it?"

"Ascot, a week ago."

"Aah yes, now I remember you," he smiled and grasped my hand. I paid him scant attention, for I had just detected sister Georgina slinking across the room in a shiny sheath dress that clung to the curves of her body like shrink wrap.

"You're the fellow who worked!" Rupert suddenly remembered, but my eyes and attention were fastened on the approaching Georgina.

"You're looking incredibly beautiful," I complimented her. She looked at me curiously as if questioning my right to be present.

"We met this afternoon when you were picking your sister up," I explained.

"Oh yes, I think I remember. What on earth are you doing here?" She asked the question in a way that made me feel like a serf who'd ventured in from the kitchen garden.

"Guy and I met at Ascot with you," Rupert interrupted. "Jolly interesting chap. He works."

Georgina demonstrated her complete indifference by reaching for a cigarette and lighting it soundlessly. She drew in deep lungfuls of smoke, which she then exhaled over us like a traveller spraying midges with insect repellent.

Olivia arrived to rescue me from Rupert's inane rambling.

"How's the little aeroplane going?" she enquired sweetly, leading me by the hand onto the patio.

"You mean the DC-3? Okay, I suppose, there's still plenty of work for it."

"No, silly, the little four-seater you keep at Biggin. I was admiring it in the hangar the other day."

"It's going fine, haven't used it much recently though. Too darned busy. What about you, still learning to fly?"

"Mm, yes, of course. I've got fifteen hours now, including five solo. My instructor says I'll start learning navigation on my next lesson. I'm really looking forward to that."

I nearly jokingly told her to let me know when she got her private pilot's licence so we could use her for ferry flying. I'm glad I didn't, it would have been unkind to raise her hopes unnecessarily.

She had almost finished telling me the details of her latest lesson when her elder sister interrupted.

"I'm trying to get John Deterding to notice me, he's the fellow in the blue shirt," she whispered to her sister, as she gestured towards a young fellow in his mid-twenties. "But that Wendy bloody Smythe is dominating his attention, and I can't get a word in edgeways. She's looking at him as if butter wouldn't melt in her mouth, the little bitch."

"Who is he to attract you so strongly?" Olivia enquired.

"One of the banking family and absolutely loaded. I've been waiting to meet him since he came back from university. He came in the most gorgeous car, a convertible Aston-Martin. Absolutely beautiful."

"People with Aston-Martins don't impress me at the moment," I commented to Olivia, who giggled. Her sister turned on me angrily.

"That's because your dull-as-ditchwater lifestyle doesn't run to exciting things like fast cars and horses and boats. Nine to five, five days a week and two days off at the weekend to go and watch the local football team. I don't know why you trouble to come here with such a chip on your shoulder. You're completely out of your depth socially."

I realised the chances of striking up any form of relationship with the beautiful but spoiled Georgina tonight were probably slightly worse than hell freezing over. Olivia and two others turned their backs and walked away as the elder sister ground her cigarette out on the carpet.

"Alcohol must have short-circuited her brain, I'm afraid." Olivia had come back with a glass of champagne, and we returned to the subject of learning to fly.

The party got better as the night wore on. Georgina passed out in the lake, where two house staff quickly retrieved her and whisked her away. The object of her attention joined us shortly after that, and proved to be a most entertaining character with a fund of amusing stories from three years at an American university.

It was past 3am before the party began to thin out.

"Come and have coffee if you don't mind drinking it in the kitchen," Olivia invited five of us. We retired to the back of the house to talk animatedly for another hour. Olivia's father must have detected the aroma of good coffee, because he joined us, armed with a bottle of very old port. The conversation turned to horse racing and he told me about his latest horse.

"Trouble is, horses and women are probably the most expensive pastimes a man can indulge in," he concluded. "Don't get involved with them if you can't afford them."

My suggestion that aeroplanes would lie in a close third place aroused his curiosity.

"I thought you said you weren't a gambling man?" he remarked, filling our glasses. I explained I didn't gamble on horses because all my assets were tied up in a fleet of old aircraft. I told him about the struggle to survive in independent aviation. He listened with interest, then told me how he'd made his fortune in the electrical appliance business. When electrical kitchen devices first came on the market in the fifties, Max Noble's factories had been there to supply them.

"Never put all your eggs in one basket, though," he cautioned. "Some of the bigger retail stores placed enormous orders with me, forcing me to neglect the smaller shops. That way they monopolised the market. Then once they'd done that, they demanded bigger discounts. Nearly drove me out of business in the early days."

"Air Links is too small for that to happen," I assured him. "The state airlines take most of the business, and we live off what's left."

As daylight broke, I departed with the last of the guests. It was Saturday, and my turn to man the office again. As I passed Biggin, I decided to take the Proctor to work. It hadn't flown for several weeks and probably needed the exercise.

Saturday morning in summertime was always an exhilarating time at the airport. Hordes of happy holidaymakers, who could normally only afford to take their two weeks' holiday at Blackpool or Southend, found they were able to fly to the Continent or Costa Brava, thanks to charter flights.

One of our Argonauts had already arrived back from Greece as I let myself into the office. Ground staff had wheeled steps up to the front and rear doors, and the first smiling sunburned faces emerged. I phoned down to the traffic office with the details for the next flight's documentation. Denis and crew arrived as I hung up.

"Good flight?" I enquired conversationally. He assured me everything had gone like well-oiled clockwork.

"Both aircraft are performing splendidly, I reckon we can get at least another year out of them before we'll need to think about winter overhauls. I wish Levitt would keep his nose out of the operational side and allow us to run it properly."

I voiced the opinion that the prestige of owning a jet airline was probably blinding the doctor to the other important aspects of the operation.

"And by the way, Jock Bryce phoned yesterday and invited us to pop over to Weybridge to look at the 200 series One-Eleven prototype. They're unveiling it to the press on Monday."

"When did he suggest?"

"Didn't say, but he thought we might like to meet up with their boffins to discuss what the new model can do. He's phoning back some time during the weekend. Want me to phone you when I hear?"

"Oh Christ, that's just what we didn't need." Denis had suddenly rushed to the window. I followed his gaze to where the second Argonaut, Hotel India, had landed and was entering the apron area. The number-four engine was not operating; the propeller was stationary in the feathered position.

"Wonder what's gone wrong?" he queried. I phoned our chief engineer at home and told him we had a problem on our hands.

"Okay, I'll get the situation under control," he promised. "If it's an engine change, we'll pull an engine out of the spares aircraft and get it over here as soon as possible. Once I've spoken to the crew, I can assess how serious the problem is."

Down on the tarmac, the captain and co-pilot were talking to the tarmac engineer. As I phoned down to the apron area, the door behind me opened to admit two people.

"How serious is the problem on Hotel India?" I asked him.

"Dunno at the moment, they're still talking to the crew. Phone back in five minutes."

I put the phone down and turned to Denis. "Nobody knows anything yet, but I think I'll alert Air Couriers of a potential problem," I told him.

He glanced up at the wall chart. "The Basle flight's due out at eleven and we'll need ground engineers to get it away before we can really do anything more. We'll swap aircraft over, then once the flight's on its way, we'll take a look at the engine. There's no point in having both aircraft grounded."

"Problems with one of the aircraft?" the elder Zucher's voice enquired behind me.

I spun round and was faced with the travel agent and our commercial manager.

"Routine maintenance on one of the aircraft," I assured the travel agent.

"We've changed over aircraft for convenience."

"What do you mean by minor maintenance? Has something gone wrong?"

"Engine failure, nothing to worry about, these planes can fly quite easily on three engines," Nathan assured him.

The travel agent reacted with some concern at this piece of news. "Will this delay a flight?" he enquired anxiously.

Nathan unfortunately beat me to the reply. "No, nothing to worry about, we've got another aircraft we use for spare parts, so we'll pull an engine out of . . ."

"We've got a back-up aircraft which will do the next flight for us," I hurriedly interrupted Nathan. "Meanwhile our engineering staff will take a look at the other machine and fix whatever's wrong with it. Could be something very trivial."

Zucher departed looking even more concerned. I turned to Denis anxiously.

"Why did he have to turn up at a time like this?" I demanded. "He never was particularly happy with our aircraft, now he's downright worried. What's he doing here anyway, and why's Nathan here on a Sunday? He should be playing golf or something."

"A group of travel agents expressed interest in seeing our operation. Nathan recognised it as a good excuse for a nosh-up and invited them down to watch us in action. He thought he'd better include Horizon Holidays in the invitation, and old Zucher accepted. Pity we had to have an engine failure on the day the eyes of most of the travel agents were upon us."

Five minutes later Tony appeared, demanding to know what all the excitement was over the engine shut-down. "Olympic's engineers in Athens topped up the oil levels on the turn-round and must've replaced one of the caps incorrectly, 'cause when we crossed France I noticed number four was using more oil than the rest. The co-pilot went back and had a look and reported oil running back over the cowl, so we shut it down an hour out of here."

"Why didn't you detect it earlier and land somewhere en route?"

"Because it was dark for the first half of the flight and we couldn't see the engine very well. And as for landing en route for a drop of oil, why go to the additional time and expense of an extra landing? The aircraft was performing okay, and I only shut the engine down when the oil quantity approached the cautionary band. Joe Phillips has confirmed the oil cap wasn't correctly replaced and says there was still sufficient oil in the reservoir when he checked it. He's topped it up to the level and checked all the caps are secure. He says it might be better in future if we check the oil caps on the walk-around check."

The apparent engine failure had in fact been a precautionary shut-down with no damage to the engine. Unfortunately, the incident had done irreparable damage to the public relations side of our airline.

The remainder of the day passed uneventfully. As I finished talking to the incoming crew, Olivia Noble arrived for her Basle flight. She looked rather serious. I waved her a warm good morning.

"Great birthday party, but I wish I hadn't stayed so long," I remarked. "Enjoyed myself immensely." Her face lit up at this news.

"Did you really? I was worried you may have felt a little left out."

"On the contrary, I enjoyed talking to your friends, especially your dad. Sounds like he's had an interesting life."

"You mean office boy ending up as chairman of the board?" Olivia's elder sister interrupted.

I eyed her warily, anticipating another insult.

"Look . . . er . . . sorry if I was bloody rude last night," she said. "I was, wasn't I?" She looked at me defiantly as she spoke. "I probably was rude. I got a bit sloshed after being stood up by a boyfriend."

My heart leaped with excitement. Georgina Noble exuded an animal-like allure that most men found irresistible, and I was no exception. I ignored the ringing phone as I beamed at her.

"Sorry, but I suppose I am rather boring compared to your other friends," I mumbled. "Anyway, I know it was a good party 'cause I had to come straight from there to work." I floundered in my attempts to sound witty and amusing.

Olivia interrupted by passing the phone to me. "Sir George Edwards calling from Weybridge."

"Hello, Sir George. Yes, I spoke to him yesterday and he told me you've got the prototype on display."

"We'd like to show it to you. Dr Levitt told me you were a bit sceptical of some of our claims for the new 200 series," the plane-maker volunteered.

"Not sceptical, but I would like to know a few more facts and figures before committing us to a million pounds worth of aeroplane," I protested.

"Fine, that's why I've phoned. We're holding a press conference on Monday, bringing all the aviation correspondents out to Weybridge to look over the new aircraft then drink a lot of our free booze."

"Dunno if I could make Monday. I've put myself down for the Genoa flight, and there's nobody else available to . . .," I began.

"No problem. Monday will be a bun fight. It'd be better to come over during the weekend, when things are quieter."

"Weekends are our busiest time," I explained. "Everybody else is flying and I'm left holding the fort. Two other directors would like to see the aircraft, but they're both flying over most of the weekend."

"Could you come over for a couple of hours?" Edwards suggested. "You'd get a lot of interesting information."

An idea had suddenly occurred to me. "It'd have to be now," I informed him. "While there's a lull between flights. Our next arrival's due here at four. How about if I pop over now?"

"It'd take you an hour and a half in this weekend traffic," Edwards announced regretfully. "We'd need two hours to show you all the facts and figures, and even that's pushing things a bit fast."

"I'll fly over," I explained to him. "I'll take off as soon as our Basle flight's departed. That's at eleven, so I should be with you by half past."

The plane-maker agreed to have somebody meet me when I arrived. I turned back to Olivia.

"Make sure you get away on time. I've got to fly over to Weybridge to look at a new aircraft while you're away."

"Who's Sir George Edwards?" the elder sister interrupted abruptly. "Have I heard that name before somewhere?"

"Probably not," I assured her. "Pretty dull character really. Nine to five, six days a week office boy who ended up as chairman of the company. Dull as ditchwater — bit out of your social circles really."

Georgina looked at me strangely for maybe fifteen seconds before exploding into peels of uninhibited laughter.

I phoned Denis and told him I was off to Weybridge in an hour if he wanted to come. He groaned wearily and said he'd only just got to bed.

"Tony and I can go another day, so why don't you report back on what you think of it?" he suggested.

I waited till the Basle flight was off chocks before locking the office and walking across to the light aircraft park. Georgina Noble had questioned me curiously about the Proctor while I was waiting.

"Can anybody own an aircraft and just fly off anywhere?" she enquired. "Don't you need a permit or something?"

"Just a pilot's licence, but they're easy to get. Ask your sister, she's getting hers at the moment."

She said something disdainful about having to spend a lot of time reading books and manuals. I told her a bit more about the aeroplane as we walked across the tarmac.

"You mean we could just get in and fly away to Deauville or Paris?" she asked.

"Well . . . er . . . yes. I'd have to work out the route to fly and do a few calculations, but basically this is a flying motorcar," I said, gesturing at the aircraft. "Which reminds me, I'm in a bit of a hurry to get to Weybridge and back again before your sister's flight returns at four o'clock. Want to come along for the ride?"

She accepted hesitantly and I assisted her up onto the wing then into the front passenger seat. I ran through the checks and we were soon on our way.

The British Aircraft Corp's aerodrome lay in the centre of the old pre-war Brooklands motor-racing track. Its connections with flying went back more than half a century to the years before the First World War, when eager young men like Alliott Verdon Roe, Tommy Sopwith, the Pashley brothers, Frederick Handley-Page and others flew their frail machines from the site.

Now, in the early 1960s, lines of BAC-111 and VC-10 jet airliners waiting to be test-flown served as a barometer of how far aviation had progressed in a mere sixty years.

Two scientific-looking gentlemen greeted me as I stepped down from the wing of my aircraft. Georgina had reached the ground before me and was breathlessly recounting the excitement of having flown somewhere rather than going by surface.

"Everybody should have their own aircraft," she enthused as I introduced her. I decided not to say anything about preaching to the choir.

"John Tiplady from the design office, and this is my assistant, Mr Jefferies," one of them replied. "Delighted you could pop over today. We understand from Sir George that you can only spare a couple of hours, so we'll take you straight to the aircraft." He motioned for us to climb aboard a mini-bus for the short journey to the hangars.

The new model One-Eleven was in the centre of the first hangar. Lights in the roof emphasised its new paint and shiny metal. George Edwards waited to greet us.

"Delighted you could come along too," he assured Georgina, although I detected he must have wondered what the dickens she was doing there. He led us towards the aircraft, pointing out salient features as we approached.

"We've retained the integral airstairs and auxiliary power unit in the tail," he explained. "The most significant changes are a nine-foot fuselage plug, increasing the seating capacity to over eighty, and production versions will have the new up-rated engines. This, in turn, has resulted in an eight percent increase in maximum take-off weight, and we've also managed a slight increase in range. Mr Tiplady will run through the operating economics after I've shown you some of the new features of the 200."

We spent the next half hour looking at galleys, hat racks, various types of seats and finally the cockpit. A bored Georgina sat herself in a first-class seat while we progressed up the cabin.

"Pity Jock or one of the others couldn't give you a better rundown on flight-deck instrumentation, but I'll do my best," Edwards apologised. "As you can see, it's a two-man cockpit with all controls and instruments duplicated for both pilots. Navigation equipment will be to Category Three approach minima, eventually allowing landings and take-offs in all but the very worst weather. We're liaising with the Royal Aircraft establishment at Farnborough over all new developments and will incorporate them as and when they come out."

I sidled into the captain's seat. The One-Eleven's cockpit was extremely well laid out, with all controls within easy reach of both pilots. Ample space had been left for flight bags, clip-boards, maps, approach charts and meal trays.

"We've hit the right formula once again with this model," Sir George assured me. "BUA, Eagle, Alitalia, Scandinavian Airlines System, American Airlines, Trans Australian, and even New Zealand National Airways are contemplating it as a Viscount replacement, which of course it is. Once the market moves, we'll initially be producing four aircraft a month, increasing to meet the demand."

Tiplady then led us to his office in the corner of the hangar, where facts and figures about the plane's capabilities had been collated. Georgina remained in the aircraft, smoking and looking extremely bored.

"Basically, your present flight times will be halved," he began. "Normal cruise is Mach point seven one — that's about 450 knots, which is almost twice the speed of your Argonauts.° With the new higher-rated engines you'll be able to operate Athens to London with a full load on a plus-fifteen day . . ."

"In less than three hours," Sir George interjected. "And above the worst of the weather. Fuel consumption in terms of seat per mile costs is lower than you're presently experiencing. That's based on 1000 hours' flying a year, which is a trifle conservative. We anticipate you'll easily exceed this figure when word gets round that you're operating jets. There'll be quite a bonus there."

Tiplady showed me various graphs relating to the aircraft's take-off performance.

"Take-off from one or two airports like Palma or Verona could be a slight problem in the middle of the day," I suggested, referring to the take-off graph. Tiplady hastily assured me the newer engines would soon have provision for water injection to further increase their power.

At the end of their two-hour sales drive, BAC had convinced me their 200 series One-Eleven would elevate Air Links from a charter company into the major airline league. I told them how I felt, adding I'd convey this sentiment to my fellow directors.

It was three o'clock when we collected a sleepy Georgina from the One-Eleven and bused back to our aircraft. Noise prevented much conversation as we flew the short distance back to Gatwick.

"Will you buy that new aeroplane?" she asked curiously, after we'd disembarked and were back in the Air Links office.

"Probably, but I'll have to get the okay from the other directors," I replied. "There's the small matter of finding a few thousand pounds for the lease. We haven't paid for our present aircraft yet."

She seemed to become quite interested when I told her this, so I gave her an approximation of the costs of running two old Argonauts and a Dakota. After two minutes her interest waned. "You fellows must be raking the money in," was her final comment.

° The speed of modern jet aircraft is measured as a percentage of the speed of sound; Mach one is the speed of sound.

CHAPTER EIGHTEEN
More Problems

The younger Zucher phoned on Monday morning and asked to speak to Pickles. He seemed rather concerned about something, and when I told him Pickles didn't work for us any longer, he paused for a rather long time.

"Where's he gone then? He never said anything about leaving," he protested. "Last time I spoke to him he was working out quotations for Dad for our winter sports flights. That was only about . . . oh, say a week ago. When did he leave?"

"About then. I was away, but when I came back he'd left."

"Did he say where he was going? Why did he leave?"

I dodged most of the questions by repeating I'd been away when Pickles left. Young Zucher suddenly rang off rather abruptly.

This and a few other factors probably resulted in the letter we received three days later from Horizon Holidays, advising us that as from next week, our weekly Thursday flights to Genoa were cancelled.

"That's seven hours' flying a week we've lost," Tony complained. "Wonder who could have got it? I'll ask around."

All the other charter operators around Gatwick vehemently denied having taken the job off us. I reminded the other directors that Horizon had a contractual obligation to fly with us, but Levitt pointed out it would be ludicrous to contemplate legal action against our best client.

"Some fast-talking commercial manager has probably convinced Zucher his airline can do the job cheaper and better. It'll only take a couple of breakdowns to convince him his customers are miles better off with us," he said.

"The elder Zucher seems obsessed with the thought of his passengers being stranded somewhere and getting to their holiday destination late," I admitted. "Pickles was good at convincing him how reliable our aircraft were. He told him about the Rolls engines and all that sort of stuff. Pity he's not around now."

Nobody could fathom why Horizon had switched to another charter operator in preference to us.

Next morning we received written notification of cancellation of one of the Friday evening flights to Greece. Denis phoned the travel agent in an attempt to discuss the matter with somebody, but was icily informed "there was nobody available to speak to him". Our weekly flying hours were now slashed by another ten hours. Our costings had been based on an assured total of 4000 hours per year, but if this figure dropped, our cost per flying hour could well rise to an uneconomic figure.

"We must find other work," I urged. "That's the job of the commercial manager. Let's get him to do it."

"Might be better to keep him out of this. Last time he found us work we lost money," Denis reminded me. "One of us can phone round the big tour operators — Arrowsmiths, Powell-Duffryn, Clarksons. Surely they must have a bit of ad hoc charter work available. What about the Ministry of Defence? Plenty of people fly for them."

Over the next week we contacted every potential client we could think of. Lieutenant Colonel Fitzwilliam at the Ministry of Defence told Tony he hadn't included our name in the list of charter operators available for government work because we'd always been too busy. "When we charter somebody, we usually need to go at short notice, so any preliminary arrangements need to have been settled in advance," he explained. "Costs, handling details, catering — all that sort of thing."

Tony informed him that we now had increased availability as a result of future proposed expansion and would be happy to take on trooping charters for the ministry. Fitzwilliam listened and promised to keep us in mind. Most of the other large travel agents gave us the run-around treatment. There was a definite reluctance to charter Air Links, but nobody seemed anxious to tell us why.

It all came clear when I spoke to a Clarksons' man one evening after a long hot tiring day of administrative work. Somebody called out to me as I walked past the restaurant bar area on the way to the car park.

"You look like a man in need of a long cool drink," Clarksons' senior sales rep informed me.

"Thanks, that's probably the first bit of common sense I've heard today. I'll have a McEwen's."

He gestured to the barman, who returned with two brimming pint glasses.

"Cheers and good health." I raised my glass.

"Busy?" he asked, starting the usual verbal sparring.

"Can't complain, always busy at this time of year. Mid-week's a bit slack though. Got any work you want us to do?" I parried.

"Naagh, sorry, not at the moment. I noticed both your aircraft seem to sit around a lot. Bit unusual at this time of year?"

"We're going through a period of change at the moment," I explained. "Can't say anything yet but next year should see some rather dramatic changes if everything eventuates." I detected a flicker of interest in his eyes.

"Bad luck about the other day, but I thought your fellow handled it bloody badly, to be perfectly frank."

"What do you mean?" I enquired with concern.

He suddenly became rather coy. I pressed him to continue.

"Well, it's none of my business, you understand, but it was unfortunate that one of your aircraft had to suffer engine failure on the very day half the travel agents in Southern England paid you a visit."

I agreed with him, but pointed out such things were part of the aviation scene. "And, in fact, it proved to be a bit of a non-event." I explained how the incorrectly fitted oil-filler cap had resulted in a precautionary shut-down.

The Clarksons' man listened sympathetically.

"Pity your commercial manager didn't know that when he tried to explain the problem away."

"Whaddya mean?" I demanded.

"He gave us a long lecture on how your aircraft often fly on three engines, then he went into a long dissertation on the problems of operating old aircraft. He even said you used wartime Spitfire engines in your DC-4s."

"Well, he's partly right. They are Merlins . . . but we don't pull 'em out of old Spitfires," I assured him, wondering where I could find Nathan and strangle him.

"Yes, well it's none of my business, but I reckon your fellow did more damage to your company's image in an hour and a half than any form of propaganda from your competitors. Old Zucher from Horizon Holidays wasn't too impressed either, he left halfway through without speaking to anybody. Looked absolutely furious. He's one of your customers, isn't he?"

I admitted we flew for him, but didn't disclose his was the mainstream of our business. We had put all our eggs in one basket when we committed ourselves to flying exclusively for him summer and winter. Now we were paying the penalty for our indiscretion.

The conversation then drifted onto other topics, as one or two other members of the travel industry joined us.

I finally got away about eight o'clock and phoned Denis.

"I think I know the reason for our cancelled flights," I began. "It sounds like Zucher's suffered a loss of confidence in us following our recent engine shutdown."

Denis listened in silence as I repeated the gist of my conversation with the Clarksons' rep.

"Nathan is a blooming nuisance around customers," he concluded. "Pickles would have been the best one to sort this mess out. He'd never have let it escalate to this point. Anyway, he's not around any longer so we're going to have to convince Horizon Holidays we're a reliable and safe airline, especially if we intend to get One-Elevens next year. Okay, I'll phone them tomorrow."

A roomful of long faces greeted my arrival in the office at eleven the next morning. Levitt, Wilson, Tony and Denis eyed me dolefully.

"Problems?" I enquired. "Did you manage to speak to somebody at Horizon?"

Denis's reply was to hand me a single typewritten page on Horizon's notepaper. The message was short and to the point.

Dear Sirs,
Horizon Holidays/Air Links Flights, Summer/Winter 1964
We wish to advise you that following a recent market survey, with effect

from June 11, we will not be using the services of your airline to transport our clients to their holiday destinations.

Alternative arrangements have been made to convey them aboard modern four-engined jet aircraft.

Yours faithfully . . .

The letter bore an indecipherable signature.

"Now I can see why you all look so po-faced," I remarked, handing the letter back to Denis. "Have you spoken to anybody at Horizon yet?"

"I've tried. Everybody's tried, but as soon as we give our name, the switchboard operator tells us there's nobody in the office who can speak to us."

"Did you ask for Zucher?"

"Yes, I even tried to get hold of the son, but he wasn't available either. Somebody's got in ahead of us and taken away our business, but I don't know who it can be. Who do we know with four-engined jet equipment?"

"Nobody has jets except the scheduled airlines like BOAC, and Horizon couldn't afford their fares. Couldn't be a foreign operator like Bal Air or Martin's Air Charter, could it?"

"Naagh, they don't have jet aircraft."

Nobody could think of a charter airline with jets.

Levitt was the first to recover from the shock. "We'd better get hold of a good lawyer," he said, dialling a London number as he spoke. "Unless we find alternative work for our aircraft, we're going to run out of cash fairly quickly. I think I know just the right firm to handle this matter for us."

The question of the mystery airline was resolved two mornings later, when the Genoa passengers reported for their flight.

We watched from our office doorway as their tour guide directed them across the terminal concourse area towards the lines of check-in counters. Proceeding past the Dan-Air, BUA, Caledonian and overseas counters, they carried on and lined up at British European Airways.

We exchanged puzzled glances.

"Zucher must've increased his prices dramatically," Tony commented. "The cheapest scheduled airfare to Genoa is more than the complete package holiday."

"Could they have got a group discount?" I suggested. Denis shook his head, vehemently assuring us international agreements forbade scheduled state airlines from under-cutting each other.

We watched as BEA traffic staff checked the eighty passengers through departure formalities. As the last passenger disappeared into the departure lounge, we hurried back to the office to see what type of aircraft they were travelling on. Down on the tarmac, a ground tug had entered the manoeuvring area with a de Havilland Comet IV jetliner in tow. The aircraft passed in front of our two Argonauts, which were parked in the overnight park, and entered the apron area.

"It is BEA!" Denis announced indignantly as the streamlined black nose

approached us head-on. The tug driver manoeuvred left onto the stand area, revealing the company name on the side of the fuselage.

"British Air Tours?" we chorused together. The aircraft slowed to a stop, and as we watched, several ground staff with the BEA logo on the backs of their white uniforms wheeled boarding steps up to the doors.

"Who are they?" somebody queried.

Nobody knew, but we all admitted having seen their aircraft here on previous occasions. Discreet enquiries in the Greasy Spoon at lunch time revealed absolutely nothing, so finally we decided to adopt the direct approach. We found the BEA station manager's office and knocked on his door. A voice bade us enter, and we found an office similar in size to ours, with two uniformed staff seated either side of a desk by the window. Denis introduced us.

"Nice to meet you, my name is Rutherford," one of them replied politely. "I'm the station manager here. This is Mr Hancock, my assistant. Now what can I do for you gentlemen?"

We wondered what was going on exactly," Denis began. "We've noticed your Comets coming in here several times recently and . . ."

"Not our Comets," Rutherford was quick to correct him. "Air Tours. They are a completely different company. We only handle them here."

"And supply the aircraft and crews," I protested. "You claim they're a different company, but they're obviously backed by your corporation."

"It wouldn't be appropriate for me to comment on the status of Air Tours, except to say that if you poked around, I think you'd discover pretty quickly that the aircraft they are using are no longer a part of the corporation's fleet.

Likewise, the aircrew are assigned to Air Tours and no longer work for BEA," Rutherford replied slowly and carefully.

We plied him with a few more questions, but learned virtually nothing. The answer to the mystery was revealed to me next morning, while I waited in the queue at the local butcher's shop.

The owner of the business was a florid-faced, rather loud-mouthed individual, who liked to boast he knew everything going on around Gatwick. I only had to listen to learn all about Air Tours.

"All a matter of common sense really, darlin'," he informed a Caledonian ground hostess at the front of the queue. "I always said when the independent airlines began stealing passengers away from the state airlines, something had to be done about it." He paused to weigh a string of pork sausages, while I waited anxiously for him to continue.

"They couldn't reduce their fares to compete with the likes of Dan-Air or Air Links, so what did they do?" He paused dramatically to wrap the sausages. "They did what I said they should have done years ago. Know what that is?"

The Caledonian hostess shook her head and reached into her purse.

"Two-and-eleven-pence, thank you. Now who's next?"

Next in line was a Dan-Air traffic clerk.

"Pound of stewing steak, is it?" The butcher reached into the fridge for a large bowl. "Now where was I?"

"They did what you said they should have done," I ventured. "Years ago."

"Oh yes, thank you squire. Now as I was saying, the independents were taking passengers away from the state corporations. So they formed their own charter airline, didn't they?"

I nodded to encourage him to continue.

"They formed their own charter airline. Anything else? Just a pound of stewing steak, was it? Yes . . . well, as I was saying, they formed their own charter subsidiary and killed two birds with one stone. Want to know why?"

Unfortunately the Dan-Air clerk wasn't interested and paid for his purchases and departed. Next in line was the wife of a Dan-Air Ambassador captain, wanting two pounds of streaky bacon.

"How did they kill two birds with one stone?" she demanded suspiciously.

"Ha-haah, that's where they've been so clever," the butcher revealed. "In one fell swoop they've solved two problems. The first is the question of the missing passengers; they lure them back to fly with their charter subsidiary. Now the other problem is what do they do with their older aircraft when they become out of date? Do they sell them off to the independents at bargain-basement prices to compete against them with? Course they don't. That all?"

"And a pound of lard."

"Pound of lard? Okay, now where was I . . . oh yes, old aircraft. What do they do with them? Put 'em on the open market for the independents to snap up and use in competition? Course they don't! They pass their Comets and Viscounts on to their new subsidiary charter line, to compete against the poor old independents with their DC-3s, Ambassadors and other old stock. Now that's what I call clever. Okay madam, that's nine-and-four-pence . . . anything else?"

"All makes extra work for us," a baggage loader at the front of the queue complained. "The scheduled airlines should stick to Heathrow . . . and I'll have a pound of stewing steak."

"Doesn't make any difference to you, my friend," the butcher assured his customer. "They're the same passengers, but now they're flying in more modern aircraft. That's what I call clever. Anything else? That's two-and-ten. Thank you. Who's next?"

I hastily made my purchase and hurried home to phone the office.

"I think I've found out who Air Tours are," I announced, repeating what I'd just learned in the butcher's.

"Denis heard much the same thing from a member of *Flight* magazine's staff," Tony confirmed. "Mat Ramsden, their public transport editor, is a friend of his and told a similar story. We should have anticipated this might happen, it's already happening overseas."

"Where?" I demanded indignantly.

"All over Europe. Look at Holland. KLM is hand in glove with Martin's Air Charter. Lufthansa's in bed with Condor Flugdienst, Alitalia and SAM, Iberia and Aviaco, Swiss Air and Bal Air. Want me to go on?"

"Hmm, I see what you mean. Wonder who BOAC will merge with?"

"Probably British United, Eagle or Caledonian, but not until the big three UK independents have fought to the death.° Whoever survives will eventually end up as part of the government conglomerate."

"It makes sense," I had to agree. "The government knocks out the competition, gets a slice of the lucrative charter market and unloads its old aircraft."

"Doesn't paint a very rosy picture for us with our twenty-year-old piston-engined aircraft," Tony observed.

"I'm afraid it doesn't. We've still got our on-going expenses, but no revenue. Any sign of any charter work?"

"None, but don't give up yet. Levitt's contacted a top law firm, who have examined our contracts. He phoned an hour ago. His lawyer told him we have a cast-iron case, the contracts are watertight. They urge us to sue Horizon Holidays for breach of contract, failure to perform, and a whole load of other things. Levitt wanted to get hold of you and Stan Wilson to see if you're agreeable to Air Links suing them."

"Course I am. The only other course of action is for us to go under. Yes, let's take 'em to court for everything we can think of."

"Good, I thought you'd feel that way. It could be several months before the case gets to court, but we can look around for any ad hoc charter work in the meantime. There's about £40,000 in the kitty, which should pay our bills until the case comes up. The DC-3 is still earning its keep on freight work, and we're sure to find something for the other aircraft."

I rang off and paused to consider our position.

° Eagle folded about 1969. BUA was taken over by Caledonian and the new company eventually became a part of British Airways.

CHAPTER NINETEEN

Preparation

The following Monday the directors attended a meeting in our solicitor's office.

"The contracts seem quite simple and straightforward," a partner explained to us. "A precedent was set when you first accepted work from them. We'll check a few technical points in the contracts — such as correctly witnessed signatures, correct particulars on documents and anything else we can think of — but on the face of it, it appears to be a flagrant breach of contract. That being the case, we'll sue for compensation. There'll be other matters in addition to that but basically the simpler we keep it, the better our case sounds."

"And how would you rate our chances?" Levitt enquired.

The lawyer laughed. "I've been in this profession too long to be drawn into a prognosis so early on in the proceedings, but my initial reaction is they're out of their minds walking out of a firm contract."

"So we should be able to recover substantial compensation?" Levitt prompted hopefully.

Again the lawyer laughed. "Hold on, I haven't finished." He held up a hand. "Horizon Holidays are a pretty big travel firm. They've been around a long time and wouldn't break a contract unless they had reasons for believing they could get away with it. While we're on that subject, can you think of any reason why they suddenly went cold on Air Links?"

"Air Tours," Tony announced. The lawyer looked at him enquiringly.

"Air Tours are a new company just starting up, with modern aircraft bequeathed to them by British European Airways," Denis explained. We then described the new situation that had arisen with the birth of the new company.

"Zucher liked our low prices, but always worried our aircraft would break down and strand his passengers overseas. He couldn't use the scheduled airlines because of their higher fares, so when Air Tours came on the scene, he saw them as the answer to his prayer."

"Modern aircraft backed up by BEA's engineering facilities, but available at charter airline rates," I explained.

The lawyer took notes as we spoke.

"Okay then, I think I've got the picture," he nodded. "It may well be the case they can afford to pay you monetary compensation in exchange for the peace of mind of flying with a government-backed airline, albeit one called by another name."

"What do we do now?" Denis was the first to ask the question that had been on the tip of everybody's tongue.

"I'll write a letter to Horizon, advising them they're in breach of their contract, and demanding they honour it and continue to use Air Links as their means of air transport. They will no doubt pass this on to their solicitors to respond to. Once we hear from their lawyers, we should have a better idea of their reasons for dishonouring the contract."

"And then?" I asked.

"Well, depending on the reasons for their actions, they'll either refuse point blank to honour the contract, citing some legal technicality, or they may negotiate."

"Negotiate?"

"They may be prepared to negotiate an out-of-court settlement," the lawyer explained. "My instinct tells me this is what they'll most probably do — offer a sum equal to the loss incurred by you, less your costs."

"Why less costs?" Tony enquired. The solicitor smiled ruefully.

"Unfortunately, costs awarded by the court rarely equal the amount of the actual costs. Their lawyers will know this and will use this knowledge to trim the amount of compensation offered."

"You mean it would cost too much in additional costs to recover the full amount?" Stan Wilson enquired. The lawyer nodded sadly.

The remainder of the meeting covered other points of law. One of the solicitor's main concerns was whether we could afford the cost of the action if we lost.

"Solicitors' fees, counsel's time, court costs, witnesses, disbursements — these could amount to several thousand pounds if they won and had costs awarded against you," he cautioned. "Can you afford that?"

Levitt reassured him on that matter, but each of us had already calculated that unless we started earning some form of revenue over the next four months, our financial resources would be exhausted before the spring. We discussed this as we left the lawyer's office.

"The DC-3 is self-sustaining," Denis pondered aloud. "The other two aircraft need to earn £2500 a month just to break even."

"Plus miscellaneous other expenses. That's twenty hours' flying if we include fuel and handling charges. If we're only going to fly twenty hours a month, we don't need a full complement of crews."

"You mean lay off a few pilots?" I enquired with alarm. Staff cuts were one of the first indications of an airline in trouble, and we didn't need to advertise our situation.

"Not immediately," Denis assured me. "But if the money starts to run a bit short, it's one option we'll have to consider."

Nobody mentioned the subject again. Over the past years we'd built up a loyal hard-working team of ground and air crew. The thought of having to condemn people like Joe Phillips, Les Smith, Timber Wood and Mike Sommerpole to a winter's unemployment was just too horrible to contemplate.

We devoted the whole of the following week to looking for charter work. Tony and Denis paid several visits to various air-charter brokers on the Baltic exchange and returned confident of being able to secure sufficient work. Nathan and I contacted every travel agent, social club or group of people likely to travel together. I quickly learned never to leave Nathan alone on a telephone.

"We've had a bit of a bad run recently with engine failures," I heard him tell one travel agent. "Fairly routine with older aircraft but it's cost us a lot of work and we wondered if you'd be interested . . ."

I hastily took the instrument out of his hand and smoothed the matter over with some fast talking. I told them our proposed introduction of modern British-built jet aircraft had resulted in temporary excess capacity. I also told Nathan never to contact clients alone in future.

Regretfully, most if not all of the travel agents had made their arrangements well before the start of the IT season. "We'll keep you in mind if we have an aircraft breakdown anywhere though," Arrowsmith's man promised us.

Lieutenant-Colonel Fitzwilliam at the Ministry of Defence surprised us by suddenly offering us four trooping flights to Gutersloh, which boosted our cash reserves slightly.

Our lawyer wrote advising us that Horizon Holidays had passed the details of the dispute to their solicitors.

"This will be a waiting game, I'm afraid," he advised us, when we phoned to discuss the case. "Unfortunately, justice is not free in this country and their solicitors will probably endeavour to drag this matter out as long as possible."

"In the hope that we run out of money before the case gets to court?" I suggested.

"I'm afraid so. Our date for a hearing could be as late as August or September, and even then they might seek an adjournment for any one of a number of reasons. Can you hold out that long?"

"No problems there," I lied. "We've got charter work running out of our ears." I thought the lawyer sounded quite relieved when I said that.

Inevitably, members of our staff came in over the next few weeks to enquire what was going on. I told most of them we were going through a period of transition.

"Next year could see us operating a fleet of modern jet equipment," I told one of the Argonaut co-pilots. His face lit up at the news.

"That's tremendous," he enthused. "I've been offered a job with BEA but I didn't want to desert Air Links in the middle of the busy summer season. That's great news about jets."

My conscience troubled me and I had to tell him the decision whether to stay or leave was his alone.

BAC kept in regular contact regarding the 200 series One-Eleven. The prototype was expected to complete its test flight schedule before the end of the year, and they hoped to introduce it into airline service by early summer.

"Freddie Laker's ordered it for BUA and there'll be a lot of attendant publicity with its introduction," Tiplady from the design office said when he called one day. "We'd like to be able to say we've reserved two options for Air Links. Sort of laying the ground bait to attract other airlines, know what I mean?"

Nathan had taken the call, and he unwittingly did us a favour for once when he gave his approval for BAC to make the announcement.

Less flying meant less office work, and I was able to contact the delectable Georgina Noble frequently. Our outings usually took the form of dinners at expensive restaurants of her choice where several of her socialite friends joined us. Owning my own private aeroplane seemed to elevate me in her estimation, and she never missed an opportunity to introduce me with the comment, "He's got his own aeroplane." Members of the aristocracy and their attendant hangers-on seemed to think owning a 300-quid ex-RAF communications hack was infinitely more prestigious than driving a £5000 Aston-Martin or Bentley. Offers to take any of them for a flight were invariably declined, however.

"But Olivia, her sister, would adore to go with you," one member of the debutante set had assured me earnestly one evening. "She's spending every pound she can afford on flying lessons." I nodded politely at this piece of information, but did nothing about it; Olivia was a hell of a nice girl, but I was more interested in spending time with her delectable sister.

Horizon Holidays' solicitors took three weeks to respond to our solicitor's letter.

"Something's not quite right here," our lawyer informed us. "They simply confirmed that their client, Horizon Holidays, has taken the opportunity to use another air carrier for all future business.

"'Another carrier' being Air Tours, of course," Denis announced.

"Precisely," the lawyer agreed. "You now need to decide what action you wish to take. Do we sue them for the consequences to you?"

"Most certainly. We've lost thousands of pounds of revenue. If you think we've got a good case, let's try to recover the money from them."

The lawyer then announced he'd like to call another meeting of the Air Links board of directors as soon as possible.

"This case will be heard in a local court before a judge," he explained a few days later. "We need to use the best ammunition available to win this case. The other side will contest it strongly. We're going to have to brief counsel."

"What does that mean? Why can't you handle it?" Stan Wilson enquired. Our solicitor then explained that in a case of this magnitude, a barrister would represent us in court.

"We're the solicitors. We prepare the case, but a barrister will stand up and present it," he informed us. "We prefer to use firms we've worked with before. One of our longest associations has been with a firm in Lincoln's Inn. We've worked together in quite a few cases now, spread over many years, and I have the utmost confidence in their ability to present this one."

"Okay then. Sounds good to me, let's use them," Denis suggested, looking at us for our opinions. We were unanimous in our agreement.

"Very well then. They're a long-established chambers specialising in contractual disputes of this nature. I was at Cambridge with two of their silks, one of whom I'll contact immediately."

"Who is this firm, as a matter of interest?" Tony enquired.

"Netherby, Driscoll and Toombes, established over a hundred years ago. Excellent firm. Two of the partners are third-generation barristers."

The name seemed to ring a bell in my mind but I couldn't fathom exactly why. My contact with the law had never gone past motoring offences.

The lawyer promised to be in contact within a week.

"The quicker we set the wheels in motion, the sooner we'll get a trial date," he explained. "In the meantime, don't contact the other party except through us."

"Do we need to keep an aircraft ready in case Horizon suddenly decide to come back to us?' Denis queried. The solicitor shook his head.

"Definitely not. If they were to decide to do that, their solicitors would inform us first, which I think very unlikely."

Everybody shook hands at the conclusion of the meeting, and three of us caught the next train home to Gatwick.

The two Argonauts and the DC-3 stood forlorn and alone in the overnight park as our train pulled into the station. The IT season was now in full swing, and every other charter company was flying maximum hours. The office seemed depressingly quiet as we entered.

"BKS Air Transport phoned twice in the last hour," the receptionist greeted me. "Sixty of their passengers to be picked up from Palma, can we do it? Phone Mr Keegan as soon as possible."

I dialled BKS's Bradford number. They were a firm similar to us, except they'd been going longer. After starting with government surplus DC-3s at the end of the war, they had now progressed to Airspeed Ambassadors and were reputed to be about to get Bristol Britannias. Their phone rang only once.

"BKS Air Transport," Keegan's voice announced. I smiled to myself. Although BKS was a pretty big operator in the north-east of England, they'd never lost the personal touch. Theirs was a team effort; it wasn't unusual to find the managing director refuelling one aircraft or the chief pilot wheeling a set of boarding steps up to another. Keegan and I exchanged brief pleasantries before getting down to business.

"One of our Ambassadors has gone unserviceable in Palma," he announced. "The passengers were due to fly out this morning, but we've told them to stay around the hotel till we call them. Our engineers are already there and reckon it'll take a full day to rectify the problem. The question is, do you have an aircraft available at short notice?"

I looked across the tarmac area to where our Argonauts waited patiently like hobbled horses. They hadn't flown for a week now and the revenue from this charter would help bolster our fighting fund.

"Sounds urgent, I'll see if we can help you," I told him. To have immediately accepted the charter would have made him wonder why we weren't flying as much as every other charter operator.

"Make it snappy, we don't want a load of grumpy passengers telling everybody about their delay if we can possibly help it. Should be about nine hours' flying for you, about 1400 quid, right?"

"Okay, our commercial manager's just advised me we can do it," I lied. "It'll be £15,045 plus handling and landing fees." I invented the figures as I spoke.

"Okay, but could you get onto it fast?" Keegan urged. "I'll confirm the terms by telex immediately."

One of the problems in the air-charter business was its heavy dependence on good faith. One phone call could send an aircraft across Europe with no signed agreement, only a gentleman's word. The rogues in aviation were quick to take advantage of this, but they rarely lasted long. In contrast, the older well-established companies built up a track record of paying on time, even though no documentary proof existed. BKS, Dan-Air, Westpoint, Autair and Air Links were in this latter category.

I phoned our chief engineer in the Beehive and he promised to have an aircraft fuelled and ready to go in an hour. Tony rounded up a standby crew, and the aircraft was setting course for the Mediterranean less than ninety minutes later.

"If this keeps up all summer we might even make a profit," I observed to Joe Phillips, as we watched the aircraft disappear into the distance.

Regrettably the BKS charter was the only real piece of work we were able to find for the Argonauts. The Dakota continued to putter away on mainly freight charters, while our two larger aircraft gathered successive layers of grime from the Gatwick industrial environment.

The weeks of enforced idleness played hell on our nerves as we watched our capital reserves dwindle. To make life even harder, we had to maintain an air of confidence that we didn't feel. We continued to maintain a full complement of crews, although one or two seasoned veterans of the charter scene recognised the impending signs of a company in trouble and left for greener pastures. The Argonaut co-pilot who'd called in to discuss the company's future came in for a second discussion. I told him we were slightly overstaffed at the moment and if he resigned, we wouldn't need to replace him. When he still hesitated, I gave him a short lecture on the advantages of working for a government airline. Two days later he returned and handed me his letter of resignation.

Levitt phoned in the middle of June to say we'd got a court date.

"Seventeenth of August. Counsel wants a preliminary meeting before then," he advised. "Any particular day that suits you?"

"Any day," Denis assured him. "There's nothing going on around here and three of us to do it. What about next Monday?"

He confirmed the arrangement with the other directors, and five of us assembled in the lawyer's office four days later.

"There are two silks in particular whom I recommend most strongly," our solicitor began. "Don't misunderstand me, the firm is absolutely first class and any member of it would do a first-class job, but both of these gentlemen are exceptional in their field."

I suddenly remembered where I had heard the name Netherby, Driscoll and Toombes. Seven years previously, I'd associated with a young law graduate when we'd both been called up for compulsory National (military) Service. This was back in the post-war years of the 1950s, when the armed services still relied on "weekend warriors" to man their ships, tanks and aircraft. Mike Parry and several others had been selected for aircrew duties with the RAF and had spent the next two years maturing into men as the Air Force spent thousands of pounds of taxpayers' money teaching us to fly. At the end of that time, the government discharged us back into civilian life to resume our interrupted occupations. Mike Parry had exchanged his flying suit, bone dome and Mae West life-jacket for the sober suiting of a city gentleman. He'd entered the prestigious law firm of Netherby, Driscoll and Toombes as a very junior barrister serving his pupillage, learning the profession from one of the firm's partners. It had always amazed me that young men were able to settle back into mundane jobs after two exciting years fighting Malayan guerrillas, serving at sea or flying high-performance aeroplanes at subsonic speeds.

"I've had previous dealings with one particular member of that firm." I interrupted the lawyer in mid-sentence and he eyed me curiously.

"Mike . . . er, sorry . . . Michael Parry. I knew him particularly well when he first qualified," I explained. "Brilliant mind, very much a lateral thinker, bit unconventional too. I'd have complete confidence in him if he were to represent us in court."

The lawyer wrote the name down and promised to relay our wishes to the firm of barristers.

We concluded our business an hour later and returned to our respective homes.

Our solicitor phoned the next day to advise us our chosen barrister was not available.

"Trainee barristers serve a three-year pupillage before being admitted to the bar," he explained. "After that they assist senior members of the firm for several years, gradually acquiring court experience."

"Mike would be well out of his three years by now," I assured the lawyer. He agreed.

"The problem is, progress is distressingly slow in the legal profession," he explained. "Your friend Mr Parry has probably been helping as a junior for several years now but won't have been entrusted with a case yet."

"Why's that?" I demanded.

"When I said progress in the legal profession was slow, I made an understatement. In fact it's virtually at a standstill."

"So how do young barristers ever get court experience?" I enquired.

"Well, don't quote me on this, you understand, but basically it's dead men's shoes. None of the senior silks want to admit young barristers to their ranks, so until one of them retires or dies, the men at the top tend to hog all the work. Provincial law firms are different, of course, but then so is their remuneration."

"So Mr Parry is fully qualified but won't get a chance to practise until somebody retires?" Denis enquired. "Sounds a bit like BOAC to me."

"I can assure you the salary Mr Parry earns is commensurate with his qualification," the solicitor retorted rather huffily. "He'd get quicker promotion in the provinces but earn substantially less than his present salary." I restrained my urge to say it sounded even more like working for the government airline.

"So we can't use him to represent us?" I concluded.

"I didn't say that." The solicitor now spoke defensively, reminding me of met men when asked their opinion of what the weather will do. They tell you every possibility, but hate to tell you which one they consider most likely. If you'd asked them the time, they'd have told you how to make a watch and you still wouldn't know what time it was when they'd finished.

"Then what did they say?" I demanded rather sharply.

"They said they didn't recommend your Mr Parry as their first choice of counsel. Bearing in mind that an awful lot of money is involved in this case, I can understand their sentiments. We need a top silk with a proven court record."

"Would it be possible to discuss this matter with Mr Parry?" I enquired. The lawyer nodded his head affirmatively.

"Most definitely. I could probably arrange an appointment for tomorrow," he suggested.

I concluded the phone call by asking him to do that.

I repeated the gist of the message to the others. Denis remarked I had an unusual amount of confidence in somebody I hadn't seen for several years.

"He had a rare genius for doing the unexpected," I explained. "He's fully qualified and probably raring to go. I'd have a lot more faith in him than some stuffy old QC who's relying on his reputation rather than his wits."

"It can't do any harm to meet him," Denis admitted. I told him we'd probably have the opportunity tomorrow.

True to my predictions, our solicitor phoned to say Mr Parry could see us next day. "I'm fully booked till late afternoon, so I've arranged a meeting at ten past five in his chambers," he informed us, and provided the address and instructions on how to get there. I promised we'd meet him next evening.

I had anticipated mild antipathy towards my suggestion of employing Mike on this case and was not surprised when the senior partner greeted us on arrival. He explained in a very patronising manner that his junior didn't have the experience required for a case of this nature. "One of our partners has agreed to accept the brief," he concluded condescendingly.

My reply that we'd prefer Mike upset him badly.

"We would not have the same amount of confidence in Mr Parry as we would have in Mr Durell," he objected.

"Is Mr Parry fully qualified for the job?" I enquired.

"Yes."

"Is he competent?"

"It depends on what you mean by 'competent'." The lawyer was talking like a met man again.

"Is he incompetent?" Tony stressed the last word.

"No, of course not, he's a very brilliant young man, almost outstanding I'd venture to say, but . . ."

"Okay, we'd like him to represent us," I ended succinctly.

Mike had been absent during this conversation. It would have been easy for his senior to have forced him to bow out of the case. The senior member looked daggers at us as we shook hands. His final remark made me feel good about employing young blood in this case.

"You realise, I hope, that it'll reflect very badly on these chambers if Mr Parry should lose the case?" he fumed.

Denis resembled Laurence Olivier as he smiled his most ingratiating smile.

"Then we'd better all ensure he doesn't, hadn't we?" he suggested menacingly.

CHAPTER TWENTY

Battle

The occasional bit of ad hoc charter work turned up at irregular intervals, but there was not enough to meet our total outgoings. Our cash reserves began to dwindle. An air of despondency hung over the office as word got round that Air Links was a bit shaky. One or two more staff members resigned to go to other jobs, and when this happened we didn't replace them.

In the middle of July, Mike Parry and our solicitor began final preparations of our case.

"We'll attack them with three main charges," the lawyers explained. "Breach of contract, loss of contractual earnings and non-payment of debt." Over the next few days they went through the contracts again, looking for legal flaws. Finally they interrogated the witnesses to the signatures and again found no problems.

"Everything seems perfectly in order," our solicitor concluded afterwards. "The other side must believe you can't afford the cost of a court action. They'll almost certainly offer to settle out of court for a lesser sum, as I explained earlier. You'd be wise to consider accepting such an offer, so you'll need to establish what minimum amount of compensation is acceptable to you."

"Winning this case won't be the end of our problems," Denis ventured over a cup of coffee a few minutes later. "We still need work for our aircraft, and Horizon won't touch us with a disinfected barge pole after this. Particularly when they can send their passengers on Air Tours."

"Not even if we re-equipped with One-Elevens?" I suggested optimistically. "British United and Eagle have seen the writing on the wall and plan to compete with modern jets. They're probably able to undercut Air Tours."

"What's our situation with BAC at present?" Tony enquired. I told him the PR department were about to announce a tentative order from us for the 200 series One-Eleven. I also mentioned that since our loss of the Horizon contract, calls from BAC had ceased.

In August we prepared one of the Argonauts for a morning of recurrent crew training. Every commercial pilot had to have performed at least one take-off and landing within the preceding twenty-eight days to remain current. Our aircraft had hardly moved for over a month, so Gibby took six of us up for a morning's circuits and landings. It felt good to get back in the air again, even though we weren't earning any money. The rest of the pilots on the training detail questioned me about our lack of work.

"Everybody else is flying to the maximum, while we hang about on the ground. This can't be good for the bank balance. What's the score?" one of the ex-Derby Airways captains enquired. Other ears listened attentively for my reply.

"BAC will be releasing a press statement shortly about our proposed re-equipment," I assured them. "I'm prevented from saying anything until then, but you only have to look around you to guess which aircraft it'll be." I stared at a One-Eleven as I spoke.

We endeavoured to contact Sir George Edwards, BAC's chairman, to discuss leasing one or more One-Elevens for next season. Our tentative plan was to assemble a small fleet of modern jet aircraft to persuade some of the smaller travel agents to fly with us. He proved rather difficult to contact.

Finally, in mid-August, we had a council of war with our legal team. The solicitor ran over the details of the case. All of us would be required as witnesses, as would members of the office staff who had witnessed signatures on the contracts.

After the meeting, I phoned Georgina Noble in her London apartment and suggested going out somewhere.

We ended up taking four of her friends to the Nightingale, probably the most expensive restaurant in Berkeley Square.

I quietly told her tonight was a bit of a gladiatorial dinner.

"What the hell does that mean?" she enquired.

"Air Links is going into battle tomorrow against the big boys," I explained. "We're going to fight to get back the passengers who usually fly with us. We're taking a big travel agent to court."

"But you already carry passengers, don't you?" she remarked with a yawn. "I thought you carried the working class, you know, the great unwashed. They couldn't possibly afford to fly with the big airlines, could they?"

"I'd certainly hate to sit beside one of them," a spoiled-looking debutante almost spilt out of her frock as she addressed me across the table. "A school friend and I once travelled third class on Southern Railways. Honestly, it was ghastly, full of wretched oiks."

I turned the conversation onto less controversial subjects for the remainder of the meal. I suspected Georgina and her friends weren't interested in gladiatorial endeavours. Money grew on their daddies' trees.

The evening ended with everybody suddenly getting up and leaving the restaurant. I found myself alone as a waiter sidled up with the bill. I looked at the total. It was £35.10s, almost all the money I had on me.

I joined the others outside on the pavement as they scrambled for taxis. Georgina and one of the men were discussing something animatedly.

"Bit off, isn't it, leaving the poor chap to foot the whole bill? Why don't we . . .," he began to protest as Georgina pushed him into the last cab.

"Shuddup fer Chrissake, the idiot's loaded," she hissed urgently, then turned as I approached. "Guy, are you all right for transport? The driver can only take five, but I'm sure there'll be another taxi along shortly." She slammed the door before she'd finished the sentence, and the cab pulled out into the late evening traffic.

I arrived home on the last train. Tomorrow promised to be rather exciting. I was looking forward to watching Zucher and his Horizon Holidays travel agency being dismembered in court.

The phone rang as I got into bed. It was Mike Parry.

"Don't worry about tomorrow. It's an open and shut case, which we'll win with costs awarded against them. Now get an early night and relax, 'cause tomorrow I'm going to take Horizon Holidays apart, financially and legally that is. And that's a stone cold certainty."

He rang off, and I was left with my own thoughts. We were now beginning to get into debt. The two Argonauts hadn't flown for three months, apart from occasional last-minute ad hoc charter flights for other operators who'd broken down.

I read through the contracts we'd signed with Zucher's Horizon Holidays. Palma, Madrid, Oporto, Perpignan, Athens, Corfu, Heraklion. These destinations represented more that 3000 hours' flying per annum at quite favourable rates. A veritable fortune. Yet Zucher had opted at the last moment to switch allegiance to BEA's new charter subsidiary, British Air Tours.

I finally went to bed with a nagging doubt in my head. Mike's last remark had left me with a feeling of insecurity. "We'll win . . . that's a stone-cold certainty.

Experience had taught me that in aviation there is no such thing as a stone-cold certainty.

CHAPTER TWENTY-ONE
Mid-course Correction

The door of the courthouse slammed behind our four shocked figures as we walked out into the gloom of a foggy August morning. Weather was appropriate for such an unhappy occasion, cold with light drizzle and mist.

"What'll you do now? Reform and regroup, I suppose?" Mike was the first to break the silence. The rest of us were still too dumbstruck to respond. It was mid-morning, and Mike Parry suggested adjourning to the Checkers pub to discuss a few details. We sat at a large table and relived the events of the case again.

Mike had somehow lacked his usual air of complete confidence when he'd met us outside the court. I'd also noticed he wasn't accompanied by any assistants. Now my feeling of doubt was confirmed. He paused for a very long time before he spoke.

"I don't know how to put this," he began.

"That's unusual for you," I tried to counter jocularly. Mike's well-known quick wit and rapport were the main reasons I'd suggested hiring him. He barely acknowledged the compliment.

"You fellows have invested a lot of confidence in me," he began hesitantly. "This case represents tens of thousands of pounds. Ordinarily the firm would've put one of their top silks onto it."

I felt the nagging gut feeling of doubt become a certainty. For Mike Parry to be temporarily lost for words, something must have gone badly wrong. We waited for him to continue.

"When you approached me and briefed me that Horizon Holidays had chosen to renege on your contracts and use the scheduled airlines instead, I examined each contract closely. In every contract they had given you rock-solid agreements guaranteeing you a minimum of 250 hours' flying per month."

"Three thousand flying hours a year, including a lot of winter flying," I interrupted, but the others gestured me into silence. Mike continued.

"Yes, well, any court in the land would have upheld those contracts."

"Would?" I didn't like the tone this conversation was taking. Denis and Tony listened intently as Mike carried on.

"Yes, I'm afraid so. Let me explain further. After our first meeting in chambers, I went through the contract documents very carefully. I could find no loopholes through which they could wriggle out of their substantial commitment to you."

Mike paused momentarily to collect his thoughts.

"As this was the first case I'd been entrusted with thus far in my career, I then discussed it informally with one of the partners specialising in contract law. Needless to say, all the partners and members of the firm had been vitally concerned that I win this case. Anyway, the partner ended up going through each document with a fine-tooth comb. We even checked the status and characters of the witnesses. Everything was in order."

I began to feel slightly better now. Maybe Mike was asking for more time to prepare the case.

"One thing you will have got from this experience is value for money," he assured us. "Late yesterday afternoon, I was summoned to the senior partner's chambers. You'll have heard of him, Sir Godfrey Denning, made his name in the Courtauld's case a few years ago. Anyway, he devoted more than an hour to questioning me on the various aspects of the case. By the time I spoke to Guy late last night, he'd assured me we had an open and shut case. He doubted it would get past the doors of the courtroom. They obviously intended to settle out of court."

My initial indignation at Mike began to dissipate. His preparation had obviously been comprehensive and very professional.

A middle-aged barman padded up to our table to take our drink orders. Normally none of us drank during the day, in case we had to fly. Denis began to order a soft drink.

"Four whiskies with ice, make 'em doubles," Mike cut short our mumbling. The barman returned shortly with a tray holding four glasses and a jug of water. Our lawyer poured a small measure of water into each glass before handing them round.

"Cheers," Tony muttered somnolently, sounding like the life and soul of a funeral. We raised our glasses.

"When I arrived in court before you this morning, I was met by the two solicitors," Mike explained. "I knew the opposing solicitor quite well, a small one-man band from Littlehampton with a bit of a reputation for shaky practice. Frankly, I was surprised at Zucher employing such a firm. Normally these people are outclassed in disputes of this nature and wisely tend to pass them on to the larger law practices. It therefore came as even more of a surprise when this snake-in-the-grass showed signs of acute embarrassment, in fact he almost apologised for his client's actions."

"What actions are you talking about?" Denis demanded impatiently.

"Okay, I was coming to that. The contracts signed by the younger Zucher are invalid, due to a technicality."

"But you just said yourself there were no loopholes," I insisted.

"There weren't any, except that your young Mr Zucher wasn't legally empowered to sign the documents. Under British law you have to be . . ."

"That's wrong!" Denis interjected. "He was an adult acting as agent for the charterers. We've done countless other flights for them and they've always paid us . . ."

"Correct," Mike conceded. "But it could be argued you were lucky to have been paid, because you didn't have a legally binding contract. Before you jump down my throat, describe this fellow Zucher to me."

"You mean the father? Well, he's the managing director of the travel business and, er . . . well actually we've only met him once or twice."

"Never mind about him, tell me about the son. What does he look like, his characteristics, interests, what's he like to talk to?"

"Well, he's about five feet two or three, sort of rather shy, especially round the girls in the office — nobody can talk to him much. Oh . . . except Pickles, and he got on with him like a house on fire. He's mad about aeroplanes, liked to come flying with us whenever possible."

"How old would you say he is?"

"Oh, about thirtyish . . . or late twenties maybe. Dunno, it's difficult to tell. He's completely bald so that must make him at least twenty-five. Yes, I'd say twenty-five or -six."

"And that's where you're wrong. In fact we were all wrong." Mike's angry fist banged the table. "Even the seniors in our firm overlooked one basic tenet of British law."

"And that is?" Denis voiced the question on everybody's lips. Surely you didn't have to have hair to sign a contract?

"Young Mr Zucher was nineteen when he signed those contracts," Mike announced slowly and regretfully. "Not even the other side's solicitor was aware of that fact until shortly before the hearing today. Your contracts were not signed by an adult, and are therefore invalid and unenforceable under law."

"But that's a load of rubbish, we've done business with Horizon for three years now. We've always dealt with Mr Zucher's son," Tony insisted.

"Yes, but hold on a minute. Remember how he came down in the school holidays to see the Argonauts when we first got them?" I reminded everybody.

"And he'd only flown once before when he went on holiday with his parents. What sort of travel agent has only flown once?"

The volume of our discussion had increased in proportion to the size of the disclosures being made. I could sense even the bartender becoming involved. Now was probably a good time to conclude the meeting.

"So we have no redress against these people?" I concluded lamely."

"'Fraid not," Mike confirmed. "Under law you don't have a valid legal contract, so there's nothing to sue them over. Maybe you should have checked up on his age or something."

Denis pointed out that you don't meet many bald teenagers, to which our lawyer agreed.

"I believe its called alopecia areata," he remarked helpfully. "A hereditary condition which can be inherited from either the male or female side of the family, but more usually the father's side."

Mike glanced at his watch and announced he'd better get back to the city soon.

"More case research and casework for the senior partners," he reflected morosely. "This case would have really got me out of the rut. If we'd won, my career would have taken off."

Somebody commiserated with him, but pointed out that at least he was still in business.

"Zucher has wiped us out," I explained. "Payments on the aircraft are two and a half thousand a month, then there's another two thousand for office rental, salaries and insurance. We'll be lucky to get out of this with anything. We'll be paying off our debts for years and years."

The barman had arrived with four more whiskies. I recognised him now as Captain Snodgrass, the chief pilot of the recently defunct Pegasus Airlines. He'd been a hard man to compete against. Under his command, Pegasus had cut every corner and bent every rule to stay in business. We'd watched them struggle in their financial death throes, until finally one day the bank had stepped in and put them out of their misery. Overnight they were closed down. Snodgrass and his crews had reported to work on the Monday morning and found the office bare. The creditors had moved in over the weekend and removed everything. Only the phones remained, and they'd been disconnected.

"Have this one on me, fellows," Snodgrass invited, screwing up the bill. "It's going to be a long hard winter ahead. What a bloody awful way to make a living, eh? It's either a feast or a famine in our business. See you next year."

"Thanks for that." Denis extended his hand, and Snodgrass clasped it momentarily before returning to hibernate behind the bar and wait for spring.

We exited the pub at 11am and I began to ask myself if I wanted a career that was either a feast or a famine.

CHAPTER TWENTY-TWO
Carrion

The sun had burned off most of the early morning mist as I drove into the staff car park next morning. Over the fence, the two Argonauts waited patiently and forlornly for the summons to fly.

It was not so quiet in the office, where white-overalled workmen were removing the last sticks of furniture. My route had taken me past the National Provincial Bank, where I'd waved a greeting at the usually effusive Cattermoull. His response had been a contemptuous stare. The news of Air Link's collapse had travelled fast.

Various airline colleagues popped their heads into the office to offer encouragement.

"It's a bummer, isn't it?" Paddy Wickens, until recently a training captain with Pegasus, bemoaned. I knew he'd been out of work more than three weeks now and was reputed to derive most of his comfort from endless glasses of Scotch whisky in the Gatwick Aero Club.

"Thanks Paddy."

"Maybe something good'll come up in the spring. Hey, did you hear Caledonian have probably won their Supplemental Carrier Certificate for the North Atlantic?"

Independent aviation was like a crowd of gamblers, peopled by those who hoped for the impossible. And the impossible rarely happened.

I called in to the bank and drew out the balance of my account, less a few pounds. From now on I was going to need ready cash, for there was a strong possibility they would freeze my account.

While the teller took an interminable time checking my balance in the back office, I had time to consider my situation.

My major assets were threefold: stock in a failed airline, a private motor car worth £600 and a private aircraft worth £300. My personal guarantees to the bank were open-ended, and I didn't dare guess what they might cost.

The car and aircraft were in my name and wouldn't be difficult for the bank to encumber. The teller arrived back with a slip of paper.

"Your available balance today is £120.11s.10d," she advised me primly. "Of course, that doesn't take into account any cheques outstanding."

I assured her there was nothing outstanding and wrote a cheque for £118.

A figure began to emerge from behind the frosted glass window of the manager's office. I could feel a pair of eyes boring into me while I wrote.

"Looking for a job, by any chance?" the voice of Blob-bottom enquired. I smiled weakly and tried to put on a brave front.

"It's a bad time to be out of work," I admitted. "Most of the airlines have finished crewing up for the summer season and I'm only current on the Argonaut."

Blob gestured me to the far end of the counter out of earshot.

"I've got to pick up some documentation at British United, then I thought we could have a pub lunch at the Aero Club — unless you have anything else to do?"

My gaze drifted towards our inactive aircraft outside on the north park. There was very little likelihood of any flying today — unless the bank came to repossess them and decided to fly them away somewhere. I told Blob lunch sounded a good idea.

I tried not to watch the hordes of departing and arriving aircraft as we drove round the perimeter road to the Aero Club. Summer IT flying was at its peak and I wasn't a part of it. I felt lousy.

The bar was deserted when we entered. Blob rang the bell, and Vic appeared and took our orders. We retreated to the snug bar, while two ploughmen's lunches were prepared.

A feeling of acute embarrassment came over me. We had press-ganged Blob into recommending a bank loan to purchase the three Argonauts. Then we were unable to keep up the finance payments, forcing the bank to move in and foreclose on us.

"Look, I'm sorry for what happened . . ." I began. Blob waved my apologies aside.

"It happens, I'm afraid, although I must say I thought you fellows in Air Links had got it right. Guaranteed cashflow throughout the year and a promise of better things to come. What went wrong? Why did Horizon Holidays renege on the contracts?"

I briefly described the events in the courthouse. Blob whistled in amazement when I told him Zucher's age had invalidated the contracts.

"That's a trick I haven't heard before," he admitted. "Better make a note of it for the future."

Lunch arrived and we took time out to enjoy it. When I thought the time was appropriate, I again raised the subject that was troubling me.

"I'm afraid we've let you down badly over this deal," I began.

"In what way?"

"The loans to buy the aircraft. When they stopped flying it became rather difficult to find two and a half thousand pounds a month for the lease purchase, plus another two thousand for salaries and office expenses. Mike Parry was confident we'd recoup the losses in court but I'm afraid even he was wrong . . ."

Blob waved the explanation away, explaining his bank had ample equity in the aircraft.

"We only loaned eighty percent of their assessed value so recovering our part will be comparatively simple. Now that we've heard the outcome of your case, we'll place the aircraft in the hands of a broker who'll find a buyer. The DC-4 Argonaut is still a competitive aircraft. I know for a fact that Flying Enterprise in Copenhagen are looking for more Argonauts. We'll dispose of them for whatever we can get and anything left over will be paid to you."

This news delighted me. I had feared the bank would hold Blob accountable for our delinquent payments. We ordered two more drinks on the strength of this, and I turned the conversation back to him.

"Doing much flying recently?" I enquired casually. He replied he hadn't flown since getting his private pilot's licence but the head of the bank's finance department had displayed considerable interest in using a light aircraft as transport between airports.

"I did a few costings for him, and the savings in overnight accommodation and time more than outweigh the cost of hiring a light aircraft," he informed me. I jokingly suggested he buy my Proctor, but he dismissed the idea.

"Anything we use must have two engines," he declared. "The bank would never subject staff to the dangers of an engine failure. I've spoken to George Miles down at Shoreham and they have a later version of the Gemini which might suit us."

"But the Gemini can't maintain height on one engine," I protested. "With two engines you have twice the chance of a failure and when it happens, you still go down."

"The new Gemini has more powerful Cirrus Major engines and can climb on one engine at maximum weight," Blob assured me. "The bank demands safety and security in everything it does."

I silently reflected that security was Blob's consuming passion.

"What'll you do now?" he enquired considerately. The question took me by surprise and I had to admit I hadn't given the matter much thought.

"Tidy up the loose ends at work, pay as many of my creditors as I can afford to, reduce my outgoings to a financial trickle and look around for a job."

"Does it have to be a flying job?"

"No, doesn't have to be. By the end of the month we'll probably all be desperate for work. There's not many flying jobs going begging this late in the season, and frankly I'd take almost anything. The Pegasus chief pilot is working in a pub in Horley to hold body and soul together. Why do you ask? Got any suggestions?"

Blob thought long and carefully before answering. "What about British European Airways? They've been recruiting since April; surely they'd be a good outfit to work for? State-owned airline, subsidised travel, government pension scheme . . ."

He winced when I related the details of my recent application to BEA.

"Yeah, they wouldn't like it when an independent pilot didn't turn up for an interview," he admitted. "They have the pick of the bunch."

I pointed out that at the time it seemed like Air Links was going places, possibly becoming as big as Eagle or British United.

"And anyway, I would have found it pretty hard to desert my friends and partners in the company for a better job," I explained. "There were the bank guarantees, plus I'd have had to find a replacement who'd do my job in the office and fly a thousand hours a year. I just couldn't have left the others in the lurch in that way. Besides which there was ample work for two aircraft. The Ministry of Supply offered us a series of Middle East trooping flights, which we turned down just to fly exclusively for Zucher. I really thought we were going places. So did other people. Did you know that Sir George Edwards and Jock Bryce came over from BAC to discuss selling us One-Elevens and VC-10s?"

"Yes I did," Blob admitted. "In fact it was probably a chance remark of mine to Sir George that planted the idea in his mind."

We gazed reflectively out towards the busy airfield.

"Of course there's always the chance of a job in the bank," Blob volunteered hesitatingly.

His earlier attempts to persuade me to join him behind vertical steel bars had not been outstandingly successful; some of us had been downright rude when we'd refused his offer. But now it was different. I was a bit wiser and realised I had eight inactive months ahead of me, at the end of which I'd compete with hundreds of other unemployed pilots for whatever flying jobs were available in the spring. There might be plenty or there might be only a few. It was always hard to predict. But one thing was certain: this would not be the last time an airline failed.

"Adequate starting salary, regular hours, luncheon vouchers, two weeks' paid holiday, good promotion prospects, low-interest home mortgage. We could use your experience and advice in the aviation finance division. It's not all writing in the ledger with a pen chained to the desk, you know."

I smiled gratefully at Blob. He was proving to be a good friend in time of need, and there weren't many such allies in private aviation.

"Thanks, but give me a bit of time to recover from recent events. I woke up yesterday expecting to win a large court case. Today I'm out of work, heavily in debt and frankly I don't know whether I'm punched, bored or countersunk. I'm going to have to find some kind of a job soon — but not today!"

After lunch I drove Blob back to the BUA hangar, where he discussed details of their forthcoming One-Elevens with Charlie Coates, the chief pilot. We looked over a pre-production test aircraft, used for crew training prior to the arrival of their first aircraft.

"One hundred percent British!" Blob announced proudly. "Rolls-Royce engines, Vickers airframe, Dowty controls and Smith's instruments. And a blooming competitive design too. Aer Lingus are rumoured to be about to announce an order for six, with options on four more." He discussed other matters with the chief pilot, and I began to appreciate how well his earlier military flying training had equipped him for the job.

I left him at the railway station at four o'clock and returned to my flat. The rent was paid till the end of the month, after which I'd move back home with Mum and Dad.

I couldn't dismiss the thought of a job with the bank from my mind. Economically it made sense. The bank offered life-long security, whereas independent aviation couldn't even guarantee your job for a year.

Next morning I prepared to fly the Proctor over to Biggin. Griff had offered to find a buyer. It was mid-morning when I began removing the control locks and covers. The day's IT traffic had already departed for sunny Spain, France or Italy, leaving the airport comparatively quiet. Less than a hundred yards from my aircraft, our Air Links planes stood impotently at rest. I reflected how ironic it would be if a charter enquiry came up now. The finance company had been quick to remove every stick of office equipment so even if somebody had wanted to charter us, the lack of paperwork would prevent us flying.

The flight to Biggin took twenty minutes. I cleared the Gatwick Control Zone east of Redhill, cruised along the top of the North Downs and joined the circuit for runway two nine. This was probably my last flight in my own aircraft.

The tower cleared me to join left hand downwind.

"Only other traffic's a Chipmunk on finals," he advised.

Feeling sad at having to part with such a beautiful aircraft, I entered the pattern and landed. The Proctor represented the last of a long line of pre-war thoroughbred aircraft — like Whitney Straights, Hawks, Puss Moths and Percival Gulls — that young aviators of both genders had used to establish international long-distance records. Henceforth, private aircraft manufacture would be dominated by American designs that were more like motorcars, with ashtrays, autopilots, air-conditioning and soundproofing, and with all the tricky foibles and fun taken out of the flying.

Griff himself marshalled me into the parking area and waited for me to emerge from the cockpit. Neither of us referred to the recent unhappy events. I handed him the aircraft logbooks and licence.

"I thought we might get £300 for her," I said, gesturing at the monoplane.

Griff nodded in agreement. "We'll advertise it in next week's *Flight* and *Aeroplane*," he suggested. "It would make an excellent club touring aircraft. I'll try asking £350, she's in nice condition. Meanwhile, do you want us to use it on charters while it's here?"

We settled these and other details and I headed towards lunch at the Greasy Spoon.

Apart from a Surrey Flying Club instructor and two members, the lunch crowd had returned to work. I carried my cup of tea and a sandwich to a window table. Out on the flight line, a couple of Chipmunks and various Moths belonging to the club rested between flights. Over in the far background, my aircraft rested in the shade of our Argonaut spares aircraft.

A rather shy-looking fellow of about twenty-five suddenly detached himself from his companions and asked if I minded him joining me at my table. I bade him be seated.

"I saw you arrive in the Proctor," he began. "Oh sorry, my name's Tim Martin, I'm a member of the Surrey Flying Club." I introduced myself and waited for him to continue. He didn't take long.

"Peter Chinn, my instructor, told me you bought the aircraft for £300," he began. I confirmed that was the price I'd paid.

"That's less than a family car," he protested in surprise. "I've been toying around with the idea of owning my own light aircraft, and something like your aeroplane would be my dream."

I told him what a delightful aircraft it was to fly. "Rather intolerant of fools and bad pilots though," I cautioned. "Get too slow on approach and she'll stall with little or no warning. Usually drops a wing too. Get too slow on the final turn in and she'll spin into the deck. How many hours have you got?"

"'Bout a hundred."

Further conversation with Tim elicited the information that he came from a family of musical instrument manufacturers and was possessed by a passion for flying.

"Had hoped to do a short service commission in the RAF. Flew with the Cambridge University Air Squadron, mainly on Chipmunks but did a little time on the dual Vampire trainer. Joined the family business after university and now only fly at weekends. The rest of the time I'm on the road, up and down the country, selling our instruments. So, as I was saying, I suppose I'd have about a hundred hours by now. Trouble is, though, aero club flying's a bit dull, rather like bumper boats. You go up for three-quarters of an hour, practise a few circuits, do some aerobatics . . . then suddenly your time's up, somebody else wants the aeroplane — come in number sixteen. If I could afford it, I'd buy something of my own to tour the Continent in. Do something different."

I told him the Proctor would make an ideal tourer. "Four seats, 150 mph cruise, good range and cheap to operate," I explained. "The only negative thing about it is the handling characteristics. It's not a beginner's aeroplane."

"A hundred hours is quite a bit of experience around here," Tim ventured.

I recognised him as a potential buyer for my aircraft, and if he bought it, it couldn't end up with a more appreciative owner.

"Look, I haven't got anything terribly important to do. Would you like a flight in it?" I suggested. He accepted with great delight.

A quarter of an hour later we had walked across to Air Couriers and I'd told Griff what I was about to do. I gave Tim the full conducted tour as I showed him how to check the outside of the aircraft, then I gestured for him to climb onto the port wing. He settled into the pilot's seat as I strapped in beside him. We spent another ten minutes going over the controls and instruments. I ran through the basic procedures for flying this aeroplane. He'd never used a constant speed propeller before, so I spent a lot of time explaining its operation to him. He seemed to assimilate everything I taught him, so it was time to go flying.

We completed three circuits, doing a touch-and-go landing each time. He was a bit confused at the way things happened faster at first, but once he began to think ahead of the aeroplane, he quickly became quite adept at handling it. On the fourth approach I glanced at my watch and saw we'd been airborne for half an hour.

"Make this the final landing, let her roll almost to a stop then turn off across the grass," I instructed. In my present financial state I couldn't afford to fly around in private aircraft all afternoon.

We parked back where we'd started and remained in our seats long after the engine had stopped. Some things have to be enjoyed fully.

"I see what you mean about fast," Tim began. "We were doing 130 knots downwind, what's that in miles per hour?"

"'Bout 150 mph, or two and a half miles a minute. London to Paris in an hour and a bit. There's not much else around here can lay heels to a Proctor."

"Do you think this would be a safe aeroplane for me to own?" he enquired. I told him I thought so, provided he didn't overload it or fly in adverse weather conditions. He'd certainly had no problems flying it today. "Keep in regular flying practice, fly at least twice a month, more if you can manage it. If you spend more than a fortnight away from flying, go up with one of the Surrey Club's instructors and get him to give you a quick refresher course to iron out any bad habits. This is a fairly demanding aircraft, the worst thing you can do in it is get too slow. Don't try and stretch a glide, it'll bite you and this bird's bite is lethal."

A lot more conversation in Griff's office finally resulted in the sale of the aircraft to Tim. Griff would continue to hangar and maintain the machine for an agreed monthly figure. The new owner wrote a cheque, which Griff handed to me. We shook hands on the deal and I walked out of the hangar £350 better off.

Several well-meaning friends called that evening and commiserated over the fate of Air Links. Olivia Noble phoned and said how sorry she was, but I didn't hear a word from Georgina. I found this rather depressing as well as unproductive, so I packed everything up next morning and moved back home with Mum and Dad. They had a dairy farm just outside Horsham, less than thirty minutes drive from Gatwick.

On the way, I deposited Tim Martin's cheque in my bank account. Cattermoull saw me, but chose not to acknowledge my greeting. My request to draw the money out as quickly as possible was rebuffed by the information that cheques required five working days to clear.

Dad had come in for lunch when I arrived home at the farm. The harvest was in and now they were busy with autumn ploughing. He greeted me affectionately and waited for me to bring up the reason for my unexpected return.

"Your room's still made up for you, towels are on the wash basin," Mum volunteered. I then explained what had happened to Air Links.

"Doesn't seem fair, somehow," Dad volunteered at the end of it. Farming also had more than its fair share of scoundrels in the 1960s.

I explained the legal ramifications of our contracts with Zucher and his Horizon Holidays travel firm.

"There must be plenty of pilots' jobs around though," Mum announced confidently. "Aircraft are flying over here every twenty minutes, full of tourists going overseas."

I smiled at her optimism. The charter companies had completed their crew training for the season, so even if they'd wanted to hire another pilot, their aircraft were fully committed to revenue flying. I quietly informed her I was looking around for alternative work. Dad's ears pricked up immediately.

"There's always a job waiting for you here," he volunteered. I thanked him and told him I needed a bit of time to review my options. The truth was I didn't really know what I wanted.

Somebody once said it was never darker than before the dawn, and that best described my mental state. After eight years in the flying business, we'd managed to build up a small but reasonably competitive business. Now a strange twist of fate had taken me back to the beginning again — jobless, heavily into debt, and a bit disheartened.

A phone call next morning summoned me to the bank. I misjudged the amount of traffic and arrived ten minutes early. I hung around the main terminal building and bought the current issue of *Flight* to check on the job market. Eagle needed experienced Britannia pilots and flight engineers; Borneo Airways in Malaya wanted Twin-Pioneer pilots, and Alfie Cope up at Newcastle needed freelance pilots. None of this interested me.

I was about to turn to the "Aircraft for Sale" section when my gaze fell upon a full-page advert for TEAL — Tasman Empire Airways Ltd, in New Zealand. I read the page with interest.

> TEAL, Tasman Empire Airways Ltd, the international airline of New Zealand, wishes to recruit experienced pilots, flight engineers and navigators.
>
> TEAL currently operates a fleet of three Lockheed L-188c Electras to Australia and the Pacific Islands, and plans to expand with Douglas DC-8 jetliners to Hong Kong, Singapore, Honolulu and North America.
>
> Applicants should have a valid ALTP or CPL with instrument rating.
>
> Interviews will be held in London this month, and successful applicants will be based in Auckland, New Zealand.
>
> Please apply to:
>
> > Captain K.A. Brownjohn
> > Flight Operations Manager
> > Tasman Empire Airways Ltd
> > Airways House
> > No. 1 Custom Street
> > Auckland, New Zealand
>
> Previous applicants are invited to reapply.

My eyes skimmed the advert with interest. Air Links' charter operations had once taken me to New Zealand and I remembered TEAL. It was a small airline operating mainly between New Zealand and Australia.

A photo of a Proctor in the "Aircraft for Sale" section distracted me momentarily. An owner in Elstree had a Mark Three for sale with low hours and good radio equipment. I was interested to see he was also asking £350 for his machine. Other adverts for Geminis, Messengers, Austers, Tigers and Prentices filled two pages.

A tap on the shoulder brought me back to the present.

"Thinking of buying a private aeroplane?" Blob-bottom asked cheekily.

"No thanks, just looking. I've just sold the Proctor for what looks like a fair price. What brings you down to Gatwick?"

"Well . . . you, actually. The bank's received an enquiry about the three Argonauts. An outfit in Scandinavia are looking for five more aircraft. Can't tell you who they are but . . ."

"That'll be Flying Enterprise, based in Copenhagen. Good operators, plenty of financial backing. They've tapped into a veritable goldmine flying Scandinavians to the Mediterranean resorts. Where do Air Links figure in this? Our creditors have closed us down."

Blob nodded, then explained the bank needed our assistance to transfer our mortgage deeds to the prospective owners. "It looks like you could come out of the deal slightly in credit. Why don't we discuss it in the manager's office?"

I found Tony, Denis, Stan Wilson and Levitt already assembled there. Cattermoull vacillated around nervously; he wasn't sure what was going on and didn't know how to treat us. I subjected him to a wide smile and long handshake, telling him how nice it was to see him again. He looked at me doubtfully before bolting for the safety of the back office.

Blob closed the door before addressing us.

"Good morning and thanks for coming here at rather short notice."

We returned his greeting and waited to hear what he had to say. It was worth waiting for.

"First of all, let me say how sorry the directors of the bank and I are about the failure of your company. All's fair in love, war and business, but this was a bit close to the mark, or so we thought. I attended a meeting yesterday where the matter was discussed, and the overall feeling was that the circumstances leading up to the cessation of operations bordered on fraud."

Our only response was an awkward shuffling of feet. Platitudes were nice, but they wouldn't pay the ever-increasing delinquent payments on the aircraft plus parking fees and other incidentals. The bank could sue us as personal guarantors for everything we had.

"And the bad news is . . . ?" Tony enquired facetiously. Blob dismissed the suggestion.

"Well I think this is good news for everybody. A Scandinavian charter operator has expressed interest in the three aircraft. We've quoted them a price, ready to fly away from Gatwick, and they seem quite happy with it. Now the question is, as mortgagees, are you prepared to co-operate with us in disposing of the aircraft to a prospective buyer?"

Tony enquired the sale price and Blob mentioned a figure that would cover the principal and overdue payments plus extraneous expenses. Stan Wilson, ever the businessman, enquired why we couldn't lease the aircraft to the prospective owners. Blob's head shook disapprovingly.

"You can try it, but I'm afraid you'd be operating alone. You'd need to buy the aircraft outright from us, as well as pay all delinquent charges and fees. Bearing in mind that the other airline has signed no contractual agreement, I think there are too many fish-hooks in such an idea to be worth pursuing. You'd also need alternative financing, because this bank wouldn't underwrite such a scheme."

Blob waited while we considered his words. Denis spoke first.

"Speaking personally, I don't fancy getting into the aircraft leasing business. Finance is a specialised business employing highly trained specialists, same as flying. My view is that for us to blunder into aircraft leasing would be as fatal as putting a financier in the left seat of one of our aircraft."

The general consensus of the meeting was we preferred to employ experts to remove the financial albatross round our necks. Blob nodded his approval.

"Okay then gentlemen, let's say it's agreed we'll handle the financing and legal side if you fellows will assist with the technical. Copenhagen wants to know the serviceability state of the three aircraft. Anybody got that information handy?"

Denis reported that the two operating aircraft were currently airworthy, but might need a day's work to return them to full flight status.

"And the third machine?"

Denis thought long and hard. "That's a bit more complicated," he explained. "Over the months, we've cannibalised parts from it to keep the other two planes flying. Now the parts will have to be replaced; I'd estimate it would take a minimum of two weeks to get the spares aircraft airworthy again."

Blob told us he'd telex this information to Copenhagen immediately, in the hope of having a decision within twenty-four hours. After a brief discussion among ourselves, the shareholders formally agreed to the National Provincial Bank disposing of our equity in the Argonauts to an unnamed buyer.

As we left the bank, I began to hope that we might all come out of the Air Links experience with a small profit.

Blob phoned just before five o'clock to advise the Argonaut deal had gone through at the agreed price.

"And I can now officially confirm you were correct in guessing Flying Enterprise were the buyers," he added. "Captain Mills has arranged for work to start immediately on all three aircraft. Copenhagen are sending their engineering people over on Monday to supervise. They stipulate the aircraft must be ready for delivery by the thirty-first of this month. That's a Saturday, just over two weeks away."

The next sixteen days were very satisfying, as our three aircraft returned to airworthy status. Air Couriers put every available man onto the task, and the last Argonaut, our Christmas-tree aircraft, was ready for its certificate of airworthiness test flight on the Friday night.

Denis and Tony did the test flight, and I went along to note down facts and figures for the test schedule. Blob came too, "to represent the bank's interests".

196

At the successful conclusion of the fifty-minute flight, we landed back at Gatwick and parked beside the other two machines. Each of us felt rather pleased that the Air Links insignia hadn't been painted over yet. I could almost feel the hundreds of pairs of eyes watching curiously as we taxied in for the last time. It would have been interesting to have heard the rumours circulating in the Aero Club that night.

Early in September, after the aircraft had been delivered, we received notices to call into the National Provincial's City office to complete the remaining documentation.

"There'll be a balance left over, which we'll distribute among you," Blob advised over the phone. "Then I thought we could have a drink together to celebrate your narrow escape from bankruptcy. Somebody we both know will be there."

Denis and Tony were already waiting when I arrived at the bank's head office. Levitt and Wilson had arranged to sign their documentation at their own banks.

Blob met us and ushered us into a large boardroom. A small bespectacled gentleman stood as we entered. "This is Mr Larsen, representing the purchasers, Flying Enterprise Lines." We shook hands as Blob introduced us.

At the conclusion of the signing ceremony we shook hands again and Air Links was now a charter company with no aircraft or assets. Blob looked at his watch closely.

"Didn't take as long as I thought. Four o'clock too early for a celebratory drink?" he enquired. Mr Larsen had disappeared the moment we'd signed the last of the documents, leaving us alone in the boardroom. We assured Blob any time was good for us. He made a quick phone call, then led us down the steps of the bank towards St Swithin's Alley.

"Best drop of bitter in the City," he confided, ducking into the doorway of a low-ceiling pub. "Four pints of your best bitter, Frank . . . er, no . . . make that five."

The tall figure of Mike Parry, our lawyer and erstwhile fellow pilot, appeared in the pub doorway as he peered into the darkened bar. We shook hands enthusiastically. Blob and Mike had both been fellow students on my RAF wings course.

Mike seemed delighted to see us again.

"Frankly, I felt I'd let you down rather badly over the case," he confided. "When I left you after the aborted court hearing on Wednesday, I couldn't imagine how you were ever going to struggle out from under such an enormous debt. So you can imagine my delight when Blob told me the good news about the sale of the aircraft. Cheers!"

We toasted the successful outcome in several rounds of best bitter. Just as the afternoon was about to dissolve into drunken pandemonium, a thought occurred to Blob. He reached into his inner pocket and retrieved three long white envelopes.

"Hey, I nearly forgot these. They should take a little bit of the chill out of the coming winter."

We tore open the proffered documents and each retrieved a cheque. Denis whistled with surprise.

"This is £532.11s.10d.! Crikey, that's better than a poke in the eye with a sharp stick. Now my family can afford to eat during the winter."

Tony and I received cheques for similar amounts.

"This calls for a celebration," I declared. "We've just risen from the ranks of the stony broke to the solvent. Okay, my round. Mike, what'll you ha . . ."

Mike Parry cut me short as he handed me another envelope.

"Open it," he instructed curtly. Curious, I slit open the top and retrieved an invoice.

"Netherby, Driscoll and Tombes, Barristers at law," I read. Denis and Tony craned over my shoulder to read what I was holding.

"For professional attendance, research, principal's time, travel expenses, cars, conduct and disbursements, £1520. Hey, what is this, some kind of a joke?"

"'Fraid not. Arbitration is an expensive business. Mind you, as I said the other day, you had some of the best legal minds working on your case."

"Yeah, but I thought they were helping you out for nothing. Your first big case and all that, y'know."

Mike shrugged regretfully. "Yes, I must admit I thought the same. Unfortunately I've now learned that in the legal profession, when a fellow is asked for an opinion on something, he follows it up with an account for professional services. Look, I'm as sorry as you are, but we really pulled out every stop for you."

"Yes, I know," I acknowledged. "Thanks anyway. It's just that for one moment I thought I'd got enough to live on, then the next instant it's taken away."

The cordial atmosphere had disappeared from our small group. Denis, Tony and I exited the pub feeling like stunned mullets. I fought my way home in the rush-hour traffic.

CHAPTER TWENTY-THREE
Security

I was beginning to think more and more seriously about the advantages of a nice secure job in the bank. Regular pay, two weeks' holiday, luncheon vouchers, low-interest loans, staff incentive scheme, sports and social club, assured pension, staff welfare scheme . . . It sounded better than endless winters out of work, watching the occasional aircraft land and take off at Gatwick until spring arrived.

Next morning I deposited Blob's cheque at the bank. After paying Mike Parry's fee, I would still have over £200 left plus the money from the Proctor. Living at home was infinitely cheaper than maintaining a flat at Gatwick and I should be able to survive relatively comfortably for six months.

Dad asked me if I'd made any plans for the future yet. I told him I was considering applying to the National Provincial Bank for a job. He was delighted with the news, and I heard him repeat it to Mum. Flying was a hazardous pastime to them. They'd been born shortly after the Wright brothers first flew and had heard of the many accidents that claimed the lives of early pioneers. The Second World War hadn't bolstered their faith in aeroplanes either. It must have been a relief to learn that I was thinking of giving up flying.

Two days later I phoned Blob and told him of my decision. He listened attentively, then asked if I'd like him to mail me the application form.

"Er . . . yes, okay. I thought you just applied and somebody interviewed you and said either yes or no," I explained.

"It's a bit more sophisticated nowadays. We have a personnel department that looks after more than 4000 employees. I'll drop a form in the post, which you can fill in and return. I'll see if they can arrange an interview for later this week."

The promised form was on the breakfast table next morning, and I returned it before the midday collection. Blob phoned me the following day and told me to report to the head office on Monday.

"Same building you came to a few days ago," he explained. "Personnel are a new department, so they're a bit full of their own importance. Remember to wear a conservative suit, grey or black, plain tie and black polished shoes. Don't judge the rest of the organisation by these people, treat the experience like our square-bashing days in the Air Force. Come up to my department when you arrive and I'll take you down there."

Monday morning found me on the 7.46am train to London. I presented myself in Blob's office just after nine, trying very hard to look like the typical city gent. I'd even left my battered flight bag behind and invested in a rather smart executive-style attaché case, which held virtually nothing. Blob eyed the whole effect approvingly.

"Very smart, specially the case. The bank has a dress code that calls for a bowler hat and furled umbrella, but you'll be told all about that when you join."

He led me down to the basement, where a large frosted-glass door proclaimed we were now in the personnel department. We waited in a large cream-painted waiting room for a rather insipid-looking clerk to appear. Blob spoke to him briefly.

"They'll get personal details from you first, then you'll have a staff interview with a personnel admin. manager. Then, after morning tea, there'll be more interviews and things. It's all rather dull stuff, but just hold your tongue and listen."

I assured him I'd do what he said. Anything was better than being out of work.

The insipid-looking clerk bade me follow him down a long corridor. He paused before a cream-coloured door, knocked and entered.

"Clapshaw, another mature candidate to be processed, Mr Prickett," he announced without interest, placing a file on the desk before leaving.

Prickett was a fellow about three years older than me, and obviously very aware of his status in the organisation. He eyed me contemptuously for a full minute, saying nothing. I felt as if I were an officer cadet again and wondered whether I should stand rigidly to attention. He finally opened the folder and examined my job application form for another minute.

"Had quite a lot of jobs, I see," he commented. Air Force, Westaway Funeral Services, Dan-Air, Air Links, SPANZ, then back to Air Links." He made a note in the remarks column. "Any job skills?"

"Er, how do you mean?"

"Well, driver's licence, trade certificate, foreign languages spoken, that sort of thing."

"Yes, I've got a driver's licence and I can speak conversational French. No trade certificates, but I passed School Certificate." He again wrote in the remarks column.

"Anything else useful? Correspondence courses, night school or anything like that?"

"No, not really . . . oh, except a pilot's licence and about 4000 hours . . ."

"No, I mean real qualifications, not hobbies, that's no use to anyone." He cut me short in mid-sentence. "What about part one or two book-keeping? Anything like that?"

"No, I'm afraid not." I hung my head ashamedly.

He consulted my form again. "Okay, now all these jobs you've had, tell me about them. How long were you in the Raff?" His pronunciation of RAF raised my hackles.

"Two years, doing my National Service."

He said something contemptuously about a lot of fellows in the bank getting exemption. I said nothing.

"Go overseas at all?"

"No."

"Which branch were you in? Accounts, secretarial, anything useful?"

"General Duties."

"Oh, is that all? Sort of general dog's-body, were you?"

"Yes, something like that."

He put a line through the remarks column and questioned me about my other jobs. He asked no details of the job, only the length of time I'd stayed with each company.

"So the longest you've stayed in one job is the second time you worked for Air Links?"

I described the nature of the SPANZ job, explaining we were working on secondment to the New Zealand company and then returned to Great Britain to resume working for Air Links. Prickett interrupted me before I could finish.

"Didn't give New Zealand much of a chance, did you? Arrived in the middle of December and left in February. Don't imagine anybody'd like that part of the world though. Full of kangaroos, sheep and flies. We had a couple of Australians working here on secondment for three months. Uncouth pair of fellows, didn't knuckle down to authority very well, called everybody 'sport' and spent an hour every day in the pub at lunch-time. We were glad when they went back."

I clicked my tongue disapprovingly and managed to restrain myself from giving him a geography lesson on the relative positions of Australia and New Zealand.

"Okay, that's qualifications and previous job experience covered. Now tell me why you want to work for the bank?" he demanded.

I thought furiously for a moment. The truth was that, apart from flying, there wasn't much else I could do. I decided not to tell him that. His beady little eyes bored into me while I floundered around for a reason.

"Well, it's a challenging job, you're a highly respected bank," I began but I could tell this line hadn't impressed. "Then there's the dozens of staff benefits, regular hours, two weeks' paid holiday, low-interest mortgages, luncheon vouchers . . . and security. I think that's the most important reason, security. It's so important in today's world."

Prickett smiled for the first time. He began to nod his head excitedly in vehement agreement.

"Security, you've hit the nail on the head," he assured me. "You'll start as a trainee . . ."

"The pay's not terrific to start with, but I could advance quite rapidly. Look at you, how long have you been in the bank?"

From that moment the interview came alive. Prickett told me of his rapid advancement through junior teller to counter clerk.

"Then they started this new department, personnel, and I became a senior clerk! I applied to work in the new department just as they changed all the titles. Now I'm a junior administration manager in personnel!"

I whistled to indicate my admiration.

Prickett carried on for another five minutes, until interrupted by a bell.

"Ten-fifteen, morning tea-time. You'd better join the others in the candidates' waiting room. I'll take mine in the junior executive common room. Look, it was good to talk to you, I've got a feeling you're going to fit into this bank simply splendidly. You could even do as well as me."

We shook hands and I mouthed something appropriate about security, as I respectfully took my leave.

Four pimply candidates were eyeing each other speculatively as I returned to the waiting room. I bade them a cheery "good morning" and received four ear-shattering blank stares in return. Further attempts to foster conversation with them were totally unsuccessful. As prospects for becoming leaders in the international banking community, I would have put each of them somewhere between Noddy and Big Ears.

After a fifteen-minute silence, a different clerk arrived to escort us to a discussion group exercise. Here we were required to debate a number of selected issues before a panel of three senior staff members. None of the interviewees stated an opinion, and I had the impression that everybody else had rehearsed their lines. As a pastime, it was slightly less exciting than watching paint dry.

By lunch-time the selection procedures were over so I went in search of Blob. We went to the same pub for lunch.

"Thanks for your help today," I began. "I'll now wait to hear the results."

Blob laughed. "Dunno what line of bullshit you fed Prickett, but he seemed to like it 'cause he phoned me immediately after your interview. I couldn't believe my ears. I was certain the pair of you would clash in the first five minutes. What the hell did you say to him?"

"Everything that you told me about the job over the last few years — regular hours, two weeks' paid holidays, security. So he liked that, did he?"

Blob confirmed the speech had gone down well.

"All five applicants will probably be accepted," he assured me. "Unless they're a complete moron, everybody gets an opportunity to make a career in banking. The cream of the crop will rise to the top, the rest can remain in the lower ranks as clerks. There's always plenty of jobs for Indians but very few for chiefs. You should hear the result within a couple of days."

Sure enough, two days later a single typewritten page on bank notepaper told me the National Provincial Bank had hired me as a junior trainee at a salary of £416 a year. Other conditions were set out, and my commencement date was two weeks away.

I read the letter a second time, then told Mum and Dad I'd got a job in London. The delight in Mum's face was a barometer of their fear of flying. In their lifetimes, aeroplanes had advanced from the fragile machines of the Wright brothers to four-engined jetliners like the Comet and 707. I had always suspected they regarded flying as a dangerous occupation.

"Wonderful news, we'll be able to take our holidays together again," Dad declared. "And now you'll be able to enjoy some sort of a social life."

I had to admit that social engagements in charter flying had occupied positions of little importance. After two or three failures to turn up to dinner invitations, hosts tended to erase you from their lists.

Now maybe this would change.

CHAPTER TWENTY-FOUR
A Change of Heading

I kept in contact with the other Air Links pilots to see what transpired for them. A week before I was due to start with the National Provincial, I met Denis and Tony in the Aero Club for an ale. Tony had received good news and bad. An application to BEA had progressed well until the medics found he had high blood pressure. This precluded him from employment with them. Simultaneously with this bad news came an offer from the British Aircraft Corporation to join them as a staff pilot at Bristol. Tony was ecstatic.

"Initially I'll be flying Herons and Pembrokes, but Jock Bryce, their chief test pilot, said there'll be opportunities to check out on the One-Eleven or the VC-10. The Anglo-French supersonic transport's also being built by BAC, so anything could eventuate later on."

Denis had quietly settled into a vacant captain's slot with Dan-Air. The job was supposedly only until the first of October, but Pluto Wilson had assured him it would become permanent.

Les Smith and Chegwidden were supposed to be starting a freight company out of Gatwick, using a Lockheed Constellation. Mike Sommerpole was hoping to join them if the venture got off the ground. Timber Wood had joined BEA.

Nobody had heard from Pickles but Denis thought he might be selling magazines or records somewhere in London.

"What about you? Found anything yet?"

I was too embarrassed to admit to having taken a job in the bank. I told them Blob had found me something with a lot of potential . . . and security.

We continued enjoying our drinks. The club was empty save for the three of us and two elderly Caledonian flight engineers in the snug bar. Outside the window, the day's IT flights were touching down on Gatwick's runway.

"I'll be moving to Filton when the job starts," Tony ventured. "If you're looking for a flat, mine's available."

I thanked him, but declined. The rent would have exceeded my annual salary. As a trainee bank clerk, I was going to have to trim my living standards rather drastically.

They finished their drinks and declined my suggestion of another. I waved them goodbye from the car park and returned to the bar.

Vic the landlord graciously poured me a half pint on the house. I sipped it in silent contemplation, while watching the Ambassadors, Dakotas, Vikings, DC-4s and other assorted airliners returning like nesting starlings. It was a clear evening, and aircraft could be seen by their landing lights twenty miles away. It was a spectacular sight. I reflected how exhilarating yet selfish an aviation career could be.

My thoughts were interrupted by the two Caledonian flight engineers beside the chimney piece. They had been there since lunch-time and were working up quite a head of steam.

". . . and if I were a young fellah, that's where I'd go," the taller of them exclaimed in a loud Scots accent. His companion shook his head negatively.

"Too far away, Andy. Ye know what some of these foreign airlines are like," he cautioned gently.

"Yon's no foreign airline; it's owned by the British and Australian governments for Heaven's sake. And it's a bonnie country, my wife's cousin lives in Dunedin. She reckons it's like Inverness only better."

I tiptoed over rather curiously. I must have had a premonition that something far-reaching was about to happen.

"And they're expanding, buying DC-8s soon, that's why they're having to advertise over here," Andy the tall one insisted. "If I were a young lad still, that's where I'd be a-heading. TEAL."

"Aye, I think ye could be right y'know, Andy. A young fellah joining them now could find himself half-way up the promotion ladder when the new jets arrive."

I eavesdropped unashamedly on their conversation. Then I remembered the TEAL advert in *Flight* magazine. I'd been so shell-shocked by other events it had slipped my mind.

New Zealand, that was a country I knew and loved. I had a lot of friends there and I would have worked there previously if the opportunity had been offered. TEAL was the government airline, small but well run. Their aircraft were modern and well maintained.

The engineer's words rang in my ears. "If I were a young lad still, that's where I'd be heading."

I was twenty-six and didn't know where I was heading.

Something compelled me to leave my beer unfinished on the counter and hurry home to write to TEAL.

Having mailed the letter of application to New Zealand House on Monday, I was surprised to receive a phone call a day later requesting me to attend an interview the next morning.

On arrival, I was delighted to find three friends — Mike Furniss, Bunny Somerville and John Peacock — also waiting to be interviewed by TEAL. We had all arrived half an hour early, which allowed us to spend time catching up on the previous three years.

Mike had survived on a variety of jobs, mainly joy-riding and instructing during the summer and anything at all during the winter. Bunny had returned to Sudan Airways clutching his new airline transport pilot's licence (ATPL), anticipating promotion to captain. The company declined to promote him, so he'd decided to seek employment elsewhere.

Only John Peacock had managed to get into an airline, as a DC-3 co-pilot. While we waited for interview, he recounted his story of how he got in with less than the magic 1000-hour total.

J ohn had become very dejected when every airline he applied to told him to come back when he had 1000 hours. His protests that he couldn't get the 1000 hours unless they employed him were ignored.

He was bemoaning his fate one night in the Bunch of Grapes to anybody who would listen. Most could offer sympathy but no advice. Eventually an old Air Force colleague, now happily ensconced in the right seat of a BEA Viscount, came up and told John to get 1000 hours of P-51 time. This was the last straw! After exam fees, tuition and the instrument-rating flight test, the poor fellow had less than £50 to last until he either got a flying job or began selling encyclopedias door-to-door.

He turned on his advisor and angrily demanded to know where the money for 1000 hours in a gas-guzzling P-51 Mustang fighter was coming from. His advisor laid a friendly hand on John's shoulder to calm him down, then removed a gold-plated ballpoint pen from his jacket pocket.

"P-51 — Parker 51, old sport," he explained, holding up his Parker 51 pen. "If you haven't got the necessary experience they want, put in a bit of P-51 time with your Parker 51."

"Isn't that illegal?" John enquired dubiously. The BEA pilot laughed.

"Only if you get caught. And anyway, you're not falsifying your logbook to obtain a licence are you? Think it over, you can always take it out later."

John did think it over, remembering that he had a DC-3 co-pilot job interview with the managing director/operations manager of Trans-Air next day.

That evening, in total privacy, he locked all the doors and windows before furtively altering the figure at the bottom of the last pages of his logbook to read 1000 hours higher.

Next morning he awoke in a muck sweat, fearful of the penalties for falsifying a logbook. He nearly altered the figures back to the correct total.

On arrival at Croydon for the Trans-Air interview, he approached a white-coated individual peering up into the wheel-well of a DC-3 and asked where he could find the airline's ops manager.

The man in the white coat stopped his inspection and told John he was already talking to him. John explained the purpose of his visit and was ushered into an office where it would be easier to talk.

The ops manager asked various questions relevant to his job application. John told him he was twenty-three, single, of British nationality and resident in Reigate. The ops manager nodded as he noted the facts down.

"Previous employer?" he enquired. John explained he'd recently left the Air Force after four years. Another nod and more writing.

"Got a commercial pilot's licence and instrument rating, of course?"

John assured him he had, adding he had passed his ALTP subjects recently. This gained an approving nod. "And your total flying hours?"

John gulped and began to blush furiously.

"S-s-sixteen hu-hundred hours," he stammered. The manager wrote the figure down while John watched anxiously, expecting him to pick up the phone and report the crime. Instead he nodded thoughtfully.

"When could you start?" was the final question. John nearly fell off his chair.

"Tomorrow . . . no, make that today," he exclaimed. The ops manager wrote at some length on his clip-board before turning to John again.

"What about starting next Monday, the thirtieth? I'll tell the pay office you're starting, and you'll have time to tidy up any private matters."

The ops manager was through the door and half-way back to his DC-3 before John caught up with him.

"You don't mean I've got the job?" he enquired with amazement. The ops manager stopped in his tracks and looked at him strangely.

"Course y'have, you're just the sort of fellow we're looking for." He lowered his voice to a confidential whisper as he continued. "You wouldn't believe it, but we get some pilots applying to us with less than 1000 hours . . ."

Now John had decided to switch to long-distance international flying, so had applied to TEAL.

While we talked, other applicants arrived for interview. From their conversations, it was obvious they were a mixture of RAF Transport Command captains about to retire and a bevy of BOAC 707 captains who had accepted early retirement. TEAL was in the job market for experienced jet pilots, and they fitted the bill admirably. I thought it unlikely that any of us — Mike, Bunny, John or I — would be offered jobs in the face of such competition.

While we waited to be interviewed, Bunny caught up on his sleep and I read the morning paper. A typist approached and, mistaking John for Bunny, pointed out that the section of his application listing interests and hobbies hadn't been completed. John told her his three main interests were flying, drinking and young women, not necessarily in that order. The typist giggled nervously, uncertain what to put on the form. Mike came to her rescue.

"Aeronautics, mixology and bird watching, no . . . er . . . better call it ornithology," he suggested. The typist wrote it down.

The interviews seemed to go fairly well, bearing in mind it seemed a foregone conclusion the BOAC and Transport Command fellows were hot favourites for the job.

Bunny was questioned at considerable length about his interests, particularly ornithology. Being fairly imaginative, he regaled the interviewer with details of a completely fictitious survey he was conducting on the Sudanese Plane Pounder, a bird that preferred airport runways as its habitat. The chairman of the interview panel was fascinated at Bunny's description of the bird's mating habits on hot runways.

When my turn came for interview, I recognised the chairman as Ken

Brownjohn, a well-known ornithologist. He was delighted when I told him I'd been to one of his lectures when he'd visited England ten years previously. I didn't bother to tell him that the reason for my attendance was to get out of a winter cross-country run at school.

Mike's interview was uneventful, although the chairman mispronounced his name several times. John went in immediately after Mike and the chairman had similar problems with his surname.

We left New Zealand House philosophical about the belief that we were unlikely to be offered jobs.

The arrival of a long white envelope three days later informed me that Tasman Empire Airways Limited, soon to change its name to Air New Zealand, had considered my application and was happy to offer me a position as a first-year Electra co-pilot at a salary of £1580 per annum. I would be based in Auckland, and a ticket for the one-way journey to New Zealand would be despatched to me once I indicated my acceptance.

I read the letter to Mum and Dad at breakfast. "This is just the opportunity I've been looking for," I told them excitedly. "I'm in at the beginning of their big expansion. At the moment they're operating three Electra prop-jets to Australia and Fiji, but when the first of their DC-8 jetliners arrives in August, they'll expand their routes to Singapore and Hong Kong, then the USA and Tahiti."

Dad was strangely quiet as I chortled with delight. I didn't notice Mum leave the room.

The phone rang; it was Mike and John.

"Heard from TEAL yet?" they enquired non-committally. I hesitated to tell them the good news, lest they hadn't been accepted.

"Yes," I admitted.

"Well?"

"I've been accepted. What about you?"

The cheers at the other end of the line eventually quietened and I learned that Mike and John had received letters similar to mine. Bunny was still asleep and hadn't opened his yet, but it looked like he'd also been accepted. We talked animatedly about when we'd depart for New Zealand.

"The sooner we get down there the better," John suggested. "There'll be plenty of others joining, so let's try and get in ahead of them." Mike and I tentatively agreed to depart as soon as possible. John had to give notice to Trans-Air.

Dad looked rather thoughtful when I returned to my unfinished breakfast.

"Congratulations," he murmured. "You've got what you wanted. You've got into a scheduled airline."

I thanked him and began planning my departure. I phoned New Zealand House and learned our tickets could be collected at the BOAC counter on the day of departure.

"I think I'll leave on Saturday," I said, half to myself. "And arrive in Auckland on the Monday, just as they're starting work for the week."

Mum had returned to the kitchen. "Will we see much of you from now on?" she enquired anxiously.

I assured her I'd probably be home once a year, adding that TEAL might expand its services to London one day. I didn't notice them exchange glances.

"Did I hear you say you're planning to leave on Saturday?" Dad enquired.

I looked up and suddenly noticed how sad he looked.

"Why, er . . . yes, I want to get down there as soon as possible," I explained rather weakly. "Does that conflict with anything?"

Mum came up to the breakfast table and spoke in a small strangled voice. "It's Dad's birthday this weekend and he'd rather hoped you could spend it with him . . . for the last time."

Guilt suddenly lashed my conscience as I realised how hard it was for them to accept I was departing to the other side of the world, probably never to live in England again.

"Of course I'll spend it with you," I assured them, wishing I didn't have to leave them at all.

Aviation is a selfish mistress, frequently demanding we leave loved ones to go off with her.

CHAPTER TWENTY-FIVE

Aotearoa-bound

I left England on Monday, immediately after Dad's birthday. We had spent a wonderful weekend together, and nobody had mentioned my imminent departure for New Zealand.

Dad drove me to the station, trying to maintain a cheerful air. We had all been very brave as we said goodbye in front of the house. Mum waved to us from the dining-room window as we drove down the lane. I maintained an air of false cheerfulness, and Dad talked about how exciting it was to be joining an airline expanding into the jet age.

"Once they're established on the North America run, they'll want to extend further on to London," he assured me hopefully. I agreed it was an obvious conclusion.

We said awkward goodbyes to each other outside the station, then I gave him a big hug. He got quickly back into the car so I wouldn't see how upset he was.

I bought the latest copy of *Flight* magazine to read on the train and this time I managed not to open it at the back pages to check the "Situations Vacant" section. I told myself I'd never need to look there for a job again.

I met Bunny, John and Mike at the BOAC air terminal, where we picked up our tickets and boarded the bus for Heathrow. The south of England was in the midst of a beautiful summer, and I savoured the sights and smells of the trees and gardens for the last time as we sped through Hammersmith and Fulham.

BOAC flew us as far as Sydney in a Boeing 707. I had looked forward with keen anticipation to flying in a modern high-performance jetliner that cruised at twice the speed of our Argonauts. The cabin crew were polite and efficient yet aloof, as though they didn't really need the job.

We departed on schedule, turning left after take-off towards Seaford. The 707 climbed easily through the clear summer air over Guildford and the North Downs. I recognised the Hog's Back, and suddenly Horsham slipped past the trailing edge of the wing. My eyes traced the road leading to our farm, and I discerned the front paddock I'd once flown over as an air cadet in my Tiger Moth days. My thoughts turned to my dear old Mum and Dad in the farmhouse four miles below. It was three o'clock; Dad would have come in for afternoon tea and they'd be thinking of me on my way to a country 12,000 miles away, never realising I was less than four miles above, craning for a last glimpse of them.

For a few moments my eyes misted with unashamed tears. Then England and the first twenty-six years of my life disappeared under a thin layer of cloud.

BOAC sped us round the world infinitely faster than my Air Links Dakota had on my first visit to Australasia four and a half years ago. We got to Sydney in just over a day, with refuelling stops in Rome, Beirut, Karachi, Calcutta, Singapore and Darwin.

TEAL had scheduled us to catch their midnight Electra for the final hop across to Auckland and had arranged for us to spend the intervening twelve hours in a Sydney hotel.

They seated us in the first-class section for the flight to Auckland, and after dinner the captain sent back a message inviting us to the flight deck. Bunny and John were fast asleep, so only Mike and I accepted.

Dawn had just broken as we entered the cockpit. An incredibly young-looking captain, Lindsay Caudwell, introduced his crew — Bob Harman the co-pilot, Alan Partridge the navigator, and flight engineer "Jake" Jacobson. All were in their twenties and thirties — quite a change from UK scheduled airlines, where most captains were in their late forties or fifties and had served in World War II.

I was impressed at the cockpit of the TEAL Electra. Whereas our Air Links planes had always looked distinctly worn, with gaps in the instrument panel where gauges were missing, this aircraft was in beautiful condition. I reflected that flying modern well-maintained aircraft was going to be rather enjoyable.

The captain invited one of us to remain in the cockpit for the approach and landing, which I watched the co-pilot perform faultlessly.

Auckland's Whenuapai Airport looked different from the previous time I had landed there with Air Links, over four years ago. Now it was mid-winter, and gale-force winds and torrential rain greeted us on arrival. I recognised the driver of a waiting taxi and he sped us into town.

We had finally made it! After years of working for fly-by-night charter companies who often folded overnight, we had finally joined a government-owned scheduled airline.

The clock in the Auckland Harbour Board building struck 9am as our taxi deposited us outside Airways House in downtown Auckland. A sign in the passenger check-in area indicated that Flight Operations was upstairs. We headed in that direction.

It seemed strangely quiet for a weekday morning. Mike pushed open a door marked "Flight Operations Department" and we followed him into a large room, which was devoid of any furniture save a number of telephones on the floor. I picked one up and listened. As I feared, it was disconnected. An adjoining office labelled "Flight Ops Manager" was similarly empty. We looked at each other in dismay.

"Don't say the blooming airline's gone out of business before we've even started!" Bunny said. I gazed at my companions disbelievingly.

"We're going to have to get home somehow," I declared, wondering how much it would cost and what I was going to do when I got there. I began to understand why my old friend Blob-bottom put so much value on job security.

Mike led us disconsolately downstairs and back to the passenger check-in area. The Electra crew had just pulled up in a cab.

"Problems?" the young captain enquired when he saw our dismayed expressions. We explained the problem, the airline appeared to have gone out of business overnight, leaving us jobless and stranded on the other side of the world. The Electra crew chuckled at our dismay.

"Don't panic just yet, the Flight Ops department moved into new premises over the weekend," the captain reassured us. "You must report to Technical House, that's over in Mechanic's Bay, the old flying-boat terminal."

"I'm driving past there on my way home," Jake, the flight engineer, added. "Can I drop you off on the way?"

Things were beginning to improve again.

We squeezed into his stationwagon, and he gave us a rundown on the airline as we proceeded along the waterfront.

"We're going through a tremendous expansion programme at the moment," he explained. "Our first DC-8 arrives shortly, and two more are scheduled for delivery later in the year. The future looks rather exciting, you've joined at a good time. We've operated three Electras on the Tasman and Pacific Islands routes, but when the jets arrive we'll expand to Honolulu, North America and the Orient."

We began to feel distinctly better as he extolled the virtues of the airline.

"Here we are — Testicle House." He pulled up outside a large unimposing building on the waterfront. We looked at him doubtfully.

"Weren't we supposed to report to Technical House?" I enquired doubtfully. The flight engineer shrugged.

"Testicle House, Technical House, same place. Just a bit of company slang that's crept in over the years. Go up the stairs and you'll find Flight Ops on your right."

Curiosity forced one of us to enquire why it was called Testicle House.

"You'll soon find out that this is where most of the balls-ups originate," the engineer explained, as he shifted into gear and disappeared into the winter rain.

We found our way to the Flight Operations department, where a clerk directed us to the Flight Ops manager's office. Once again we met up with Captain Brownjohn. Windows on two walls gave spectacular views of the Waitemata Harbour where not many years ago, TEAL and Pan Am flying boats had alighted and departed.

Brownjohn's office contained a wooden desk and several uncomfortable chairs, the sort associated with prison waiting rooms, with the front legs slightly shorter than the rear. Pictures of various sea birds adorned the walls, and the bookcase appeared to contain more bird books than technical manuals.

"Welcome to Tasman Empire Airways, soon to be re-christened Air New Zealand," Brownjohn greeted us with a smile. "I'll introduce you to the rest of the operational staff, but first my secretary wants to check who's here."

Yvonne, his efficient-looking secretary, entered the office and began reading from a list of names.

"Mr Martin . . . oh, sorry, he arrived yesterday . . . Mr Gosling here yet?"

We explained who we were and she quickly produced our files. Brownjohn fidgeted in his chair while we confirmed the details of our licences, experience and personal details, then offered us a conducted tour of the Flight Operations department.

First stop was the Aircrew Scheduling department where a rather harassed-looking individual was surrounded by an angry crowd of arguing young females. Brownjohn muscled his way through them.

"Hugh Bromley, head of aircrew rostering, ex-RNZAF flight engineer now working for us on the ground." He caught Hugh's attention and introduced each of us in turn. "I'll leave you with Hugh, he has all the details of your courses and can answer any questions you may have."

Brownjohn then quickly departed the scene.

Hugh Bromley, usually referred to by his nickname, Huge Anomaly, broke away from the argument to consult a clip-board. Frantic searching through the pages on it failed to produce any record of us being hired.

"Are you sure you've got the right airline?" he enquired anxiously. We were quick to reassure him on that point. He shuffled more papers and suddenly resolved the dilemma.

"You're air hostesses!" he explained apologetically, pointing to a typed list containing our names.

"I'm blooming well not!" Mike assured him in a deep voice to dispel any sign of femininity. This failed to convince Huge Anomaly.

"Here's a list of newly hired hostesses, and you're on page two," he argued, pointing to his clip-board. Five minutes of dispute failed to convince him, and we began to run out of patience. I began to understand the reason for the building's nickname "Testicle House". We'd only been in it a few minutes and they'd managed to balls things up for us already.

"I'll send you to the company tailor for a uniform fitting," Hugh decided, scribbling on an order pad. Mike's patience suddenly snapped; he advanced on Hugh and towered over him menacingly.

"Tell 'em I want the hem of my skirt well above the knee and give my blouses a plunging neckline," he hissed angrily into the scheduler's face. Hugh backed away in alarm.

"We can't have you dressing up as women, not in our airline," he informed us, his back pressed hard against the wall.

"Why not, I'm a blasted hostess, aren't I? Don't your hostesses wear feminine uniforms? I thought that only happened in Aeroflot . . ."

Further discussion was cut short by a bald, serious individual interrupting Hugh.

"Got the list of new pilots handy? I want to know if any of them have navigator's licences. We're going to be critically short of navs once the new DC-8 services start."

Huge Anomaly had begun to introduce us. "Mr Furniss, Mr Somerville, Mr . . ."

"Welcome to TEAL," the newcomer interrupted. "Haven't got navigator's licences, have you?"

Mike glanced at the interloper. "Get lost!" he invited, for he had more important matters to discuss with Huge Anomaly before exchanging polite trivia with this clerk. Hugh shuffled his feet nervously.

"Er . . . this is Mr Lawton, the chief navigator," he mumbled. I gulped nervously. Our first hours in the airline had gone badly. First the company had apparently gone bust overnight, then we'd been reduced in rank from pilots to air hostesses, and now Mike had told the chief navigator to get lost.

Joe Lawton, the company's chief navigator, was too nice a fellow to be put off easily. He extended a welcoming hand.

"Welcome to the company," he smiled easily. "We need a lot of new crew. It's good to have you joining us."

We each shook his hand and muttered something appropriate.

"Now then, I suppose you haven't got navigator's licences, have you?" Joe enquired hopefully. He beamed with delight when two of us admitted we had.

"Excellent! We'd like to use you in a dual capacity, for a bit more pay of course, but only if you're agreeable."

Mike still felt slight resentment over his recent demotion to air hostess.

"I'm afraid that won't be possible. You see, according to Hugh here, we're air hostesses not pilots. As a matter of fact I was just ordering some uniform blouses when you arrived," he replied. Huge Anomaly was nodding as Mike spoke, pointing to the list of names as confirmation.

Joe Lawton grabbed the list and located our names on the second page.

"What was your previous job?" he asked me.

"Argonaut captain, mainly round Europe."

The chief navigator peered at the typewritten sheets suspiciously.

"Why the hell did Brownie put 'em in cabin services?" he demanded of Hugh, who shuffled nervously.

Comprehension suddenly lit the navigator's face. He tore the stapled pages apart and pointed to the heading on the second page.

"These are pilots!" he informed Hugh indignantly. "Somebody stapled the wrong pages together and mixed up the pilots and hostesses."

Hugh peered at the second page closely before admitting we were pilots. We breathed a collective sigh of relief.

Joe Lawton now took charge. "You're on the next Electra course, starting Monday," he advised us. "That'll give you four days to arrange accommodation and generally get sorted out. Daily transportation to the training school at Mangere will be provided."

We listened happily, grateful to have escaped the ranks of air hostesses. Huge Anomaly departed to quieten the lynch mob of angry young females who'd just learned they'd apparently been hired as pilots and not air hostesses.

Joe continued. "You'll need to draw the various technical manuals from Stationery before the course starts. Digger Dawson is the technical librarian in charge of all that. You should find him at the other end of the building, Room 212, corner office. You can't miss it."

We exited Flight Operations and went in search of Stationery.

After proceeding down a long corridor to the far end of the building, we found Room 212. Repeated knocking brought no response. John tried the handle, and the door opened easily. Inside, two white-coated painters on tall trestles were painting the ceiling. The rest of the room was bare except for a portable radio blaring forth pop music.

"Stationery?" John shouted above the noise of the radio.

"Moved," one of the painters replied. His partner nodded in agreement.

"Stationery have moved," he affirmed.

We looked at each other with despair. In our first morning the airline had gone bust, we'd almost been demoted to air hostesses, and now Stationery had moved.

Life in an international state airline was not quite what we'd imagined.

When we finally found Digger Dawson he issued us each with a complete set of manuals. These comprised a large Lockheed Electra flight manual containing all the required technical information about the aircraft, a performance manual, a route guide, and a voluminous company manual titled "Part A", which told us everything we needed to know about company procedures, from how to address royalty to which shoe to put your left foot into.

As we were departing, the librarian enquired whether we required accommodation. Only I needed somewhere to live.

"Captain Boothwaite runs a boarding house in Ring Terrace," he informed me. "Quite close to here. Call in and see what he's got available."

I noted down the address and we departed.

TEAL provided a week's accommodation, after which we were expected to have found somewhere to live. The week would soon pass, so next morning I phoned Captain Boothwaite and arranged to call round.

"Mendelsohn Mansions, large concrete building on the left side going towards the Harbour Bridge," he explained. "Can't miss it, see you about twelve then."

It was further from my hotel than I had imagined, so it was early afternoon before I found the address. Mendelsohn Mansions was a large drab concrete structure on a steep hill overlooking the harbour. In front and below, the courts of the Herne Bay Tennis Club broke the monotony of terraced houses. Although rather nondescript in its architectural style, it was reputed to be the only building in the Southern Hemisphere designed by the celebrated German architect Erich Mendelsohn.

I proceeded through a broken wooden gate into a small garden, where a petrol-driven lawnmower had been left running unattended. Exhaust fumes and noise filled the area. Walking past the machine, I followed the directions of an arrow pointing to "Reception".

The inside of the house was as uninspiring as the outside. It had, in the words of smart architectural magazines, "seen better days".

A large sitting-room lay beyond the reception area. Two big moth-eaten sofas and half-a-dozen matching armchairs lay exhausted round the perimeter of the room. A framed sepia-tinted picture of "Highland Cattle" hung over a cold fireplace. Two similar prints — one called "Stag at Bay" and the other "Monarch of the Glen" — adorned other walls of the room.

I was about to ring the bell in the reception area when a female voice bade me enter. I advanced into the sitting-room, expecting to meet the owner of the voice, but nobody appeared. Instead my gaze was met by a sad-eyed boxer dog, which stared at me solemnly. I coughed politely several times, then enquired if anybody was in.

No reply. I walked through the room and out onto a balcony commanding a magnificent view of the bridge and harbour. Suddenly the voice again told me to come in. I hurried back into the sitting-room.

"Come in, come in. Stoppit dammit." The boxer had become even more mournful, and I had found the owner of the voice — a white sulphur-crested cockatoo.

An upstairs door banged as I approached the magnificent bird, and a dishevelled fellow in his late forties, clad only in singlet and shorts, hurried down the stairs. He gawped at me for several seconds.

"Er . . . hello, my name's Guy," I explained nervously, fearful lest he mistake me for an intruder. "Digger Dawson gave me your name and . . ."

It was difficult to make myself heard above the noise of the revving lawnrmower.

"What are you?" he shouted above the din. My puzzled expression told him I didn't understand the question. "Are you a pilot, navigator or engineer? Traffic? Not male cabin crew, are you?" he enquired.

I explained I was a new co-pilot joining the company. He nodded as I spoke.

"Yeah, Brownie did mention there was a new course of mushrooms starting Monday. Looking for accommodation, are you?"

I nodded affirmatively.

"Okay then. There's a room on the second floor that'll suit you. Nice and quiet so you can study when you have to. The rent's £33.7s.6d. a month and that includes your breakfast. You can afford that, can't you?"

At that moment the lawnmower spluttered and stopped, out of petrol.

I assured Captain Boothwaite I could afford the rent. Further discussion was interrupted by a statuesque blonde lady descending the stairs and joining us.

"You must be Guy," she proclaimed, holding out a hand. "I'm Marie and I see you've met my husband, Frank." A fourth voice, identical to Marie Boothwaite's, joined the conversation. "What do you think you're doing?"

Husband and wife simultaneously shouted at the parrot to keep quiet. Marie turned to me apologetically.

"That's Mellow Yellow. Frank brought him back from Australia after the war. Don't take any notice of him."

At first it was difficult to ignore the bird, who invariably joined in whenever a conversation was in progress. Eventually I learned to turn a deaf ear to him.

Three days later I moved into Mendelsohn Mansions.

Most of the other tenants worked for one of the two New Zealand Government airlines. In addition to TEAL, which operated internationally to Australia and some of the Pacific Islands, there was New Zealand National Airways, which operated only within the country.

The first human tenant of the Mansions to introduce himself was Mike Hawk, a tall slim TEAL navigator.

"Welcome to Menopause Mansions," he greeted me. We conversed for several minutes, and I learned that he too had only recently joined the airline from the Royal Air Force. Subsequently I found he possessed a lively sense of humour that frequently brightened life in the Mansions.

Other occupants were a Viscount captain with National Airways, and Don Robertson (Robbie), a chief purser with TEAL. Like me, they occupied single-room accommodation.

The best accommodation was the top floor, which had been converted into a single luxurious apartment commanding magnificent 360-degree views of the city and harbour. The tenants were Clarence and Leslie, proprietors of an art gallery in Parnell village. They were usually referred to collectively as the two Parnell Queers, which didn't seem to worry them at all. There was a third occupant of their apartment, a tiny chimpanzee named Baby. The name was very appropriate for the creature was treated as if he were their child. They dressed him in expensive infant's clothes, kept him in a playpen full of baby toys, and took him for twice daily outings in an expensive English perambulator.

The other rooms in Mansions housed various aircrew, ground engineers and traffic staff, who tended to come and go a bit. It wasn't unusual for the place to contain a complete Electra crew from captain through to junior hostess.

Huge Anomaly, the bumbling head of rostering, soon learned to take advantage of this when yet another serious foul-up occurred in Testicle House. He only needed to make a quick phone call to the Mansions to procure an urgently needed crew member for a flight. This was rather inconvenient for the person concerned if he or she were on a day off and had made other plans. The matter was soon resolved with simple Kiwi ingenuity: half a dozen bottles of beer were kept handy to the phone, so that when Hugh required a particular crew member, the one concerned could quickly snap open a bottle, take a sip and announce regretfully, "I'm sorry, Hugh, but I've had a drink today."

Frank and Marie Boothwaite completed the cast of characters in the establishment. Frank had originally flown TEAL flying boats on loan from the

RNZAF during the war. Afterwards, he'd exchanged his Air Force uniform for that of a TEAL captain and continued flying the same aircraft and routes in peacetime. The graceful flying boats had eventually been replaced by land planes and he'd subsequently commanded Douglas DC-6s, Lockheed Electras and was soon to convert onto the new DC-8 jetliners.

He was a tall skinny individual in his mid-forties who attempted to combat the ravages of age by dying his greying locks with brown hair colouring. Unfortunately for him, this turned it not brown but orange, leading Mike Hawk to comment at breakfast one morning that "Captain Boothwaite is turning prematurely orange."

My first few days taught me how hard members of the company played. The day would start with breakfast in the sitting-room, looked down on by "Stag at Bay", "Highland Cattle" and "Monarch of the Glen". With ten or so people seated at one table, conversation could sometimes get quite noisy and animated. Mellow Yellow loved chatter and activity and would add to the cacophony by flapping his wings and contributing the occasional squawk or inane phrase.

Bosca, their boxer dog, was the exact opposite. He preferred to spend breakfast lying in everybody's way, mournfully eyeing passers-by or licking his genitalia with the gusto of an alderman drinking soup. This must have met with Marie's disapproval in the past, for occasionally Mellow Yellow would call out "Stoppit, stoppit, dammit," in Marie's voice. The dog would then shame-facedly cease his libidinous licking and gaze slowly and sadly round the room, trying to locate the voice. Finally, with a deep regretful sigh, he would fall half asleep on the floor, keeping one eye open for any food scraps that might fall from the table.

On weekends or holidays, or when some weren't working, the day's activities would usually be arranged at breakfast. This might be sailing, going to the beach or shopping.

For those of us on training courses, breakfast on weekdays was a race against time to catch the company transport to the airport at eight o'clock.

The first week of the Electra course taught me that if TEAL folk played hard, they also took flying very seriously. For reasons that I found out about later, students on courses were referred to as "mushrooms".

Every weekday morning we mushrooms bussed to the technical training school at the new international airport, still under construction for the new DC-8s.

There were ten other students on the course, seven co-pilots — including Bunny, Mike and John — and three flight engineers. Most of the other co-pilots had left NZ National Airways to join TEAL; except for Warbler, an ex-BOAC captain who'd decided to return home to his native country. The flight engineers — Jack Kingfisher, Bob Falconer and Warwick Underwood — were all ground engineers from the TEAL hangar.

Lectures were held in a medium-sized classroom with a whiteboard adjacent to the lecturer's rostrum and a slide projector in the middle of the class. The instructor would lecture from the rostrum, occasionally drawing the necessary diagrams on the whiteboard. When a particularly complex diagram like an electronic circuit was required, the classroom curtains were closed and the projector switched on to beam the diagram onto the whiteboard.

Air-conditioning had not been installed at that stage, so the classroom could get very hot by mid-morning. The combined effect of heat, darkness and the projector's hypnotic hum induced feelings of great drowsiness.

The technical course started with an introductory speech from the chief ground instructor, himself a licensed aircraft engineer. He explained the format of the course, which would be of twelve weeks' duration, with an examination every Friday. At the end of the ground course, we would undergo conversion flying training. He told us to work hard and wished us all good luck with the exams. Timetables were then handed out, and I was relieved to see the first lecture was on air-conditioning. I breathed a silent prayer of relief that the company had started with an easy subject. Or so I thought.

By 4pm I had begun to doubt my ability to stand the academic pace of the course. The Electra's air-conditioning and pressurisation system was incredibly complex, unlike the comparatively simple aircraft I had flown previously. The Electra's system was electronic and involved complex diagrams of cabin programme shafts, electronic sensors, zero negative sensing relays and a lot more to confuse the mind. The main electronic diagram was so complicated that previous students had dubbed it the "Fairisle jersey". Most of the other pilots were having problems with the course. To make a bad situation even worse, some of the American terminology was baffling to us.

I was about to approach the instructor at the end of the first day and tell him the course was beyond my technical comprehension, but the other members of the course said it for me. The instructor remained unfazed and assured us that all new aircrew made the same comment on the first day, but eventually got through the course successfully. I discreetly said nothing and caught the transport back home to start an evening's study.

The course continued through until the beginning of December. Lectures would start at nine o'clock and continue till midday, when we adjourned for lunch in the Greasy Spoon staff cafeteria. This was usually our main meal of the day and very reasonably priced, so we tended to stock up on soup, steak, chips and tomatoes, and then dessert. This enabled us to study in the evening without having to go out for dinner.

Unfortunately, the effect of a heavy lunch affected our concentration in the afternoon, especially when the temperature in the darkened classroom neared thirty degrees and we struggled to hear the instructor's dull monotone above the projector's hypnotic hum. It proved too much for Bunny one afternoon.

At lunch-time we had discussed the Torrey Canyon disaster, where a super-tanker had run aground on the rocky Cornish coast in England's West Country. Millions of litres of crude oil had spewed onto the picturesque Cornish coastline, threatening to damage one of Britain's finest natural beauty areas. In an effort to prevent the oil being washed ashore, RAF fighter bombers had been called in to bomb the site to ignite and burn off the oil before it came ashore. The morning's newspapers had been full of pictures of RAF Hunter ground-attack aircraft carrying out bomb and rocket attacks on the stricken tanker.

Bunny must still have been thinking of these things when the afternoon lecture commenced.

The subject was the Electrical System, a particularly difficult and tedious topic with many complex electronic circuit diagrams to study. The needle of the classroom thermometer had passed thirty degrees as the quiet-voiced instructor pulled the blinds down and turned on the projector . . .

The captain clung to the wheel of his stricken vessel as the first aircraft wheeled into the attack. Captain Somerville had selflessly given his crew the order to abandon ship; nothing could survive the effects of napalm and rockets from the attacking enemy aircraft. The last lifeboat was rowing away from the threatened vessel as the heroic captain steered the ship into deeper water. The first aircraft delivered a salvo which hit the bridge beside Bunny's left ear with a deafening bang. The bridge structure collapsed under the impact and Bunny was thrown to the deck . . .

Bunny picked himself up from the classroom floor and gazed up at our ring of grinning faces. Somebody helped him to his feet as he struggled in his semi-conscious state to remember where he was.

"Projector bulb blew," John Peacock explained. "You must have nodded off and your head was resting against the side of the projector when the bulb blew with a terrific bang. You awoke with a tremendous yell and said something about life-jackets. Then you must've fallen to the floor."

The laughter subsided, the instructor replaced the blown bulb in the projector, and Bunny resumed his seat, determined not to fall asleep again.

Every Friday afternoon we were examined on the systems taught during the week. After the exam we were free for the weekend; this was an excellent scheme, for it removed the necessity to study over the weekend. Students could return to the classroom on Monday morning, refreshed and ready for another five days of lectures.

We would start on new subjects, maybe hydraulics, avionics, weather radar or de-icing, subjects on which we would be examined four days later. Meanwhile, the previous exam results would be published on Wednesday, and anybody unfortunate enough not to achieve the pass mark would be given the opportunity for one re-sit at the end of the course. Several people had to take re-sits.

Towards the end of the course, lectures began to centre on less specific subjects such as company organisation, NZ aviation law, Pacific climatology and aviation medicine. With the exception of aviation law, we were not examined on these subjects. They were categorised as "nice to know" rather than essential knowledge.

Our teachers for these subjects were practising aircrew. A training captain taught four of us the essentials to pass the aviation law exam to validate our foreign licences. At the conclusion of his lecture, he handed round a selection of old exam papers with the advice to research the answers before exam date.

Climatology was taught by a very experienced line navigator. His knowledge of the geography and weather patterns of the area were phenomenal. He started his lecture by drawing from memory a map of the eastern Australian coastline, then New Zealand, Fiji, Samoa and Tahiti, before proceeding to describe the various weather patterns encountered in each area. His delivery was droll and deliberately humorous. We listened spellbound as he got his message across, for this was the voice of practical experience talking to us.

". . . then there was this Dutch fellow, Buys Ballott, who liked to stand with his back to the wind," he would start like a practised storyteller. His audience clung to his every word and rarely questioned anything he said. I only heard him doubted once, and that was on the subject of Wellington winds.

"Very tricky place indeed," he began. "Damaged three aircraft at the opening of the airport. The problem is wind shear, sudden changes in speed or direction . . . or both. The place gets very strong winds originating through Cook Strait, but basically there are only two types of Wellington weather, it either blows a gale from the north or from the south."

The ex-National Airways pilots on the course exchanged doubting glances. Their previous job had taken them into Wellington sometimes five times a day. They had experienced every type of Wellington weather.

"But I've been there on a calm day when there's not a breath of wind," one of them ventured to protest. Our instructor looked at him understandingly.

"So have I," he agreed. "That's when both winds blow at once."

The last subject in the technical ground course was aviation medicine, usually abbreviated to AvMed. This was a comparatively new topic in 1965 and was taught by the company medical officer, Dr Fred Platts. Dr Fred was a founder member of TEAL, having been present twenty-five years earlier, when RNZAF personnel had helped form the airline.

Our class of pilots and flight engineers now joined a mixed bevy of newly hired stewards and air hostesses. We quickly got to know the hostesses, especially a curvaceous little blonde. Several minutes' quick conversation before the lecture started revealed she was a former nurse, engaged to an orthopaedic surgeon in Wellington. To emphasise her words, she displayed a spectacular diamond engagement ring on her left hand.

Further conversation was cut short by the arrival of Dr Platts. He eyed his audience speculatively before beginning to talk about food poisoning.

"Still quite a problem up in the Islands on the Coral Route," he explained. "Despite the company's efforts to keep conditions sanitary aboard our aircraft, problems still arise in the high temperatures. As aircrew, you must avoid drinking dirty water at all times and remember to eat different meals at staggered times when flying."

Some may not have understood him, so he explained further. "If one pilot has fish, the other should choose meat or vegetarian, never the same. If the food looks or smells suspect, don't touch it. Choose something else or wait till you're back on the ground."

We listened attentively as the doctor continued his AvMed lecture with a description of the various maladies that may affect international travellers.

"Cholera can be contracted in any warm climate where poor hygiene conditions exist," he cautioned, then went on to list most of the diseases prevalent in the tropics: yellow fever, smallpox, dengue fever, tetanus, typhoid, malaria, filariasis, beri beri, blackwater fever, rabies, dysentery, sleeping sickness. The list was long.

When he saw the depressing effect such a long list had on his audience, he gave us some good news.

"Before going flying, you'll be immunised against all these diseases by a single injection against tetanus, typhoid and para-typhoid, called TAPT. It's a selection of every drug you're likely to need."

"Sort of like a cocktail," John whispered to me in an impressed voice.

Doctor Fred continued. "There are a few unpleasant side effects from the injection. The surrounding area will be extremely sensitive for several days, maybe even a week. Some of you might experience lack of appetite, drowsiness, possibly even nausea or vomiting. It will certainly prevent you enjoying golf, squash or tennis."

He paused momentarily to let the information sink in.

"Any questions about TAPT?" he enquired. The lecture was almost over.

The cuddly blonde held up her hand bearing the spectacular engagement ring. "Will it prevent me having children?" she enquired anxiously.

Dr Fred ignored a few sniggers from the audience and gazed at her kindly. "I wouldn't rely on it if I were you," he advised her.

The lecture ended in a ripple of laughter and the doctor departed for his office, leaving our class with a newfound respect for this quiet man.

222

In the years ahead, he was to prove a good friend and ally to anybody who became unfit to fly. He felt his job was to keep us flying rather than find reasons to ground us. Regrettably this attitude is rarer today.

CHAPTER TWENTY-SIX

The Mushroom Treatment

Before starting flying training we needed pilots' licences. This involved taking a physical examination with Dr Platts and also passing the Department of Aviation's law examination.

John, Bunny, Mike and I made appointments to see the doctor at midday on Monday. We arrived in Testicle House a few minutes early and found the Flight Ops Christmas party in full swing. Huge Anomaly staggered up to us, a beatific smile on his usually haggard face.

"Good of you to find the time to come to our party. How's the course going?" he slurred, spilling beer over himself. We explained we had come for a medical examination, but would be delighted to join in the fun afterwards. Meanwhile, we needed to find Dr Platts' medical section.

Hugh courteously escorted us there.

"Three gentlemen for commercial pilot physicals," he informed Dr Platts' nurse, banging his glass of beer on the counter top.

The nurse took one look at us and sent us off to provide specimens. "You'll find glass jars in the bathroom," she said, pointing at an adjacent room. "Bring them back here when you've finished. Dr Platts is delayed a few minutes but won't be long."

Hugh began to berate the nurse for the doctor's delay as we disappeared to the bathroom. She ignored him.

We returned two minutes later, each bearing a full jar. Hugh had given up on the nurse and now directed his attention to us.

"There's a few minutes to wait so come and join the party?" he suggested.

"Thanks but we'd better not. Might affect our blood pressure or eyesight," we replied regretfully, setting the three jars on the counter top. Hugh tried unsuccessfully to change our minds.

"It's a Kiwi tradition, the staff Christmas party. Surely you don't want to break a tradition?" he implored, gesturing with both hands.

We were adamant in our refusal not to join the party until we had completed our medicals.

Hugh accepted our reasoning. He picked up his full glass and reeled back to the party.

It took Dr Fred less than an hour to assess us as fit to hold New Zealand commercial pilots' licences. We were now free to join the staff Christmas party, where things were heading towards a noisy crescendo. Everybody was talking at once as we forced our way into Flight Operations. Joe Lawton, the chief navigator, immediately pounced on us.

"Merry Christmas. Come and join the festivities." He steered two of us by the elbow towards a long table laden down with New Zealand fruits, cakes, meats, salads and seafood. An opposite table contained the liquid refreshment: various juices, wines, spirits and a solitary keg of beer, which people seemed to neglect in preference to other choices of drink.

"You haven't got a drink!" Joe accused us. "What can I get you?"

John and I collected glasses and were about to fill them from the beer keg, but Joe returned and steered us towards the wine. "Have you tried our New Zealand chardonnay?" he enquired. "They say it's as good as the French. Or would you prefer something a little stronger? Glass of Scotch maybe?"

"Beer will be fine," we assured him.

"I'd stick to the wines or spirits if I were you," he whispered confidentially. "We've had a report from Hugh the beer's gone off."

The final academic hurdle before starting our conversion flying training on the Lockheed was the aviation law exam. The New Zealand Department of Civil Aviation had scheduled the next exam for 10am on Wednesday. This gave us a day to run through the old exam papers together. By examination date, we were reasonably confident of success.

Mike arrived early at the exam venue with Bunny in tow. To miss this exam would mean a long wait until after the Christmas summer recess, so each of us had been careful to arrive in good time.

The allotted time for the exam was three hours, but after half this time most of us had managed to answer all the questions. My request to hand in my answer book and leave early was denied by the stern-faced invigilator, who pointed to a notice at the top of the exam sheet: "Time allowed: Three hours. Candidates may not leave before the allotted time."

After an interminable wait, the supervisors collected up the answer books and released us. I left the rather stuffy exam room and breathed fresh air gratefully.

"No problems there, were there?" Mike greeted me cheerfully. The questions had contained no surprises for us and had all been repeated in previous examinations. We were about to find somewhere for lunch when John realised Bunny was missing.

"Must have sneaked out early," he suggested.

"Naagh, nobody was allowed out till the official time was up. Where the devil is he? Couldn't still be in there, could he?"

We returned and found our companion sleeping, his head resting on top of his desk. We roused him and he looked round dazedly. "What . . . where am I? What time is it?"

"Time to go, you blithering idiot. You didn't fall asleep during the exam, did you?" we implored.

Bunny sheepishly admitted he had dozed off after the first few questions

After we'd taken the aviation law examination, New Zealand's Civil Aviation Department issued us with student pilots' licences for our flying training. Bunny and I were assigned to a young ex-Air Force fighter pilot, Captain Mayn Hawkins, who had joined the company less than two years previously. The syllabus comprised twelve hours' flight time for each pilot under training. TEAL didn't believe in flight simulators; they argued there was no substitute for the real aircraft. They wrote off two aircraft in training accidents before they realised their error.

The flying training was lengthy and comprehensive. Each training detail was four hours, split into two-hour spells for each student. Training was conducted at the new international airport in the early morning, as the aircraft were required for commercial flying during the day. The session would start with breakfast in the staff cafeteria, followed by a comprehensive briefing on the day's exercises. These might include stalling, recovery from unusual attitudes, fuel dumping, then back to the airfield for various types of circuits — low-level bad-weather circuits, three-engined circuits, flapless circuits and others.

A few of the exercises were too dangerous to be taught in the aircraft and were better suited to a flight simulator, where a crash situation could be resolved by simply pressing the "reset" button. But as TEAL didn't have a simulator, they had no choice but to teach these exercises in the aircraft.°

The Lockheed Electra was an exhilarating aircraft to fly, with four Allison turbo-propeller motors, each rated at 4000 horsepower. The giant four-bladed paddle propellers almost spanned the entire wing leading edge. Flight controls were hydraulically boosted and delightfully light. The aircraft handled like a late-generation World War II fighter and was probably as fast.

Unfortunately, when the hydraulic power to the flight controls was turned off, the manual forces required to move the controls were excessively heavy. The agile Electra became very cumbersome to control as the aircraft was transformed into an unwieldy, hard-to-manoeuvre piece of machinery.

And when the throttles of the four turbo-prop engines were closed to flight idle, air flow over the wings was drastically reduced and the aircraft dropped like a stone.

Unfortunately, both these manoeuvres — hydraulic boost off and flight idle approaches — had to be performed by TEAL pilots under training. And they had to be performed simultaneously!

As each briefing session commenced, we wondered whether today was the day for boost off/flight idle approaches. Captain Hawkins had already demonstrated a flight idle approach, wisely overshooting from 200 feet. I had attempted a boost-off approach and landing, which went well until we crossed

° This is no longer the case. Air New Zealand today have an impressive fleet of simulators for each type of aircraft. Some of these are so realistic that all flight training is completed in the simulator. On the 747-400 for example, the first time a pilot gets to fly the real aircraft is with passengers. Flight simulators have contributed greatly to air safety.

the threshold of Auckland's southwesterly runway. A nor'westerly crosswind blowing over the hangars caused moderate turbulence on finals. As we passed through 100 feet, we entered this turbulence and the port wing dropped. I tried to apply a touch of right aileron to pick it up, but manual control was ponderous and slow. The strength of both arms was insufficient to deflect the controls fast enough. Captain Hawkins lent his strength to the wheel and, all too slowly, the wing began to lift.

Fortunately for everybody, the flight engineer, a very experienced aviator nicknamed "Scratchy" Poole, had second-guessed this could happen, so had kept his hands on the hydraulic power levers. Seeing our two pairs of hands struggling to gain control, he selected the hydraulic power back on again and the wing lifted. I overshot from the approach and as we levelled out down-wind, we looked at each other and agreed it was a ridiculously dangerous manoeuvre to practise.

Flight idle approaches were equally dangerous, and to combine the two was about as safe as sending a girl into a rugby-team shower. We dreaded the final session, when we would be required to demonstrate our ability to perform boost off/flight idle approaches. There was no tolerance for error, and I firmly believed there was a strong likelihood of damaging the aircraft badly. At that time a very macho attitude towards flying prevailed, possibly engendered by the many ex-wartime aircrew in the company. If we had protested against these dangerous manoeuvres, we new pilots would have been labelled as "sissies", and would still have had to perform them as part of our check-out.

Fortunately for us, early one morning two experienced captains proved how dangerous it was. Captain "Sea Jay" Cutter and Nobby Clarke were doing such a manoeuvre as part of Sea Jay's biannual competency check. As they hurtled towards Auckland's runway, I suspect the speed may have become a few knots too slow or windshear may have affected them. The tolerance for error on this type of approach was zero and they had gone outside it.

When "Sea Jay" pulled back the control column to halt the aircraft's rapid rate of descent, it failed to respond, hitting the ground and disintegrating. The fuel tanks ignited and the whole aircraft became engulfed in dense black smoke. The crew struggled from the cockpit in zero visibility and managed to reach safety. Nobody was killed, but a perfectly good aircraft was destroyed.

This unfortunate event saved Bunny and me from having to perform boost off/flight idle approaches. The company quickly removed these exercises from the flying training syllabus, and only the charred remains of Electra ZK-TEB remained to remind us all of the foolhardy manoeuvre.

The final daylight-flying training detail was the biannual competency check. Mayn Hawkins and I met at breakfast for the acid test. If I failed this check flight, my future in Air New Zealand would be doubtful. Like all executions, this one was scheduled for dawn. Bunny didn't show up for breakfast, which surprised us. His love of food was already well known.

Mayn Hawkins briefed me without waiting for Bunny, and we proceeded to the aircraft. The flight engineer for my check flight was Scratchy Poole again. Mayn acted as co-pilot for the detail. Basically the flight went as earlier training flights. The check captain/co-pilot would close a throttle to simulate a failed engine and I would then carry out the vital actions and fly a three-engined approach and landing. I also had to demonstrate other emergency manoeuvres. After an hour and ten minutes, Mayn Hawkins announced the next landing was the last.

I taxied in and parked on the ramp. Mayn finished writing up his training report, signed it and handed it to me to read. I had passed.

"Okay. Got any questions? Don't forget to use only symmetrical reverse on those three-engined landings. Otherwise it was all okay. See you on the line."

Scratchy Poole shook my hand. "Welcome to TEAL," he effused. "We hereby promote you from the rank of mushroom to first officer."

I thanked him, and forgot to ask why new aircrew were called mushrooms. I looked at my watch. It was 10am.

"Bit early for a celebratory drink in the pub, I suppose?" I ventured. Mayn and Scratchy looked at each other aghast.

"Jeezus, you've got a lot to learn in this company, Guy," Scratchy warned me. "It's never too early when somebody else is shouting."

We repaired to a grubby little pub near the airport, nicknamed the Mangere Hilton, and toasted my elevation to the first officer ranks. After several pints of New Zealand bitter had slaked our thirsts, Scratchy asked me how I'd found the course.

I told him I'd found the amount of technical detail they threw at us mind-boggling. They couldn't expect us to retain more than twenty percent. He agreed.

"And 9am to 4pm is a long time to spend in a classroom," Mayn Hawkins added. "You can't be expected to retain everything they tell you, so they tell you too much, hoping some of it will stick."

"Much of the information is superfluous shit you'll never need to use," Scratchy declared. "It's hard sitting in a darkened classroom, looking at a screen, trying to understand some complicated diagram."

"At least the mushroom treatment is over," Mayn declared. "From now on the training will be more practical."

I suddenly remembered. "Why do they call us mushrooms?" I enquired. Scratchy took a swig of his beer before replying.

"Because they treat you like mushrooms," he explained. "Keeping you in the dark and feeding you shit."

Mike Furniss, Derek Stubbs, John Peacock and Barney Ruffle had also checked out satisfactorily by now. Only Bunny remained to be checked out, and nobody knew why he'd missed the final training detail.

Having demonstrated their ability to fly the Electra, new pilots then began route familiarisation training. This required us to operate into every airfield used by the Electras, under the supervision of a training captain.

It was now Christmas time. John Peacock's first route familiarisation flight was with Captain "Sea Jay" Cutter, one of the pilots who'd recently walked away from the Electra boost-off training accident. The experience seemed to have heightened his machoism. Sea Jay was a legendary character who had joined TEAL after collecting a Distinguished Flying Cross for distinguished wartime service in the Royal Air Force.

His post-war flying career had been equally legendary; Brownie had appointed him to pioneer TEAL's Coral Route to Tahiti via Fiji, Samoa and the Cook Islands. It was not difficult to imagine this tough character diving from his moored flying boat into some tropical lagoon with a stick of gelignite in each hand to blast away coral heads from his intended take-off path. Sea Jay did everything the hard way; he was hard on himself and equally hard on anybody under his command. His idea of route familiarisation training could be best described as sado-masochistic. He preferred his trainees to learn from their mistakes. It would never have occurred to him to tell you something to prevent you making that mistake.

His crew reported at flight despatch an hour before scheduled departure time. John Peacock, feeling very much the new boy, hovered in the background while they checked the flight plan and paperwork.

"Melbourne weather looks marginal, but we've got Sydney as an alternate airfield," Sea Jay declared. "Anything in the notams?"

Partridge the navigator drew his attention to an active military danger area en route, and the co-pilot observed that the Melbourne automatic meteorological broadcast was temporarily off the air for maintenance. Normally the aerodrome weather was broadcast on the local (short-range) beacon, so that arriving aircraft could learn the landing condition and the runway in use before they commenced descent. Sea Jay scanned the notam.

"Yes, okay. I see they're broadcasting the weather on Plenty," he acknowledged. Plenty was a beacon used to home aircraft towards the aerodrome. Once within range of its emissions, the aircraft's radio compass would point towards it, telling the pilot in which direction to head to overfly it. On this occasion, the beacon was also being used to broadcast the weather information.

John sat in the right seat and began the pre-flight checks; the other co-pilot assisted him in this lengthy task.

He did reasonably well for a first line-flight, apart from mispronouncing a few Maori names of en route positions. Partridge handed him position reports (aireps) at regular intervals and Sea Jay spent the rest of the time questioning John on operational matters.

After three hours and forty minutes, they approached the Australian coast at Merimbula. They had navigated by the stars while over the ocean. The remainder of the flight would be along airways, with radio beacons dispersed at regular intervals for them to home to. The process was comparable to the "cats' eyes" seen on the road at night, the beacons marked the centre of the airway. John tuned the radio compass to the Merimbula beacon. Sea Jay noted his actions and enquired whether he was getting Merimbula. The new co-pilot confirmed he had tuned and identified the beacon.

At this moment, the hostess came to the cockpit with four breakfast trays.

"Take a quarter of an hour's break for breakfast, then we'll talk about the arrival," the captain suggested. John readily agreed to the suggestion. The flight had been hard work, answering Sea Jay's interminable questions, sending position reports, drawing up the passengers' flight progress chart and monitoring the en route and destination weather. The other co-pilot climbed into the co-pilot's seat during John's absence.

"Tough going up there?" the chief steward remarked kindly as John left the cockpit. John rolled his eyes heavenward.

"Yeah, was a bit. Couldn't seem to do a thing right, I even pronounced some of the place names incorrectly . . ."

The steward smiled encouragingly. He had first flown with Sea Jay in flying-boat days and knew what a hard task master he could be. He placed a meal tray before John and left him to enjoy it.

Meanwhile, in the cockpit, the pilots were endeavouring to pick up the weather on the Plenty beacon.

"Still out of range, captain," the other co-pilot commented. "Should come in before we commence descent; we're still 180 miles out. The last forecast was okay. Wind from the south; lowest cloud was 500 feet, broken."

Sea Jay nodded. He would have preferred the information before he commenced the descent.

John arrived back from breakfast shortly afterwards.

"Ready to hop back in?" the other co-pilot enquired. John nodded and they swapped seats.

"They want a call here," Sea Jay informed John, pointing to a reporting point on the chart. The co-pilot noted they had just passed over it. He pressed the transmit button.

"Melbourne, Tasman Echo Charlie. Er . . . we crossed Merim . . . b . . ."

"Merimbula." Sea Jay corrected John's pronunciation of the Aboriginal name.

"Er . . . yes, Merimbula, flight level two nine zero, estimate Won . . ."

"Wonthaggi," Sea Jay interrupted again.

John completed the position report and sat glum and despondent, irritated at the way the captain had chosen to humiliate him.

Sea Jay smiled and told him to cheer up, they'd soon be there. John smiled weakly.

"Tasman Echo Charlie, do you wish to route direct to Fenton's Hill?" the Melbourne air-traffic control suddenly enquired. John located the position on the chart; a direct clearance would save a few minutes.

"Tell him yes," Sea Jay shouted.

"Melbourne, New Zealand Echo Charlie, roger on the direct routing."

ATC gave them a course to steer to the position. All was quiet for a few minutes. It was 1am and they were the only aircraft airborne. The other co-pilot was tuning into another radio beacon ahead. He wrote on a message pad and handed it to the captain.

"Using runway one seven, Captain," he observed. The captain nodded.

"Echo Charlie, cleared to descend when ready to flight level one eight zero, wind is a light southerly, quite a nice night." The Australian controller suddenly cleared them. John acknowledged.

"Are you getting Plenty?" the controller asked a few minutes later. They were in descent and the cockpit workload was about to increase significantly. John paused.

"Tell him!" Sea Jay commanded.

"But he can't possibly want to know whether . . ."

"Tell him you're getting Plenty!" Sea Jay bellowed. John looked distraught.

"But I'm not," he protested. "I've been in the training school for three months and haven't . . ."

"Tell him!"

John shrugged resignedly. An order was an order; he pressed the transmit button and was about to begin a long dissertation on his non-existent love life. Before he could speak, the other co-pilot spoke for him.

"Roger, Melbourne, we have received the weather information on the Plenty beacon, understand runway one seven is in use."

Sea Jay muttered disappointedly. The new co-pilot had wriggled off the hook.

They landed on Melbourne's southerly runway and taxied in to begin the turn-round procedures for the return flight.

The flight back was equally unpleasant. Sea Jay questioned and abused John for a further four hours. The only bright thing was the strong tailwind that made the flight an hour shorter than the one to Melbourne.

Bunny was rostered to fly with the chief pilot of the Electra fleet, Jack Curtis, an ex-World War II bomber pilot referred to as "The White Fox" because of the colour of his hair. Jack was an excellent instructor and a real gentleman to fly with.

Regrettably, Bunny didn't get to fly with him . . . but that's another story.

CHAPTER TWENTY-SEVEN
Strangers in the Night

I commenced my co-pilot route training with the Beaver, a jovial little Scot who seemed more concerned that his domineering wife had a good seat for the flight than in bombarding me with questions. Our night flight to Sydney was pleasantly uneventful. The Beaver gave me a few tips and pointers, but otherwise left me to settle into the routine of flying for a new company. We arrived at Sydney, where a fresh crew waited to take the aircraft on to Wellington. The sun had just crept above the horizon as we boarded our crew bus. It was Christmas Day.

The King's Cross hookers were finishing a hard day's night as our crew transport pulled up at the Manhattan hotel in Sydney's red-light district. The captain's wife disembarked first, leaving her husband to manage their bags.

A Sydney milkman drew up in his horse-drawn milk truck as we exited the bus.

"Coming up for a drink, Milky?" the navigator suggested. "It is Christmas time."

The milkman began to decline the offer regretfully. "Gotta get Daisy her breakfast," he explained. "She gets irritable if it's late."

"Daisy, is that your wife?" the Beaver enquired sympathetically.

"Naagh, Daisy's me bleeding 'orse," the Australian explained, gesturing towards the front of the milk cart, where several of the cabin crew were feeding boiled sweets to his white horse.

"She seems happy enough for a few minutes, why don't you come up to the crew room for a quick noggin. Do you prefer Scotch or brandy?"

Milky's tongue ran over his lips in thirsty anticipation. "Is that French brandy?" he enquired, eyeing a bottle protruding from somebody's flight bag.

"Yep. Says on the label it's over 150 years old," Scratchy Poole replied. "Might go off if we don't drink it fairly soon."

The milkman saw the sense of this argument and agreed to join us for a Christmas drink. "Only one though," he insisted. "Daisy's waiting for her breakfast."

A King's Cross hooker (complete with miniature poodle) eyed us professionally from her pitch as we trooped across the forecourt.

"Anybody feel like a good time? Only ten quid," she suggested to the Beaver, who was struggling with his wife's bags. He generously suggested she bring the poodle up to the crew room for a Yuletide drink instead.

"Still cost yer ten quid," she replied, with no trace of the spirit of Christmas in her voice. The Beaver's Scottish ancestry came to the fore; he countered with an offer of ten shillings. The street walker was appalled.

"You must be bleeding joking," she replied indignantly. "Make it a fiver."

The captain shook his head. "Ten bob, take it or leave it," he declared flatly. She turned away indignantly.

"I'm selling sex, not peanuts," she spat at him. "You won't get anything decent for ten bob." She tugged angrily on the poodle's leash and returned to her street-corner pitch.

Ten minutes later the whole crew were celebrating Christmas on the top floor of the Manhattan hotel. Several introductions were made, and the Beaver introduced me to his wife, a formidable lady with piercing eyes and iron-grey hair.

Over by the window, Milky enjoyed the magnificent view of Sydney Harbour as he downed a fourth brandy. Twenty stories below, Daisy was feeling distinctly neglected. Her Christmas had been all too short — a few boiled sweets, then everybody had disappeared upstairs to celebrate, taking her prospect of breakfast with them.

"Merry Christmas, Daisy old girl," Milky called. "Fancy a drink?" His horse whinnied derisively and waited for her master to return.

"She probably does need a drink, left there in the hot sun," a plummy-voiced hostess declared. "I'd never leave my horse neglected like that." The junior steward, an amateur jockey, agreed with her. They fell into angry discussion over the matter.

After an hour of festivities, the effects of the long night flight and the alcohol began to take their toll on us. Scratchy Poole, the hostess and two stewards had already left the crew room with a bag of boiled sweets. As I departed, the Beaver and his wife were also leaving.

As we headed for the lift, the milkman had a sudden fit of conscience and decided to return to work. A lengthy wait ensued until a porter appeared and told us the lift was temporarily out of service.

"Godda larch piece of freight coming up," he explained. "Shouldn't be longer 'n ten minutes or so." He shot a furtive glance at the milkman before hurrying downstairs.

The captain's wife announced they weren't waiting ten minutes for any lift and dragged her husband towards the stairs. The milkman decided to follow. Together we walked down fourteen flights.

Milky became quite distraught when we arrived at the hotel forecourt.

"Me 'orse, where's me bleedin 'orse?" he cried. To our surprise, the milk cart was still in front of the hotel but the horse was no longer between the shafts. Somebody had released Daisy from her chains.

We had just begun searching for her, when a whinnying sound from above drew our attention. We craned our necks to locate the noise. Fourteen floors above us, Daisy gazed happily out of the crew-room window, chewing contentedly.

"Merry Christmas, Milky old boy," she seemed to say in a plummy voice. "Thanks for the drink."

The onlookers began to snigger at the ridiculous sight, but the captain's wife was not amused.

"It's cruel," she proclaimed, tugging her unwilling husband across the hotel forecourt. "Its disgusting, bestial, I refuse to have anything to do with that kind of behaviour." She paused at the corner of the street as she spoke. Her husband looked miserable.

A chuckle from behind made him turn round.

"I told yer you wouldn't get anything decent for ten bob," a voice whispered from the shadows.

Christmas brought an unpleasant surprise for Bunny.

Captain Brownjohn, the flight operations manager, had reviewed the progress of the new co-pilots and engineers under training. The introduction of the three DC-8 jet aircraft meant a doubling in size of the company, and promotion to command would be rapid in the near future. Already a few captains had progressed to training captains in less than two years and the trend would continue. Any new entrant displaying undesirable tendencies needed to be brought in line as quickly as possible. It was considered that those who failed to conform were best dismissed during their six months' initial probation period. All new entrants were aware of this and endeavoured to give the company their best effort. But in Brownjohn's opinion, Bunny was not trying hard enough. His exam results and his instructor's comments certainly indicated this.

Brownie told Yvonne, his secretary, to summon Bunny to the office at 9am Monday. She phoned the message through to Bunny on Friday, giving him the weekend to ponder the reason for the summons.

Monday came and the flight ops manager purposely kept the delinquent waiting until 9.15am to let him sweat. He motioned to Yvonne to show the co-pilot into his office.

She hesitated in the doorway before speaking. "I'm afraid Bunny . . . er, First Officer Somerville . . . hasn't arrived yet," she began.

Brownie frowned with surprise — normally any member of his flying staff would be scrupulously punctual for an interview involving disciplinary action that affected his flying career. Before Brownie could reply, Bunny's dishevelled bulk hurled itself into the office and skidded to a halt on the proverbial mat.

"Bunny Somerville, sorry I'm late but I slept through the alarm. Have a lot of trouble . . ."

Brownjohn gestured for him to sit down and shut up. He picked up Bunny's file and read it thoughtfully. Experienced pilots were becoming thin on the ground and he didn't really want to dismiss this one, but his career in the company so far had been disappointing. He eyed the offender for several seconds before speaking.

"Mr Somerville," he began in a solemn monotone. "I have reviewed your record of employment in this company and I must tell you I find it disappointing."

Bunny nodded sympathetically and wisely said nothing.

"You joined us from Sudan Airways in August and attended Number 24 Electra conversion course. Your record tells me you achieved minimum pass marks in all subjects except hydraulics and electrics, which you failed."

He silenced a protest from Bunny, who had begun to explain that the subjects he had failed in were always taught after lunch.

"The chief ground instructor attributes this to your tendency to fall asleep during lectures," he told the silent pilot. "However, I am happy to see you passed the remaining subjects at a second attempt."

Bunny brightened visibly, glad to have brought some happiness into the flight ops manager's day.

"However, I see that you missed aviation medicine a few days later and offered the excuse that you overslept."

Bunny's head dropped in shame.

"When the time came to validate your foreign licence, the record indicates you didn't complete the law paper and so failed the exam."

"I fell asleep," Bunny mumbled. "It was a hot day and I'd had a big . . ."

Brownie shushed him to silence. "Mr Somerville, this pattern has continued. You missed your final flying training detail with Captain Hawkins."

He glanced at the head bowed in shame. The co-pilot was taking the rebuke hard.

"Mr Somerville, our training facilities are stretched to the maximum, and we cannot tolerate lateness for flying training when an aircraft has been taken out of revenue service for you."

The flight operations manager paused in his delivery. The message was obviously getting through to the first officer for his head was still hung low in abject humiliation.

"You even missed your first line-training flight," Brownjohn continued. "And again the excuse was that you overslept."

Bunny's head dropped lower.

The flight ops manager closed the personal file containing details of Bunny's misdeeds and addressed him directly. He was satisfied with his handling of the matter, the poor fellow was beside himself with shame, there was no point in turning the knife in the wound. A kindly warning now and he'd be a reformed man. There was no need to dismiss him, despite the entreaties of the instructional staff.

"Mr Somerville," he concluded. "Our company is currently embarked on a programme of tremendous expansion. Pilots who joined the company less than two years ago are now captains." He paused theatrically.

"I now have to decide whether to sacrifice the effort and expensive flight time spent training you as an Electra pilot and dismiss you."

He paused to allow the severity of his statement to sink in to the huddled form before him. The poor fellow was truly shaken by the interview. Brownie wondered if maybe he'd been a bit too hard. He decided to release him from his misery with a few kind words.

"Mr Somerville," he continued. "The choice is yours."

Bunny continued to bow his head in shame.

"Mr Somerville?" he repeated.

A very quiet but distinct snore came from the somnolent form. Brownjohn approached the still figure and gave it a prod to make sure it was asleep. Satisfied, he tiptoed to the outer office.

"Give that officer a cup of strong black coffee and the standard letter of dismissal when he wakes up," he instructed Yvonne.

Bunny was given a month's salary and a ticket back to England. He eventually ended up flying for a freight company out of Hong Kong. Most of the work was night flying which suited his life style admirably.

Route familiarisation training continued for the rest of us, learning the various routes and airfields we would fly into, and ensuring we were up to standard operationally. This usually took a month to accomplish and ended with a final route check with a training captain, after which the new pilot was cleared for line flying.

It was company practice to share the flying "leg for leg" — which meant the two pilots would alternate in handling the aircraft. While one flew, the other handled the radio communications, assisted en route and performed checklist items with the flight engineer. During route training, new co-pilots were given the occasional landing at the various airfields served by the Electra fleet. These included Melbourne, Sydney, Brisbane, Tontouta (New Caledonia), Nadi, Pago Pago, Auckland, Wellington and Christchurch. The intention of route training was to produce a pilot not only technically proficient at handling the aircraft, but also conversant with the route network and company standard operating procedures. The company had no time for individualists or one-man bands; they wanted their aircraft flown their way.

A few of the initial landings during route training were less than perfect. John Peacock, in particular, did more than his fair share of "grand piano" landings. Barrie Gordon, his training captain, was a particularly patient instructor, who tried earnestly to teach John the art of putting the Electra gently onto the runway. But John continued to thump the Electra onto the ground.

After one particularly bad landing into Wellington, the instructor's patience evaporated. He angrily informed John he wasn't accepting any responsibility for the atrocious landing. He handed John the public address microphone and told him to apologise to his passengers for the heavy arrival.

John took the microphone. "Ladies and gentlemen, this is your first officer speaking," he began. "Captain Gordon has asked me to apologise for that dreadful landing . . ."

After parking outside the Wellington terminal, Captain Barrie Gordon didn't relish having to mix with the angry passengers in Customs while waiting for his bag. He decided to resolve the problem by donning the co-pilot's jacket, leaving John the captain's.

The ploy seemed to work. Several passengers remarked on the firmness of the landing to John. He decided to shift the blame. Approaching Captain Barrie, who was still attired in John's jacket with two gold rings, he told him in a stern loud voice. "That's the last blooming landing I let you do!"

Shortly after this, John's landings improved dramatically and he became one of the smoother pilots in the Electra fleet.

Flying training of the flight engineers on our course took considerably longer to complete, since none of them had previous flying experience. The requirement for the issue of a flight engineer's licence was 200 hours of flying instruction. This usually took three or four months. Consequently their training continued long after the last co-pilot had checked out.

I was on several flights when Scratchy Poole trained Jack Kingfisher. Whereas our pilot training had usually been fairly low key, allowing us to learn from experience, the engineers were constantly hounded. Frequently Scratchy would interrogate his student: "What would you do now if a propeller oversped?" or "What would be your first action now if the pressurisation failed?" Other variations on the theme were constantly fired at the student. During engine start he would suddenly ask the maximum turbine inlet temperature for start, a figure we had all learned, but one most pilots had difficulty in recalling at short notice. Five minutes later, as we began taxiing, he'd want to know the minimum hydraulic pressure for the brakes.

Over a leisurely drink with Scratchy during a Sydney stopover, I remarked on the severity of Jack's training. The usually light-hearted engineer suddenly became very serious.

"Our flight engineers are professionals," he informed me. "Most are recruited from our ground engineers. When we recruit flight engineers, there are twenty applicants from the hangar for every position. Consequently we can pick and choose. We take the ones we believe have the best temperament for flying, not necessarily the most academically brilliant. We prefer engineers with a practical turn of mind, so that when an engine starts to over-temp during start, they don't wait for it to reach the overheat limit before shutting it down. They watch how fast the temperature is rising, and if they think it's going to exceed the limit, they shut it down in plenty of time and prevent damage to the engine."

I thought of my incident during training when the wing had dropped during a boost-off landing. Scratchy had anticipated that it might happen and was ready with his hands on the switches to turn the hydraulic power on again if required. Now he was preaching what he practised.

Scratchy continued. "Our flight engineers are lifetime professionals, unlike those in the American airlines, where a new pilot starts in the engineer's seat, doing a job he knows and cares very little about, just waiting for the day he can move into the co-pilot's seat. Our blokes spend the first six or seven years on the ground maintaining the aircraft. By the time they're selected for flying training, they know the machine intimately. They'll spend the rest of their professional lives in the engineer's seat."

I had listened to Scratchy's sermon with surprise. Once again it had been brought home to me that TEAL aircrew worked as hard as they played. Scratchy hadn't finished.

"People think we're harsh on our engineers during training, and I suppose they're right. But the task of the engineer is to monitor the aircraft systems while the pilots concentrate on the flying. Once, maybe twice, in their career, the thoroughness of our training will pay off and save an aircraft, and probably many lives."

I didn't know it then, but Scratchy's words were to be proved strangely prophetic in the next few weeks.

By the end of February, most of the co-pilots on our course had completed their route training and passed the company final route check. They were now cleared for line flying.

There were two exceptions who hadn't made the grade. Bunny had already departed, and another pilot hadn't measured up to the company's standard of flying. He received additional training to try to help him attain the necessary standard and was given a second final route check, which he again failed. After discussion with the training staff, the Airline Pilots' Association (ALPA) and the pilot himself, Brownjohn reluctantly decided to dismiss him.

The arrival of the three DC-8 jetliners had more than doubled the passenger carrying capacity of the airline, creating an urgent demand for aircrew.

Although there was no shortage of pilot and flight engineer applicants, the company had to advertise extensively for cabin crew and readily accepted any cute long-legged beauties able to fill in application forms.

The training of new co-pilots and flight engineers ran parallel with the training of future captains and newly recruited air hostesses. Many of the hostesses were ex-nurses, school teachers or typists who had tired of life on the ground and decided to savour the excitement of a flying job. A few had flown previously, either with National Airways or overseas companies. Air hostessing had become a glamorous occupation, and the majority of applicants were extremely attractive.

Inevitably, romantic liaisons developed when a crew found itself in an overseas city, far from family restraints and with a large wad of expenses to pay for meals and entertainment.

The main overseas city where Electra crews spent their nights away was Sydney. The company housed us in the Manhattan Hotel, a large multi-storeyed building in the centre of the King's Cross red-light district.

The administrative side of the hotel was run by Miss Fartingale — a magnificently upholstered, elderly spinster with a bosom like a buttoned Chesterfield sofa and a disapproving face that would make a lemon curdle. She assumed all male aircrew were sex fiends and took on the self-appointed post of chaperone, endeavouring to ensure the female members of the crew were accommodated as far away from their male colleagues as possible. To confirm the success of her chaperoning, she patrolled the hotel corridors at night and always appeared in the dining-room promptly at 7am to note who arrived together. As she cruised round the tables at breakfast, with her lantern jaw and enormous bosom jutting out challengingly, she resembled a Spanish galleon under full sail.

Inevitably the new hostesses became the target of amorous approaches from male flying staff. Most approaches were subtle, but some were downright blatant. One very innocent-looking Scottish girl, who had flown extensively with a British charter airline before joining Air New Zealand, was summoned by the captain at the end of her first flight. She hurried to the cockpit.

"Miss Murray," he began, his eyes roaming over her trim figure. "It is a custom in the airline business for a new hostess to spend her first night-stop with the captain." He paused to allow his words to sink in. The hostess eyed him speculatively. He was twenty-five years her senior, sweaty and rather overweight. Not a prime specimen of New Zealand manhood and certainly not her idea of Adonis.

The crew awaited her reply with interest. She was a beautiful girl. Would she obey the orders of her commander?

"Carptin," she replied in her delightful Highland burr. "Thenk yee faw the honourrr . . ."

The pilot was smiling in gleeful anticipation. ". . . but it'd kill yee!"

Often a new hostess was invited to the hotel bar for a pre-dinner drink with her crew. Suitors jostled for position beside her. Dinner followed, and four amorous males exercised their charm on the solitary female in their midst. Some became downright unpleasant towards the end of an evening and virtually ordered the girl to their bed; others were more subtle, and used charm and guile to achieve the desired result. Time was of the essence on these occasions; there were only a couple of days to win a heart before returning to life back home. Love in the airline business was not the dying note of a distant violin, but the triumphant twang of an overstressed bed spring.

The more sophisticated girls learned to fight poison with poison. When a stuttering navigator named Jabberwocky made meaningful suggestions to one of the senior hostesses at dinner one night, she ignored him. This only inflamed his desire, so finally she told him bluntly she wasn't interested.

For a few minutes her tactic worked, but soon Jabberwocky was harassing her again.

"I s-s-say, w-w-what about coffee and b-b-brandy in my room?" he suggested.

The hostess assured him she was perfectly content to stay at the table and enjoy the company of the rest of the crew.

Jabberwocky was not discouraged. "C-c-come on up to my room, it's quieter and we can relax without all these people looking on," he persisted.

The hostess realised he wasn't going to be easy to shake off. "What did you have in mind when we get to your room?" she demanded loudly.

Jabberwocky looked embarrassed for a moment, but soon began making meaningful suggestions. "The view is wonderful and so is the bed," he assured her. "I'd like to share it with you and then . . ."

Other suggestions followed until finally the girl's patience snapped.

"You mean you want to bonk, don't you?" she exclaimed angrily. The rest of the crew pricked up their ears. Jabberwocky stuttered and stumbled before admitting that was his intention. The hostess transfixed him with a piercing glare.

"Well why don't you fuck off and leave us all in peace?" she suggested sweetly.

Jabberwocky slunk from the table, his crew's laughter ringing in his ears.

One of the less subtle approaches was employed by "Shorty", a diminutive navigator who stood five feet nothing in his uniform socks. Shorty had become enamoured by a tall statuesque hostess on his flight. The girl was under training and finding the work very different from her former occupation of research chemist. She probably didn't have time to notice Shorty during flight.

Late at night, under the influence of too many after-dinner liqueurs, the navigator tapped quietly on the girl's door, being careful not to attract the attention of Miss Fartingale. When this produced no reply, he knocked louder, and finally attacked the door with a portable fire extinguisher. This roused the former research chemist, who remained behind her firmly locked door and enquired who was there.

"It's me, Shorty, your navigator," her intending suitor replied. "Let me in."

"It's 2am," she protested.

"I only want to talk," Shorty assured her. "Just for a minute."

"But I've got an early start," the girl informed him. "What on earth do you want to talk about?"

"I'd like to get to know you a little better," the navigator explained.

"You will, after we've flown together tomorrow . . ."

"I want to get to know you now. Open the door."

"No way," the hostess assured him. "I'm going back to bed. Good night."

Shorty decided to be blunt. Friendly persuasion hadn't worked.

"Open the door," he shouted through the keyhole. "I want your body." The hostess's former training as a research chemist came to the fore.

"I'd rather give it to science," she informed him frostily. "Good night."

CHAPTER TWENTY-EIGHT

Opportunity Only Knocks Once

Romance was not always initiated by the male. Val Gammon, a senior hostess in the company, took a liking to Warwick Underwood and suggested a post-flight nightcap would be rather nice when they got to their hotel. The young engineer accepted.

He had no sooner got to his room when the phone rang. Val enquired whether he preferred champagne or brandy. Warwick chose brandy.

He hurried to her room and found her lounging on the sofa in a wispy peignoir. An ice bucket and two champagne glasses waited on the coffee table. "I decided we'd have champagne," she whispered seductively. "Brandy would make us sleepy and I didn't want that." Her hand rested lightly on Warwick's thigh as she spoke. Warwick licked his lips in eager anticipation; this was going to be good. He smelled expensive perfume as she reached across him for the champagne. She purred contentedly as Warwick's arm encircled her waist.

Abruptly the magic was broken by a knock on the door. The flight engineer looked at her disappointedly.

"Have you invited somebody else?" he enquired incredulously. Val shook her head.

"No way," she insisted.

Warwick followed her to the door, a glass in his hand.

Another more urgent knock prompted her to push the engineer into the bathroom. "Hide in there while I see who it is," she urged.

Warwick entered the bathroom and closed the door.

"Who is it?" she enquired anxiously.

"This is your captain," an authoritative voice informed her. "Open the door please."

Val opened it to find Captain Sea Jay in the corridor, clutching a bottle of duty-free Scotch.

"I thought you might care to join me in a nightcap," he explained, holding up the Scotch as he sidled through the door.

"I don't like whisky," Val lied. His eyes fell on the champagne.

"So I see, but you shouldn't drink alone," he commented. Val was smart enough not to reply. The pilot dumped himself on the sofa and began removing the wire foil round the champagne cork. He began his romantic approach.

"I don't think we've flown together before," he began. "I noticed you as you came aboard in Auckland. I was immediately attracted to you." He moved along the sofa towards her. Val moved away.

"What a bonza perfume. Did you get it in the duty-free store?" he enquired, his eyes seeking to penetrate the diaphanous silk of her nightgown. The hostess moved to the end of the sofa. He removed the cork and the champagne bubbled and burst forth.

"We need another glass," he announced, moving towards the bathroom. Val got there first and emerged with a tooth glass, having ignored the anxious glance of Warwick Underwood imprisoned in her shower. The captain poured the wine.

The next three-quarters of an hour were high drama. Captain Sea Jay tried to force his attentions on Val while Warwick Underwood listened from his hiding place in the bathroom. The wine level dropped with time and Val wondered what would happen if the captain visited the bathroom and found the flight engineer.

Such thoughts were farthest from Sea Jay's mind, however. He had thrown subtlety away after the second glass and was trying unsuccessfully to convince Val she was being offered the amorous experience of a lifetime. She successfully fended off his advances.

Finally the bottle was empty and the captain realised he wasn't going to score that night. He thanked her and rose to leave.

"Very pleasant evening, we must do it again," he observed.

"Must we?" Val murmured under her breath. In the bathroom Warwick Underwood began to breathe a sigh of relief. The captain was about to depart.

Sea Jay moved towards the door. "Goodnight then," he muttered with disappointment.

"Goodnight, Captain. Don't forget your bottle of Scotch."

Sea Jay hurried back into the room and retrieved the whisky. The act of bending to pick it up affected his metabolism slightly. "Mind if I use your bathroom?" he enquired.

Val turned pale. Her secret was about to be revealed. She thought furiously. "Er . . . it doesn't work."

Captain Sea Jay frowned. "That's not very good. The hotel manager should know better than to put TEAL crews into substandard rooms."

The hostess nodded in agreement. "I've notified maintenance," she lied. In the bathroom, Warwick listened with bated breath, fearful that the captain might investigate.

"What's the problem with it?" the captain demanded suspiciously.

"The light doesn't work," Val replied. Warwick heard her and removed the bulb from its socket before Sea Jay opened the door and tried the switch.

"Probably the bulb," he suggested. "Phone me in the morning if they don't come and fix it."

Val held the bedroom door open as the captain walked out. He found himself facing the disapproving glare of Miss Fartingale, finishing her final patrol of the evening.

"I thought I heard voices," she accused Sea Jay.

The captain looked confused. He was caught coming out of a hostess's bedroom with a bottle of Scotch and a guilty expression.

"One of my crew had a defective room," he explained unconvincingly. "Light doesn't work in the bathroom, needs a new bulb."

Miss Fartingale stole a glance at Val, who shook her head in silent disagreement.

She flicked the switch and the bathroom flooded with light. She looked at Sea Jay enquiringly. He muttered and mumbled something unintelligible before skulking back to his room.

"Men!" Val protested to the spinster. "They never give up, do they?" The doughty spinster nodded in agreement and patted the hostess's arm reassuringly.

"I'll be listening out for the rest of the night, dear, so don't worry about a thing. Have a good night."

"Thank you, Miss Fartingale, I'm going to have a wonderful night now," she assured her before closing and locking the door. Miss Fartingale resumed her night vigil.

Warwick Underwood had emerged from exile in the shower and now stood beside the coffee table. Val approached and kissed him seductively on the mouth. Warwick responded hungrily.

"Miss Fartingale says I'm to have a good night and not worry about a thing," she informed Warwick huskily, her tongue seeking his.

"Better do as she says," the engineer replied, nibbling her neck. "After all, she's got us trapped here till morning."

244

CHAPTER TWENTY-NINE

Visitors

By the end of May, the engineers on our course had completed the 200 hours' flying required for the issue of a flight engineer's licence.

Jack Kingfisher completed his final route check on the last day of May, 1965. Scratchy Poole was the check engineer. Jack landed back at Auckland looking as if he'd been tortured on the rack for twelve hours.

"How did it go?" Mike Furniss enquired sympathetically.

Jack shuddered at the recollection. "He asked everything," he reported. "Limitations, emergency procedures, operating techniques, regulations. Every air intake and drain hole, he wanted to know what it did and where it led from. The walk-around check took a full hour. Anyway, at the end of it all he announced I'd passed."

"Now you can relax a bit and enjoy flying the line," somebody suggested.

"Yeah, until the next biannual check, then I'll need to know all the emergency procedures and limitations and everything else again."

Jack didn't know it but he was going to need that knowledge sooner than he thought. A lot sooner . . .

By the beginning of March, the checking-out of the pilots on our course was over.

As we became more conversant with the idiosyncrasies of the routes we flew — Wellington weather, Melbourne's Air Traffic Control, Christchurch's nor'westerly conditions, Nadi's cyclones and Samoa's crosswinds — we were able to concentrate on enjoying flying the Lockheed Electra, an exhilarating aircraft to handle.

I continually marvelled at the skill and ease with which the senior captains coped with situations both in the air and on the ground. While we younger pilots had to work hard to fly the Electra accurately, the older ex-wartime captains frequently came in high, fast or off the centre line. As we neared touchdown, a sudden wind shear or gust of crosswind would bring them back to the right place at the right speed. Their ability to predict these phenomena and overcome them was uncanny, and frequently reminded us of how little we knew.

On the ground the same held true; the ex-wartime pilots were way ahead of us in most ways. An event involving Dusty Miller, Jabberwocky and the beautiful princess was proof of this.

When we weren't flying, the two main pursuits away from home were getting to know the hostesses and gambling. A wave of gambling fever engulfed the flying department and became almost the sole topic of conversation. If New Zealand played Pakistan at cricket, somebody would bet the Kiwis would win by five wickets. Betting on horse racing also occurred, but as we were often away flying when the race was televised, interest seemed to wane on the horses.

Most bets were struck on mundane subjects. One afternoon, while a group of us were enjoying a leisurely lunch-time ale, a pair of blackbirds landed in the garden bar of the Rex Hotel. Scratchy immediately bet the next round of drinks that the male blackbird would fly away first. Bets were struck, and Scratchy emerged the winner. We later found he frequently gambled on this particular incident and usually won by betting on the male. His rationale was that the average female blackbird couldn't make up her own mind, so followed her husband.

Even during quiet moments in flight, wagers would be struck on what time we'd get to the next reporting point, or the temperature in Brisbane when we landed.

When conditions were smooth during cruise, and the workload light, captains were happy to welcome the occasional visitor to the flight deck. This was before the days of hijacking, when aviation security wasn't a problem.

On one occasion, Don (Robbie) Robertson, the chief purser on our flight, told Captain Dusty Miller there was an elegant lady in first class who'd like to visit the flight deck. Dusty told him to bring her up. She was gorgeous!

The exquisite creature entered the Electra cockpit and introduced herself in a throaty European accent. She was in her early thirties, and her coiffure and fashionable clothing indicated wealth.

Dusty chatted for five minutes, introducing each crew member and explaining what they did, and pointing out the more important aircraft controls. She revealed she had been holidaying in New Zealand while her husband attended a United Nations conference in Geneva.

"Pity you couldn't have accompanied him to Switzerland," somebody commented. She wrinkled her nose in distaste.

"Diplomats and politicians, they can be so very boring," she explained. "Old people bore me, so I prefer to go my own way."

Further conversation revealed she was the wife of the Finnish ambassador to Australia, and was on her way back to Sydney after two weeks touring New Zealand.

Kiwis are fanatically proud of their country, and the next thirty minutes passed quickly as the four aviators told her the places to visit on her next trip. Dusty wrote down a few place names for her on a message pad, which she accepted gratefully.

"What a shame you have to go straight back to New Zealand," she observed sadly. "I would like to have entertained you and learned more about your beautiful country."

Jabberwocky began to explain they had two days in Sydney before taking the next service back to Auckland. Further discussion was interrupted by Sydney Control calling the aircraft.

"Tasman Echo Alpha. Theesizz Seedney Control, tyke uppa heading of three zero zero and confirm altitude," a nasal Ocker voice instructed. Dusty wound the heading knob onto the required course, while the co-pilot confirmed their altitude. Jabberwocky returned to his chart table and plotted the change of heading.

When things settled down again, the beautiful lady had left the cockpit. Only an elegantly engraved visiting card and a lingering trace of her perfume remained to remind them of her visit.

Air Traffic Control came up with a late descent clearance, and the crew were kept busy for the next twenty minutes.

After arrival formalities, the crew bus sped them to the Manhattan Hotel. The cabin crew raved on about the Finnish diplomat's wife.

"She must be loaded with money," the junior steward observed. "Didja see 'er jewellery? Must've cost 'er old man a king's ransom."

"He can afford it; he's a prince."

"Yeah but the poor old goat's seventy plus."

No wonder diplomats bored her, Dusty and his crew mused as the bus sped them through Surrey Hills and Darlinghurst. Her husband's friends were probably the same age.

By the time Miss Fartingale had assigned rooms, it was close to lunch-time. A card fell out of Dusty Miller's pocket as he changed out of uniform. He retrieved it and read the engraved printing.

Princess Kristal Larsen
Apartment 800
Greycliffe Apartments
Vaucluse
Ph: (02) 888 19543

An idea suddenly occurred to him; picking up the phone, he dialled Kristal Larsen's number. He would invite her for lunch and tell her a bit more about New Zealand.

To his dismay the number was engaged. He finished changing and tried again.

Kristal Larsen answered immediately. Dusty introduced himself again and the voice on the phone gurgled with delight. "How amusing. I was trying to call you to thank you for such an interesting flight in your aircraft."

"It was a pleasure," he assured her. "I called to enquire whether you'd care to hear a bit more about New Zealand over lunch?"

Kristal Larsen replied she'd love to, but her butler and kitchen staff were preparing a welcome home luncheon for her.

"Why don't you share it with me?" she suggested. "Then we can talk all afternoon if we want to."

Dusty readily agreed, and arranged to meet her in half an hour. Kristal told him she'd look forward to that and rang off.

Her phone rang again almost immediately . . .

A glance at his watch told Dusty Miller he was running late. He emerged from the Manhattan to find Jabberwocky taking the last cab off the rank.

"G-g-going my way, Captain?" the navigator stuttered.

"Dunno, I've got to get out to The Bays fairly quickly . . ."

"Hop in, I'm going that way myself. The driver can drop you off."

As the cab whisked them through the streets of Sydney, Jabberwocky asked Dusty where he was headed.

"Vaucluse."

"Any particular address?"

Dusty thought frantically. He didn't want this young navigator to discover he was meeting Kristal Larsen for lunch.

"Just anywhere, the main street will do fine," he lied.

The cab dropped Dusty off, and he rechecked Kristal's address. A half-minute walk brought him to her luxurious apartment block. He entered the foyer to find a surprise waiting.

"G-good morning again, Captain," his navigator greeted him, pressing a button to summon the lifts.

"What the devil are you doing here?" the pilot demanded.

"Probably the same as you, paying the delectable Mrs Larsen a visit. She wants to hear more about New Zealand."

"You can't, she's invited me up to lunch . . . and anyway, you're not a New Zealander, what would you know about the country?"

"Oh really? I can probably tell her as much as you can," Jabberwocky countered. "She never mentioned your name when I phoned."

"How did you get her number?"

"I copied it from the card she left in the cockpit."

At that instant both lifts arrived simultaneously.

"I'll race you for a pound!" Jabberwocky cried, leaping into the nearer lift.

Dusty threw himself into the other elevator and arrived at the eighth floor just ahead of the navigator. Jabberwocky grudgingly laid a pound note in the pilot's upturned hand.

An elderly English butler answered their knock.

"Captain Miller and his navigation officer, your highness," he announced grandly, ushering them into the apartment.

Kristal Larsen emerged from the lounge area looking enchantingly elegant. She had brushed out her blonde hair, and it now cascaded over her suntanned bare shoulders.

"Captain, how kind of you to come for lunch after such a long flight," she cooed, obviously delighted to have company. "And you've brought your navigator to keep you on course and ensure you don't go astray."

Dusty muttered he'd intended to come on his own, but their hostess had disappeared onto a balcony. He sidled up to Jabberwocky.

"Why don't you piss off?" he suggested quietly. "Neither of us is going to get anywhere if we both stay."

"Give me one good reason, Captain," the navigator replied indignantly. "She prefers mature men. You're much too young for her."

"On the contrary, she's obviously tired of her stupid old prince and wants a bit of excitement with somebody her own age . . ."

Further conversation was precluded by Kristal calling from the balcony.

"Cocktails or sherry, gentlemen? Or there's champagne if you prefer it."

Dusty and Jabberwocky were led onto a balcony commanding breath-taking views of Port Jackson and the Sydney Middle Harbour. Glasses of champagne appeared miraculously in their hands. The navigator proposed a toast.

"To friendship," he began, ignoring Dusty. "May ours prosper."

Kristal clinked her glass with his, and seemed to positively glow with pleasure. Dusty Miller fumed, and racked his brain for ways of getting rid of Jabberwocky.

Their hostess led them to a laden table. Dusty remarked on the wonderful selection of seafood.

"Jennings, my butler, gets it fresh. Every morning he goes down to the market," she explained to the captain, resting her hand on his. "Here, let me help you to a Balmain Bug, or perhaps you'd prefer a few Sydney rock oysters . . . ?"

Conversation flowed easily over luncheon. Kristal asked innumerable questions about life in the flying business, and the two men learned about life in diplomatic circles.

"But I much prefer to mix in younger more exciting circles," she explained.

"And your husband?"

She suddenly became very serious. "You New Zealanders may not understand this very easily, but in European society there are many arranged marriages for financial, social or political reasons. My husband and I were married at the instigation of our families."

Dusty and his navigator listened attentively as she continued.

"My husband was an aristocrat in the days when our country was a Russian province."

"Before the Russian Revolution of 1917," Jabberwocky murmured.

Princess Kristal nodded.

"My husband was twenty when the revolution broke out. He emerged with a chestful of medals, Finnish nationality, his Russian title and precious little else. He excelled himself again in World War II, and was eventually rewarded with a diplomatic post in the United Nations."

"And how did you meet him?" Dusty enquired.

"My family were wealthy through timber and dairy produce. Father introduced us at a reception at our house in 1950. I was twenty-one, beautiful, rich and recovering from a broken love affair."

She paused briefly to collect her thoughts. The two aviators waited silently for her to continue.

"My husband was elderly but active, socially prominent and titled. The marriage was arranged by my parents and provided everything we wanted. My new husband was at last able to sustain a lifestyle appropriate to his position, and I shed my *nouveau riche* image and became a princess. It was everybody's dream — houses in Helsinki, St Moritz and Fort Lauderdale and an ambassador's residence in Sydney."

"Sounds an idyllic existence," Dusty observed.

"Oh, it is. My husband and I are good friends. I appear beside him at official functions as the dutiful wife, and when out of the public eye we lead our separate private lives. He loves diplomacy and the thrill of political manoeuvring, I enjoy more immediate excitement — travel, skiing, sailing, sports cars. I'd love to be able to fly."

The aviators remained silent while Jennings removed their plates. Kristal suddenly brightened.

"Now for a surprise! I'm going to make crêpes Suzette. It's my speciality." She hurried into the kitchen as she spoke. Soon the rattle of pots and pans indicated she was busily engaged in the production of dessert.

Dusty Miller took a reflective sip of his wine and addressed Jabberwocky.

"Look, there's one too many of us here. One has to go and leave the other to entertain her highness."

"Agreed," the navigator responded. "It's obvious she prefers me."

"Rubbish! You heard her say she thinks she'd like to fly. That was a subtle invitation to . . ."

Princess Kristal interrupted to enquire whether their glasses were empty. A smell of burning summoned her back to the kitchen. Dusty continued his argument.

"You're being bloody selfish, so I'll tell you what we'll do. We'll spin a coin and the loser leaves."

"I'm not leaving, Captain."

"Don't be such a bad sport. C'mon, you can spin the coin, I'll call heads." He handed Jabberwocky a coin. The navigator tossed it in the air. It landed on the floor, rolled several feet, and disappeared off the balcony.

Dusty watched it fall eight floors and vanish into a drain. "Got any more good ideas, Captain?" Jabberwocky enquired, disappearing into the kitchen to help Kristal.

Dusty sat and glowered; he was going to have to come up with something good.

Kristal's pancakes were as delicious as her promise and the liqueur induced a sense of languor to the diners.

"Mm, you know what I'd like now? An hour's sleep then a swim," she murmured, stretching as she rose from the table. She pecked both fliers on the cheek and disappeared into her bedroom.

Dusty glared at Jabberwocky. "You're behaving bloody stupidly," he accused the other. "We can't both stay."

"Then why don't you push off back to the hotel?"

"Not unless you come."

"Is that a promise?"

"Yeah, but no sneaking back here again. We'll both go in the same cab."

"Agreed."

They rose and tapped on the princess's door. It opened at the lightest touch to reveal their hostess snuggled under a duvet.

"Thank you for such a delightful luncheon," they chorused.

The expression on her face portrayed her disappointment. "But I thought we were going for a swim . . ."

"Later," the captain replied.

"We have a matter to attend to," Jabberwocky explained. "I'll phone you tomorrow."

The captain propelled him out of the penthouse onto the landing. Jabberwocky pushed the button for the lift and they waited in sullen silence. The navigator didn't know it, but Dusty hadn't given up yet.

Both lifts arrived simultaneously. They hesitated indecisively over which to take.

Dusty thrust a pound note into Jabberwocky's hand. "I'll race you!" he exclaimed, heading for the nearer lift.

"You're on," the young navigator announced, hurling himself into the other.

Dusty Miller paused at the lift and sighed at the impetuosity of youth. Jabberwocky had reached the ground floor as the captain turned and knocked on the penthouse door. It was opened immediately by a delighted princess.

"Ready for that swim?" the sage captain enquired. "You look a little sleepy still . . ."

CHAPTER THIRTY
Morning Becomes Electra

Jack Kingfisher had to wait ten days for his first line-flight as a fully checked-out flight engineer. The company training reports were sent to the Civil Aviation Administration in Wellington for evaluation before a full licence was issued. Jack waited impatiently at home. The neighbours began sniping enviously at his leisurely lifestyle when they saw him pottering round home every day while they went off to work.

Finally, one foggy morning, Flight Engineer Officer John Kingfisher donned his new uniform and prepared to drive to work. The telephone rang as he kissed his wife goodbye.

"Weather's pretty crook at the drome," a flight despatcher reported. "Runway visual range is less than 100 yards, looks like we've got an indefinite delay. Stay at home near the phone, we'll call when we want you."

Jack struggled with his impatience. After waiting so long for this day, the weather was robbing him of the satisfaction of his first line-flight.

A second call from Flight Despatch an hour later was the same. "Stay in bed till we call you," the voice instructed, not realising Jack had been up and dressed since 6.30.

The engineer gazed out the family-room window at the indistinct form of his car waiting outside in the mist and fog. Struggling into a windcheater, he collected a chamois leather from the laundry and cleaned the fog from the windshield. The time was 8.30.

Jack's nextdoor neighbour, a loud-voiced character who managed a secondhand car business, found time for a quick greeting as he hurried towards his stationwagon.

"'Nother day off? Gawd you airline people have it easy," he remarked, fumbling with his car keys.

Jack began to explain the situation, but the man was already driving away. He contented himself with a venomous glance at the receding vehicle, reflecting that everybody seemed obstinately convinced his job consisted of five-day weekends with occasional interruptions for trips to Bondi Beach, Nadi or Tahiti. Attempts to explain only produced envious banter. Nobody wanted to hear about the struggle to become a flight engineer — the waiting for an opportunity, job interviews, months of training, study and exams. Jack comforted himself with the thought that most criticism was prompted by envy. Even he had to admit that flying was infinitely better than his previous job as a ground engineer in the hanger — despite Scratchy Poole breathing down his neck all the time with questions.

The call to work finally came at quarter past ten. "Visibility is going up and down like a whore's drawers, but met reckon it's improving," the flight despatcher told him over the phone. "Departure is re-scheduled for midday. Can you get here by eleven?"

Jack assured him he could and replaced the receiver, an optimistic smile lighting his face. It finally looked as if he might get airborne on his first flight.

"'Bye dear, have a good flight and don't worry about all those questions," his wife called from the front door. He waved back happily. Today was different; the questions were over, and he was now a fully qualified flight engineer. He could relax and enjoy the flight.

The anticipated clearance in the weather didn't happen until 12.30, by which time Jack had completed his external pre-flight checks and was seated in the Electra cockpit with the other crew members.

Captain Harold Thompson, a craggy ex-RNZAF Catalina pilot, and comman-der of today's flight, directed his attention towards the new flight engineer.

"First flight after checking out?" he enquired.

Jack admitted it was and they swapped views on the rigours of airline train-ing. Both agreed it was tough. Finally, when conversation had slowed to a halt, the captain addressed his crew.

"Okay then, this will be a normal take-off on runway two three. Engineer, I'll open the throttles to take-off power and you'll line 'em up for me. If we have an emergency before the decision speed, I'll call aborting, simultane-ously closing the throttles, applying brakes and selecting reverse thrust on the engines. If an emergency occurs after decision speed, I'll continue to take off. The flight engineer will carry out the appropriate emergency procedure on my command, monitored by the co-pilot. Are there any questions?"

The three crew members nodded their understanding of the captain's take-off brief. Each understood the most important point: if anything happened before decision speed, the captain could close the throttles and stop within the remaining runway length. Above decision speed, it was better to continue accelerating to flying speed rather than attempt to stop on the short amount of runway remaining.

The door to the rear of the cockpit opened, letting in clouds of fog-laden air, and the face of a traffic clerk appeared. He was clutching the load sheet.

"Weather's clearing rapidly now, skipper," the clerk reported. "We hope to get you away in ten minutes, the passengers are boarding now."

The captain nodded his understanding as he checked the load sheet.

Ten minutes later the Lockheed Electra moved slowly away from the ramp under the power of its four Allison turbo-props. Harold Thompson called for the take-off checks.

"Flaps," the new flight engineer read from the checklist.

"To take-off position," the co-pilot reported. The engineer also checked their position.

"Airways clearance?" They paused in the checks while the co-pilot called the control tower for clearance.

"Air traffic control clears Tasman Echo Alpha to the Sydney airport via flight plan route, climb to flight level two five zero," an anonymous voice in the tower began. "After take-off you are cleared for a right turnout after Westpoint. Cleared for take-off."

The clearance was repeated and confirmed correct.

"Tasman Echo Alpha, have a good trip," the controller called. The co-pilot rogered their acknowledgement as they turned onto the runway and the captain advanced the throttles.

Jack Kingfisher concentrated on lining up the indications of the four engines as their fifty tons of aircraft accelerated down the runway.

"Power set," he announced. The needle of the airspeed indicator on the pilots' instrument panels crept towards flying speed. As they accelerated through 100 knots, a thicker layer of fog-laden air drifted across the runway.

"Weather's thickening up a bit out here," the captain observed and removed his right hand from the power levers as the co-pilot called decision speed. The aircraft continued accelerating as the captain concentrated his attention on the runway centre white line.

When it happened, they were five knots below flying speed. A light backward pressure on the control column had lifted the nose wheel from the runway and further back pressure was about to get the aircraft airborne.

A large flock of sea birds, quietly minding their own business on the smooth surface of the fog-enshrouded runway, suddenly had their morning ruined by the sight of four whirling discs of Electra propellers bearing down on them out of the mist.

Their leader squawked the alarm. The first two birds to get airborne were mercifully beheaded by the number-three propeller before their decapitated remains were sucked into the engine airscoop, leading to the whirring blades of the forward compressor. The minced remains then entered the engine hot section for roasting before being spat out the jetpipe. Any fast-food vendor would have been impressed at the speed of the process.

On the panel in front of the flight engineer, the horsepower gauge of the number-three engine wavered indecisively at the unaccustomed fare before dropping towards zero. The engine's automatic propeller feathering mechanism sensed the drop in power and feathered the propeller, turning the blades edge-on to the airflow to reduce air resistance.

"Engine failure number three, propeller has auto-feathered," Jack called instinctively. The aircraft was now flying on three engines, a configuration it was designed to handle. It would climb away easily.

More sea birds on the runway struck the windshield, reducing visibility still further with their blood, gore and feathers.

Captain Harold Thompson was continuing his rotation of the aircraft's nose skyward, when the remainder of the birds hit the number-four engine, splattering it with more remains. The beheaded corpses of six of them entered the engine and stalled the compressor. The horsepower gauge of that engine didn't even fluctuate before plunging to zero. Other indications became chaotic as the enormous propeller windmilled in the airstream.

Jack couldn't believe his eyes. "Engine failure number four," he heard himself say.

The last three birds to leave the runway were struck by the wing tip, which killed one instantly and injured the other two. They fell to the runway.

Keeping his head below the level of the windshield, lest some birds come through the toughened perspex, Jack still found time to note the indications of the number-three and -four engines. He was about to repeat the second engine failure call when he heard a stifled exclamation from the captain. Suddenly the nose wheel was back on the runway, the throttles were being pulled back into reverse thrust and maximum wheel-braking was being applied.

The two operating engines on the port side commenced their braking action, swinging the Electra towards the edge of the runway. The captain juggled rudder pedals, nose wheel steering and throttles to remain on the concrete. As the runway continued to unwind out of the fog, none of the crew knew whether sufficient length remained to stop before the chilly waters of the Manukau Harbour claimed them. They were in a situation not covered by any manual, an eventuality so unlikely that no aircraft manufacturer or airline had even considered it, namely double engine failure on take-off. To have continued the take-off would have resulted in the aircraft rolling uncontrollably towards the failed engines, plunging inverted into the ground.

The sound of breaking crockery from the galley testified to the efficiency of the Electra's brakes. The aircraft decelerated rapidly; Jack raised his head cautiously above the lower level of the windscreen and caught his first glimpse of the approach lights at the end of the runway. The captain gave a last fierce jab on the toe brakes and the Electra ground to a halt, less than ten yards from the end of the runway.

The aircraft lurched again as he moved the port engines out of reverse and applied the park brake. The four crew members took their first gulps of air in thirty seconds and looked at each other. Nobody said a word at first, then "Shit!" was repeated four times.

"Tell the tower we've aborted our take-off, will you? " The captain was the first to regain his composure. The control tower would assume they were safely airborne through the fog. Unless they called them, they might clear another aircraft to take off while they were still on the runway.

"Roger, Echo Alpha. Understood, are you going back for another attempt?" the tower controller enquired. The four crew members looked at each other incredulously. Go through that again?

"No way!" they chorused.

Jack ran his eyes over the engineer's instrument panel. Something was wrong; the turbine inlet temperature of the number-four engine was rising inexplicably. The voice of Scratchy Poole, his meticulous instructor, echoed in his memory: Engine fire number-four engine. Whaddya gonna do about it then?

A warning bell sounded in the cockpit. "Engine fire number four, Captain," Jack reported, checking that the throttle was closed, cutting off the fuel and ignition switches and reaching for the fire extinguisher control.

"Fight the fire," the captain commanded. "Co-pilot, monitor his actions and complete the checklist items. Take your time and get it right."

The co-pilot ran through the checks. Fire extinguishant sprayed into the engine and doused the fire.

"Engine secured, checklist completed," Jack announced. The captain nodded approvingly. A potentially catastrophic situation had been averted. He released the brakes and the blood-splattered aircraft began to limp back to the ramp area. Its crew grinned ruefully at the astonished expressions of the ground staff as they taxied in.

The number-three propeller was still in the feathered position, with pieces of seagull clinging to the leading edges and cuffs. Around the lip of the air intake on top of the engine, traces of blood, skin and feathers bore witness to the fate of the first three birds to strike the aircraft.

Externally the number-four engine was a bloodied mess, reminiscent of a poulterer's slab at Christmas time. The exterior of the cowl and the wing leading edge out to the wing tip were a brilliant shade of red. Even the starboard navigation light, normally green, was tinted red. Heavy soot deposits round the tail pile and a curious smell like roast chicken bore witness to the recent fire in number-four engine. Around the nose of the aircraft, every nook, cranny and air intake was crammed with pieces of seagull. Above each red-tinted windscreen, a line of white feathers, resembling an old man's eyebrows imparted an aged expression to the Electra.

The experience had also aged John Kingfisher! He emerged from the aircraft as the ground staff began inspecting it. Scratchy Poole was talking with the captain as Jack reached solid ground. The training engineer beckoned him over.

"Captain Thompson's just told me how well you handled this emergency," he began. "You did bloody well, especially for your first flight on the line."

Jack could think of nothing to say. The captain nodded approvingly at the training engineer's words. Scratchy patted the young engineer on the back.

"Good work, keep it up. Now do you understand why we give you such a hard time during training?"

Jack had to agree. His actions had been automatic when things began to go wrong.

The aircraft was ten days in the repair hangar before it was ready for service again. The passengers were trans-shipped to a later flight that day, and Jack Kingfisher and the crew were sent home. New Zealand aviation had to wait a few more days for Jack to join their professional ranks.

Jack drove home cautiously; he was beginning to shake a bit now that the whole thing was over.

He parked in his driveway and noticed his neighbour had just come home for lunch.

"Got the rest of the day off, I suppose?" the man bawled across the fence. "Gawd, you airline blokes have it easy . . ."

Jack looked at him pityingly. "Yeah, piece of cake isn't it?" he agreed.

He kissed his wife affectionately as he entered the house. She smiled at him pleasantly.

"Had a nice flight, dear? I bet it was much better without all those questions being thrown at you . . ."

At the end of February, South Pacific Airlines of New Zealand, the private enterprise airline, ceased operations. An ever-increasing financial debt, some of it resulting from the unnecessary legal battles over routes, finally forced the rebels into liquidation. The great government clobbering machine had won.

Bob Anderson and Rex Daniels, the founders of the airline, flew the last service into Auckland's new international airport. As they walked away from their Viewmaster aircraft for the last time, jobless and penniless, both must have wondered what the future held for the loyal staff of SPANZ.

The five-and-half-year struggle had achieved wonders for New Zealand domestic air travellers. Competition from SPANZ had forced the government National Airways Corporation to upgrade the interiors of its aircraft and improve the standard of service. The tiny airline may have finally been asphyxiated by the behemoth, but its spirit lived on in the improved service aboard NAC.

The government airline refused to acknowledge they'd regained their monopoly on scheduled air travel.

"Of course the public still have a choice," a senior executive insisted. "They either fly with us or take the train."

M y first flight after check-out as a co-pilot was with Captain Brownjohn, the flight ops manager. We positioned an empty aircraft to Wellington early in the morning, prior to operating the morning scheduled service across to Sydney.

Although I had spoken to him only once since joining the company six months ago, Brownjohn remembered me.

"Good to see you checked out," he greeted when I reported to flight planning office at five o'clock. "Although, the way things are going, I think you'll probably be back in the training school before very long."

"A DC-8 course?" I enquired. He nodded.

"With the continued expansion to Hong Kong and Singapore, plus the probable return of our landing rights in Tahiti, we're going to need a further ten pilots for the DC-8. They'll have to come from the Electra fleet, leaving a requirement for ten new co-pilots for the Electras. We're also short of navigators, and another six flight engineers start training next month."

T he airline was really expanding. In addition to the DC-8 co-pilots to be trained, Electra captains were being converted onto DC-8s and the jet co-pilots were returning to the Electra for training to command. To produce ten more DC-8 pilots involved putting thirty-five pilots back into the training school. This may seem unbelievable, but consider five captains and five co-pilots transferring from the Electra to the jets:

Course No.1: Five Electra captains return to the training school for command jet conversion.

Course No.2: Five DC-8 co-pilots return for an Electra command course, so they can replace the captains on course No.1.

Course No.3: Five Electra co-pilots return for DC-8 co-pilot jet conversion, so they can replace those on course No.2.

Course No.4: Five more Electra co-pilots join course No.3 to increase the number of DC-8 co-pilots by five.

Course No.5: Ten new co-pilots are hired to replace the ten Electra co-pilots transferred to the jets.

This would total thirty pilots in the training school for at least two months. Five training captains (at least) would be involved in converting these thirty pilots, bringing the total number in the training school to thirty-five.

The time it took to reach a command position was at that time less than two years. Several Electra captains were in their mid-twenties, having joined the company less than twenty-four months previously.

This shortage of aircrew worked to the advantage of some of my comrades in SPANZ — Swooper Cooper, Alan McGreevy, Jack Griffiths, Keith Walsh, Jack Budd, Laurie Barclay, Ralph Simpson and Jack Humphries joined the company. Mount Cook Airlines snapped up Geoff Williams as their chief pilot. On the ground, Jim Haskell, Thos Caldwell and Brian Rhodes joined the company in flight operations.

Unfortunately, a few other senior pilots of the defunct SPANZ were still hunting for work. Bill Pattie, the smiling ex-fighter pilot with the scar on his face which he got from "defending the honour of a woman", had approached Alan Kenning, the cold-hearted head of NAC Flight Operations, to enquire into the possibility of being hired to fly the ex-SPANZ routes now inherited by NAC. The reply had been a long cold stare from the fellow fighter-pilot whom Bill had flown alongside in World War II.

Brownjohn and I completed the flight planning formalities and he suggested I flew the empty sector to Wellington. He would fly the next to Sydney. He proved to be a pleasant captain to fly with; I was impressed that he knew the names of all his crew — Ernie Swann the chief purser, Alan Martin the flight engineer and "Fez" Partridge the navigator.

I landed on runway 16 at Wellington in good weather conditions. After a ninety-minute turnaround we departed for Sydney, and reached it after four and a quarter hours' flying.

That evening Brownie introduced us to a restaurant a few hundred yards from our hotel. The food was excellent and the wine flowed freely. Brownie discussed generalities, but mainly his passion — ornithology. He remembered I'd once attended a lecture he'd given at Charterhouse.

"How are you enjoying flying with us?" he enquired unexpectedly. I assured him my short time in the company had been most enjoyable. He ruminated on this for a few moments.

"Do you know any other pilots or navigators, who might be interested in joining us?" he asked. "We need more experienced pilots, but our main concern is to find enough navigators. I may have to go overseas again to recruit."

I listened to his remarks with interest. I felt sure there were plenty of experienced pilots flying for the independent British companies who'd be happy to join the security of a scheduled state airline. I told Brownjohn my feelings on the subject. He listened with interest.

"The employment market has changed a lot recently," he explained. "Most state airlines — Qantas, Swissair, British European, plus the American carriers — are hiring. People are less inclined to go round the world for a job when they can work in their own country."

I remembered my interview with him. There had been plenty of well-qualified applicants for the job, yet he'd turned down some of the most experienced. I mentioned this.

"Experience isn't everything," the ornithologist explained. "I personally don't pay much attention to a man's experience or personal particulars on his application form."

I was surprised. If he didn't heed a job applicant's particulars, how on earth did he select pilots for the company? He must have guessed my question.

"I give first preference to people with birds' names," he explained. "No selection method is perfect, but mine seems as good as any other. We don't have many failures."

I thought back a few months. "It didn't work for Mr Somerville," I reminded him cautiously.

He acknowledged the fact. "But Mr Somerville didn't have a bird's name," he reminded me. I thought of a few of the aircrew I'd met, "Fez" Partridge, Mayn Hawkins, Barney Ruffle, Jack Finch, Alan Martin, Ernie Swann and of course John Peacock. I realised I had probably been accepted on the strength of having attended Brownie's ornithological lecture at school. The most surprising part was that his method of selecting pilots seemed to work as well as any of the more sophisticated ones used by larger airlines.

After six pleasant days flying the Tasman out of Australia, we got home to New Zealand in time for the weekend. Brownie bade me farewell outside Customs and suggested I call in to his office if I thought I could help him locate pilots or navigators in the UK.

The following Tuesday I found myself in town, so I called into Testicle House. Brownie's secretary, Yvonne, informed me her boss was at an all day meeting and suggested I call back the following morning.

I was about to depart when Mike Furniss appeared. We conversed briefly and I decided to tell him about Brownie's pilot selection procedure.

"He doesn't pay any attention to experience or qualifications," I told him.

Mike looked disbelieving. "How does he select them then?" he demanded. Yvonne was sniggering in the background.

"Well, you know he's quite a prominent ornithologist; in fact he's written one or two books on the subject?"

Mike nodded, but still looked puzzled. I continued.

"Well, he told me recently that whenever possible he selects people with birds' names."

Mike scoffed at the idea. "How did you get in then?" he demanded.

I told him about Brownie's lecture I'd attended at school.

Mike thought for a moment.

"You know, there's a surprising lot of Drakes, Kingfishers, Cox, Sparrows, Robins and Starlings in the company," he admitted thoughtfully.

"Not forgetting John Peacock, Robin McGrath or Harry Swift," I added.

Mike thought a bit longer. "Wonder how I got in?" he ruminated.

Yvonne stopped her typing for a second. "That was a slip of the tongue," she explained. We waited for her to continue. "Captain Brownjohn selected the birds' names first. Fortunately for you, Mr Furniss, he confused your name and Mr Peacock's."

"What difference did that make?"

Yvonne blushed a little as she started to explain. "Captain Brownjohn got 'Furniss' and 'Peacock' a bit mixed up."

"What do you mean?"

Yvonne's blush deepened. "Well, when he dictated the names of the successful applicants to me, he called you Furcock and Peaniss. I thought I knew who he meant, so I sent letters of acceptance to both of you."

Mike Furniss gave me an astonished look. "What a hell of a qualification to be accepted on," he observed ruefully.

As TEAL flew between the major Australian and New Zealand cities only once or twice a week, the work pattern on the Electras was very pleasant, with lots of time spent in Sydney or Nadi waiting for the next aircraft to come through.

For reasons connected with accommodation costs and flight-time limitations, we rarely flew return trips out of New Zealand. Instead, a typical week's work would be to fly from Auckland to Sydney, taking off at midnight and arriving early on Monday morning. We would get to the Manhattan Hotel by breakfast time, and a fresh crew would take the aircraft back to New Zealand. Another crew would then fly it up to Nadi and spend three or four days there, while yet another crew flew from Nadi back to New Zealand.

The Nadi service was only twice a week so a crew could look forward to several days' lazing in a luxury hotel at company expense when rostered for such a flight. A crew of ten young people left in a tropical paradise with pockets bulging with generous expenses found plenty of excitement and amusement on such layovers.

Everybody was content with the Electra work pattern except the company, who were desperately short of aircrew and resented having us lazing around in foreign countries when we were needed to fly.

Brownie gave Huge Anomaly, the bumbling head of rostering, the task of devising ways of using our time more efficiently. Hugh accompanied us on a midnight departure for Sydney. His intention was to gather a few background facts before making any recommendations. Captain Alan Potts, an extremely conscientious pilot who put most of us to shame with his dedication to the job, commanded the flight. Hugh checked in with the rest of the passengers and was invited up to the flight deck during cruise.

Jake Jacobson the engineer and I were engrossed in conversation when the roster-maker came into the cockpit. Jake was expounding the merits of the sleek BOAC Comet jetliner, which was also en route to the same destination. It left forty minutes after us, travelling 140 mph faster and 12,000 feet higher.

"What a machine! Those lucky blighters cruise at 500 miles per hour above the worst of the weather," the flight engineer observed enviously. Huge Anomaly craned forward to peer through the cockpit eyebrow windows at the sleek form above. I mentioned they'd be landing half an hour ahead of us and would be back in Auckland in time for morning tea. Hugh became quite excited at this snippet of information and jotted something down on a notepad. We continued to discuss the operational merits of the Comet, while Alan Potts checked the latest Sydney weather broadcast.

When we landed two hours later at Sydney's Kingsford-Smith airport, the Comet was already boarding its passengers for the return flight. Hugh Bromley caught us up as we walked across the tarmac towards Australian Customs and Immigration.

"Staying at the same hotel as us, Hugh?" the captain enquired. Hugh shook his head, he was continuing back to Wellington, then across to Melbourne for the night. We expressed our sympathy. Sixteen hours in an aircraft, albeit as a passenger, was a long and tedious day. I comforted myself with the thought that it would convince Hugh not to extend our duty time to such lengths, even if flight-time limitations had allowed it.

The crew bus deposited us at the hotel for three days off in Australia. I didn't think any more about this flight until several weeks later, when our work pattern changed rather dramatically.

A day off in Sydney would normally start with a visit to the back bar of the Rex pub at midday to check who else was in town. On this occasion, Scratchy Poole and Jabberwocky were already in attendance, celebrating the recent promotion to command of Jack Priest, an ex-RNZAF fighter pilot and aerial top-dresser. We spent the early part of the afternoon christening Jack's promotion, before embarking upon a discussion of the problems of the world. When we headed off in search of food about 7pm, nobody felt the slightest trace of pain. Alan Potts had long left us by this time to spend an early night in his room reading his manuals.

More alcohol was consumed over dinner by which time I began to feel a little the worse for wear. I returned to the back bar of the Rex for one last toast to Jack's recent command then headed home to bed.

Scratchy Poole and Jabberwocky were made of sterner stuff and continued carousing with their captain, finally staggering back to the Manhattan at midnight. Each had forgotten until now they had an afternoon departure for New Zealand.

Jack Priest demonstrated his command skills by deciding it would be more politic to take the back stairs to his room rather than risk running into a check or training captain in the lift, who might register concern at the pilot's inebriated condition so soon before a day's flying duty. As Jack led his flight engineer and navigator stealthily up the back stairs, he became aware of somebody descending. He recognised the flight operations manager. Jack froze dumbstruck and stared fixedly at his boss as they passed on the stairs. Only Brownjohn spoke.

"Good morning, Captain Potts," he greeted Jack Priest disapprovingly.

A fortnight later, our state of euphoria was broken by the publication of the next month's roster. Instead of flights terminating in Australia or Fiji, with three or more days lazing in the sun, our rostered duties consisted of short flights followed by an unknown duty.

"What the hell does 'Pax BOAC.450 AKL' mean?" Mike Hawk the navigator appealed over breakfast in the Mansions one morning. Nobody knew. Frank's parrot remained silent and Bosca gave a deep sigh and went back to licking his genitals under the table.

Huge Anomaly was preening himself in the rostering section when four of us arrived to find out the meaning of the new roster symbols. The phone rang before we could ask him. "It means you passenger home by BOAC Comet after operating your service," he explained to the caller. "BOAC leave for New Zealand an hour after you land, so you'll be home in time for morning tea. When we need a crew to operate the return service two days later, we'll passenger them over by the same method. This way we get better utilisation of crews instead of having them lazing around overseas where we can't use them. It's called cost-effectiveness."

He paused to allow the caller to consider the new scheme. I reluctantly had to admit to myself that it seemed to make more sense to have aircrew where they could be utilised. Mike Hawk disagreed.

"If you leave Hugh in control, he'll end up with all the aircraft in Australia and all the crews in Auckland," he warned.

Hugh's new rostering system started off well, and our monthly flying hours increased while our time away diminished. We began to cast envious eyes towards the DC-8 fleet, whose crews were beginning to spend as much as nine days away on shopping trips to the USA and Orient.

At the end of four weeks, Huge Anomaly's first "cost-effective" roster had worked exactly as planned. I did seventy-five hours' flying and thirty hours as passenger aboard the comfortable BOAC Comet. First-class food and service were excellent so it wasn't too arduous a duty to fly all night to Australia, change quickly out of uniform after landing and board the Comet, where a champagne breakfast would be served to us at 37,000 feet on the way home from work.

Nevertheless, we missed the bonhomie and excitement of a few days away from Auckland.

The crunch came on the second roster. John Peacock flew as Jack Priest's co-pilot and told me the story afterwards.

"We flew over to Sydney and another crew took the aircraft back to New Zealand," he began. "We passengered home aboard BOAC."

I nodded my understanding; everything seemed straightforward.

"After we landed at Auckland, the Comet then did a double-banger flight to Nadi and back, bringing the crew that normally waits up there back to New Zealand.

I couldn't see any problems with what John had described. He continued.

"Three days later, the general manager was booked to fly to Sydney for an important IATA conference, along with an Electra crew to operate the morning Electra service back to New Zealand."

I listened for signs of trouble. I didn't have long to wait.

"Unfortunately for everybody, the Comet hit a seagull on take-off and had to return to Auckland on three engines."

I could begin to detect a hint of trouble now. The Comet was a rare bird in southern skies and a replacement engine would have to be flown out from London.

Mike Hawk, the navigator who'd been so scathing of Huge Anomaly's cost-effective rosters, came into the conversation at this point. He'd already heard the whole story from the lads in Crew Control.

"So what do we blooming well have? Just what I warned you all about," he glared at me triumphantly as he spoke.

"Mike's right," John confirmed. "The crew for the Sydney-Auckland service were back in New Zealand and worse was to come. After the Sydney service the Comet was scheduled for a return flight to Nadi."

"Taking another crew up to Nadi," I exclaimed.

The others nodded their silent agreement. Only Mike spoke.

"So the result is exactly what I warned you all about when this crazy new cost effective roster system of Hugh's first started."

I began to see the light. "You mean all the aircraft are in Sydney or Nadi?"

Mike finished the statement for me. "And all the crews are in New Zealand," he roared.

I paused, stunned. Looking towards Brownie's office I noticed the frosted glass door was shut, an ominous sign for whoever was inside.

On this occasion it was Huge Anomaly. I could see the back of his neck flushed a vivid shade of red while he tried to explain away the massive hiccup in his cost-effective roster system. He never succeeded; instead Brownie quietly removed him from his position as the head of rostering and appointed him to something more appropriate to his rare blend of talents: officer in charge of emergency procedures. To a man of his calibre, an emergency or two a day would be a piece of cake after the hazards of cost-effective rostering.

Huge Anomaly ultimately went down in the Airline Hall of Fame as the first man to get all the aircraft overseas and all the crews at home.

Meanwhile, the old roster system, with days spent lazing in the sun in Fiji or propping up the back bar of the Rex, was reinstated.

CHAPTER THIRTY-ONE
Trained to Fly

A recent computer survey to establish the ideal characteristics for captains of new generation airliners concluded that while experience is a desirable attribute, younger pilots tend to adapt more quickly to space age technology. "The ideal new generation jet captain would be fourteen years old with 10,000 hours flying experience," the computer concluded.

With the commencement of DC-8 services to Honolulu, North America and the Orient, TEAL changed its name to Air New Zealand.

One of the perks of flying for Air New Zealand was transport to and from work, for management realised the undesirability of leaving a private motor vehicle in the carpark for a week or more.

I arrived back in Auckland one evening to find I was the only member of the Electra crew requiring transport.

"The DC-8 service from Hong Kong landed just after you," Chris Giles the duty despatcher advised me. "Probably be quicker for you to get a lift with them. They're coming out of Customs now."

When the DC-8 crew arrived at the pick-up point, I recognised their captain as Lindsay Caudwell, the incredibly youthful-looking pilot who'd flown me across the Tasman when I first joined the company over a year ago. Lindsay was one of those light-skinned people who could easily have passed for ten years younger than his twenty-seven years. The expansion caused by the arrival of the DC-8s had resulted in much promotion, and Lindsay was now a DC-8 captain.

The transport pulled up, and Lindsay beckoned me to get in with his co-pilot, navigator and flight engineer.

Most of our aircrew lived in West Auckland in those days, which made travelling time from the new international airport about fifty minutes. Lindsay had mentioned earlier he was spending the evening at his parents' house in Remuera, which meant he'd be dropped off first. His wife and young family were waiting at the house to start their Christmas party.

Once on our way, conversation inevitably turned to flying. I gathered the approach to Hong Kong had been a harbour circuit onto runway 13. This is a spectacular procedure, where the aircraft is flown below the height of the luxurious apartments on Hong Kong island, then across the masts of ships anchored in the harbour before banking right and descending to skim between the tenement apartments northwest of the airfield. Anybody who has experienced this approach can testify to the excitement of seeing lines of washing flash past the wing tips as the aircraft nears the runway on final approach.

The co-pilot, who was on his first Hong Kong trip, had clearly been impressed by the harbour circuit.

"I thought we were about to collect a load of Chinese laundry when you flew between those apartment buildings," he joked to Lindsay.

The cab driver sneaked a quick glance at the youthful captain in the seat beside him.

"Do you fly the new DC-8s?" he enquired with surprise, and was impressed when Lindsay admitted he did.

As we continued into town, conversation turned to the subject of Hong Kong shopping. Lindsay was nursing a large box wrapped in gift paper, no doubt a Christmas present for his lucky five-year-old son. The navigator enquired what was in the box.

"Electric train set," Lindsay replied. "The very latest — twenty feet of track, locomotive, carriages, controller, electric points, lights, siren, the lot. Unobtainable in New Zealand."

Everybody was impressed. The recipient of such a wonderful gift was indeed very lucky.

As the cab turned into Remuera Road, somebody asked Lindsay what his next duty was.

"Back to school Monday, I'm afraid," he admitted ruefully. Ground school was an integral part of life on the DC-8, route briefings had to be done for each airport before you flew to it. We muttered something appropriately sympathetic.

Lindsay pointed out his parents' house to our driver. A middle-aged lady paused at the front door as we turned into the driveway. The youthful captain wrestled his precious train set and suitcase out of the cab, and his mother embarrassed him in front of the crew by welcoming him home with a big hug. His children were too busy partying in the back of the house to worry about Dad coming home. Lindsay had disappeared into the back of the house to start assembling his precious train set before the cabby realised he'd left his captain's briefcase in the taxi. The navigator delivered it to the front door, and we resumed the journey home.

"Was this your first flight with Lindsay?" the navigator asked the co-pilot conversationally.

"Yeah, I've only been in the company a year and most of that time has been on courses. First the Electra course, then the DC-8s arrived and I was on one of the first courses. Things are happening pretty fast at the moment, two members of our course are scheduled to go back onto the Electras as captains next month."

Subsequent conversation ranged round the subject of expansion and promotion. The company route structure was expanding rapidly and soon there wouldn't be enough pilots available in New Zealand.

"Dunno what we're going to do for pilots then," the navigator commented. The cab driver had listened in to the conversation as we sped along the southern motorway.

"You must have some pretty young pilots flying in your company," he finally ventured. "That captain I just dropped off, he looked very young. What did he mean when he said he was going back to school on Monday?"

The navigator and co-pilot exchanged conspiratorial winks.

"He is a bit young," the navigator admitted. "Still at school in fact."

"Big boy for fifteen though," the co-pilot added. The taxi driver nearly spun off the motorway at this piece of information.

"Didjer say fifteen?" he exclaimed, fighting to keep his cab on the road. We nodded.

"Yep, fifteen and mad about aeroplanes. Knows everything about DC-8s," somebody volunteered. The cabbie exhaled a surprised breath.

"Fifteen, eh? Bit young to be a captain, isn't 'e?"

We agreed he was, but the co-pilot assured the driver Lindsay had all the required licences and qualifications.

"The company's desperately short of pilots, so they gave him the job. He's a blooming good little aviator, I might add."

"Whadda 'bout his school work though?" the cabbie protested. "I heard 'im say he was going back to school on Monday."

The co-pilot nodded.

"Yeah, that's right. He only flies for us during his school holidays, never during term time," he explained. "Oh, except when we get really short, then we sometimes pull him out of school for the day. He doesn't mind, but his parents don't approve.

The cab driver expressed his astonishment. "Fifteen and a captain of a four-engined jet? Bloody amazing, I've never heard anything like it! How old were those Spitfire pilots in the Battle of Britain?"

"Oh, early twenties usually, but they'd left school," the navigator explained. "Lindsay's taking School Certificate this year, so he can't fly for us full time. We'd have the truancy officer after us if he did."

The cab pulled up outside the flight engineer's house.

"What's he gonna do when he leaves school then?" the cab driver enquired incredulously. The navigator and co-pilot were having great difficulty in not convulsing with laughter.

"Last time I asked him, I think he said he wanted to be a train driver," the engineer remarked with a straight face. "Thanks for the lift. So long chaps."

CHAPTER THIRTY-TWO

Lost at Sea

The return to the old style of rostering, where we spent considerable time overseas, was welcomed by all of us. But it almost cost seven aircrew their lives.

The first hint of trouble came at breakfast time when Flight Operations rang the Mansions. Mike Hawk took the call and listened with concern to the voice on the other end.

"Trouble in Nadi, two of our fellows and six others missing at sea. Search and Rescue have been looking for them since dawn, but nothing yet. We need an Electra captain and co-pilot to stand by."

"What happened, did one of our aircraft come down in the ocean?" Mike enquired.

"No other details available yet. Tell Ruffle or Gosling to stay near the phone in case we need them." The caller rang off before Mike could reply. He returned to the lounge looking very serious.

"That was Testicle House," he said, addressing the five of us sprawled in armchairs listening to the radio. We eyed him without interest.

"Not another balls-up, surely?" somebody enquired suspiciously. The airline had barely recovered from Huge Anomaly's cost-effective rostering system.

"This one sounds really serious," Mike confided. "They didn't say exactly what happened, but it sounds like two crew and six passengers are missing at sea. Number Five squadron are out looking for them."

The atmosphere suddenly became very serious; if one of our aircraft had ditched at sea, loss of some lives was almost inevitable.

A quick look at the Electra roster revealed that Ian Gemmell, a young Electra captain, had flown the Thursday evening Nadi service, with Derek Stubbs as his co-pilot. The navigator and flight engineer weren't known to us. We packed overnight bags and waited for things to develop.

Ian and his crew had been on the first evening of a Nadi layover. The company accommodated its crews at the Skylodge Hotel, a rather primitive structure by today's international hotel standards. Nevertheless, stopovers in Nadi were tremendous fun.

The hotel consisted of two blocks of rooms adjacent to the bar and dining-room area. It was run by three colourful characters: an Englishman, Pete Slimmer; a Scotsman, Jock Mills; and an Irishman, Paddy Doyle. These three ran the hotel efficiently and created a tremendous atmosphere of conviviality among guests and staff.

Paddy Doyle was an enthusiastic yachtsman and owned *Seaspray*, a half-keel mullet boat. He had invited the Electra crew out in her for a day's sailing next day.

Only Ian and his co-pilot, Derek, accepted the invitation, so Paddy extended the offer to the resident Pan-American crew. Five of them accepted: the American captain, his co-pilot and three of the stewardesses. None of the Americans had previous sailing experience, and Gudrun, the younger girl, was apprehensive because she couldn't even swim. However, the prospect of sailing in tropical waters conquered her fears. After all, Paddy and the New Zealanders were experienced sailors.

Next morning, the seven guests helped Paddy load gear and equipment aboard the vessel in Denauru Marina, southwest of the international airport. It was 9am when they prepared to push off from the jetty and head her out into Nadi Bay.

Anybody looking at a map of the area will notice the coastline curves gradually round to the northwest, culminating in the town of Lautoka. Northeast of the international airport, the outline of the 1200-foot high Sabeto mountains resembles the somnolent form of a warrior lying with his hands clasped across his chest. The locals call him Mocemoce Ni Tuwawa "The Sleeping Giant".

Nadi Bay, to the west of the airport, is almost totally encircled by a chain of small luscious tropical islands curving round to the south. Many of them have been given names that conjure up visions of the romantic history of the South Seas. Castaway Island, Musket Cove and Plantation Island lie to the west while Beachcomber and Treasure Island lie further away to the northwest towards the outlying Mamanuca Group.

Ian handled the tiller as they pushed off. Paddy hoisted the sails, and the vessel heeled gently under the effect of the light southeasterly trade wind. The Americans watched and assisted as best they could. This was their first experience of small boat sailing and the New Zealanders showed them where to sit so that their weight would prevent the vessel heeling excessively.

By midday the trade winds had increased to a boisterous twenty-five knots, making the boat difficult to handle. Paddy gestured for Ian to head towards a nearby island for lunch.

Seaspray's shortened mullet-boat keel ran up onto the coral beach and the American pilots waded ashore with the anchor. The girls assisted Paddy to bring the provisions ashore, carefully ensuring nothing was dunked in the ocean as they waded through the surf.

The Fijian cooks in the Skylodge had provided a veritable banquet for the sailors. Gudrun extracted a bottle of Dom Perignon champagne from the wine chiller and confessed to having dreamed of drinking French champagne from a conch shell on a beautiful tropical desert island.

Paddy quickly fulfilled her ambition. They already had the champagne and the tropical island so he would search for a conch shell. He soon returned with a suitable shell, which he filled with the sparkling wine.

"Compliments of the Skylodge." He filled everybody's glass and they drank a toast.

After the meal, Ian conferred with Paddy and Derek. The offshore wind had continued to strengthen and they debated whether to head back to the mainland. After some discussion the three experienced sailors decided they were competent to handle the boisterous conditions.

Half an hour later they had pushed off from the island. *Seaspray* came alive in the increased wind, with Ian steering and Derek manning the sheets. Paddy again showed the Americans where to distribute their weight to prevent the vessel capsizing.

By mid-afternoon they had completed a long downwind reach to the northwest of the Bay. Conditions had changed from exhilarating to difficult. The swell had increased, and seawater kept coming over the side, keeping the American pilots fully occupied with bailing.

The girls, wet and chilled, huddled together and began to experience the initial feelings of seasickness. Ian made a decision to go about and return to shore. Because of the wind direction, their return would be longer, entailing a series of crosswind tacks. He gave the signal that he was going about.

The prow of the mullet boat pointed round into wind as Derek manipulated the sheets and prepared to transfer his weight to the other side. The Americans watched to see which way to move.

It was unfortunate that a sudden change in wind direction to the northeast occurred as Ian commenced the manoeuvre. He had already moved across to the windward side as the boom swung across. The unexpected gust from the northeast heeled the mullet boat in an unexpected direction, causing Derek to momentarily lose his footing and fall to the leeward side.

Taking this as a sign they should also move their weight to the leeward side, the Americans moved in the same direction. The ship's rail disappeared into the next wave and the ocean poured into the boat. Ian kept the tiller over and beckoned for everybody to lean on the upwind side, but it was too late. The mast dipped into the sea and the sudden intake of water slowed them to a stop.

They struggled to prevent items of equipment floating away as the hull settled on its side a few inches below the surface.

After rescuing Gudrun, the non-swimmer, from the water, eight of them sat up on the side of the submerged hull and wondered what to do next. Bailing was out of the question, as the vessel was below the surface. Paddy was first to size up the situation.

"We'll sit tight until we're spotted by another vessel," he instructed. "The wind and tide will eventually blow us onto one of the islands. If necessary we can paddle towards an island when we see one."

Statistically their chances of being spotted were good. One of the many fishing or pleasure boats would be certain to sight them shortly. Meanwhile the trade winds were blowing them towards the large number of tiny islands to the north-west.

Or so they thought.

From their position on top of the submerged hull, visibility in the high seas was less than twenty yards. Even the mountains of Viti Levu were out of sight.

After three hours in the water, Ian called a council of war. The effects of strong winds and constant immersion had begun to make them shiver with cold. The combined effect of salt spray and the sun's rays had brought up blisters on their unprotected skin and lips. They decided to follow Paddy's plan and stay with the boat. They sighted several pleasure craft returning to shore at the end of a day's enjoyment on the water, but none heeded their frantic waving.

The sun began to slip below the western horizon, and the trade winds lost their strength. They heard the sounds of music and laughter from a last passing charter boat as the sun disappeared below the horizon. Derek realised with a sudden sickening dread they were probably going to have to spend a night in the water.

Meanwhile, their fortunate colleagues ashore were preparing for a party. Ian's navigator and flight engineer had spent their day basking beside the Skylodge's pool, while the chief purser and two of the hostesses had mounted a sortie on Nadi's duty-free shops. All five met as they returned to their rooms.

"What about meeting in the bar before dinner, say about six?" the navigator suggested brightly. The evening's pleasure was about to begin with tropical cocktails; dinner, dancing and socialising would follow. He let himself into his room and was about to step into the shower when a thought struck him. Picking up the telephone, he dialled the captain's room.

The call was answered after six rings.

"G'day Ian, Jack here. How was the sailing?" he enquired cheerily. A deep Fijian voice told him he was speaking to the roomboy; the captain was not in the room. The navigator replaced the receiver and turned on the shower. Ian and Derek were probably having a few drinks on the boat and would join them later. Or maybe they'd decided to introduce the American girls to one of the local Indian restaurants.

It was after sunset when he joined the small group of guests at the bar.

"How was the sailing?" the junior hostess enquired brightly as everybody exchanged pleasantries. The navigator explained he hadn't gone sailing, only the captain and co-pilot had ventured out. Two Americans at the bar overheard the conversation and came over.

"Say, excuse us but are you the Noo Zeelund crew that went sailing today?" the burly Pan-American flight engineer enquired, introducing himself and the navigator.

"Yes and no. Only two went out, we stayed behind. They should be back soon."

The Americans muttered something about this being the only time they'd known Keenan to be late for cocktail hour.

"Is Keenan your friend?" the New Zealander replied.

"Yeah, sort of. He's our co-pilot, and Keenan sure likes his drop of whisky when the sun goes down. I've never known him be this late for drinks before."

They assured him the missing mariners would soon appear. Further discussion was interrupted by the arrival of a thirsty Qantas crew, and soon the bar was filled with the sound of laughter and good-natured badinage. The plight of the eight mariners was quickly forgotten.

Sixty miles away, over on the eastern side of Fiji's main island of Viti Levu, the RNZAF's No. 5 (Maritime) Squadron had completed the day's flying operations from Lauthala Bay. Two of their four-engined Short Sunderland flying boats nodded on their moorings out in the bay, while a third, hauled up onto the slipway for routine maintenance, resembled a beached white whale. Only the duty crew remained, ready to take off if required for a mission.

The squadron, formed in Fiji during the Second World War, had a proud record. Its task had been and still was to provide maritime surveillance, search and rescue, supply dropping and emergency air transport when required. The detection equipment carried aboard the venerable flying boats was rudimentary and outdated by modern standards, consisting mainly of World War II ASV.6.C. radar and nine pairs of Mark One human eyeballs. The squadron commander continually stressed to his aircrew that the human eye was probably the most reliable piece of equipment aboard their aircraft.

Certainly the squadron's World War II record of successful rescues confirmed his view, for most had resulted from visual sightings.

The inevitable card game started in the crew room as darkness fell. The nine members relaxed with the knowledge that the chances of being called out on a night mission were minimal.

Out at sea, Ian Gemmell guestimated their position. It was five hours since they had capsized and he calculated the combined effects of wind and tide were drifting them northwest towards the outer chain of islands in the Mamanuca Group. The trade winds had died to a light zephyr and the stars of the Southern Cross were reflected in the ocean's calm. The Pan-Am crew conversed quietly, anxiously reassuring themselves they would be picked up at daybreak. Ian and Derek squinted in the dark, hoping to glimpse a passing island. The combined effect of sunburn and salt spray had turned everybody's skin into a source of intense pain. Hunger and thirst combined with the pain to make the night even more uncomfortable. Despite this discomfort, the New Zealanders were optimistic of their chances of being washed ashore onto an outlying island.

Over at the Skylodge, Pete Slimmer, the duty manager, watched as hunger drove his hotel guests from the bar into the dining-room. A glance at his watch made him suddenly realise Paddy Doyle was now half an hour late relieving him as night manager. Normally this wouldn't have been a problem, but tonight Pete and his wife were giving a dinner party and it was important he was home to host it. A sudden burst of laughter from the dining-room

272

made him wonder whether his Irish colleague was perhaps telling the guests some of his famous stories and had lost track of time. He headed towards the sound of laughter: The Qantas and Air New Zealand crew were swapping tall stories again. He waited for the New Zealand flight engineer to finish his yarn before attracting his attention.

"Seen anything of Paddy tonight?" he enquired quietly. "He usually comes into the bar some time during the evening."

"It's funny you should say that," the New Zealander replied. "He and Ian Gemmell went sailing with a few others this morning and nobody's seen them since."

Alarm signals began to sound in Pete's brain. His partner was usually scrupulously punctual for duty and would never be more than a minute or two late.

"Has anybody heard whether they're back yet?" he asked a trifle anxiously.

The New Zealand flight engineer shook his head. "Nobody," he confirmed solemnly.

"I'll go in the car and check whether their boat's back in its berth," Pete announced. The New Zealand navigator and engineer followed him out of the restaurant.

Ten minutes later they were standing beside the empty marina berth, straining for a sight of Paddy's boat anywhere out in the darkened marina. The hanging mooring lines told them the sailing party were still somewhere out at sea.

"I'd better inform the police," Pete decided, leading them back to the car. "They'll alert the emergency services."

"There's not much anybody can do till daybreak," the navigator commented. "There's no moon tonight and it's as black as the inside of a cow out there."

Pete located a phone and dialled the emergency number. After half a dozen rings a sleepy Fijian voice answered.

"Ni san bula, Fiji Emergency Services. Fire, police or ambulance?"

"Police, this concerns seven missing persons."

"Stand by, I'm transferring you."

After several clicks and scratches, the duty sergeant in Nadi Police Headquarters came on the line. He listened while Pete related his concern.

"I'll transfer you to the Search and Rescue co-ordination centre," the police officer announced. Less than a minute later, Pete was speaking to the duty officer at Search and Rescue HQ at Nadi airport.

The duty officer listened as Pete repeated his story.

"Do you know what time they departed?" the Fijian enquired.

"Round about nine this morning. They took packed lunches, intending to be back in time for dinner." A glance at his watch told him it was now 10.30pm.

The duty officer had picked up a second phone and was dialling a direct line.

"Five Squadron operations room, Squadron Leader Tomkins," the captain of the duty Sunderland crew answered on the first ring.

"SAR headquarters here. We've had a report of a missing boat. Well . . .

not missing exactly, but it hasn't returned. I'll transfer you to the caller."

"Can you describe the type of vessel?" the flying-boat captain demanded.

"It's a half-keel mullet boat, light-blue hull, white sail. Not the most comfortable place to spend a night in, beside which, one of those aboard was due back for work at nine this evening." Pete realised his chances of making it home for their dinner party were now significantly less than zero.

"SOB?"

"What the hell's that?"

"Oh, sorry . . . 'souls on board'. How many people in the vessel?" the Air Force pilot enquired.

"Er, let me see. There was Paddy . . . and the two Kiwis and . . . er . . . four or five Pan-Am crew. About seven or eight."

The pilot noted down the information as Pete spoke. Today's strong winds and high seas could have taken them far away. Behind the pilot, his crew had interrupted their card game to listen to his half of the telephone conversation.

"Seven or eight people missing in a small boat," he advised his co-pilot.

"Can't do much till daybreak," the other commented. "Then we'll initiate a Dumbo." Dumbo was the code name for a search and rescue mission.

The flying-boat skipper nodded as the duty officer's voice continued.

"Probably got blown ashore on one of the outer islands," the pilot commented to the duty officer. "Anybody checked the beaches?"

"Negative, there's a hell of a lot of coastline and most of it round here would have a thousand copulating couples on it at this time of night. It'd be impossible to check in the dark. We'll get a light aircraft to patrol the beaches at first light."

"Okay, I'll put my crew on Incerfa, that's the uncertainty phase of a search. I'll upgrade this to full Alert or Distress phase before we start searching. We'll take off before dawn and arrive over the search area at first light."

The pilot picked up another phone and was connected to the senior air traffic controller. Behind him, the navigator had begun calculating the time of first light from his nautical almanac.

"Tower? G'day Jim, Ted here, duty crew. Sorry to spoil your evening but we've had a Dumbo. It's only at the Incerfa phase at present but it'll go to full Alert at daybreak. We'll need the flare path laid out for a night take-off about 5am."

The next call was to the Nadi police HQ.

"Give me a description of the missing vessel. Length, colour of hull and sails, plus details of any emergency equipment carried."

The Fijian police sergeant fielded the enquiry to Pete Slimmer, now back at the Skylodge. He provided a detailed description of the vessel.

"The light-blue hull and white sails won't stand out very well, but Paddy Doyle's an experienced sailor in these waters," he ventured. "Ian's an excellent sailor too, and young Derek's pretty knowledgeable. Dunno about the Americans, though. I heard one of the girls say she couldn't swim."

"Shit, that's just what we didn't need! Any life-jackets or emergency equipment on board?"

"'Fraid not. Paddy only used the boat for pottering around in, close to the shore."

The flying-boat pilot finished copying the information down before turning to his air signallers.

"Load a Lindholme gear and two containers plus medical supplies for eight. Brulidine cream for exposure, oxygen supplies, shark repellant, rescue lines, life-jackets, flares, loud-hailers, plus the full first-aid kits. All the usual stuff — stretchers, blankets, splints, food and drinking water. Oh, and see if a couple of orderlies from sick quarters can come along."

The signallers nodded as the captain spoke. "Okay, got it. Anything else skipper?"

The pilot ran through a mental list of equipment needed. Medical supplies, nutrition . . . He'd been through this exercise many times before.

"No, just the standard list of equipment," he told them quietly. The signallers got up to leave as a last thought struck the pilot. He gestured quietly to one of them.

"Just one other thing, flight sergeant," he murmured. The other waited expectantly.

"What's that, sir?"

"Body bags. Bring eight and pray to Christ we don't need them."

The eight crew members departed on their individual tasks. The flight engineers would supervise the refuelling and pre-flight the aircraft; the navigators would check the navigation and electronic equipment then draw the necessary charts from the ship's library; the signallers would check over their radio equipment and install the appropriate frequency crystals and the pilots would review the mission profile to establish the best area to centre the airborne search.

When everything had been prepared for the morning's sortie, the Sunderland crew retired to their bunks for a few hours' rest.

Aboard the submerged hull of *Seaspray*, Ian Gemmell reviewed their situation. It was now 2am. They had been in the water ten hours, seated on the semi-submerged hull. Earlier, the five men had spread the spinnaker to provide shelter from the elements. He could sense the American girls becoming despondent at their chances of rescue. He forced himself to be more positive, reasoning that the rest of his crew back at the hotel would have noted his absence and alerted the authorities by now.

"Should have the first aircraft overhead in about three hours," he proclaimed in a voice more cheerful than he felt. The stewardesses regarded him listlessly. Throughout the night he had insisted they call the roll every five minutes, since it was impossible to count the number of heads in the dark; anybody falling asleep could slip quietly away into the ocean.

"Derek? Jack? You still here Paddy? Keenan? What about you, Gudrun?"

"Still here, Captain."

"Okay, hang on for just a little longer. What about you, Peggy, you still with us? Peggy?"

"Yeah, she's still here with me but very tired."

"Never mind, we're all a bit that way. Is that you Estella?"

"Si, Captain. I'm all right."

"Okay everybody, let's try to keep awake, otherwise we'll fall into the water. Anybody thirsty? We can open some soft drinks."

Thirst had been their constant companion; they were fortunate to have rescued a few cans of soft drinks when the boat capsized.

"Okay, tonight's big decision for you, Jack." He gestured towards the Pan-Am captain. "Coke or Fanta?"

"What the hell's Fanta?" the American pilot demanded curiously.

"Sorta soft drink. Fizzy and tastes of orange. Try it, you'll enjoy it."

"I'd prefer a beer. Bring me a Budweiser and a packet of peanuts, will you?"

"Coming right up. Want to order dinner yet, sir? I'll bring you the menu."

The constant badinage was a vital part of maintaining morale aboard the waterlogged hulk. Once morale and the will to keep going disappeared, so would their chances of surviving the nightmare.

The Pan-Am captain flipped open his tin of Fanta and consumed the warm contents slowly. His eyes and ears strained for the sound and sight of a line of waves breaking on a shore, but the dark tropical night revealed nothing.

Back in New Zealand, Captain Brownjohn grumbled irritably when his bedside phone rang. Mrs Brownjohn mumbled something unintelligible, turned over and went back to sleep. The operations manager switched on the bedside light and groped for the instrument. Twice in the previous week their daughter Anne-Marie had called him out in the early hours; once when she'd lost her car keys at a party and the second time when her car ran out of petrol half a mile from home. It was getting a bit too much.

"Where the devil are you this time? Do you realise what the time is?" he snarled into the mouthpiece.

"Yes. Sorry to disturb you, Captain, this is Crew Control. We've just had a call from the Electra crew in Nadi. The navigator rang to tell us Captain Gemmell and his first officer are missing."

"Whaddya mean missing? They're not due to fly back till Thursday. Why've you called to tell me this?"

"Missing as in lost, Captain. They went sailing with a few others and didn't return to the hotel by dinner time."

"Probably socialising somewhere else. They don't always have to eat in the hotel."

"We thought of that but their boat isn't back in its berth. Five others were with them and they haven't returned either. Sailing conditions became a bit boisterous in the afternoon and the authorities think they may have run into trouble."

Brownjohn's mind quickly grasped the situation. They would probably have stayed within the Nadi Bay area so even if they'd capsized, any passing ship or aircraft should be able to detect them.

276

"What's being done about it?" he demanded.

"Nothing yet, Captain, it's still too dark, but a Sunderland's due overhead from Lauthala Bay at first light. A number of boats and light aircraft from Nadi will start searching about then too. Search and Rescue think they're probably washed up on a beach or one of the nearby islands. They'll check the foreshore and inner islands first."

"Okay, let me know when they find them."

"Will do, Captain." The other rang off.

Brownjohn glanced at his watch. Four o'clock in the morning. He should hear something before breakfast.

News of the crew's disappearance broke at breakfast time. Captain Geoff White and first officer Barney Ruffle were told to be ready to dead-head up to Nadi that afternoon.

"What the dickens for, I thought we'd stopped that cost-effective rostering system?" one of them complained. The officer on duty in crew control explained the reason.

"We'll let you know when they're found, but in the meantime make sure you're ready to go if we need you."

Two hours before daybreak, Tom French, an Australian charter pilot who existed on the hand-to-mouth business of flying tourists round the islands, woke and made himself a thermos flask of coffee. A few hours earlier, Nadi Search and Rescue had contacted him to enquire whether his Piper Tri-Pacer was available to participate in a search. Tom readily agreed; a full-blooded search would boost his revenue considerably.

Fiji Airways pilots reporting for duty at 7am were told to keep their eyes open for a missing sailboat lost a few miles out in the bay.

Charter-boat operators and owners of private yachts were similarly alerted.

By the time the duty officer at Nadi Search and Rescue HQ was relieved at five o'clock, he was confident the missing yacht would be located by breakfast time.

"Probably becalmed half a mile off the coast," he grumbled to the officer relieving him. "Dunno why there's such a fuss really."

About this time, Peggy began to lose hope. Cold, hunger and sea sickness had reduced her morale to the point where she consistently failed to respond to the regular roll calls designed to ensure her survival. The skin on everyone's face was raw from constant immersion and exposure, and now a school of sea lice made life even more impossible.

The Pan-Am captain changed places with one of the other girls and tied Peggy and himself together.

"Hang in there, honey. It'll soon be light and they're gonna find us. Whaddya going to have for breakfast when we get ashore?"

The girl's vacant stare made him suddenly realise she might not survive till daylight.

Ian Gemmell had begun to call another roll as Derek detected a slight lightening in the sky to the east. Dawn comes rapidly in the tropics and it would be daylight within twenty minutes. He forced himself to concentrate on the pleasures of being rescued; a long cool drink accompanied by the biggest bloodiest steak imaginable followed by a week's sleep. No . . . make that two weeks.

And it was probably only an hour away.

Peggy slipped into the water yet again and the Pan-Am captain found he no longer had the strength to pull her out. Summoning one of the other girls to help, the two Americans slipped into the water either side of Peggy and held her semi-conscious face out of the water. Ian observed their actions anxiously.

The situation was saved by a present from the heavens. The sky to the east was definitely lighter now, and Gudrun began to discern the shape of the Sleeping Giant mountain range.

"Look everybody, I can see a light. It's an aircraft coming to rescue us."

Sure enough, a light brighter than any of the other stars had appeared low down in the east. The yacht's crew watched as it changed colour and seemed to come nearer.

"It's getting brighter. It's coming towards us. It's a plane, they've found us!"

The news roused the semi-conscious Peggy from her torpor and she became excited at seeing the bright light.

The eight watched as it became brighter in the pre-dawn sky. The light kept changing from white to yellow then red, green, blue, white. Five of them cheered as the light grew brighter.

Only the New Zealand and Pan-Am pilots knew what it really was.

Brownjohn didn't need to call a meeting in his office at 9am. Doug Keesing, the chief pilot, Joe Lawton the chief navigator and two operations officers were already there.

"You don't think Captain Gemmell planned a two-day sailing jaunt, do you?" Keesing suggested. After three hours of searching by ships and aircraft, not a sign had been found of the overdue yacht.

"Possible, but extremely unlikely," Brownjohn assured him. "Paddy Doyle, the boat's owner, was due back that evening and they only took food for a day. I'm afraid they're still out there somewhere."

Over at Number Five Squadron HQ, in Lauthala Bay, the navigation leader in charge of the search operation finished ruling lines on a large-scale plotting chart.

"We've searched the whole of the Nadi Bay area," he informed his commanding officer. "Not a sign of anything and nothing from other ships or aircraft either. They must have drifted further out to sea."

The senior officer inspected the chart intently. "What do we know about the crew?" he enquired. "Are any of them experienced sailors?"

"Three are. Doyle, the ship's owner, is an experienced coastal sailor, lived up here for years. There are two New Zealanders aboard, pilots, both have done a bit of sailing. The rest are Americans, Pan-Am crew from San Francisco. We don't know much about them."

The CO picked up a pair of dividers and marked off a distance. "Assuming they were about here when they ran into trouble . . ." he marked a point in the centre of Nadi Bay, " . . . and assuming they've been in the water since 2pm yesterday, the wind and tide would've drifted them nor'west to about here." With pencil and plotter he drew a line north-westward towards the outer Yasawa Group of islands. "My guess is they've drifted past every other island and are heading towards deep water." He turned as somebody knocked on the operations room door.

Two pilots and a pair of navigators entered and saluted the senior officer.

"Morning, sir. No news yet, eh?" The captain of the relieving crew addressed his commanding officer. "I would've thought they'd have found them by now."

The senior officer brought him up to date on the situation.

"Wind's going to increase in strength during the day and we're expecting a high swell, which will make visual detection difficult. We'll concentrate the search to the northwest towards the Mamanuca and Yasawa groups. We've searched every square mile of the Bay area since daybreak and there's no sign of them there."

"You'll proceed to a point northwest of the Yasawas and direct your search in towards Nadi," the lead navigator briefed them. "If they're anywhere, they'll be there. Now if you're ready, I'll give you the search co-ordinates."

"And if they're not there?" the captain enquired.

"We won't consider that yet," the CO reproved him. "But if they're not, they're either at the bottom of the ocean or in some shark's belly."

The ensuing silence lent dramatic emphasis to his words.

Back in Air New Zealand flight ops Auckland, Brownjohn had a bit of housekeeping to do. Neither of the missing aviators' next of kin had been advised of the mishap. It was important to contact them before they heard anything on the radio. He scanned the aircrew roster to see who was at home.

"Dusty? Brownie here. Could you come to my office as quickly as possible. Something urgent."

A similar call to another crew member was made, and before long both engineer officer Geoff Freer and Captain Dusty Miller arrived in Brownjohn's office simultaneously. Brownjohn motioned them to be seated and provided the details of the previous day's events.

"Every available ship and aircraft has scanned Nadi Bay since dawn," he emphasised. "Five Squadron are sending a second Sunderland to the outer islands, in the belief they may have drifted out there during the night."

"What would you like us to do?" Dusty Miller enquired.

"Dusty, I want you to go round to Ian's house and tell his wife the basic facts, that Ian went out sailing yesterday morning and hasn't returned yet. Tell her they're looking for him and his crew, and hope to locate them shortly. Nothing more than that. Geoff, you live near Mangere Bridge, call round to

Derek's parents and tell them the same thing. Emphasise we'll contact them as soon as we hear anything, and tell them not to believe everything they hear on the radio."

Brownjohn followed both men as far as the flight operations department where he joined his colleagues in silent contemplation, wondering what the devil could have gone wrong.

The bright light to the east was further away than the observers on the submerged hull of *Seaspray* had at first realised.

"It doesn't seem to be getting any closer. Why's that?" Gudrun protested. It was now almost daylight and aircraft would be taking off to search for them soon.

"We should see the first aircraft any time now." Ian broke into their conversation.

"But what about that aircraft there? Why doesn't he come down and find us? He's been there for ten or fifteen minutes," one of the girls protested indignantly.

Ian exchanged glances with the Pan-Am captain. Both had recognised the planet Venus the instant it appeared over the horizon. Both knew it sometimes rose just before the sun, making it the morning star. Each of them had recognised it as a godsend, a morale booster when spirits were lowest just before dawn. Peggy would probably have slipped into unconsciousness and drowned if Venus hadn't rescued her so fortuitously.

"I'm afraid that's the morning star." Ian suppressed a rueful smile. "It's a bit further away than you imagine."

"That's nonsense, somebody aboard was signalling with a lamp, I saw different-coloured lights. No star does that, it can only be an aircraft."

"Venus is one of the brightest stars in the heavens," the Pan-Am captain interrupted her. "Diffusion through the atmosphere causes it to change colour like that. More people have mistaken Venus for another aircraft or a UFO than I've had hot breakfasts. Sorry folks, that was a false alarm but I think I can hear something now."

It was now fully light, and the first rays of the morning sun rose above the Sabeto mountains to the east. As an accompaniment to this event, the deep sound of aero engines could be heard faintly in the distance. All eyes scanned the southern horizon. The arrival of the first search aircraft would ensure their spirits remained buoyant.

"I think I see it!" Estella attempted to stand on the submerged hull and ended up in the water. The others laughed uproariously as they retrieved her.

"Yeah, there it is." The Pan-Am co-pilot pointed to the right of the rising sun. "What kind of an airplane is that for God's sake?"

"Flying boat," Ian explained. "Short Sunderland. As soon as he sees us, he'll land on the water and pick us up. We'll be home in time for breakfast, folks. How do you like your coffee. Black with plenty of sugar?"

An air of delighted excitement enveloped *Seaspray* as the Sunderland thundered past five miles to the south. As it drew abeam, they expected those aboard to see them and alter course towards their frenetic signals. Instead, the aircraft carried on past.

"Why he no come this way?" the volatile Estella demanded indignantly.

"He's carrying out a square search," Ian explained. "He'll be back again shortly." The echoing sound of aero engines gradually faded.

"He'll be back," Ian repeated.

Paddy Doyle pulled the spinnaker out of the water.

"We've got to make ourselves as visible as possible," he instructed. "It's difficult to detect objects in the water when you're flying past them at two miles a minute. Spread the sail out to attract their attention, make us more conspicuous."

As he spoke, the sound of the flying-boat's engines could be heard increasing in the distance again.

"He's coming back!" Ian encouraged everybody. Sure enough, the noise was much louder now.

The eight sailors found renewed energy to stretch the spinnaker along the length of the boat. The engines increased in volume, and soon the Sunderland could be seen flying back on an easterly heading.

"Everybody wave to attract their attention. Come on everybody, wave!" Estella ordered. Eight pairs of eyes followed the flying boat as it flew past less than a couple of miles to the south.

"He'll continue out to the east then turn back and pass overhead on his next sweep," Ian assured the excited crew. Once again the flying boat flew past and continued on until it disappeared below the eastern horizon.

As the Sunderland disappeared, a de Havilland Heron fifteen-seater airliner became airborne off Nadi's westerly runway and climbed out to sea, before turning back onto an easterly course for Samoa. The highest peaks of the Sleeping Giant required them to reach 5000 feet before heading across the main island of Viti Levu. Aboard the Heron, Captain Neil Ganley had delegated the flying to his co-pilot, while he scanned the Bay area for signs of *Seaspray*.

"Keep climbing. Maintain 115 knots," he told his co-pilot. "We've got to reach 5000 before setting course over the beacon." The tiny Heron climbed at 900 feet a minute while the captain scanned the sea to the south and west.

"Sunderland's below us so they must've sighted something," he commented to the other pilot as they pierced a thin layer of strato cumulus. "Okay, turn back towards the field, we should make 5000 easily now."

The co-pilot concentrated on his flight instruments as he banked right. Ganley's view of the water was severely reduced by the plane's banked attitude. Neither pilot saw *Seaspray*'s crew waving excitedly as the plane flew directly overhead.

Breakfast had finished at Mendelsohn Mansions when the telephone roused Bosca from his mid-morning siesta.

Frank Boothwaite had left for a Sydney flight, the two Parnell queers were already at work in their art gallery, and those of us not flying were enjoying a leisurely read of the morning papers.

Marie picked up the receiver and listened for several seconds before gesturing to Mike Hawk.

"Probably about my leave request," he grumbled struggling out of his armchair. "Hello this is Hawk."

He listened intently for forty seconds then rang off.

"That was Flight Ops on the phone," he told the room. "They still haven't found Gemmell and co. There's a bit of a scare on up at Nadi." He then filled in further details.

"Shouldn't be hard to find them." Don Robbie protested. "Even if they're in the water, there are plenty of islands to swim to. Knowing their luck, they're probably marooned on a tropical island with a couple of luscious-looking females and a case of booze."

"As a matter of fact there were three Pan-Am hosties with them," Mike admitted.

We discussed the matter at length and came to the conclusion they'd be found in plenty of time to operate their flight home the following day.

The sun had passed its zenith and *Seaspray*'s crew had given up signalling to passing ships and aircraft. The wind had increased to a twenty knot sou'easter, and an eight foot swell made their lives unpleasant. Seasickness had struck everybody during the morning and an air of despondency hung over them like a leaden pain.

The high seas had reduced visibility to a matter of yards, making it difficult to detect surface vessels until they were almost upon them. Aircraft were heard long before they were seen, and the searching flying boat had twice flown directly overhead without seeing them.

They had been in the water twenty hours, and the dark colour of the sea persuaded Ian they were drifting through the island chain into deeper water. From their semi-submerged position on the hull, the high seas made it impossible to observe adjacent islands. Ian conferred with the four men on the best course of action.

"We can't rely on being spotted by a boat or plane," Derek concluded for all of them. "The blue hull and high seas make us virtually indiscernible to searchers. Meanwhile, we're probably drifting further away from land."

They knocked the problem round for a considerable time and concluded that once they drifted out into the deeper waters of the Pacific, their chances of rescue would be minimal. Fatigue, exposure, hypothermia, hunger, seasickness and the ever-present chance of shark attack would combine to make their demise inevitable. Unless they were rescued soon, the deep waters of the Pacific would be their last resting place.

Knocking-off time in Technical House was officially 5pm, but anybody calling by telephone would be lucky to get an answer after quarter to five. The office staff and flight ops team were usually well on their way to the bus stop before the bell on the Harbour Board building struck five times. But this evening was different; nobody had left the office.

It was almost 7pm when the phone rang on Brownjohn's desk. Doug Keesing and various flying and operations staff paused in the midst of their discussion to eavesdrop. The ops manager listened for perhaps thirty seconds, grunted something unintelligible and rang off.

"Phone Captain White and Mr Ruffle and tell them to catch the evening TAI flight to Nadi," he instructed the senior operations officer. "They'll operate our Saturday morning flight back to Auckland."

The others nodded their understanding. That evening's TAI flight was the only connection with Fiji until tomorrow. It would be prudent to have replacement pilots up there.

"A wise precaution," Joe Lawton agreed. "They can always dead-head back again if we don't need them."

Brownjohn surveyed the circle of faces around him. He directed his gaze at the senior operations officer.

"Contact Mrs Gemmell and young Stubbs' family. Arrange for somebody to stay with them over the next twelve hours. I don't care who it is, friends or family. I'm afraid it's not looking too good."

"Isn't that a bit precipitate?" Joe Lawton suggested. "They're probably washed ashore on one of the outlying islands. It's only a matter of time before they're picked up. There must be fifty pleasure boats operating in the Nadi Bay area and at least a dozen aircraft . . ."

Brownjohn interrupted his chief navigator. "An RNZAF Sunderland has scoured the area since first light. Additionally, every boat and aircraft has been instructed to keep an eye out for them. They've criss-crossed the area, yet nobody's reported a thing. It's after dark in Fiji now, and all the charter boats have returned home. The police have questioned everybody. Nobody's reported a sighting." He paused momentarily to allow the impact of his words to sink in.

"In the circumstances, I think we must assume they are lost," he ended gravely.

The effect on the gathering was dramatic. Clerks and typists exchanged astonished glances. One of the office girls began dabbing her eyes. Nobody spoke for half a minute.

Joe Lawton was the first to break the silence. "Not necessarily lost," he suggested. "There's always tomorrow. People have been picked up after weeks at sea."

"In the tropics without food, shelter and water? I don't think so," Brownjohn advised him. The navigator remained silent.

"Let's see what tomorrow will bring." Gus Knox, the senior operations officer, was the only other person to speak.

"Realistically, I think it can only be bad news. That was Search and Rescue on the phone." Brownjohn spoke slowly and deliberately to control his emotions. "The search has been officially called off."

CHAPTER THIRTY-THREE

Search Abandoned

To be precise, the search had been halted officially at sunset. A second Sunderland headed back to a night landing at Lauthala Bay, and the various ships and light aircraft returned to the island. One of the last to receive the summons to return was Jack French, the pilot of the Tri-Pacer. Local knowledge had convinced him *Seaspray* and her crew would have been washed ashore onto one of the tiny islands in the Bay. All day he'd concentrated his search on the islands around the Nadi area, initially surveying the inner-lying islands to the north and west, flying round at low level for signs of wreckage or survivors. He'd continued his search to the west and south before heading towards the outer chain of islands. When the recall signal came, he was circling Qalito Island, twenty miles west of the international airport.

With a sign of resignation, he acknowledged the instruction and turned onto an easterly heading for the airport. Previous experience told him the *Seaspray* crew's chances of surviving another night at sea were not good.

Tom French would have put the crew's survival chances at zero if he'd witnessed their actions four hours earlier, when they committed what many armchair experts would have told them was a fatal mistake for those lost at sea. They'd abandoned ship.

Their supply of drink had run out long before, and the waterlogged hull now afforded them little or no buoyancy support. They had managed to remove a flotation bag from between the thwarts for Gudrun to cling to and one of the other girls relied on a plastic container for support in the water. Morale began to decline with their ebbing strength. If they drifted into open water, death would be inevitable.

Ian surveyed the situation. The five men were probably the best swimmers. *Seaspray* was gradually sinking beneath them and would soon lose the last of its buoyancy. When that happened, they would be left floundering in the water, hungry, thirsty, weak and with two members of their party unable to swim very far. It would be better to make a raft from the spars and ropes and attempt to tow the girls to land.

He discussed the options with the others. All agreed it made sense to leave the waterlogged hull and tow the girls on the raft. Paddy Doyle would provide protection from shark attack by patrolling round them with his spear gun.

And so, after lashing loose pieces of timber into a makeshift raft, the party of eight abandoned the ship and began the slow and excruciatingly long swim back to land.

Once in the next four and a half hours they were threatened by sharks. Derek saw them first — white reef sharks swimming twenty feet below them. Realising there was nothing he could do if they attacked, he kept silent. The sharks surfaced and circled for several minutes in wide orbits, gradually drawing closer. The larger of the two predators drew close to Ian before abruptly veering away. Its partner approached from the rear, its triangular fin cleaving the surface of the water as it swam, its open jaws revealing rows of saw-like teeth. When it came within three feet of them, Paddy clubbed it with the speargun. In pain, the shark swerved abruptly away and dived to safer water. Its companion sensed panic in the water and turned to renew its attack. As it neared them, Paddy fired the speargun beside its head, purposely aiming away from the sleek body. The percussion of escaping air alarmed the shark and it fled. Neither of the predators returned. Had Paddy aimed to hit the fish, it is certain the scent of blood in the water would have excited other predators into a feeding frenzy. Death by shark attack would then have been a foregone conclusion.

By mid-afternoon the swell had reduced, and they were able to discern the distant mountains of Viti Levu to the east. Of more immediate interest was a tiny island less than a couple of miles away. The four swimmers pulled the girls for another two and a half hours before collapsing exhausted on its sandy shore.

On regaining their strength, they surveyed their situation. Although they had reached dry land, they were not yet rescued. They had reached Malo Malo, one of many tiny islands in the Bay. Now they must attract the attention of a passing ship or aircraft.

The problem was how to do this. Several times earlier, the RNZAF Sunderland had thundered directly overhead at less than a thousand feet, yet nine pairs of searching eyes had failed to detect them. Other aircraft flying into and out of Nadi's international airport, plus occasional passing ships, had also missed them.

Ian and the Pan-Am captain surveyed the tiny island and concluded their best plan would be to lay out some form of message on the beach. With assistance from the others, they laid out rocks and branches on the foreshore in the shape of letters large enough to be visible from the air.

After an hour's work, they surveyed the result of their labour. Lines of debris spelt out their message on the sand.

The effects of twenty-two hours without food hit them simultaneously. They barely made it back to the shade of a small clump of coconut palms before collapsing exhausted on the sand. Paddy realised nightfall was not far off and rescue could still be days away. They would need sustenance until they were picked up. He went in search of anything edible to sustain them during their wait.

It took less than five minutes to complete a search of the island. Sand, fallen palm fronds, shells and thousands of rocks and stones were all he found, until he looked up at bunches of green coconuts in the crowns of the palms. Paddy was too weak to consider climbing up the trunk of a palm. He looked around for something with which to knock the nuts down and his gaze fell upon the speargun. A triumphant grin lit his face as he formulated a plan to obtain one of the life-giving nuts. He would shoot it down.

Taking careful aim at the centre of the lowest bunch, the Irishman squeezed the trigger. Another problem was about to occur.

Compressed air spearguns are designed to be fired below the surface of the water, where the effect of the gun's tremendous kick is reduced by water resistance. Unfortunately for Paddy, firing the gun out of water greatly magnified the force of the gun's reaction, causing its energy to dissipate in the wrong direction. The effect was comparable to dropping a depth charge in three feet of water. The gun's mechanism slammed back into Paddy's face, breaking his nose. Blinded by blood and pain, the Irishman staggered back, clasping his face. The American stewardesses woke with a start and hurried to bathe the wounded area with cloths soaked in seawater, laying the injured man down to recover in the shade of the palms.

Despite the mishap, Paddy had managed to bring down a coconut, which provided them with food and drink. The eight members of *Seaspray*'s crew soon felt sufficiently revived to take turns to act as observers on the two sides of the tiny island. They carried branches to attract the attention of passing ships or aircraft. Several of these went by, but none close enough to see their signals.

The sun's rays were casting long shadows on the sand when the observers detected the welcome sound of aero engines approaching from the northwest at low level. As the Air Force Sunderland appeared, everybody waved palm fronds and articles of clothing to attract the attention of those aboard. The giant flying boat was heading directly for the island, climbing gradually. Individual rivets and oil stains became visible as it passed overhead and continued on its southeasterly track. Disbelief registered on the faces of those left on the island.

"He must have seen us, he flew right over the top," Estella wailed, but the Sunderland continued eastward without deviating.

"Probably turning into wind to land," Derek suggested optimistically. Eight pairs of eyes followed the aircraft as it continued climbing on a path towards the mainland.

"Could he be returning to refuel?" one of the Americans suggested. Ian nodded hopefully, but he knew the flying boat would have taken off earlier from Lauthala Bay with fourteen or more hours' fuel. It didn't need to refuel. If it was returning to its base, it could only mean the end of the search. The sun was declining into the western ocean; soon it would be dark.

"There'll be other aircraft," the New Zealand captain encouraged everybody. "Don't give up yet." His words encouraged the others to keep hoping, yet realistically he reasoned the Sunderland had probably completed its daylong search and reported finding nothing.

The duty officer would have had to weigh up whether the cost to the New Zealand taxpayer justified continuing the search after no sightings had been made.

Ian and Derek watched sadly as the Air Force machine climbed higher to clear the mountains along its flight path back to Lauthala Bay. Neither voiced aloud what they suspected; the Search and Rescue Authorities had concluded they were lost at sea and called the search off.

Further to the south, a small high-winged monoplane could be discerned heading back to the airport. It was too far away for its pilot to be able to detect their message on the sand.

Back in New Zealand, the news of eight people missing at sea finally broke. Earlier that evening, the New Zealand Broadcasting Corporation had received a preliminary news flash from Fiji, advising that ships and aircraft were patrolling the Nadi Bay area for eight missing tourists. No further details had been provided.

As darkness fell on Auckland, an RNZAF spokesman released a detailed press statement containing details of recent events. Brownjohn had already advised his missing pilots' next of kin that the search had been called off. Simultaneously, the American Consul General in Auckland conveyed the news to Dave Morgan, Pan-Am's New Zealand area manager, who immediately passed the buck to Pan-Am's Pacific Headquarters in San Francisco.

By 7pm the Air New Zealand flight ops department was empty save for the crew control officers maintaining contact with other routine flights.

Back in Mendelsohn Mansions, an anxious crowd gathered round the small black and white television set in the lounge. The newscaster finished reading an account of the circumstances surrounding the accident and turned to the next news item.

Frank Boothwaite turned down the volume on the television.

"Not looking very good for them, is it?" a National Airways pilot resident in one of the back rooms commented.

"I'm afraid it's probably all over," Frank stated gravely. "Nobody can survive for twenty-four hours in those conditions. If the sharks haven't got them, hunger and fatigue will have by now. The Air Force would have scoured the Bay with a fine-tooth comb before calling the search off. Even if any of them were still alive, which I doubt, they wouldn't last another night at sea."

Nobody challenged Frank's opinion. During twenty-five years of flying in the South Pacific, he had taken part in many air–sea rescue attempts and knew how slim the odds of survival were.

"Without some sort of device like a heliograph or distress flares, survivors are almost undetectable in high seas," he announced regretfully. "From what I hear, Paddy Doyle's boat had none of those things aboard."

Discussion ranged round this subject for a while, then seven of us decided to go out to dinner.

News travelled a lot slower in the South Pacific in the mid-sixties and it was after 10pm when Tom French's momentous news reached the New Zealand Press Association's newsroom in Auckland.

Tom had received the recall signal at fifteen minutes after six, and pointed the nose of his tiny Piper Tri-Pacer back towards the mainland. He climbed to 1000 feet to escape the light turbulence at lower level.

No aviator or mariner likes it when colleagues go missing, and Tom was no exception to the rule. He was saddened by the unsuccessful outcome of the search, even though he'd profited from seven hours' flying at full charter rate.

Levelling out at 1000 feet, he reached for his unopened thermos flask. It had remained untouched in his flight bag since before first take-off at dawn. The strong black coffee fortified him somewhat and caused him to ponder yet again on the fate of the crew of *Seaspray*. If Tom had been a gambling man, he'd have staked his day's earnings the survivors would have made it to an inner island, but he'd flown round every one in the area. He replaced the cork in the flask and called Nadi Approach Control on VHF.

"Tri-Pacer Alpha X-ray requesting joining instructions, five miles south-west, field in sight."

"Alpha X-ray cleared for a straight-in approach, runway in use zero nine, one DC-6 clearing the cross runway, call on short finals."

Tom altered course thirty degrees left to intercept the extended centre line of the east-west runway. His new flight path took him abeam a tiny island two miles off the coast. It had been one of the first he'd circled in his busy day's flying. As the pilot commenced his descent prior to landing, his gaze lingered momentarily on the island. It was about three acres in area, with wide sand beaches and a clump of coconut palms on the southern side. Tom circled the island at 600 feet, idly thinking what a wonderful retirement home he could build on it. There would be a seaplane ramp on the northwest side, sheltered from the prevailing winds, and a single-storey two-bedroom New Zealand Lockwood house nestled in the shade of the palms. There might even be enough soil for a bit of lawn in front of the house and a vegetable garden at the side. It looked idyllic.

"Tri-Pacer Alpha X-ray carrying out one orbit of Malo Malo," Tom transmitted.

"Roger Alpha X-ray, see any sign of survivors?"

"Negative, just daydreaming."

"Roger, call when finished. No other traffic."

Tom circled the island at 500 feet, still thinking what a wonderful retirement home it could be for somebody wealthy enough to afford it.

Rounding the south side, he noticed with irritation that persons unknown had strewn boulders and logs on the beautiful silver sand beach.

"Damned tourists will wreck every beauty spot eventually," he cursed. "Tin cans, plastic bags, rubbish left all over the place." His thoughts were interrupted by the unexpected appearance of two red-skinned figures running out from the palms. Only when they began pointing at the rocks on the beach did he notice the message they formed: "8 OK".

Dropping down to less than 200 feet above the water, he flew along the line of surf. More figures emerged from the palms and ran down the beach waving branches. He counted six as he flew past.

"Nadi approach from Alpha X-ray, I have sightings of six plus persons on Malo Malo."

"Alpha X-ray, you're hard to read, confirm on final approach?"

Tom firewalled the throttle and climbed to 1000 feet to improve the radio signal.

"Negative. Present position four miles southwest the field, orbiting Malo Malo. I think I have survivors in sight."

Extending the flaps, he descended and flew low and slow along the beach. Eight figures stood in a line at the water's edge, waving and pointing at the letters on the sand as he flew past at low level.

After Jack French had confirmed his discovery, the senior air traffic controller in the Nadi tower picked up the telephone and spoke urgently into it.

Ten miles away at the Texaco oil refinery on Vinda Point, the coxswain of the company launch *Retriever* received instructions to proceed at high speed to Malo Malo.

"Light aircraft reported sighting eight persons apparently alive on the island. Sounds like they'll need food, water, medical treatment. Get 'em back here as soon as possible, a medical team will meet you on arrival."

The launch's twin Perkins grumbled into life before the controller finished his message. The note of the diesels rose to a belligerent roar as the coxswain firewalled the throttles and headed south into the Bay.

Twenty minutes later *Retriever*'s prow crunched gently onto the coral sand of Malo Malo. Two boatmen jumped over the side and helped Ian and the Pan-Am skipper assist three girls and an injured Irishman into the launch. The crew began to dispense sustenance and basic first aid to the fortunate eight, while the skipper sped them back to shore.

Fifty-five minutes after being summoned to the rescue, *Retriever* was unloading survivors onto the wharf. An ambulance crew and Police Emergency Service vehicles were the first to greet them. After a brief discussion, the drivers agreed to convey the survivors back to the Skylodge.

Paddy Doyle spoke to the hotel before boarding the vehicle. "Tell the chef to have eight steaks ready when we arrive in half an hour," he instructed. "And keep the bar open."

"I'm afraid the dining room's closing in twenty minutes . . ." a waitress began, until the Irishman convinced her in his inimitable way to keep it open.

The blistered survivors were greeted by their fellow crew members as the Emergency Service vehicles pulled up outside the Skylodge. Sympathetic hands gently helped them from the vehicles.

"Gotta cold beer for eight thirsty sailors?" Ian was the first to speak. Pete Slimmer gestured towards the bar.

"Followed by the biggest, bloodiest, juiciest steak on the island, rare as you like," Derek added, hobbling slowly and painfully into the hotel.

Geoff White, the relieving captain, had already phoned Brownjohn with the good news. Simultaneously the New Zealand Press Association received details of the rescue from Search and Rescue Headquarters in Wellington.

Frank and Marie were still up when we returned from our rather sombre meal in a nearby café. Frank greeted us with a tremendous smile.

"They're safe, back in the Skylodge, enjoying their first food for thirty hours," he announced gleefully. "Fellow in a light aircraft found them."

"Anybody injured?" Don Robbie enquired concernedly.

"Nobody. Apart from severe cases of hunger, thirst and exposure, they're apparently in surprisingly good shape after what they've been through. I imagine the Skylodge is attending to their hunger and thirst."

A spontaneous cheer rose from the throats of those of us who'd been struggling to come to terms with the probable deaths of two colleagues.

Back in Fiji, one final disappointment awaited the survivors. They'd hobbled to the dining-room where eight enormous steaks appeared by magic. Derek cut off a succulent slice and raised it to his mouth. To his dismay, he was unable to get it past his parched and blistered lips. The others encountered the same problem. They found the only sustenance they could take was ice cream, and the steaks remained uneaten on their plates.

Miraculously the event had ended successfully; no lives were lost, no permanent injuries sustained and eight people had learned the lesson of the sea.

The sea is unforgiving to those who ignore its warnings and treats them with contempt. Only those who brave its dangers comprehend its mysteries. And those unfortunate enough to succumb to such dangers are reluctant to reveal its secrets once the enigmatic waters have closed over their heads.

Twice more in the years ahead, Nadi would play host to life-threatening situations involving hundreds of lives on the ground and in the air. *But that's a very long story . . .*